My Feet

630 miles on th

I.S.B.]

Copyright ©

Dedication

For Dad, with love. You were the best.

Also by Julia R May

Walking Pembrokeshire with a Fruitcake

Walking with Offa

Pedals, Panniers and Punctures

Walking with Hadrian

I've Cycled Through There

Cycling Across England

Cycles and Sandcastles

Bicycles, Boats and Bagpipes

A Week in Provence

Bicycles, Beer and Black Forest Gateau

Dawdling Through The Dales

Cycling Through a Foreign Field

My Feet and Other Animals

630 miles on the South West Coast Path

When two friends planned a long distance walk on England's South West Coast Path they thought the toughest challenge would be the walking itself. But the biggest obstacles to be overcome were not the 630 miles of footpaths, or the soaring ascents and descents of the cliffs. They were the unforeseen factors that cannot be planned for but which transform a journey into an adventure. Factors such as a torn calf muscle, recalcitrant underwear, two days of torrential rain and gales, two weeks of the hottest July temperatures for years, high tech equipment designed to help but determined to hinder, the capriciousness of public transport and a host of B&Bs all competing for the title of Worst Accommodation in the West.

'My Feet and other Animals' is a candid and often hilarious account of their journey through some of the most spectacular coastal scenery in England. If you are a keen rambler or just an armchair walker with the desire but not the energy to experience a long distance walk, then this is the book for you. It will give you a taste of the pleasure, the pain and the sense of achievement to be gained from the simple act of putting one foot in front of the other.

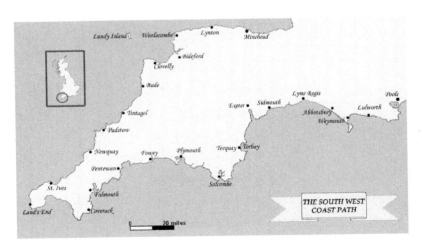

MINEHEAD to PADSTOW

"Oh, I've just had an idea; you could keep a diary!"

"A diary?" I echoed.

"Yes, then I can see what I've missed," replied Chris. "A book, even! And get it published!"

"Yeah, sure."

It was the last week in June and I was spending my lunch hour sitting in Chris's lounge. I seemed to have spent numerous lunch times there throughout that spring. Chris was off work and had been for several months but it was not until that moment that I realised just how envious she was of me. In a matter of days I would be setting off on a walk that we had talked about for weeks.

Outside the window the hornbeam tree danced in the rain and wind. When I had first started calling in to see Chris at lunchtime, the tree had been a bare skeleton. As winter had given way to spring, the hornbeam had slowly dressed in its grey-green foliage, and by late June was now fully clothed. Together we had watched the blackbirds building their nest in the creeper covering the neighbour's house. Time had advanced and as we sipped cups of tea we had watched the adult birds flying in and out, feeding their brood.

Several degrees farther south and with the moderating effect of the surrounding sea, summer would have reached Devon and Cornwall sooner than in Lancashire. The trees would be in full leaf, the countryside would be verdant and alive, and if it didn't stop raining the paths would be very wet under foot!

I glanced at my watch, my lunch hour had already stretched to an hour and a quarter and I had a fifteen minute drive back to work. Never mind, I could soon make the time up and the boss was very understanding, especially as she was the one I was visiting! I gulped the last of the tea and stood up to leave. Chris hobbled to the door with me.

"The next time you see me I will have walked 164 miles from Minehead to Padstow!"

"Get lost, you make me sick!" was her response. Then, more seriously: "I'm really jealous you know. Don't forget that diary!"

I ran through the downpour to the car, calling a hasty good-bye over my shoulder. Oh, this weather was terrible – would it never stop raining? As I reversed up the drive I could see Chris standing dejectedly in the doorway. I suppose I could keep a diary, I thought, nothing lengthy just a brief account of the weather ("rain, rain and more rain") and the scenery ("fog, fog and more fog") that sort of thing.

So that is how I came to pack a little notepad amongst the clothing, food and waterproofs in my rucksack. As it transpired, that little notepad and the larger one I bought to replace it were used more than the waterproofs in the end. And the 164 miles that summer were to stretch to 630 miles over a period of four summers, until I finally completed the whole of the South West Coast Path.

Tuesday 30th June

I wouldn't have been walking the 164 miles from Minehead to Padstow, through what looked set to become the wettest summer on record, if it had not been for a holiday excursion to Bournemouth. I just happened to pop into a bookshop there and some time later popped out; £4.99 the poorer but clutching a book called "500 Mile Walkies" by Mark Wallington – one man and his dog along the South West Coast Path. Mr. Wallington and Boogie the dog walked the path in its entirety in 1982. I was limited by time and money to a mere 164 miles in fourteen days. Since reading the book I had wanted to follow in their footsteps; the south western corner of England held fond memories of childhood holidays, not to mention adult holidays and, a keen walker, I saw the distance as a challenge.

When I announced I was going to do the walk, initial reaction was mixed, but mainly negative. Most people expected me to be attacked and my body dumped in the Atlantic. My husband went so far as to express concern as to whether the mortgage would be paid off should my body not be recovered.

"It's not safe, a woman walking on her own," he said.

I think I managed to persuade him I would be okay with a mobile phone, personal alarm, whistle, big stick and pre-booked accommodation. Although I suspect the deciding factor for him was the thought of a nag-free two weeks without me!

I was not looking forward to telling my mum, I knew she would worry. That's what mums do, it's part of the job description. So when her initial reaction to my news was "Oh you lucky thing!" I was pleasantly surprised, until she asked who was going with me.

"Er, no-one, I'm going on my own."

That's when the worrying and motherly concern began.

Only one person had been encouraging about walking on my own, which was hardly surprising because it was her fault that I was going to be walking alone. Back in April, Chris and I were both off work with leg injuries: mine a damaged Achilles tendon, hers a torn calf muscle. We felt confident that by the summer we would both be fit and well; and so we planned a walking holiday. The best laid plans of mice and women do not always work out. I was soon back at work, Chris however, wasn't. Her injury seemed to be no better and if anything, was worse than when she did it on New Year's Eve.

Now the sort of picture which springs to mind for any injury received on New Year's Eve involves a person very much the worse for drink, attempting to scale Nelson's Column. Chris has always been quick to point out that as the driver in her party that night she had not had a single drink. Neither was she in the vicinity of Trafalgar Square. Still, it serves as a warning for anyone considering attending a barn dance at the local village hall!

On the last day of June, bereft of companionship but not of enthusiasm, I boarded the train to Taunton. I had given the cats a kiss goodbye, given the houseplants a drink of water and given Roger, my husband, a plan of the kitchen, a crash course in washing machines and a pizza takeaway menu. I was ready for adventure and hadn't a clue what I was letting myself in for (but then again neither did Roger!)

4

In my rucksack was everything I would need for two weeks on foot: mobile phone, packet of sandwiches, nail clippers, bar of chocolate, clothes, bag of crisps, waterproofs, water bottle, list of Bed and Breakfasts I was booked into, fruit, oh yes and a map and guidebook. Strapped to the back of my rucksack was my shiny new walking pole.

Was it my imagination? As I got off the train at Birmingham New Street Station my rucksack seemed a lot heavier. After a struggle I managed to look over my shoulder and the top of the rucksack, only to find I was carrying a commuter and someone's suitcase impaled on the walking pole. I disentangled myself, apologised profusely and legged it to the ladies.

Why is it that designers of public toilets do not consider the mechanics of getting into a cubicle? I struggled to squeeze into a space two feet by four feet, whilst opening and closing the door behind me and attempting not to step into the toilet. Add to this a thirty litre rucksack stuffed to exploding point and a walking pole with a mind of its own and you will understand my difficulties. Eventually, after an argument between the walking pole and the toilet roll holder, I took my rucksack off and successfully entered the cubicle, backwards.

Afterwards, as I struggled back into my rucksack, I felt something give. A strap? My shoulder? The walking pole (curse it)? Er, no. My bra. The contortions necessary to fit both arms into a rucksack harness and heave it onto my back had undone my bra. Back I went into a toilet cubicle to fasten my bra. When I emerged, by that time at risk of missing my connecting train, I decided not to bother putting the rucksack back on. I staggered towards the platform, the rucksack in my arms, until three porters took pity on me and carried it on to the train.

I knew what to tell mum when I rang her, in answer to one of her earlier questions: "What will you do if you're attacked?" I would simply drop my rucksack on my assailant's toes and if that failed to finish him off I would introduce him to my walking pole.

I had attempted to keep the weight of my rucksack to a minimum and thought that I had been remarkably conservative in my packing. However, after staggering along under its weight on railway station platforms, I was beginning to wonder how I would manage traversing rugged cliff top paths for the next fortnight. If I once sat down with the rucksack on my back, would I ever have the strength to stand up again? I decided I would weigh the rucksack at the first available opportunity and I was able to do this in the public toilets at Bristol Temple Meads Railway Station. I placed the rucksack on the scales and pushed my twenty pence piece into the slot on top of the electronic weighing machine. The digital readout displayed "16 lbs". The machine then demanded to know my height, I entered 5'6" which obviously gave the machine considerable cause for concern; it thought for a moment before displaying the words "seriously underweight… please try again". Sixteen pounds! That was the equivalent of two large babies, sixteen pounds of potatoes, over a stone in weight! Thank goodness I wasn't camping!

The train arrived at Taunton behind schedule, a leaf on the line or something, cutting it very fine if I was to catch the hourly bus to Minehead. As the train pulled in I jumped off and pulled on the rucksack, sag went the bra (no time to sort it out) and I sprinted out of the railway station. I just had time to register a sign that said something about a bus stop for Minehead being 100 yards on the left. Checked the watch, ten minutes to find a bus with "MINEHEAD" in the window – but where was this promised bus stop? I couldn't see a bus stop.

After a 100 yard race down the high street, at speeds which would have shamed Linford Christie and worried a heart specialist, I collided with a slow moving student. To my gasped demands for directions to the bus station, he took in my rucksack, pole and Lancashire accent, translated my request into his own dialect and began to speak. Students are notorious for taking drugs these days (when were they not?) but this was the first I'd met who was on Prozac. What's the hurry? Life's a breeze. Relax. Chill out. Why worry? He gave considerable thought to my question; couldn't he see I was in a hurry? He spoke slowly and unclearly in a West Country burr, which at any other time I would have found endearing. Basically I had to go straight on and turn right at Next. It would, he said, take me ten minutes. A quick glance at my watch told me the bus left in four minutes.

If ever they make another series of Treasure Hunt, I'd get the job. I sped down Taunton high street like Anneka Rice in search of a pink clue, with a clock in my head ticking down the seconds to zero. As Next came into view a bus with "MINEHEAD" in the window passed me going in the opposite direction. So then I had an hour to find a toilet, take off my rucksack, fasten my bra and find the bus station.

One hour behind schedule I boarded the bus for Minehead. But what on earth possessed me to go upstairs? Going up wasn't too bad but coming down – with the rucksack and pole – amongst a group of ten assorted Americans and their children and their rucksacks and their prams, was a little bit tricky. When my feet did touch Minehead promenade I looked around to find I was pushing a pram with a toddler in it. One of the American ladies was complaining that a rucksack had undone her bra and one of the American gentlemen was extracting my walking pole from his anatomy. We sorted ourselves out in the spirit of entente cordiale and set off in opposite directions.

I bought a postcard with "MINEHEAD" on it, donned my walking boots, zeroed my pedometer and took my first step on the South West Coast Path. Oh, and in case you're wondering about the sign in the railway station giving directions to the bus stop, let me set your mind at rest. Before leaving Taunton, the bus turned into the railway station car park and drew to a halt by a pole with a green and yellow sign on top that said bus stop! How I had failed to see it I did not know.

That morning I had boarded the train and left behind a miserable, rainy Lancashire. By the time I was half way up North Hill at Minehead off had come various layers of clothing until I was stepping out in just a T-shirt and walking trousers. I walked into a Somerset evening with birds singing and the sun shining. Maybe this weather boded well for the rest of my walk.

If things seemed to be improving weather-wise, my pedometer was another matter. After two solid hours of walking I checked my distance. Quarter of a mile! Even allowing for the weight of my rucksack I wasn't going that slowly, surely? At that rate, I calculated, it would take me until September to reach Padstow and that would be walking non-stop. I didn't have enough holidays for that!

After a lot of stomping from one foot to another I realised the pedometer was not registering the majority of steps. So, after careful thought and further experimentation, I clipped it onto my waistband over my right hip. I didn't exactly catch up after that but the pedometer did make more sense of my distance.

The path to Porlock was a mixture of woodland trails and open moorland. As the path reached the top of the cliffs I could look across to Selworthy Beacon, although the chocolate box village of Selworthy with its quaint thatched cottages remained hidden from view. This was one of the rare parts of the walk where the coast path was actually some distance from the sea. The nature of the sloping cliffs necessitated that the path follow a route often over a mile away from the sea. Heather and bilberry bushes covered the hillsides, the purple flowers of the heather promising a dazzling display of colour as summer advanced into autumn. Unable to resist, I risked tumbling headlong down the slopes, as bent over double – and still wearing my rucksack – I picked handfuls of juicy bilberries, smearing my face and hands with the purple stain in the process, what a mess I must have looked.

The footpath was very well sign posted and by 6 p.m. I reached a confluence of four paths above Hurlstone Combe. The South West Way acorn symbol pointed down the combe. Surely the path did not go down there? The gradient was severe and the ground was covered with scree, a safe descent looked impossible. But the map confirmed that the route did indeed lead down into the combe. Leaning heavily on my walking pole, I slithered down the precipitous slopes of Hurlstone Combe. It was a sharp long descent and by the time I reached the bottom my knees were aching and my legs were trembling. From the bottom of the combe a level path continued towards Bossington. Here, the sea had washed the pebble ridge onto part of the footpath and new signposts directed the walker inland. I followed the edges of fields of wheat, passing hidden farmhouses and cottages until I suddenly emerged in Porlock.

The Bed and Breakfast establishment I was booked into was a large detached house on a quiet road. From my bedroom window I looked down into a beautiful garden with flowerbeds, vegetable plots, manicured lawns and an aviary. Behind the high boundary hedge, Porlock Hill loomed in the background. My room had tea making facilities and I collapsed wearily into a cup of tea. If I were this tired already, having walked less than 9 miles, what would I be like by the end of the next day?

Supper that evening came from the one and only chippy in the village. Having scouted out a quiet bench to eat them on, I had my chips where many who'd had theirs' had gone before; and read the gravestones.

Wednesday 1st July

The day dawned cloudy with a promise of rain. It was my ninth wedding anniversary! It rained then as well. I left the B&B laden down with calories, hoisted my rucksack onto my back and was reminded that I really should do something about that bra fastener.

As I followed the road down into Porlock Weir I drank in the scents of the morning: roses, honeysuckle, the sharp tang of seaweed blown in from the sea, the pungent aroma of bad eggs as a car passed me, its catalytic converter not yet warmed up.

At Porlock Weir the weather tried to deliver on its promise of rain. Fortunately it only tried half-heartedly and soon gave up. I used the toilets there to fasten my bra, whilst at the same time making a mental note not to drink four cups of tea at breakfast in future.

I was walking to Lynton, the path for much of the morning going through woodland. The flowers of the wild garlic had long since died but the pungent aroma lingered on the air. The bluebells too were over, I imagined how the woodland floor would have looked two months earlier, a carpet of blue and white flowers. At Culbone church I stopped and looked inside. This tiny church was in the Guinness Book of Records as the smallest church in England, seating only thirty people at a squeeze and still in use! The churchyard was a popular burial place for one family in particular – the Redds. Nearly every other gravestone bore the name. Were these to become the Rudds of R.D. Blackmore's Lorna Doone?

Blackmore had not been the only literary person to enjoy this part of the world. The Napoleonic Wars, not surprisingly, deterred a lot of gentlemen from doing a Grand Tour. Some of them visited North Devon instead, rather sensibly I think. Coleridge was one such to do so; being interrupted by a person from Porlock he was unable to finish Kubla Khan.

I think I caught a glimpse of a red squirrel in Culbone Wood, I could not be sure because I only spotted its tail and some greys do have a reddish tinge but I hoped for the sake of our native squirrel population that it was a red one. The rest of the squirrels that I saw were grey. The guidebook urged me to be alert for sightings of deer, alert I was but fortunate enough to spot one I was not.

From Culbone church I climbed to Silcombe Farm, following an alternative route, the original path having been diverted due to land slides. For the next few miles I walked through fields and beside hedgerows watching pheasants and rabbits. Suddenly a stoat emerged from a high bank in front of me and began to run directly towards me. I stopped and watched it, hardly daring to breathe. The stoat continued advancing until there were no more than a few yards between us, then he turned and disappeared into the hedge.

The diversionary route carried me through several farms. Approaching one farmyard I could hear a dog barking frantically. Signs posted on gates and walls screamed 'Private' and pointed toward the direction of the footpath; obviously this farmer did not like walkers. As I stood reading the plethora of signs to ensure I did not inadvertently stray from the path, the dog continued to bark and howl. I had no wish to delay my crossing of the yard and wanted to be certain of my escape route at the other side before I entered the yard through the gate in front of me. I opened the squeaking gate, the noise sending the dog into more frenzied fits of barking, and as I walked hurriedly across the yard I could see his nose rammed into the gap at the bottom of a barn door. The dog was beginning to throw himself against the door, the whole structure shaking in its frame. Hoping the door would hold, I scurried across the yard to the gate bearing a footpath sign. Fumbling with the latch, I noticed the dark red splotches on the concrete floor by the gate. Blood? Had some walkers not made it through the yard before the dog caught up with them? My panicked fingers struggled to open the gate, time seemed to slow down as it does in bad dreams. With every passing moment I expected to feel sharp fangs sinking into my backside. Realising that I had been pulling the gate when I should have been pushing it I finally succeeded in opening it and escaping into the field, slamming the gate behind me.

Safely beyond the farm I passed a group of youths, staggering along under the weight of very large rucksacks. They were backpacking, although from the size of the packs they all carried I think each one had five-man tent all to himself. If the stoat had been warm in his fur coat, these boys must have been melting. Whereas I was ambling along in a T-shirt, they were all wearing several layers of clothing and the youth that brought up the rear (trudging wearily several yards behind the others) was wearing waterproofs!

Shortly after passing the youths it became my turn to experience discomfort with my apparel. A stone had worked its way into my boot and jammed itself beneath my heel. I endured it until I reached a conveniently sited bench before removing my boot. I shook the boot and felt inside, satisfied the stone had gone, I put the boot back and carried on. Immediately, the stone rematerialised, this time under my big toe. It felt the size of a small boulder and I was forced to stop and remove the boot yet again. Still nothing inside it! I banged the boot against the path but no, nothing came out! Perhaps the stone was inside my sock, or stuck to the bottom of it? I checked the sock, took it off, turned it inside out, shook it, examined my foot. No sign of any stone. I replaced the sock and boot and set off once more.

Ah, yes, I'd got it that time! I was prematurely confident, within a few strides the stone was back yet again. Now I was beginning to lose my patience! Off came the boot and there, barely visible to the naked eye, was a microscopic piece of grit. I picked the grit out of the boot, placed it well out of reach of the path, put the boot back on again and continued. Success at last, the foreign body did not come back!

After Glenthorne Plantations the mixed woodland gave way to rhododendron and then open moorland. I stopped for lunch on a seat overlooking a rocky promontory called Sir Robert's Chair, with the sun by now blazing down. I was not really hungry but lunch was a habit I found hard to break. I was to discover as the walk progressed that I could manage to walk all day with little need for lunch, fuelled by gargantuan breakfasts that I never had when at home.

By mid afternoon The Foreland loomed ahead and I took a path towards the old lighthouse down Coddow Combe. At this point I was actually following an old road. I soon became aware of a stick on the road in front of me. As I drew nearer I realised it was looking at me. This non-stick (sorry about that) was the highlight of the walk so far. I was looking at an adder! We stared at one another for a few seconds before I came to my senses and began a frantic fumble for my disposable camera. You cannot take a spur of the moment picture with one of these cameras. First you have to dig it out of your pocket, then you have to wind the film on, then you have to compose the subject and then, and only then, can you take the bloody photograph. The adder didn't have time to wait while I did all this; she slithered off before I even got as far as the composing stage!

The lighthouse was a bit of an anticlimax after the adder, but I descended The Foreland, passed Countisbury and walked down into Lynmouth on a high. The path crossed fields, getting closer to the road before eventually joining it for a short distance, then turning right away from the road towards the seafront.

At Lynmouth I could, for 50p, have ascended to Lynton on the cliff railway. But that would have been cheating! I was jolly well going to walk every foot of this coast path from Minehead to Padstow if it killed me! As I reached the summit of the cliff path at Lynton, wringing wet with perspiration, breathless and with heart pounding, the first thing I saw was a sign directing me to "Cottage Hospital and Health Centre". Was this prophetic I asked myself? The sign had obviously been placed at the end of the steep path by someone with a rather dry sense of humour.

I received a warm welcome and a cup of tea and chocolate biscuit at the B&B in Lynton. The landlady lived alone and seemed glad of my company. After only two days walking by myself, I too appreciated someone to talk to and we chatted companionably as I drank the tea and munched the biscuit. Then, feeling very much refreshed but not particularly hungry, I went in search of an ice cream. Everything seemed to be closing in Lynton so I splashed out, paid my 50p and descended on the cliff railway to Lynmouth. The only shop still open selling ice cream was on the harbour front overlooking the Rhenish Tower. The tower and part of the harbour it stands on were washed into the sea on that fateful night in 1952 when a flash flood on Exmoor turned peaceful Lynmouth into a disaster area. Looking at Lynmouth now, almost half a century later, it is difficult to believe it was once the scene of such terrible devastation; twenty-eight people lost their lives that night. The visitor centre in Lynmouth tells the story in sobering detail.

I was not in luck as far as the ice cream was concerned. Instead of the creamy Devon-made variety I had been hoping for, the shop only sold a massed produced version, bearing little resemblance to frozen cream. Margaret Thatcher "inventor" of cream-less ice cream, made with milk and vegetable oils, had a lot to answer for! Whether her career move from food scientist to politician was a good thing is open to debate, as far as ice cream was concerned the damage had already been done.

By the time I had discovered there was no traditional ice cream to be had, the cliff railway had closed for the evening. So, once more I trudged up the hill to Lynton. At the tiny local Spar I bought a yoghurt and some chocolate which I had for supper. I had walked over fourteen miles that day, sleep should have come easily but it didn't. The bed, like most of the furniture, was old and I fought to find a comfortable position on the sagging, lumpy mattress.

Thursday 2nd July

That morning I woke to the sound of wind screeching through the open bedroom window. It crossed my mind to wonder if I would be blown off exposed sections of the cliff path that day; I needn't have worried – that would not happen until Cornwall! I decided that my best plan would be to make myself as heavy as possible, so with that in mind I went down to breakfast. It beat the previous days by grapefruit and a mushroom. The fried bread however, could have better been described as soaked. Had I rubbed myself down with the fat that oozed from it I would have been all set to swim the Channel.

By 8.50 a.m. I was once again on my way, conscious of calories to burn off. Leaving Lynton I turned right at the Town Hall and promptly got lost. This was the first time and I hoped it would be the last. I trudged up and down paths in the Valley of Rocks, cursing the guidebook and the lack of signposts, before eventually realising I should have been on the road. The Valley of Rocks was spectacular; a remnant of the Ice Age, complete with wild goats which I was lucky enough to see. Evidence of ancient settlements has been uncovered in the valley and it is a popular tourist haunt, the whole area around Lynton and Lymouth being known as Little Switzerland.

At Lee Abbey, an abbey no longer but now a hotel, I turned off the road and left the coast path, which at that point followed a toll road for some distance. The alternative recommended route wound through a wood where I saw more squirrels, all grey ones this time. Back on the official route once more, it was not long before I was tempted off it again by a sign pointing to Woody Bay Beach. The tide was almost in and I sat on the rocks munching a packet of crisps and enjoying the peaceful morning. A lady walking her dog soon left and I had the cove to myself.

This seemed an opportune moment to make a toilet stop. Now I suspect men don't realise how lucky they are – not to have to struggle with belts and buttons and not having to crouch in a most undignified position reminiscent of a toddler on a potty. Several minutes later, having battled with trousers that were clinging to me with sweat, I was back at my rucksack feeling very much relieved. Not a moment too soon! A party of school children and four teachers suddenly appeared from nowhere. A potentially embarrassing moment had been narrowly missed, or I would have undoubtedly been the most memorable sight of that school trip! I could just imagine what the conversation would have been like when they arrived home.

"Did you have a good time then?"

"Yes mum, there was this woman on the beach…"

I climbed the lane from Woody Bay; the sounds of the children's laughter soon muffled by the trees. A Royal Mail van was driving slowly down the lane, bouncing over the rutted cobbles on his way to deliver mail to the few isolated houses. The properties were set back amongst the trees and I envied the owners their seclusion, what a beautiful, peaceful place to live!

The woods on the next section of the path were called hanging oaks. I didn't know if this referred to the way the trees hung onto the steeply sloping hillsides or because of how the branches hung with their heavy cloaks of mosses and lichens. No air pollution here! Sitting, chattering in the branches was a jay.

As I descended wooded slopes into Heddon's Mouth, dropping over three hundred feet in a short distance, I met a lady and her dog that I had passed the previous day. She was walking circular routes of the area, staying overnight in the same place. We greeted one another like old friends. A lot of people had expressed concern about a woman walking on her own; it was encouraging to note that I wasn't the only one doing it.

It was an arduous climb from Heddon's Mouth after crossing the stream by an old hump backed bridge. The path zigzagged in a long series of switchbacks up the steep hillside and I was forced to make frequent stops to catch my breath. The day had become quite hot and with my exertions, so had I! Climbing from Heddon's Mouth I left the woodland behind, the nature of the landscape changing as the path crossed fields of short-cropped scrubby grass.

A procession of three young men passed me, striding out along the path. They were all using a pair of walking poles, and the action of their poles and the fast pace they were travelling at reminded me of cross country skiers. Each of them handled the poles like professionals. I couldn't even manage one pole without tripping over it or getting into difficulty!

I had been greatly concerned about my Achilles tendon before setting off. So it was somewhat of a surprise when, nearing the descent into Sherrycombe, my left knee gave a scream of protest. I carried on, attempting to ignore it but after a little while my left hip came out in sympathy and I had to lie down. Perhaps it was the continuous pounding on my knee, I don't know. After half an hour it felt better, so donning my rucksack (tonight I would definitely fix the bra fastener) I set off again. The pain began immediately and continued all the way down into Sherrycombe and all the way up the other side. I forgot about the pain, for a while at least when, halfway up the hillside I spotted four Exmoor ponies.

At 3.30 p.m. I reached the top of Great Hangman, 318 metres (1043 feet) above sea level; the highest point of the South West Coast Path. I had walked almost from sea level at the bottom of Sherrycombe, but the views made the effort worthwhile. The pain in my knee suddenly gone, I was on a high of endomorphins. I had to talk to someone! Sitting down by the cairn, I took out the mobile phone and rang Chris, afterall she should have been sharing this with me. She wasn't in; I left a garbled message on her answer phone and rang Roger. It was his day off and I expected him to be out but he wasn't, he was watching Wimbledon.

"It's me. I'm at the highest point on the coast path and the views are fantastic!" I raved.

"Oh, hello. Tim Henman has got through to the semi finals, the last Brit to do that was Virginia Wade!"

Maybe you had to be there to experience the excitement. At that moment not even Henman could have felt the euphoria that I did.

From there it was a gentle stroll all the way into Combe Martin. But I left the official route once again to detour to the top of Little Hangman. The altitude might not have been as great but the views were still impressive. To the east, Great Hangman and the coast I had already traversed. To the west, the land stretched away beyond Combe Martin towards Ilfracombe and Morte Point hidden from view, where I would walk the next day. To the south, the hills of Exmoor and their mantle of cloud. To the north, the waters of the Bristol Channel, a bright blue in the afternoon sun and without a cloud as far as the horizon.

Great and Little Hangman are named, not for any dark past history but from the Celtic language and basically mean little and large sloping hills. Personally I prefer the story of the sheep stealer who tied a sheep around his neck, as he was climbing a stile the sheep struggled and slipped from his shoulders, strangling the thief.

The last part of the path into Combe Martin was a riot of wild flowers. Their rainbow colours dazzling the eye. Campion, foxgloves, honeysuckle, clover and dog rose scented the air. The water at Wild Pear Beach was a many shaded blue due to the seaweed and rocks beneath the surface. The rain shelter just before the end of the path an unusual metallic blue, different, but at least it had not been vandalised, yet.

Entering Combe Martin I left the Exmoor National Park, the only national park through which the South West Coast Path runs. Combe Martin lays claim to being the longest village in England. Strung out along a road it consists predominantly of Edwardian architecture but its history stretches back far beyond the early nineteen hundreds. Lead and silver were mined here in ancient times, to be sold to visiting Phoenicians - an event which had been commonplace in much of the region, as I was to discover in Cornwall the following summer.

I had travelled fourteen miles again that day and was desperately in need of a pot of tea. The first thing I saw in this mile long village was a sign: "Cream Teas £1.95". I was sat at a table loading clotted cream onto a scone before you could say "Minehead". It occurred to me then that this was the first time I had ever sat in a café on my own; the barriers you will break for a cream tea!

One hundred yards up the road and I came to my B&B for the night. Ever since making the booking I had been looking forward to meeting the landlady. On the telephone she had sounded a real character – and she was. She ushered me in, exclaimed over the distance I had walked, showed me to my room and went off to put the kettle on. Five minutes later she was bellowing up two flights of stairs that my cup of tea was ready. I descended to the lounge to find a cup of tea, a plate of biscuits and a cream scone! Whilst I was washing down the third scone in less than half an hour, the door bell rang. There were two more walkers just booking in.

"There's a young girl just arrived, walked all the way from Lynton she has!" I could hear.

This was the first B&B where I was not the only guest. Another walker was staying and the two new arrivals were French, proving how popular the South West Coast Path really is.

After a shower and time to digest the scones I wandered down to the seafront and, tempted by the smells emanating from one particular shop, had a fish and chip supper. It may appear to the casual observer that I had eaten rather a lot in rather a short space of time but over the years my stomach had been trained to cope with such things, and it wasn't as if I wouldn't burn off the calories. I calculated I would need 4000 calories each day of my walk, if I over ate then I could always do a bit of exercise when I got home!

For the time being there was nothing particular I had to do – shopping, vacuuming, ironing etc. - and so I people watched. Recreational activities for the young of Combe Martin fell into four distinct categories depending on age.

The children under ten, or thereabouts, whiled away the time in front gardens, watering their younger sisters with watering cans. Those without younger sisters, or friends with younger sisters, played World Cup Football.

"I'm Shearer."

"No you're not, I am."

"I'm Ronaldo."

"He's no good anymore."

"Yes he is."

"No he's not, the manager should never have selected him!"

Was there to be no escape from the dreaded game for me?

The boys on the brink of puberty, just discovering hormones, body hair and the opposite sex, skateboarded in front of the museum. They performed tricks, or at least tried to, in an effort to impress the watching girls. You could almost smell the testosterone coming off them, at one point it threatened to mask the smell of malt vinegar on my chips.

The older teenagers had outgrown skateboards, having latterly discovered the internal combustion engine. They wheel spun around the car park. Their mating calls were screeching tyres, wailing car alarms and screeching, wailing Tina Turner songs played at full volume on their car stereos. After a while it became difficult to differentiate one from the other.

The males of the species inhabiting Combe Martin who had reached maturity, had outgrown not only skateboards but also cars and Tina Turner. They played with the big boys' toys – jet skis. I have to say these definitely looked the most fun, the jet skis that is, not the young men; no Tina Turner and less painful than a skateboard if you fell off.

14

Friday 3rd July

The day started off cloudy, so I dressed in walking trousers thinking I could always change into shorts if the weather improved. The weather did improve and I spent most of the day trying to find somewhere secluded to change.

One would imagine that on a long walk in the countryside there must be somewhere isolated enough to quickly change but this stretch of coast in particular was proving so popular that I was constantly meeting other walkers. In fact I had spent a good deal of time saying "Good morning", so much so that I was beginning to consider making a tape recording in order to save my vocal cords from excessive wear. It had got to the point that, as soon as I saw anyone, I immediately said a cheery "Morning". This did start to get a little embarrassing however, as I was still using the same greeting when the sun was setting, receiving strange glances as a result.

Breakfast at the B&B in Combe Martin that morning was even better than the previous ones, no mushrooms but beans and fried potatoes and two loaves of different breads on the table. I shared a table with the French couple, fortunately their English was better than my French, which runs to shut the door and whatever will be will be, a little limiting in conversations.

"'allo!" they greeted me as they seated themselves at the table.

"Bon jour!" I replied, feeling rather pleased with my own accent. With mounting confidence that I had not forgotten quite as much French as I thought I had, I decided to attempt an introduction.

"Ich bin Julia."

One look at their faces informed me I had made a slight mispronunciation. Yes, very slight: my accent may have been French but the words were German. We conversed in English after that.

I left Combe Martin heading for Ilfracombe and Woolacombe. I had gone no more than 50 yards down the road before I heard an unusual call. Song thrush? Blackbird? Willow warbler? Mynah bird? No, landlady! I had set off without handing in my key and the poor lady was frantically trying to catch me up, hampered by an arthritic hip.

After a short section of beech lined old coast road, the scenery changed from that of previous days. The magnificent headlands were still appearing around every corner but the wooded slopes of Exmoor gave way to moorland and sheep pasture. I found myself missing the trees. A mornings walking led me by secluded bays, caravan sites, a golf course, a hotel – once a Victorian castle, and a coastguard lookout station to Hele and from there to a hill top overlooking Ilfracombe.

Looking down from the top of Hillsborough, Ilfracombe spread out before me. Set around a harbour it looked very picturesque but the first thing I noticed was two enormous sand castles or were they cooling towers? I could not decide which. They dominated the landscape and the eye was drawn to them to the detriment of everything else. As I later found out, these eyesores were called "The Landmark". They were certainly that, amongst other things. Had I been naming them I would have plumped for "The Monstrosities". Apparently they had been designed to deflect the wind coming in off the sea; previous buildings on the site, following more traditional designs, had been storm damaged, so at least their appearance was born of practicality.

I had planned to stop at Ilfracombe for lunch. I knew just what I was going to have, where I was going to buy it and where I would sit to eat it. A Ginster chicken and mushroom pie, from a chippy, overlooking the harbour. Eight years previously I had had exactly that lunch in that location and I intended to relive it, or re-eat it if you like. Why is it that when you really look forward to something it rarely turns out as you expect?

I got to the fish and chip shop and was just about to enter when I noticed a poster on the door. "Holland's Pies" it said. I had not come all this way to eat a pie made ten miles from where I lived! Mortified with disappointment I plodded further along the harbour wall. Joy of joys! A second chippy, this one selling Ginster's pies.

I sat on the harbour wall in the sunshine, dodging herring gull and pigeon you-know-what, eating my pie. It still wasn't as good as I remembered. Only one thing was different from eight years ago – Roger was not there. That couldn't affect the taste of a pie, could it? No, they just don't make pies like they used to; either that or my taste buds are failing me.

After my near embarrassing episode of the toilet stop at Woody Bay Beach the previous day, I had decided to make use of the facilities every time I came across public toilets, irrespective of whether I needed them or not. With this in mind I used four different public conveniences on my way through Ilfracombe. By the time I had got to the last one, the zip on my trousers was so hot from constant use it was approaching melt down.

"Ilfracombe," said my guidebook, "is the largest holiday resort in North Devon," and it showed. Don't get me wrong, it's a nice place, very touristy. This was the first place where I had seen amusement arcades. I pondered on a strange bird call (surely not my landlady again?) until I realised it was coming from a mechanical parrot outside one of the arcades. There were signs everywhere: "Have you paid and displayed?" "Do not feed the seagulls!" "This is a working harbour."

As I walked up the hill along Torr's Walk, I breathed a sigh of relief. I was leaving the madding crowds behind. Civilisation was all very well but only in small doses; denied the companionship of a good friend on this walk, I craved solitude.

For a while the path followed the old coach road before dropping down into Lee Bay, I pitied travellers of centuries gone, imagining how the coach would have rocked and bucked its way from Ilfracombe over the hill to Lee. Just before Lee, the single-track road I had been following became progressively steeper until it seemed I was travelling down a one in two gradient. Looking closely I imagined I could see the holes left by climbers' crampons! Then into Lee and out the other side by an equally steep but this time, up-hill route.

As I got ever closer to Morte Point the guidebook kept insisting I should be able to see Lundy Island. I couldn't, it was too hazy. But, as I reached and rounded the end of Morte Point, Lundy appeared. In the distance, just visible behind Baggy Point, that I would pass the next day, I could see Hartland Point. It would be almost a week before I reached Hartland.

Just then I was approached by a walker, who asked me if I had seen any seals. The guidebook had said there would be some but, like the Exmoor deer, the seals were proving elusive.

After ten minutes walking I arrived in Mortehoe, which came as a bit of a surprise as I was expecting to arrive in Woolacombe. I stopped at the village shop to ask directions to my B&B on Georgeham Road near Woolacombe. The word "near" in the address should have warned me; near translated as two miles inland from Woolacombe.

The shopkeeper gave me directions and then added: "You'll have to go up a one in five hill!"

I gulped, "In that case I think I'll have a pint of milk please."

As it turned out the shopkeeper had been optimistic; the hill – all one mile of it – was one in four.

I drank my milk and ate some chocolate coated raisins whilst sitting on a bench gazing across the two mile stretch of golden Woolacombe sands. Feeling much refreshed I then set off to scale the steep Challacombe Hill to Georgeham Road. On the way I passed Potter's Hill.

"Mmm," I thought, "I bet there's a good view of the beach from up there. What about going up Potter's Hill?"

"No!" Screamed my knees.

"Yes," said my stupidity, so up we all went.

Rabbits darted into the bracken at my approach. Part way up the hill I became aware of an unpleasant smell, I soon discovered the cause: my presence disturbed a jackdaw in the process of disembowelling a very dead rabbit. It could have been worse; I could have still been eating my raisins.

If I had cared to sit on the top of the hill for four hours I could have watched the sun set over Lundy. However, I had travelled sixteen miles and was getting tired. So after a quick check with the map in my guidebook, I took a path down the landward side of Potter's Hill to join up with the road climbing Challacombe Hill. I began to severely doubt my guidebook. If this was a footpath, where were all the foot prints? There weren't any unless you counted the cloven variety! And that's another thing, why do sheep and cattle always use footpaths as latrines?

At long last I joined the road, although I had to scale a five bar gate bedecked with barbed wire to do so – it was either that or pole vault the hedge; the guidebook seemed to have got it wrong about the footpath. After a further half an hour of walking along a lane I found my B&B and received another warm and friendly welcome. The landlady brewed a huge pot of tea, supplied a mountain of biscuits and told me to help myself to the fruit bowl. Feeling much better, I had a hot shower in a bathroom to die for and went to bed.

Saturday 4th July

Weather-wise the morning was the same as the previous ones: cloudy but with a promise from the weathermen of sunshine to come. I shared a breakfast table with a married couple on holiday for a few days and we soon began chatting about walks in the Lakes and the Dales. When they discovered I was walking to Braunton that day they very kindly offered me a lift, it seemed they hadn't quite grasped the idea that I was walking because I wanted to but it was considerate of them nevertheless.

This was a farmhouse and the breakfast was all one would expect of such a place. There was even a toaster in the dining room so you could have as much hot toast as you liked. I viewed the toaster with mixed feelings; I do love hot toast and with some breakfasts it had been luke warm before I ate it, on the other hand though, I did tend to have problems with electricity. I had nearly fried myself once trying to free a muffin from my own toaster with a knife; the shock had sent me across the kitchen in one direction and the knife in the other – a good job Roger hadn't been standing in the way at the time! And at work I had killed an expensive electrical appliance, something my colleagues would not allow me to forget. So it was with some apprehension that I put the bread in the toaster and pushed the switch. I need not have worried, the toaster was idiot proof and the toast was perfect.

Half an hour later I was setting off, in shorts this time – the waistband was not as tight as the one on my trousers! No doubt because I had put shorts on that day, the weather tried to rain although only briefly but it was to be the coldest day of the walk so far.

Beaches were to dominate the walk more on that day than on any other day of the walk that summer. The day began with a long walk through sand dunes behind the beach at Woolacombe before turning right at the end of the long beach and climbing up onto Baggy Point. I followed the footpath around Baggy Point where I came across a dead slowworm. This is in no way a criticism of the worm's speed, just a description of its lack of life. Further along the path was a flock of sheep, very much alive. The lambs were as large as their mothers, only distinguishable by their un-shorn fleeces.

As I watched two of the ewes began to have a disagreement, butting and shoving each other. Pretty soon the rest of the flock had formed a circle around the fighting pair. Other sheep started to join in the scuffle until the altercation had developed into a free for all, with several fights taking place. Amidst all this one lamb was desperately trying to get a drink of milk and getting pushed this way and that in the process. Not liking violence, I left them to it and continued down to Croyde.

On the little road to the beach, every car that passed me had a surfboard fastened to the roof rack. Croyde, like Saunton and Woolacombe and numerous other beaches on this coast was very popular with surfers, even having their own "Baywatch" lifeguards. I tried to count the number of surfers at Croyde, bobbing on their boards waiting for a wave but I ran out of fingers and toes before I had counted a quarter of their numbers.

Little shops sold wet suits, dry suits, boards, Malibu boards and Boogies. I thought Malibu was something to do with coconut and white rum; and wasn't Boogie the dog who had walked this path with Mark Wallington? Was there a factory somewhere making commemorative Boogies?

Full of questions and feeling very ignorant I continued along a path above the road to Saunton and the Saunton Sands Hotel. The hotel was a very large, very white and very posh building, a Union Jack flew from a flagpole and liveried doormen stood to attention outside the grand entrance. I skirted around the grounds of the hotel and emerged onto Saunton Sands, a three-mile stretch of surfers' paradise. The child in me surfaced and unable to resist the beach (no I didn't make a sandcastle) I took off my boots and socks and went for a paddle. I was still paddling when I passed Braunton Burrows Nature Reserve and reached Airy Point two hours later.

One of my pet hates in life is litter. It was depressing to note the detritus of humanity on the high water mark. Plastic bottles, fishing lines and bits of net, plastic buckets, the non-biodegradable remains of sanitary protection, bread crates, German bread crates, two oranges, one onion and, ironically, a dustbin.

Jellyfish washed up by the tide reminded me of an incident two summers ago at a beach on Anglesey involving a friend's dog and one of these ancient stinging creatures. After spotting several I paid more attention to where I was putting my bare feet and slightly less to the views.

On reaching the Saunton Sands Hotel I had been presented with a choice of routes. The inland option involved some road walking and a golf course. My chosen route was preferable and only to be avoided if the nearby military ranges were in use. I had walked more than half way down the beach before several army Landrovers emerged from the dunes and onto the wide stretch of sandy beach. My initial concern that I might have to retrace my steps and divert inland were quickly dispelled when it became apparent that the soldiers were not on manoeuvres but were simply enjoying themselves. The Landrovers glided over the beach, weaving between one another and spraying up sand in a graceful four-wheeled ballet. After a few minutes the vehicles turned and headed back into the dunes in single file, exiting stage left.

As I progressed down the beach, the estuaries of the Taw and Torridge rivers opened up before me. Looking along the opposite shores of the estuary I could see Instow and Appledore. Further along the horizon I struggled to locate Westward Ho! and Clovelly. Hartland Point lighthouse was an intermittent flash barely visible on the far headland.

At Airy Point I replaced my socks and boots and turned inland through the dunes. I was on familiar territory in the dune system, having visited Ainsdale dunes every summer for several years with the field trips at work. I had little difficulty identifying evening primrose, scarlet pimpernel, ragwort, marram grass, pennywort, dwarf willow, vipers bugloss and many others, their flowers and foliage colouring the area. Many people think of sand hills as barren places but they are not and the plants and creatures inhabiting them illustrate succession well, providing a useful example for ecology studies, not to mention convenient undergrowth to hide in when there are no public toilets in the locality.

Into Braunton, my stop for the night, I followed a tedious path along an embankment running beside the muddy edges of the river Caen. The occasional wading bird or skylark provided much needed distraction. The first building I came to was a little factory producing surf boards, the second building manufactured surf wear. It was good to see that tourism had brought jobs to the area not just in the retail industry but in manufacturing too.

Braunton was reached, for the last few hundred yards, along an old railway line and past an old open field system, a preserved piece of history. The route at this point was part of the Tarka Trail, a popular cycleway as well as a footpath. So, tired and weary, I spent the last minutes of that day's walking constantly diving into hedgerows and bushes to dodge fanatical cyclists who, despite all the notices posted along the path, did not have bells to warn walkers of their silent approach.

I had somehow managed to get sunburnt despite the often cloudy weather. The friction of the straps each time I took off or put on the rucksack aggravated the sunburn. It had reached the stage where I was considering wearing the rucksack in bed rather than endure the agony of the straps rubbing down my arms. I stopped at a chemist to buy some lotion to ease my burning arms and asked directions to the Bed and Breakfast. Although I did not notice at the time, the lotion contained lanolin and whilst it did ease the burning, it also left a greasy residue. For days after I was baffled, trying to locate the source of a smell similar to that of old chip pans, it took me some time to realise that the odour was coming from my shirt. The residue of the lotion had transferred itself to the sleeves of my shirt and by the end of the walk, the shirt smelt rancid. On returning home from the walk, it took several washes and much contact with a certain brand of fabric conditioner before the shirt began to emanate the fresh smell of summer meadows.

I found the B&B without difficulty and was soon settled in what had formerly been a child's bedroom. After a cool shower, anything too hot and my sunburnt skin threatened to spontaneously combust, I headed out in search of food.

There proved to be quite a selection of eating establishments to choose from. I was tempted by the appetising smells wafting from an Indian restaurant. The idea of dining alone did not appeal to me, although the deciding factor was the possibility of digestive repercussions and toilets were few and far between on the coast path! In the end I sat with a chicken burger and chips and watched the youths of Braunton. It was a Saturday evening in a small Devon town. Unlike Combe Martin, with a beach to jet ski from, entertainment in Braunton was much more limited and obviously many of the kids who lived there found it boring and too quiet. I would have enjoyed growing up in such a place, not interested in night-clubs and large social gatherings and with the town so near to beaches and countryside and cycleways I would have found it far more interesting than any large town or city. But then, as I was discovering on this holiday, I didn't need a lot of organised entertainment or company to be happy.

That evening it was oestrogen that washed over my chips. If the population of Combe Martin had seemed to lack many young girls, Braunton had a surfeit. Groups of teenage girls stomped around, smoking cigarettes and trying to look sophisticated in platform trainers. Feeling distinctly unfashionable (but decidedly more comfortable) in leggings and sensible jogging trainers I headed back to the B&B. This was the first one to have a television in the room, I lay on the bed and watched the weather forecast; no rain predicted, yet. Before going to bed I dowsed my arms, neck and face in calamine lotion and prayed for a cloudier day to come, my prayers were answered, the next day was not only cloudy but also considerably cooler.

Sunday 5th July

Breakfast proved to be a little embarrassing that morning. Not because of anything I did, such as throwing ketchup all over the table as I had done once in Llandudno, or spilling my cup of tea. I shared a table with a young couple and though I tried to make conversation to ease the tension, they answered in monosyllables. On other mornings conversation had flowed easily, maybe they just weren't morning people but then neither was I.

My guidebook graded this day's walking as easy, sixteen miles following the river estuaries through Barnstaple and onto Bideford. I did not need the walking pole that day and so I tied it to the back of my rucksack. We still had not gelled as a team, the walking pole and I, it had taken me some time to become accustomed to the different lengths it needed to be, depending on whether I was going up hill or down. Things had seemed to be going fine and I thought we had reached an amicable working arrangement when suddenly and without warning, the telescopic walking pole had lived up to its name. At the time I was on a steep, rutted section of the cliff path before Lynton, going downhill and so leaning quite heavily on the pole. The next thing I knew I was face down in a patch of bracken, unable to move because of the weight of the rucksack pressing down on top of me. I felt like an incapacitated tortoise, laid there feebly kicking my legs. The pole had chosen that moment to telescope into itself!

I recovered my dignity and gave the pole a stern talking to, I think I might even have sworn at it. But the pole was planning revenge and, later on, it got it. This time, instead of telescoping, it wriggled out of my grip, hooked itself onto a pocket flap on the leg of my trousers and, with a bit of help from my own momentum, ripped the pocket half off! When I had booked into my B&B that night I had borrowed a needle and thread and sewn my trousers back together.

So, on the Sunday I did not have to worry about handling the walking pole. It was strapped to the rucksack, safely out of harms way, what could go wrong? Nothing, or so I thought, but the pole was feeling left out. At first it kept slipping round and tapping me on the elbow to remind me it was still there. I would push it back; it would slip round again. After a while this began to get a little bit wearing. Eventually I became annoyed and threw it back over my shoulder so hard that it whizzed over the top of my rucksack and bashed me on the other elbow.

For I while after that I walked along nursing my funny bone and the walking pole seemed to settle down. It soon got bored again though and started up a rhythmic tapping against my rucksack. As time went by this knocking grew to be as irritating as a dripping tap. I am ashamed to admit that I gave in to it in the end. For the rest of the day I carried it in my hand, gripping it firmly by the neck.

For much of the day the path followed the line of the old railway. The railway had survived Dr Beeching only to be closed in 1970. At this point on the walk the South West Way was combined with the Tarka Trail, for this was Tarka the otter country. The Tarka Trail is a combined footpath and cycleway and, as on the previous day, I spent a lot of time leaping out of the way of cyclists.

Leaving Braunton the route passed Chivenor Royal Marine Base with its high chain link fence, razor wire and lookout towers. Guards watched me as I watched greenfinches and bullfinches flitting amongst the bushes lining the path. At Heanton Court, once a family home and now a hotel, the path ran alongside the estuary. The tide was out and I ventured down onto the mudflats. Silly me! Yes, I did get a better view of the wading birds, just before they all flew away, I also got splashes of mud up the back of my legs. I attempted to wipe the mud from my trousers using a paper tissue, this was not a great success and I walked into Barnstaple covered in mud, rather smelly mud at that, where I was able to wash it off to some degree in the public toilets.

I decided to get some money out of my post office account but it was Sunday and Barnstaple was shut. For the shop-a-holic all you could do in Barnstaple on a Sunday was buy a paper, eat a burger or get an exhaust fitted on your car.

I had opened the post office account knowing that in many of the places I would be staying there would be no banks or building societies, as I did not want to be carrying a lot of cash about with me the post office seemed like the best solution. The cash machines were working and so I decided to see if I could remember the P.I.N. of my post office account. I couldn't. I knew it had four numbers - that was the easy bit; I thought the numbers included five, four and two but after that my recollection got a bit hazy. I tried one set of four numbers. I tried a different combination, then another. At that point the A.T.M. spewed my card back and informed me I had tried too many times.

"Your P.I.N. has been cancelled!" it gloated.

Oh well, I would go to the post office tomorrow, I told myself.

Along the estuary towards Instow it began to rain. The rain was not heavy and after a short while it stopped, although the sky remained cloudy for the rest of the day. Family groups of cyclists were not deterred by the sun-less day, passing me in their droves. A couple went by on a tandem, they were obviously not married – they weren't having an argument. A father overtook me with half a child's bike attached to the back of his own.

"I hope you're pedalling," I heard him say to his young daughter.

"Yes, daddy," she lied, leaning back with her feet swinging below the pedals.

"Well it doesn't feel like it!" came his reply.

Despite a toilet stop at Barnstaple, I soon found myself in need of another. There were none along the path and so I detoured inland to the village of Fremington where P.C. was marked on my map. A newer map would have shown a housing estate in place of P.C. I walked the half mile back to the footpath, searching all the way for a secluded bush!

At Yelland Marsh, an R.S.P.B. Nature Reserve, I turned off the cycleway to follow an alternative path that shadowed the curving shoreline of the estuary. Signs for private property and warnings of deep excavations and buried asbestos greeted me. This had once been the sight of a coal fired power station; the fuel had been shipped in from the mines of South Wales. Like many of the mines, the power station was no more. It seemed strange that such an industrial scar existed side by side with a nature reserve.

The path kept to the seaward side of the C.E.G.B. site. Taking heed of the warnings I stuck religiously to the path, unlike two men who wandered over the grass covered mounds; why is it some people think signs do not apply to them?

Mother Nature had set about recolonising the site and in places it was impossible to tell there had been a large industrial complex there. Further along however, near to the quay – purpose built for the landing of the coal – nature had been defeated. Transformers, buildings and pylons stood abandoned, for some reason they had not been demolished like the rest of the structures; it was a depressing site. The tide had washed debris and litter into the channel by the side of the quay, the water lay stagnant and malodorous, the stench an assault on the nostrils. I was overwhelmed by the ugliness, in life the power station could have been little worse than the fetid corpse that now remained.

I walked on around the next bend in the estuary where I came upon a family of mallards. May be nature hadn't given up after all.

On I walked through Instow, back once more on the old Okehampton to Ilfracombe railway line. The walk might have been easy, following the flat river estuary all day, but it had been relatively uninteresting when compared with previous days. Before, there had been a new view around every corner; on this stretch of the coast path there were no corners, no incentive to be spurred on to the next headland or the next dip in the path. For much of the way the line stretched ahead, mile after monotonous mile, with bushes lining each side. The consolations though were the array of flowers, shrubs and bird life. Honeysuckle, privet, wild strawberries, scabious, dog rose, birds foot trefoil, meadow sweet, lady's bedstraw and many more added colour and perfume to the walk. I watched shags, swans, ducks, gulls and numerous other birds feeding on the water and the mudflats. Cormorants stood facing the sun, their wings spread open to dry. Greenfinches, wrens, blackbirds, robins, sparrows and many others flew along the path and between the hedges. On some parts of the estuary sheep grazed on the sparse grass. Not the Swaledales I was accustomed to seeing at home but a different breed that I was not familiar with: short legged, with little, round faces. I wondered at that point, for some unknown reason, how Chris was getting on with her leg.

I reached Bideford at about half past five that evening. I had been walking with hardly a break for eight hours. My calf muscles were cramping and sore to the touch. I found myself wishing I had caught the ferry from Instow to Appledore, saving my body the discomfort of those last few miles. My pedometer informed me that I had walked just over 17 miles that day but these were easy miles, not like the knee-cracking miles over cliffs that I had traversed on previous days. So why did my calves ache so much?

I had to ask for directions to my B&B and chose a taxi office to do so. The man behind the glass window, surgically attached to his short wave radio, noticed my rucksack, mud splattered trousers and glazed eyes. For a moment I thought he was going to insist I hire a cab but he pointed me along the road, past Safeway and down a turning to the right.

Now, unlike Chris, I do not have a fetish about Safeway, I can take it or go to Asda instead. However, at the thought of a piece of freshly cooked Safeway roast chicken, I began to salivate like one of Pavlov's dogs. The thought spurred me on until I reached the superstore, where I remembered it was Sunday and the shop would have closed over an hour and a half ago.

I found the Bed and Breakfast and I would like to say that after a hot bath my calves felt a lot better, I'd like to but I would be lying. They continued to ache all evening and only just managed to carry me as far as a kebab house where I bought supper.

I sat on a bench in Bideford park overlooking the Armada cannons and opened the plastic tray containing my kebab. Oh! All the ingredients were there; they just hadn't been assembled. After a lot of messing about I managed to cram chicken and salad into the pitta bread: and it was delicious – as it transpired, that kebab was the best supper of the entire holiday.

That night I had a double bed all to myself. I slept right through, not waking once: the best night's sleep I had had so far.

Monday 6th July

In the morning I checked that my walking trousers had dried over night, they had and I went into the bathroom to have a shower. In the daylight and with my glasses on I was horrified to notice that there was a tide mark around the bathtub. The previous evening I had washed my muddy trousers in the bath, on emptying the bath I had failed to spot the line of mud and soap scum that was left behind. Shamed at my own slovenliness, I used the liquid cleaner to remove all traces of the tidemark before finally having a shower.

Breakfast was a solitary affair that morning. I munched my way through it admiring the array of family photographs displayed around the dining room and tried to ignore the neighbour in the house opposite the dining room window peeping at me from behind her net curtain.

I did a quick trolley dash around Safeway, buying roast chicken and other goodies for lunch. As I loaded up the rucksack and swung it onto my back I promised myself that I would definitely fettle the bra fastener that night.

I headed next for the post office, with the intention of withdrawing some money from my account. I was in for a shock, not only did I need the cheque slips, which I had, but I also needed the chequebook, which I had not. In an effort to minimise my luggage weight I had only brought a few cheques, not the entire book. Result: I was unable to withdraw any money over the counter! So, the post office account I had opened specifically to simplify finances for the trip was useless. Not only that but my normal bank account was rather unhealthy because I had transferred funds from it into the uncooperative post office account.

I left the post office, emerging onto the quayside and spent some time struggling to do mental arithmetic in order to see if I had enough available money to finish my holiday. Many brain-taxing minutes later I came to the conclusion that I should have enough; if the worst came to the worst I could always go into my unofficial overdraft. I used an A.T.M. to withdraw £60 from my Co-operative Bank account. I did not feel comfortable carrying that amount but the alternative was running the risk of spending all my available ready cash and starving until I got to Bude and more A.T.M.s.

Seeing potential muggers everywhere, I set off for the Tarka Trail information centre, located in a refurbished railway carriage. I had passed it the previous day but it had been closed. It was still closed and so I retraced my steps over Bideford Long Bridge (consisting of 24 arches and built in 1535) and headed back through the town towards Westward Ho!

Bideford was for many years North Devon's major port. The former prosperity of the town is reflected in the architecture of the buildings lining the streets rising up the hill from the quay, and the tree-lined main street fronting the still busy jetty.

As I left Bideford it had begun to drizzle and I was wearing my waterproof jacket for the first time. Before reaching Appledore the rain stopped and so did I, shedding the jacket with a sigh of relief. Although it was made of breathable fabric, I became hot when wearing it because of the rucksack, which prevented the back of the jacket from breathing properly.

The path to Appledore still followed the line of the estuary but time seemed to go so much quicker than on the previous day. Whether this was because I was feeling fresh with no pain in my calves, or because the path was no longer along a straight disused railway line, I wasn't sure.

I passed under the modern towering concrete bridge of the North Devon link road, carrying traffic away from the cramped streets of Bideford. The last time I had visited the town, several years previously, the bridge had not been completed and heavy traffic thundered over the old bridge and through the narrow streets, squeezing around the sharp bends. The new bridge had done much to ease the congestion.

Just before Appledore the path detoured inland, passing the back of Appledore Shipyard, one of North Devon's largest employers. The sound of heavy machinery echoed inside the large hanger-like buildings, cranes dominated the skyline. Although the site was ugly and noisy it was also optimistic: jobs were being provided in an area that otherwise depended on the seasonal tourist trade, fishing and agriculture; and according to the guidebook the skills of the shipyard were much in demand.

Appledore is a tiny port with a history of seafaring dating back over one thousand years. At the other end of the village from the noisy modern shipyard there is a much smaller yard building wooden vessels. As well as fishing boats this yard has been responsible for the creation of full scale working replicas of historic ships including the Golden Hind.

I liked Appledore; picturesque cottages lined the quayside and it seemed to consist of little more than a few houses, a shop, a pub, a church and of course, the shipyards. At West Appledore the path followed a lane between rows of cottages, once the homes of sea captains. All the house names reflected the town's nautical past: Captain's Cottage, Hove To, Gannet's Nest, Capstan Cottage, Golf Cottage. Golf Cottage? Oh yes, according to the guidebook, the county's oldest golf club, founded in 1846, was located on the nearby Northam Burrows. It didn't seem particularly old to be merit the title of the oldest in the county – but if the guidebook said so, it must be true!

I soon reached Northam Burrows Country Park, another dune system at the mouth of the Taw and Torridge estuary. Across the estuary were the dunes at Braunton Burrows, I had walked around them two days and over twenty miles previously. The guidebook seemed to delight in telling me that these dunes were a mere 900 yards away! Soon Baggy Point and Saunton Sands with its white hotel came into sight.

The Country Park was a popular place, with an informative visitor centre and tiny souvenir shop and, rather incongruously, a recycling centre. Many people apparently came here for exercise – for both themselves and their dogs. Devon seemed to be big on doggy litter bins. Unfortunately though, not all the dogs could read the notices and I found myself, on more than one occasion, narrowly avoiding putting my foot in it.

I sat on a bench and scoffed my chicken, bread roll, crisps, chocolate, fruit and yoghurt. That little lot should keep me going until teatime! Ahead of me lay Westward Ho! As the day brightened the coastline stretching away to Windbury Point became visible. Hartland Point remained little more than a promise further westward, hidden behind a bank of low-lying cloud.

It was only eight miles from Bideford to Westward Ho! Although I had taken the day at a leisurely stroll, stopping for quite a while to linger on the dunes and for an even longer while to eat my lunch, it was not quite four o'clock when I arrived at the Bed and Breakfast. Not surprisingly there was no one at home and so I set off to explore the town.

At the beginning of the last century Westward Ho! did not exist. At that time the area was no more than a few farms and a gentleman's' club. At the outbreak of the Crimean War, Charles Kingsley, a local lad living at various times in Clovelly and Bideford, fired with patriotism wrote the novel Westward Ho! from where the growing settlement took its name. Kipling, a frequent visitor to the area, used the United Services College there as a base for his novel Stalky and Co; basing his characters on friends and himself who attended the college.

Westward Ho!'s famous literary connections were for me its one redeeming feature, with the exception of the toilets, which I will deal with later. The town, snuggled between a wooded hillside and a rocky beach, was otherwise a rather dour collection of houses, amusement arcades, a caravan park and a few shops (one of which was a surf shop). Before coming on holiday I had not realised how popular surfing was in this area, imagining it was concentrated mainly around Newquay in Cornwall. As I passed a house in the town I was startled to see a body hanging from an upstairs window. When I gave it more than a cursory glance I realised the "body" was a wet suit put there to dry and not a suicidal tourist driven to the limit by the lifeless, soul-less town. It must be hell living there on a bleak, wet winter's day.

If you hadn't noticed I was not much impressed by Westward Ho!, my own fault probably. (And apparently Kingsley did not like the place much either, taking no pride in the use of his book's title). I think I had been expecting more: more shops, more cafes, more life! But then I doubtless would not have liked it if there had been more – it would have been too urban for me. Fickle: my mum always said I was fickle; she was right.

I bought my first Devon ice cream of the holiday, with clotted cream on top and wandered along the promenade eating it. The townspeople were very proud of their sea wall; numerous plaques commemorated its construction. The council had painted it, and so had the vandals.

Passing some toilets, I popped in. Due to the number of public conveniences I had used on the walk I felt I had become a bit of a connoisseur. The Egon Ronay of the lavatory, if you like. A purveyor of porcelain. The ladies toilets (I can't speak for the men's) at Westward Ho! ranked top of the pots of all toilet facilities between Minehead and Padstow; I will go further – they were the best public toilets I had ever been in. They were spotlessly clean, if I had had any food left I could have eaten it off the floor. Paper and soap were to be found in abundance. Tubs of geraniums and pansies were everywhere – on the floor, hanging from the walls, behind the sinks. If you were the sort of person who liked to read whilst on the loo (disgusting habit) there was even literature available in the form of leaflets for things to do and places to visit.

Had the immaculate condition of these toilets anything, I wondered, to do with the fact that there was an attendant on duty? I could not leave without complimenting her and picking up a leaflet for a cider farm.

The toilets near the bus depot at Taunton, whilst not on the walk but on the way to it, came a close second. Equally clean, their flowers were of the plastic variety. Most of the other public lavatories I used on the holiday were average: no paper, a bit of graffiti here and there, that sort of thing. The ones at Tintagel had been a bit smelly but they were much in demand – King Arthur and all that. I was sure the toilets at Birmingham New Street would be very adequate once renovation work was finished, providing the micturating public did not happen to be carrying a large rucksack. The public conveniences on the harbour at Padstow were frankly disgusting - there's no excuse for sanitary bins not being emptied regularly. The toilets in Clovelly, half way down the cobbled street had won a Loo of the Year award. They were in an unusual octagonal building and each cubicle had its own sink and hand drier but they still didn't beat, in my opinion, the ones at Westward Ho!

When I arrived at the B&B for the second time the landlady was in. She showed me up to my room on the second floor of the large Victorian house, apologised for the broken door lock and left me to unpack and freshen up. The bedroom was huge with a high ceiling and bright blue walls. I had a choice between a double and a single bed. I put the kettle on and then the television, just in time to watch a smiling weatherman predict rain for the next day in the south and west. Why were they always so cheerful when it was going to rain? Were they on commission from the water companies?

The bathroom did not look as if it had been altered since Victoria's reign. The toilet was of the old variety with a high tank mounted near the ceiling and a chain, the noise of its flush could be heard throughout the house. The floor was covered with linoleum, once bright but now cracked and faded with age. A pair of leaking taps dripped into the rust stained cast iron bathtub. Despite the rust marks the bath was clean and the water was piping hot.

After a nice cup of tea, a hot bath and change of clothes and footwear I went out to reconnoitre the takeaways of the town. The choice was not vast: a full fish and chip shop and an empty fish and chip shop. Working on the principle that there is always a queue at Harry Ramsden's, I chose the full one. Fifteen minutes later I was sat on a bench on the promenade eating chips and a turkey stick, and very good they were too!

It was a lovely evening, high wispy clouds floated across the sky and the sun shone down. The town and its beach were full of holidaymakers, spilling from the caravan park. I walked down onto the beach, took off my trainers and, as so often happened after a day spent walking, I went for a walk. I paddled along in the ebbing tide back along the shoreline of Northam Burrows, before turning back towards the town to watch the sun sink into the sea.

I sat on the pebble ridge that protects the Country Park from the sea and struggled to put damp, sandy feet into my trainers, a sensation I have hated since I was a child. I remember my dad being forced to carry me back from the sea to my shoes, risking getting his own feet wet in the process rather than me having to walk across the sand. If I did happen to get sand on my feet, my poor dad would go down to the waters edge and fill a bucket so that I could rinse my feet clean. I appreciated his kindness now even if I hadn't at the time.

With another cup of tea, herbal this time, I watched the weather forecast at the end of the ten o'clock news. The forecaster still smiled and still predicted rain for the next day. What was a little rain? I didn't care, I was enjoying myself and nothing the weather could throw at me could spoil my mood of ebullience. Ha! Watch this space! In a decadent mood I chose the double bed and settled down for the night.

Tuesday 7th July

The start of the second week and that day I would clock up one hundred miles. This was to be the first continental breakfast of the trip and I had anticipated that I would still feel hungry afterwards, surprisingly though, I didn't. I pigged out on cereal, toast, chocolate filled croissants and hot chocolate before setting out feeling more full than on any other morning.

The previous evening had been very clear and sunny and Tuesday morning, despite forecasts to the contrary, was the same. Once again I found myself following the path along a disused railway line. After a short while it branched off and for much of the way hugged the cliffs close to the shoreline. At Cornborough Cliffs I came across the remains of lime kilns. In many places the path twisted up and down through woodland, dropping to sea level and the pebbly beaches on the way to Buck's Mills.

At Babbacombe Mouth I took advantage of the privacy to make a much needed toilet stop, not the first and by no means the last of the walk. In a hurry to complete the task before a fishing boat, rambler or search and rescue helicopter came along, I inadvertently knocked the pedometer from my waistband. In trying to catch it I accidentally managed to push the reset button and so I never did see 100 miles come up. I sat on the beach staring dejectedly at the pedometer, now reading 0.00. I had been so much looking forward to seeing it change from 99.99 to 100.00. My sense of disappointment was profound. Ridiculous if you thought about it: I would have had to walk for quite a distance, not watching where I was going but staring instead at the pedometer clipped to my side, all the time risking twisting an ankle or falling over the edge of the cliff. I considered tapping the pedometer until the reading increased to 97.00 which is what I had last noticed my mileage recorded at. In fact I did try this but after ten minutes and with a very cramped finger I realised that I would probably still be sitting there tapping away when the sun went down.

I ate a bar of chocolate to cheer myself up, then set off again. When the pedometer reading reached 3.00 I paused to reset it, at least then I knew I had walked 100 miles.

Through woodland the path began a rather steep descent to Buck's Mills. It was at this point that I became aware of the sound of muffled voices behind me. At first I assumed I was being followed by a pack of singing boy scouts and decided to pause to allow them to pass. Around a bend in the path a single walker appeared and with him came the boys' voices. A ventriloquist? The voices were not those of a group of scouts, rather a group of singers. The young man was carrying a rucksack with a radio in it, played at full volume. How sad that he felt unable to walk and listen to the birds, the wind in the trees, the sound of the waves on the shore etc. etc. but needed the companionship of a rapping, wailing pop group. He politely thanked me for letting him pass and carried on ahead of me into Buck's Mills.

Buck's Mills had at one time suffered from rather a lot of inbreeding if the guidebook was to be believed. I half expected to come across a community of two headed, twelve fingered outcasts, instead the only people I saw were fellow tourists reading the menu outside the tiny tea rooms. I had intended to partake of a cream tea at Buck's Mills but as I approached the single main street from the footpath I noticed radiohead had had the same idea. Instead I decided to press on and put some distance between myself and the latest musical offerings of Radio One.

The route led me through ancient woodland at Keivill's Wood, skirted a small sewage works – a startling find amidst the trees - and continued along the edges of fields where tall grass grew waiting to be turned into hay. I soon began sneezing and remembered, too late, that I had not had an antihistamine tablet that morning. Cattle grazed in other fields and had also, it seemed, been in the wood, where the path had been churned into deep ruts by their hooves.

I stopped for a drink, in Barton Wood, sitting on a fallen beech trunk and noticed with disgust two empty drinks containers discarded by thoughtless walkers. Why were people quite happy to carry full bottles, food wrappers and crisp packets out on a walk; but incapable of carrying the empty and therefore lighter wrappings back to a litter bin? Muttering to myself about litter louts, I picked up the plastic bottle and waxed carton. The bottle still contained some spring water and so I emptied it. The carton, with a straw in the top proved difficult to drain. I put both into a plastic bag and looped the handles through the waist strap of my rucksack as there was no room to fit the bag into the rucksack. For the remainder of the day I carried someone else's litter until I reached a bin. The bag bounced along with every step, swinging behind me and knocking into my thighs. It soon became apparent that (a) the carton still contained quite a quantity of orange juice; (b) the carton was gradually draining into the plastic bag; (c) the plastic bag had holes in the bottom and (d) the back of my legs and the bottom of my rucksack were being sprayed with stale orange juice. Result: I spent the rest of the afternoon cursing anyone who ever dropped a molecule of litter anywhere.

Soon the path emerged onto Hobby Drive, built in the nineteenth century by prisoners of the Napoleonic War. I followed it for quite a way as it wound around the contours of the hillside, crossing streams, all the time amongst beautiful woodland scenery. On two occasions I had cause to wonder if I was experiencing déjà vu, as the drive seemed to bend across streams identical to each other. Suddenly and without warning the drive ended and I was in Clovelly.

The steeply cobbled street leading down to the harbour was crowded with donkeys and tourists. Clovelly was a tourist trap but a carefully preserved one. This mainly due to the foresight of Christina Hamlyn, lady of the manor at the turn of the century, who refused to allow motor vehicles to enter the village street. Even today the only form of transport allowed on the cobbled street has four feet and brays!

Clovelly is possibly the most photographed village in Devon. It even merits its own large visitor centre with a huge car park above the village. Narrow cottages huddle together, clinging to the steep hillside. Colourful hanging baskets adorn the whitewashed walls. Open doorways frame low ceilinged rooms. Cats of all colours seem to be everywhere, sunning themselves in the safe traffic-free community. Holiday makers scramble down the cobbled street to the harbour before trudging slowly back up the hill; the faint hearted can ride up in a Landrover by a different route. The harbour itself still shelters a tiny fishing fleet, protected from the sea by a stone pier that was built by the local Carey family whose dominance in the area spanned over four hundred years.

I followed the directions sent to me by the owner of the Bed and Breakfast, up a steep, narrow lane, and out onto the road at Lower Slerra, half a mile above the village. I knocked on the door of the cottage but there was no answer. Disappointed at having walked up the steep hill for nothing, I turned to head back to the village, intending to have some tea before returning to the B&B later in the evening. As I crossed the road in front of the cottage I heard a clipping noise and retraced my steps. In the garden at the side of the cottage, shrouded by a large overhanging privet hedge, was the landlady, perched on top of a precarious ladder and wielding a large pair of hedge trimmers.

"Mrs. May!" I shouted over the noise of a passing coach.

"Mrs. Merrifield?" she replied, turning and nearly over-balancing the ladders.

Abandoning her gardening she came round to the front of the cottage and ushered me into the large, deceptively rambling interior. My room was under the eaves of what would once have been a thatched roof. Fire risk and insurance premiums had dictated that a more practical slate roof had been substituted at some stage of the building's history.

The landlady made me welcome with a huge pot of tea and a chat about Lundy Island where I was visiting the following day (I was staying in Clovelly for two nights in order to take a day off from walking). Then after a shower and a change of clothes I set about unpacking and sorting out my dirty laundry.

The logistics of clean clothing for the two weeks while I was away had given me considerable difficulty. I could not carry fourteen days supply of clean clothes, not without the services of a Sherpa at any rate. In the end, in true "Go With Noakes" fashion I had posted a parcel of clean clothes to the B&B at Clovelly before setting off from home. They had arrived several days before me and so I packed up my dirty clothes to send home.

I had decided to take four sets of underwear and wash them out overnight. The idea being that if they had not dried by morning I could pack them up and unpack them the next night to finish drying. At Porlock on the first night there had been a kettle and a teapot in the room. As I was wringing out my freshly washed socks that night I had been struck with inspiration. I was, after all, a technician – accustomed to resourcefulness and problem solving. (I had stood by once and watched a fellow technician cut chocolate cake with a credit card in a plastic bag when no one had a knife: we were an inventive bunch!) My underwear dried really quickly draped over the kettle and teapot. I employed this technique to great success at all the B&B's that had tea-making facilities in the rooms.

Roger had objected to the notion of receiving a parcel of dirty clothes. There's no pleasing some people! A colleague at work had offered to pay me for the privilege of getting such a parcel, although he did say he wasn't too interested in any socks. Perhaps if I had put more thought into this aspect of the planning I could have recouped some money!

After organising my clothes and parcelling up the dirty ones I set off back to Clovelly with food on my mind. I sat on the harbour wall, relaxing in the sunshine. The two inns didn't start serving food until 7 p.m. and the tea room had closed for the day. At the village shop-come-post office I bought a pasty, crisps, biscuits, chocolate and a drink, then as an after thought a home-made lemon meringue ice cream ninety nine with clotted cream. Staggering up the cobbled street I ate the ice cream. Surprising how difficult it is to eat an ice cream when you are out of breath!

Back at the B&B I sprawled on the bed, ate my supper and watched the television. After phoning Roger with a progress report and instructions to expect some dirty clothes in the post, I went to bed.

Wednesday 8th July

I was dining alone once more, other guests were not expected until the evening. Not many of the B&Bs gave a choice when it came to how the egg was cooked, this one did.

"Would you prefer your egg fried or scrambled?" I was asked.

"Fried please," I replied, I'm a sucker for dipping bread in the yolks.

"That's right, scrambled," the landlady answered and disappeared before I could correct her, leaving me sat there with my mouth open.

Oh well, I thought, scrambled would be a nice change, and they were.

This was my day off, my day of rest from walking. As it turned out it was to be my first day of injury. Ironically the mishap occurred not when I was on terra firma but whilst I was at sea. Basically it was Chris's fault. At her suggestion I had planned in a rest day, just in case by this stage of the walk I had begun to feel the effects of walking everyday for a week. Good idea Chris! Without that rest day I would have been okay – free from injury – so yes, I feel justified in blaming her.

I had arranged to spend the day on Lundy Island. During the summer trips ran regularly to the island from Ilfracombe, Bideford and Clovelly. Embarkation dates at Clovelly fit in well with my schedule, plus the distance to sail was the least from all of the three ports. The ship that operated the service to Lundy, the M.S. Oldenburg was unable to dock at the quay in Clovelly as the tide was out. Therefore a tender was provided in the shape of a motorised bath tub.

I admit the accident could have been worse. I could, for instance, have fallen between the Oldenburg and the tender and been crushed to death by their hulls and got my sandwiches ruined in the process. Obviously that didn't happen or I wouldn't have written this.

To board the Oldenburg you had to climb up from the tender, stepping onto the gunwale with the help of the ship's crew yanking at your arms. Not a problem in a sea as calm as a millpond or if you happen to be seven feet tall with an incredibly long stride. The sea was not calm. I am not seven feet tall. I pity the vertically challenged visitors to Lundy!

Just as I put the toe of my boot on the Oldenburg's deck, the swell dropped and the tender dropped with it, the much larger Oldenburg was seemingly unaffected by the swell – she did not drop. Me, with 99% of my weight resting on my foot still in the tender, also dropped. Up on the deck, my other foot had no option but to drop with the swell, the tender and the rest of me. It was snatched off the Oldenburg, my shin smacked into the edge of the deck and was then scraped downwards.

Just as suddenly as the sea had dropped, it rose again and the next second I was aboard the Oldenburg. I hobbled away to a quiet corner to lick my wound, but not having the flexibility of a contortionist was unable to do so. Instead, not daring to look at my leg, I spent the next hour and a half of the voyage gritting my teeth and watching Hartland Point lighthouse flashing through the mist.

When I finally did pluck up courage to look at my leg it was difficult to see where my leg ended and my sock began. Through a layer of trouser leg, one thick walking sock and one thinner sock I had taken off a lot of skin. Bits of skin stuck in my sock. Bits of sock stuck in my leg. I took out my first aid kit and used an antiseptic wipe to clean the area (I knew where my socks had been!) None of my plasters were long enough to cover the skinned bit of leg, in the end I used two but even then part of the adhesive was covering the wound. By the evening a nice lump had developed and a bruise was beginning to form.

Crossing to Lundy the sea grew rougher and rougher. A couple seated in front of me had been sickeningly affectionate at first. Gradually as the waves increased, the snogging decreased until it finally stopped. They both took on a greenish hue and spent the rest of the voyage with their heads on the table.

Lundy Island is owned by the National Trust, who lease it to the Landmark Trust – nothing like complicating matters is there? It is a wildlife haven and a truly beautiful, rugged place. A windswept lump of granite standing sentinel over the Bristol Channel. Travelling west from Lundy the next landfall is North America. The island has a long history. Its name derives from the Norse language and means puffin. Parts of the island are also named after animals: Gull Rock, Gannets' Rock, Gannets' Bay, Seals' Rock, Dead Cow Point, Mouse Island, Rat Island; although whether all these creatures are still in residence there is questionable – especially the ones who gave their name to Mermaids' Hole! In the thirteenth century a castle was built for Henry III on the southern tip of the island. Other buildings include lighthouses, a farm, tavern, church and even a ruined hospital.

The island is not just host to day trippers. With a permanent population of eleven and accommodation available for those visitors wishing to stay for a few days, the island is more than just a nature reserve, with supplies needing to be shipped in and waste shipped out. At the landing beach, new work was underway on a jetty, the money coming from a recent lottery grant. Whilst this would improve access, I could not help feeling it would take away some of the charm of landing on the island. Until work on the landing stage was completed the islanders continued to use an old, mobile wooden jetty. A tractor was employed to push the jetty into the sea in a much practised and smoothly conducted operation.

My guidebook provided details of a walk around the southern half of the island and, never one to turn down a walk, I followed the route laid out. At the south-western tip of the island, I stopped for lunch. Across the water, the lighthouse at Hartland Point winked out. To the left were Clovelly and the coastline from Westward Ho! Beyond Hartland Point were the cliffs I would be traversing in the following days. On this holiday at least, I was getting my first glimpse of them.

I had got a packed lunch from the owner of the B&B that morning. There were the usual sandwiches, cake, biscuit and fruit. What were unusual were the fillings in the sandwiches. The first one was egg – okay, the second was a bit more unusual – cheese and piccalilli, not a combination I would have thought to try myself but good nevertheless. I ate them sat on a rock, peering down at the rocky shores below and wishing I had brought a pair of binoculars: could those specks in the distance be seals? After much squinting I realised it was a patch of seaweed.

I followed the cliff tops along the western shore. The bird life was tremendous, not just gulls and other sea birds but moorland birds as well. I cut across the island, barely half a mile wide, to make my way back to the landing stage on the leeward side. I would have liked to trace the path the whole way around Lundy but I only had three and a half hours - it would have been a route march. I contented myself with seeing a smaller area of the island but at a more leisurely pace.

The contrast between the western and eastern shores was striking. The west, buffeted by the Atlantic, was wild – strong winds and often high seas. The vegetation consisted of short-cropped grasses, trefoil, ling, sea pinks and a few other hardy plants. In comparison, on the eastern shores, away from the pounding Atlantic, the vegetation was lusher and more verdant. Bracken grew rampantly. Foxgloves, heavy with flowers, bowed majestically. Trees, although short and stunted in the thin rocky soil, grew on the eastern cliffs, their twisted branches covered with lichen and mosses.

Although I saw numerous species of birds, I was not fortunate enough to see any puffins. Neither did I spot any seals on the shores below. The last remaining cows had been shipped from Lundy years ago, only sheep, rabbits and ponies grazed there now.

With ten minutes to spare before leaving the island, everyone seemed to be heading back down the track to the beach to board the ship. I hung back, not wishing to get in amongst a large group. I sat on a bench overlooking the beach, from where I could see that no one had yet begun boarding the Oldenburg. Voices coming from the direction of the tiny village soon materialised into a youngish couple. Whereas the majority of visitors seemed to have explored the island, this particular couple must have spent their time inside the Marisco Tavern, named after pirates that at one time used the island as their base. They stumbled down the rutted track, arguing at the tops of their voices. All the way back to the mainland they toured the ship, talking to anyone polite enough to listen, and breathing beer and whisky fumes over their captive audience. I sat alone at a table, keeping my head firmly in a magazine, praying they would not pester me. The sound of their drunken laughter, loud voices and curses could be heard all over the vessel. It was a relief to disembark, not just because of the choppy seas.

Due to the tides, the Oldenburg took all the passengers back to Bideford. Those like me, who had boarded at either Ilfracombe or Clovelly, were then driven by coach to their final destinations.

Back in Clovelly, I wandered down the cobbled street, stopping at the New Inn, where I had a meal. I took my half of cider and went to sit down in a quiet corner of the quiet pub to await my cauliflower cheese. Whilst I waited I noticed a sign on a nearby door: "Ladies". Fitting that description loosely and bearing in mind my resolution of the previous week to use any I came across, I went in. It obviously wasn't my day. On flushing the toilet, I somehow cut my finger on the broken handle of the cistern.

It stopped bleeding quite quickly but as soon as I picked up the fork it started again. In the end I had blood on the fork, the napkin, the table, the crockery and the cauliflower cheese. Then to top it all, someone turned the television on and tuned in to the World Cup! I was sitting next to the television and so it seemed that all eyes in the room were now turned in my direction.

I ate my meal rather self consciously, feeling that each time I raised the fork to my mouth I was impeding the view of the couple sat at the next table. They appeared to be watching the football avidly. As the meal and the match went on I seemed to be loosing the ability to handle a knife and fork; the bleeding finger didn't help any. The heavy wooden table was positioned just too far away from my seat to making eating easy, even perched on the edge of the seat I was forced to lean forward for every mouthful. As a piece of tomato landed in my lap, closely followed by a dollop of cheese sauce, I comforted myself that if the couple had noticed, it hardly mattered as I would never see them again anyway. Wrong! As it transpired they were staying at the same B&B that evening, a fact I only discovered at breakfast the next morning where, fortunately, I did not have to share a table with them.

Leaving the New Inn, I passed the little shop, I fancied another lemon meringue ice cream but unfortunately the shop had closed. I reflected on my foresight when on Lundy, where I had bought two bars of chocolate. At least I wasn't without supper, just to fill the gaps, you understand.

When I arrived at the B&B I phoned Roger.

"Hi, it's me. Has my underwear arrived yet?"

"No, and I'm not unwrapping it when it does!"

"I suppose you're watching the football?" I asked.

"Trying to," was the terse response. "I'm missing you," he added as an afterthought.

"I'm missing you too." I replied, trying to make amends for interrupting his viewing pleasure.

"Are you?" he asked sounding somewhat surprised, "You don't usually say that."

"No, well I have just had some cider."

Thursday 9th July

My first thought on waking that morning was that in a week's time I would be back at work. Depressing thought! When I looked out of the window I was further depressed. It was raining. The wind blew the rain horizontally past my bedroom window. It looked like I was about to find out just how good my waterproof socks really were.

Late the previous evening I had heard some other guests arriving but when I went down to breakfast they had not yet got up. As on the previous day I was told to help myself to cereal, prunes and grapefruit. Once again, I chose grapefruit in preference to prunes. That morning though, the dish of grapefruit segments was larger. What's more, even though there would be three people at breakfast there was still only one dish of each. Perhaps, I reasoned, the landlady would bring in more for the other guests. I picked up the bowl of grapefruit and the spoon, set them down at my table and began to eat. The spoon was a little bit big I thought, as I consumed what was probably an entire tin of grapefruit segments. When I had eaten them all I replaced the dish and spoon on the sideboard and helped myself to cereal.

I was part way through the cooked breakfast when the couple who had been seated in the pub the previous evening, appeared. The landlady brought in another large dish of grapefruit and the spoon and put them next to the dish of prunes on the sideboard, telling the other guests to help themselves. That is when realisation began to dawn. The couple put cereal into their bowls then spooned a few prunes and grapefruit segments on top, using the large serving spoon that I had been cramming into my mouth a few minutes before! I kept quiet, amazed at my own stupidity. I had eaten enough grapefruit for three people and probably consumed a month's worth of vitamin C in five minutes! In my own defence I think I should just say that at other B&Bs there had been grapefruit followed by cereal, which is what had led me to think the entire dish was there for the eating.

It was 9.30 before I set off that morning, wrapped in my waterproof coat. Although the rain had stopped, the vegetation was very wet. As a result of my tendon injury I had bought a new pair of boots. They were cut low around the ankle, with nothing to press against the tendon but had the sole and support of a conventional walking boot. Unfortunately they were not waterproof and so I had purchased a pair of breathable, waterproof socks. The boots quickly became saturated but the socks did their job and my feet stayed dry, although it was a strange sensation to be squelching along in sodden boots whilst still having dry feet.

The path from Clovelly travelled through woodland for the first mile or so. It was very peaceful. At the first of several shelters, I shed my jacket. The sun was trying to come out and, as had happened on many other days since leaving Minehead, it looked like the weather would improve as the day went by.

I was suddenly startled by a young squirrel, disturbed by my approach. He leaped across the path in front of me, shot up a tree trunk and darted away jumping from branch to branch; bringing a shower of moisture down on top of me. He was the first of several squirrels I saw that day.

Shortly after that I was amazed and thrilled to see a mole on the path ahead of me. Completely oblivious to my approach he ambled along, zigzagging across the path. I was able to get to within a couple of yards of him before he became aware of my presence. Then, quick as a flash, he darted down a nearby hole.

Earlier in the walk I had been studying my map when, out of the corner of my eye, I had seen a mouse, or possibly a shrew, dart into a hole right next to my feet. I had seen plenty of shrews. Unfortunately, all the ones I had seen had been run over. I had found at least four in this way on sections of the path that followed roads for short distances. I was beginning to suspect that a special sub-species of shrew existed in Devon, exhibiting similar tendencies to lemmings; choosing to throw themselves under the wheels of passing cars as opposed to over cliffs. As there was no shortage of cliffs they could have chosen I reasoned that perhaps they didn't like heights.

I passed several summer houses in the woods to the west of Clovelly, in various states of repair, from the renovated shelter known as Angels Wings because of the intricately carved joists, to a very dilapidated stone structure now much overgrown and, I am sad to say, vandalised. From this final summer house the guidebook suggested following a "steep but safe" path down to sea level at Mouth Mill. For steep but safe, read steep and slippery and incredibly overgrown. I should have realised how bad the path would be by the evidence of its disuse; in places it was difficult to see the path due to the encroaching plants. By the time I knew just how steep and slippery the path was it was too late to turn back. I descended rapidly in an uncontrolled flailing of arms and legs before loosing my footing altogether and arriving at the bottom of the hill on my backside. The bottom of my rucksack and the bottom of me displayed large patches of mud and there were bits of tree and bracken stuck in my hair.

I dusted myself down and ventured out onto the rocky beach to photograph Blackchurch Rock. This rock stands as high as a house in the middle of the beach and has two natural archways carved by the eroding action of the sea. I returned to join the path by the side of the old limekilns and began the ascent up another steep wooded slope to the cliff tops and the open fields at Brownsham Cliff.

From there the path followed the edge of fields all the way to Hartland Point. Grazing cows watched my progress with bovine curiosity, one even walking with me to the stile at the other end of the field. On I went, passing fields of wheat, barley and oats, the crops a waving sea in the breeze.

Presently the domed tower of the M.o.D. radar station at Hartland Point came into view. To my left were fields, to my right the gorse-topped cliffs with the turquoise sea below and Lundy on the horizon.

I had seen numerous butterflies during my walk and large, fat, hairy, syrup-coloured caterpillars were abundant. Just before Hartland I saw marbled whites and brimstones for the first time.

At Hartland Point, as well as the radar station, coast guard hut and lighthouse, there was a tiny refreshment hut; "open in season" said the guidebook. The trouble was it failed to say which season: it was closed. It looked like I would not be having an ice cream after all.

I crossed the car park over the subsiding strip of tarmac, reading signs warning of landslides. As I rounded the point I took one last look back at the coastline, tracing my steps all the way around to Morte Point in the distance across the water. Saunton Sands Hotel, my nemesis, stood out white on the far off shore. The sight of it had haunted me for the better part of six days, visible on nearly every day. Each time I had looked across Bideford Bay, there it stood, an ugly white scar on the land. Turning, I followed the path south along Blagdon Cliff, that was the last I saw of Saunton Sands and its hotel, when I turned to look again it had gone, hidden from view, exorcised.

From Hartland Point it was a relatively short walk to Hartland Quay and my hotel for the night. The cliffs and beaches illustrated the geology of the area, the rock strata clearly visible and very impressive along this section known as the iron coast. After several dramatic climbs up and down the cliffs, crossing shallow streams in the bottom of the valleys, I reached the narrow road leading down to Hartland Quay.

There has been a quay at Hartland since the reign of Elizabeth I. It was only with the coming of the railways in the last century that it became no longer economically viable to repair storm damage to the quay. Standing watching the evening tide pounding against the rocks I could appreciate the damage a storm could inflict. My guidebook helpfully suggested I visit the museum there, but it was closed by the time I arrived. I contemplated visiting in the morning before resuming the walk until, that is, I discovered the museum only opened at 11.30 a.m. by which time I would be well on the way to Bude.

The hotel was old, functional but clean, the architecture reflecting the location with thick walls, low doors and small windows. Concessions had been made to the building to bring it into the twentieth century: electricity, running water and fire doors and extinguishers. I carefully read the fire drill notice pinned to the bedroom door and fervently hoped there would not be cause to evacuate the hotel in the middle of the night. "Do not stop to collect any personal belongings" instructed the notice. If I adhered strictly to those instructions in the event of a fire, I would be stood on the quayside with the other guests, wearing nothing but an embarrassed expression. I had not brought a nightie on the principle of travelling light!

Along with the expected furnishings – bed, chest of drawers etc, my room contained tea making facilities, colour T.V. and an oil filled radiator. I took a hot bath in one of several bathrooms along the corridor and once more washed out my underwear and trousers. Returning to my room I switched the radiator on to its highest setting and arranged my clothes, socks and very soggy boots around it to dry.

Leaving the hotel I followed the road inland to the tiny village of Stoke. The good people of Stoke were obviously a pious bunch – religion came high on the agenda. The place consisted of a smattering of houses, a post box, a telephone box and a church the size of a small cathedral. The church, dedicated to St. Nectan, is actually the parish church of Hartland, a somewhat larger village a few miles further inland. St. Nectan was a Welsh missionary who travelled to Cornwall in 500 AD. The poor chap would have been better off staying in Wales as he was beheaded by robbers!

I passed a sign pointing to Saint Nectan's Well and on impulse decided to try to find it. I slipped down a set of slimy stone steps and into a dark tunnel of shrubbery. The path seemed to double as the bed of a tiny stream and I began to wonder if I had somehow misread the sign. To my left, hidden in the shadows of the overhanging branches I noticed a wooden structure which I at first assumed was an outside privy, closer examination revealed it to be the well. With a feeling of anticlimax I stumbled back up the damp path and out onto the road, to receive strange glances from a farmer passing by on his tractor. I checked but no, it was not my mistake, the footpath sign really did point down the way I had come.

Back at the quay I ventured into the old inn abutting the hotel and with no difficulty at all, found a quiet table. It seemed the only other occupants, apart from the bar tender and the cook, were a well-preserved fisherman (pickled from the inside out) and his dog. I ordered chicken and mushroom pie and chips, followed by nut sundae and clotted cream. Two seconds after the pie and an enormous basket of chips arrived, so did the dog. With an expression that said "My master spends all his money on rum and none on dog food, please can you spare me something?" the dog settled down underneath my table. I set about the business of demolishing the pie and tried to ignore the pitiful eyes staring up at me from the level of the floor. When only three chips remained I could stand it no longer, with a sacrifice Saint Francis himself would have been proud of, I gave the mutt my last chips. He gobbled the chips and with a canny sixth sense he got to his paws and ambled away; how did he know I had no food left? The answer was simple: he didn't, what he did know was that a recently arrived family of four had just been served and kids are suckers for pathetic canine expressions. When I left the pub I had to stride over the dog, lying supine by a table groaning under the weight of four pies and four baskets of chips.

Outside my room I fumbled for the door key, thinking how hot the corridor seemed. It was nothing in comparison to the temperature inside my room; those oil filled radiators certainly throw out some heat! The trousers and socks were dry; the boots although considerably drier than when I had left, were still quite damp. Unable to bear the temperature (I hadn't been this warm since Mexico) I turned off the heater, opened the window as wide as it would go and went to bed. In the middle of the night I awoke freezing cold. I got up, closed the window, put an extra blanket on the bed and went back to sleep.

Friday 10th July

The first thing I did was check my boots – bone dry. The second thing was to stick my head out of the window, I couldn't see very much, so the third thing I did was to put my glasses on. The weather was once again overcast but dry. After a quick bath I went down to breakfast. The dining room in the hotel was enormous; I spent nearly as much time finding the table corresponding to my room number as I did eating my breakfast.

As I set off after breakfast I was aware I had a hard days walking ahead of me: fifteen miles and a lot of steep river valleys to negotiate. This was the section of the walk I had been dreading the most. I had read somewhere that to complete the entire South West Coast Path one had to climb over 91,000 feet, the equivalent of three times the height of Everest. As I planned the walk I felt confident that by allotting myself a reasonable mileage each day I should be able to achieve my goal. With only a week to go I was suddenly beset with doubts. I voiced my concerns to no one, I was committed, people had reached far into their pockets to sponsor me, and I could not back out even if I had wished to – not that I did. But was I really fit enough to walk twelve or fifteen miles each day, day after day, with or without my Achilles tendon letting me down? May be I was expecting too much of myself. My mood in that last week prior to departure swung from high exuberance to deep anxiety. Fortunately, after only one day of walking, all doubts left me; there was nothing I had experienced before that could compare with the freedom I felt and the sense of achievement I attained with the ascent of every contour and at the end of each day. I had no one to rely on but myself, I ate when I wanted and what I wanted, wandered off the track to follow other routes whenever the fancy took me and rested when and where I chose; in short, I was having the time of my life. At the same time I regretted that Roger, my parents or Chris were unable to live the experience as well. The pictures I painted with words and the images I captured on film could not do justice to the atmosphere and the scenery.

On this stretch of coast there was much evidence of erosion. I passed numerous fences that ended in mid air, the wire supporting broken off fence posts that dangled over the cliffs. On several occasions the path had been re-routed and signs warned of the dangers of straying from the path.

By mid morning the clouds had cleared from the coastline at least, although clouds were still amassing over the hills inland. I walked along listening to the songs of skylarks and the less melodious calls of stonechats and whitethroats. I passed the much written about, Speke's Mill Mouth and its spectacular series of waterfalls and paused to watch the surfers before walking through rough pasture where sheep grazed to the cliff top fields at Milford Common.

At the ancient hill fort of Embury Beacon I took a break. There was a strong signal on the mobile phone and so I rang Chris with a progress report. I enthused about the wildlife, the scenery and the weather (according to the forecasts it was raining at home).

"You'd really enjoy it, it's a shame you weren't able to come."

"Get lost, you make me sick!" was her envious response.

Getting lost was not a problem that day as I followed the coastline southwards. The path through the cliff top fields was clearly visible and I soon came across a herd of young Friesian heifers. From a distance one of the animals appeared to be covered in clumps of mud and seemed all the more endearing for it. Was it therapeutic to cuddle a cow I pondered? I was within cuddling distance before I realised the mud wasn't mud at all but rather unpleasant looking warts or growths of some kind. What did cow pox look like? Was it still around? Was it transmitted to humans? Was I still contemplating cuddling a cow? Was I hell!

At Welcombe Mouth the footpath crossed Strawberry Water (lovely name) then began a steep ascent to the cliff top. I puffed slowly uphill.

Crunch!

"Oops, sorry snail."

Crunch, crunch!

"Sorry, sorry."

Wildlife was fated to suffer that day under my big feet.

At Marsland Mouth I had another break on the beach and met two couples holidaying together. They were not really kitted out for walking and it transpired they had parked over the hill and just slithered down the hill I was about to stagger up. There were the usual greetings, the usual questions and the usual looks of astonishment when I explained where I had walked from and where I was walking to. Then one lady asked me if I was doing the walk for charity.

I had to admit that I was raising money for the Alzheimer's Disease Society. Primarily I was walking for purely selfish reasons: I wanted to. The idea of raising money had been an afterthought; the choice of charity, in light of my Dad's recent diagnosis, an obvious one. My success relied on the generosity of colleagues, friends and family, particularly my mum who seemed to have badgered everyone she met, waving a sponsorship form in the air wherever she went, nice one mum!

Leaving the red faced breathless couples to contemplate their own ascent I set off once more. At 1.35 p.m. I crossed the footbridge spanning the tiny river Marsland and stepped into Cornwall. I had been unaware of moving from Somerset into Devon on the previous week and was only conscious of leaving Devon that day because of the specific reference to it in the guidebook. I don't know quite what I had been expecting – a large sign displaying the Cornish emblem or "Now Entering Cornwall" such as is found on the side of roads, perhaps. But there were no such border signs and in a way it did not really matter, I was walking in an area of outstanding scenery and the political divisions of man had little influence on the nature of the countryside. Bylaws governing land management may differ but nature still had the greatest authority. What petty County Council ruling could hold sway over the action of waves and wind on the cliffs?

The path climbed four hundred feet to the top of Marsland Cliff. Part way up I stopped to admire the view. Okay, okay, I admit, I was exhausted! My heart and lungs could not keep up with my legs' demands for oxygenated blood and I ground to a halt. My gaze moved from the scenery to the wild flowers bordering the path and that's when I noticed I was standing on a mouse! Not all of it, poor thing, just its tail.

The mouse had braced itself against my boot and was heaving away trying to free its tail. Feeling very guilty, I quickly lifted my foot. The mouse glared at me, dusted itself down, smoothed out the hairs on its tail and, with as much dignity as it could muster, walked across the path and into the undergrowth.

I had not been in Cornwall five minutes when the weather suddenly changed. So much for my boasts to Chris about the sunshine! Out came the waterproof jacket but I forestalled putting on the waterproof leggings, to do so would be a total surrender to the rain. I was lucky; the rain remained quite light and my legs, thankfully, remained quite dry. The wind picked up and clouds rolled in over the cliff tops. Before long visibility was reduced to less than one hundred yards, then fifty.

After descending Henna Cliff, I turned inland towards Morwenstow. At one time this had been the parish of the eccentric parson Hawker. The hut he built out of driftwood still stands on the edge of the path overlooking the sea, a much needed shelter for walkers in bad weather. Although I doubt many of the walkers would take the time to write poetry or smoke opium whilst they sheltered there, which is just what the parson apparently did!

The path inland ran alongside an electric fence, at one point crossing the fence by a stile. Aluminium has several properties that result in its widespread and varied use. It is light weight, yet relatively strong – ideal in fact for walking poles. It is also a good conductor of electricity. The human body, consisting mainly of water, can in the right conditions act as a good earth.

As I clambered over the stile, holding my walking pole in the middle, instead of by the rubber, non-conducting, handle, I made contact; the pole touched the fence. I wouldn't say I was shocked but I did get a bit of a surprise! I told you I had problems with electricity didn't I?

After that little incident, as I slithered along a very muddy track to the village, I made every effort to go nowhere near the fence. This was not easy; the path was narrow and very slippery in places and it had been churned up by a herd of cows, which didn't help any. When I felt myself loosing my balance I ended up stamping down into a quagmire in order to save myself from a second frying.

A few minutes later a very wet, muddy me made it to the Old Rectory Farm Tea rooms. I half expected to be denied entry on account of trailing mud everywhere, but no, there were no shortage of tables that day even though the car park was full of cars. From behind steamy windscreens families peered out at the mist and children drew rude pictures in the condensation.

The Old Rectory was a very old rectory: full of olde worlde charm – Inglenook fireplaces, beamed ceilings, old oak settles and stone flagged floors. It was also full of jars of jam, chutneys and preserves ranged along shelves and displaying prominent "For Sale" signs. A table by the kitchen door displayed a vast array of home-made cakes, pastries and biscuits; the Queen Anne legs splaying under the mass of calories. The choice was immense and I struggled to decide, tempted to ask for a slice of everything. I had not realised how much I was in need of a pot of tea and the huge slab of carrot cake that I eventually decided upon. I left Morwenstow feeling revitalised and took a different path back to the coast.

At Higher Sharpnose Point I stared seawards. The guidebook recommended the views. I probably would have too, had I been able to see any views! Was it not for the sound of waves eroding the cliffs I would not have known I was even staring in the right direction, for 360o the views were exactly the same – fog.

Although the clouds were still rolling in over the cliffs and sweeping inland along the valleys, it had at least stopped raining. As I paused part way up another incline, I noticed a lizard sitting perfectly still on a clump of dead gorse. It sat immobile until a gust of wind came along, then it shot into the undergrowth.

Cleave Camp, a satellite tracking station, was shown on the map. When I passed, the only thing I could make out in the fog was a chain link fence and I was so close to that I got friction burns on my nose! Ahead of me a strange shape loomed out of the mist, it metamorphosed into a cow. I was in the midst of a herd of beautiful Jersey cows and their calves. Most of them were lying down. What was that old wives' tale? When the cows are lying down… their legs are tired? No, no – got it – it's going to rain! Perhaps one of the herd could get a job at the Met. Office, they were certainly better at forecasting.

As I climbed Warren Point the clouds suddenly lifted. I turned around and literally did stand back in amazement. On the cliff tops to the north, revealed to me for the first time, were all the satellite dishes of Cleave Camp. I had walked right past them in the fog, totally unaware of their presence behind the perimeter fencing.

At Steeple Point, despite the clearer weather, I missed the path down into the valley. I followed what I assumed to be the correct one, only to find that after one hundred yards or so it began to climb. With an audience in the car park below watching my every move, I retraced my steps before eventually finding the correct path. Did I feel a fool!

Bude wasn't too far away. I passed an earthworks, a tank trap and then an enormous field of peas. From the evidence of empty pea pods scattered along the path it appeared that some walkers had already begun their own harvesting. I refrained from the temptation, yes – amazing food available and me not indulging, but this was someone's property after all, not like the wild bilberries. I didn't want my halo to slip!

On the last steep descent of the day I reached a couple of bungalows, I knew immediately they were bungalows – they were labelled as such on the map! It seemed that neither bungalow had mains sewage connection and if the smell were any indication the septic tanks were in urgent need of emptying.

At 7 p.m. I arrived in Bude, only to find it wasn't Bude it was Crooklets. Shortly after 7 p.m. I arrived in Bude, although if I had known what was awaiting me there I think I would probably have carried on going.

The town was not at all how I remembered it. Which just goes to show how unreliable the memory can be. Particularly as I think I had been remembering the wrong place.

I had been walking since 9.30 that morning, I was tired and I was hungry (what's new?) I fancied a kebab but could I find a kebab house? No! I must have walked another mile just looking for one. Being unable to find anything other than fish and chip shops, I decided to have fish and chips.

I joined the end of the queue in the chippy only to find it wasn't a queue at all but just a gang of lads hanging out and trying to impress the girl behind the counter. I joined the end of the correct queue, taking out one of the lads with my rucksack and walking pole in the process. His mates picked him up off the floor and I apologised profusely. As the line inched forward so did I. My pedometer must have been feeling left out, so it dived off my waistband and crashed to the floor in a most embarrassing bid for attention. When I got to the front of the queue, I encountered something I had not come across earlier in the trip – a language barrier.

"Is your fish skinless?" I asked.

"Pardon?" replied the girl with a puzzled expression.

"Is your fish skinned?" I simplified.

"Pardon?" she queried again.

"Do you take the skin off your fish before it is battered?"

"Sorry, do we what?"

With an audience of about six local youths and a growing queue behind me, the conversation was taking on a farcical quality. I felt my cheeks turning red with embarrassment.

"Do you remove the skin from the fish?" I tried.

"Yes."

Ah! I thought, now we're making progress.

"Some of the fish." She qualified.

I was beginning to think it would be easier if I just had a portion of chips and a pickled egg, which was silly – I didn't like pickled eggs. Neither do I like battered fish with the skin on, which seemed to be the norm in the south of England although not in the north.

"Steve, do you skin the fish?" she bellowed in the direction of the fryer.

A red face, running with sweat, appeared over the top of the fryer and eyed me quizzically. Who was this foreigner trying to place a stupid order, his expression said.

"Only the cod," he answered.

"Right, well in that case can I please have cod and chips?" I asked the girl.

"Pardon?"

I repeated my request and she began to assemble the order.

"Salt and vinegar?"

I did not dare risk more confusion, so I just nodded vigorously. Do Cornishmen and Lancastrians share a common language? At least the currency was the same. Taking the parcel of fish and chips, I squeezed past the youths, who moved as one to get out of the way of the rucksack and walking pole, and left the chippy as red faced as fryer Steve.

Within a minute of leaving the chip shop, I walked past a kebab house. Typical. Who knows, I might have faired better talking to a Greek Cypriot than a Cornish Celt! Had I not gone through so much to get the fish and chips, I might have been tempted to get a kebab and see how much of both I could eat. But the fish and chips were worth the effort and embarrassment I had endured to get them. The way my luck was running I would have probably ended up with dog kebab, hot chilli sauce and the runs.

As I set off in search of my Bed and Breakfast for the evening I paused to look at the beach. The tide was coming in and a cold wind was blowing from the sea. Yet a few (fool) hardy souls were on the beach wearing only swimming trunks, splashing out into the waves. Silly sods.

The leaflet that the owners of the B&B had sent described the location of the house as only 500 yards from the A39. What the leaflet failed to say was that the A39 was one mile inland and at the top of a rather steep hill. There was one consolation: a Safeway supermarket just down the hill from the B&B. No guesses where I would be buying lunch the following day!

I rang the doorbell at the B&B, which immediately resulted in frantic barking from inside the house. As the landlady opened the door the stink of wet dog rushed out at me, in the wake of the smell came the two dogs responsible. Ignoring their owner's commands to heel they vied with each other to stick their noses into my crotch. I tried to politely shove them away whilst trying not to breathe at the same time. I was shown to my room, which thankfully did not smell of dog. This was not the first place I had stayed that had had dogs; it was, however, the first one that had smelly dogs. I was committed; I had booked in advance and paid a deposit. But more to the point, it was almost nine o'clock, I was exhausted and the nearest hotels and guest houses were back in Bude, one mile away.

I told myself it was not too bad, the bedroom was okay (or so I thought at the time), there were a kettle and a television and a large double bed. What I needed was a nice long hot bath.

The bathroom smelt of dog. In the bath and the shower cubicle there were rubber anti-slip mats. The type of mats that could, if not cleaned properly, produce a nice line in pink mould. The mats had not been cleaned properly. Now why did that not surprise me? There was no way I was going to run a bath and lie down on top of the fungi ridden mat. I took the shower option, figuring only my feet would be in contact with the mat. When I got back to my room I washed my feet again in the sink. For the next few days I spent a lot of time checking the colour of my soles to make sure they weren't turning pink.

I made a pot of tea, inspecting the inside of the teapot first for any festering old bags. Then I went to bed, briefly. Drawing back the quilt I stared in horror and disgust at the sheet underneath. It was covered in hairs, dog and human. I spent the night sleeping on top of the bed, fully clothed in leggings and a sweatshirt, trying not to think of what lay beneath me. My skin crawled at the mere thought of lying naked between the sheets. What delights would breakfast hold? Hairy Kennomeat?

Lying there in the darkness, unable to sleep, I vowed that I would complain in the morning. I would dress, pay and leave without breakfast - I could get something at the café in Safeway. Full of indignation I rehearsed what I would say, I would be succinct and polite but with a steely tone in my voice that implied I was not to be tangled with. That night one of the two lurchers slept somewhere near my bedroom. It snored, all night.

Saturday 11th July

After a few hours sleep things smelt just the same but at least the snoring had stopped. I practised my speech about standards, hygiene and dog shampoo. Then I washed and dressed and went meekly into breakfast, saying not a word.

Displayed conspicuously in the dining room were certificates for aromatherapy and faith healing; a shame there wasn't one for hotel and catering. I sat down at the only table and began examining the cloth and cutlery for signs of dog; it looked okay. A different lady from the one I had seen the previous evening, entered the room and invited me to help myself to fruit juice and cereal.

"Did you sleep well?" she enquired.

Here was my chance, with my speech ready prepared I took a deep breath and ineffectually replied:

"Well actually, I could hear one of the dogs snoring all night." I sat there mentally kicking myself for my cowardice, why had I not taken the opportunity to complain? Why was I such a wimp?

"That's strange, you couldn't have heard the dogs, they sleep out at the back of the house. Unless it was one of us, we have both got colds at the moment."

"Oh," I replied weakly.

"I suppose it might have been our other guest, her room is opposite yours."

Two minutes later the other guest arrived and I thought it likely that she was the phantom snoring champion. Frankly, she was weird. She was wearing a grubby skirt and blouse, both a size too small, the underskirt showed three inches below the hem of her skirt and her legs were clad in sagging knee high woolly brown socks. Her greying hair, piled into a bun on top of her head was making and succeeding in an escape attempt. I could not decide her age; it could have been anywhere from forty-five to about eighty. She sat down opposite me and whilst she was preoccupied dispensing cereal into her bowl and all over the tablecloth, the cooked part of my breakfast arrived. I surreptitiously scanned the plate for traces of dog. All clear. Surprisingly the breakfast was not too bad, not a dog hair or chunk of Kennomeat in sight, furthermore the dining room did not smell of dog, well, not too much, or perhaps it was just that my sense of smell had been over-stimulated and gone on strike.

As we ate breakfast we discussed my walk.

"My friend had planned to come with me but she tore her calf muscle and wasn't fit in time." I explained.

"Oh, I bet she's really missing you!" she replied. (Just how friendly did she think we were?)

Conversation turned to wildlife; she mentioned seeing Exmoor ponies and I felt I had to say something but why, oh why, did I mention the adder? She ranted on and on about how dangerous they are, I should be careful, a German lady she had met had killed one with a stone (why?) and ought I not to report the sighting to someone?

I attempted to explain how adders are shy creatures who will slither away to hide if they hear someone approaching. It fell on deaf ears. She continued her diatribe. I was tempted to tell her more people died from tedious breakfast conversation than poisoning by adders.

What with the hairs, the stench, the mould and the fellow B&B'er I nearly ran out of that guest house. As I paid one of the ladies she suddenly said:

"Don't forget to sign our visitor book on your way out."

"Oh, yes, okay," I stuttered.

What could I write? In the end, I left the comments column empty; secretly wishing I had the nerve to write: "Try washing your smelly mutts, but not with the laundry!"

I walked out onto the busy main road and inhaled deeply. A juggernaut rumbled past and I gulped in a lungful of diesel fumes. Ah, that was better, no more essence of dog!

First stop was Safeway. I had never been in a supermarket that sold surfboards before. Bude was a black spot on my walk: language difficulties, no kebab, the worst B&B ever (it had made Fawlty Towers look like The Ritz) and the Safeway in Bude did not sell in-store roast chickens! I stood dejectedly in front of the delicatessen counter, what could I buy for lunch to make up for the lack of roast rooster? I settled for marinated strips of chicken, cookies, muffins and a new fun camera (not that I ever became hungry enough to try eating the camera – just that I had taken all the photos on my other one).

It began to rain as I got into the centre of Bude, so I stopped and donned my jacket. As the rain was only light I foolishly decided not to put on the waterproof leggings.

I crossed the canal by the locks (canals, apparently, are a bit of a rarity in Cornwall – probably due to the language barrier between the Cornish and the Irish navies who used to build them). Sadly, by the time the canal was completed demand for its use had declined and Bude now survives mainly on tourism and a little light industry. The path climbed over Efford Down, a SSSI and along to Widemouth Sands. It was Saturday morning and again, like Croyde on the previous Saturday, the human seals were out in their hundreds. Well, okay there might not have been hundreds but there were a lot! I was beginning to think they were the nearest I would come to seeing a seal.

Just after Widemouth and some convenient public conveniences, it began to rain harder. I looked around for somewhere sheltered where I could put on the leggings. I needed somewhere dry because I would have to take my boots off to put the leggings on. By the time I did find shelter, my legs – the fronts at least – were saturated.

At Millook, where a tiny stream had once powered a waterwheel, I found an unusual makeshift stone and wooden shelter on the edge of the pebbly beach. Under the cover of the overhanging eaves, I sat on an upturned milk crate and ate my lunch. My legs steamed. A snail crossed the pebbles in front of me. Snail's pace was an apt description: it was in no hurry, undaunted by the rain, it went about its business. Every so often it would retract one of its antenna as a drop of rain fell on it. I decided I liked snails. I bet they didn't smell of dog!

The weather had defeated me in a sense. I had been forced to wear waterproofs. Oh, well, at least for the first ten days there had been nothing worse than a spot or two of drizzle and a bit of mist and fog.

That afternoon the weather deteriorated rapidly. My boots were saturated. My waterproof socks, the one on my left foot at least, began to fail. My specs steamed up from my raggedy breathing on all the ascents and ran with water constantly. My nose began to run. Everything was running! Except my feet!

The scenery should have been spectacular but I could not see very much. The weather had reduced visibility and the water on my glasses created a distorted image. I kept my head down and trudged on. I pondered on one gentleman who I had read about; over a series of holidays he had walked the entire South West Coast Path – all 630 miles of it, with only one hour of rain the whole time! He must have chosen drought years to do it.

Gales had been forecast. Gales I got! At Dizzard the wind started to practice. By Pencannow Point it had practised enough and the gales began. The path followed a very exposed route along a knife edge to the tip of Pencannow Point. Here the wind was at its fiercest. I was frightened of literally being blown over the cliff. It was a real possibility and it took all my strength, leaning on my faithful walking pole, to stay on my feet. I progressed an inch at a time, bent double by the force of the wind.

A group of walkers approached me coming up the hillside; they were all having similar difficulties battling with the gale force winds to walk and stay on their feet. At least if I did do a Mary Poppins off the Point someone was there to see it. We passed, shouting hellos to be heard above the noise of the storm.

"How far are you going?" bellowed one of them.

"To Crackington Haven," I screamed.

"You're almost there then!"

My reply of "Thank goodness for that!" was torn away by the wind and we continued in opposite directions. How, I wondered, did he withstand the pain of the rain whipping against his bare calves? Every drop that hit my face and hands stung as if it were a stone.

As I began to descend Pencannow Point, there was an exceptionally strong gust and I was blown off my feet. I was lucky; I was below the level of the cliff top. I fell sideways into the heather, unharmed. Winded, I lay in the vegetation and quite absurdly noted the beauty of the flowering bell heather covering the slopes and in particular one delicate flower just inches from my nose. As I struggled to my feet, I risked a glance down into the valley to get my bearings. I had no idea how far I was from Crackington Haven; unable to see clearly to read and with the map and guidebook becoming saturated, I had long since shoved them into a pocket. For the last few miles I had been relying on the signposts, I hoped the other walker's idea of "not far" was about three yards.

Through the driving rain I could make out a cluster of houses and a car park. It wasn't until I reached the bottom of the hill that I could be sure I had reached Crackington Haven. The only thing left to do was find my accommodation for the night. It was barely three thirty - a little early to squelch up to the B&B, once I did arrive I had no intention of venturing out again. My waterproof jacket was suffering from perspiration and precipitation overload and needed to be thoroughly dried, my feet felt like I was wearing buckets full of water and if I got any wetter I was at serious risk of dissolving.

I stumbled into the almost deserted café and shed rucksack, pole, jacket and five gallons of rainwater. My spectacles steamed up, I attempted to wipe them with a napkin but the water flowing down my hands saturated everything I touched. Leaving my glasses on the table I picked up the menu and perused it, holding it inches away from my nose and screwing up my eyes to bring the words into focus. I ordered a Cornish cream tea and waited for my glasses to clear.

As I waited, I became aware of a voice that seemed to be addressing itself to me, asking how far I had walked. I peered myopically around, trying to locate anyone who might have spoken. A lady and her husband were just seating themselves at a nearby table. We soon began chatting about walking and the weather. They told me of a 75 year old gentleman they had met the previous summer, who was walking the path all in one go.

It reminded me of all the people along the way that I had either met or been told about. People from all walks of life: pensioners, scouts, couples, single women, English, Dutch, French, German, Canadian, American and others whose accents I had been unable to identify. All of them drawn to the South West Coast Path, some walking long sections, others just doing a little bit at a time. The foreign visitors not doing the usual touristy things one might have expected, such as London, Stratford on Avon, Cheddar Gorge and Wordsworth's Grasmere. They had chosen to holiday in Britain, walking a footpath. So many Brits went abroad – myself included – did they realise what they were missing? Wildlife, fantastic scenery, delicious food and gale force winds.

I finished the cream tea, put my specs on and struggled back into my jacket and rucksack. Amazing! After nearly a fortnight I had still not fixed my bra fastener!

Squelching with every step I walked up the hill and found my Bed and Breakfast. I hoped they would be able to put my clothes somewhere to dry out. I need not have worried, the guest house owners were obviously accustomed to wet walkers. I was ushered in and assisted out of my rucksack.

"If you want to take all your wet things off here, I can take them away to be dried," offered the landlord.

Had I taken him at his word I would have been stood there with nothing on! Everything was wet. I decided that as soon as I got home I would look for a new waterproof jacket, in the meantime perhaps they had an iron I could borrow to pep it up a bit? I wriggled out of jacket, boots and leggings, which were then whisked away, brave man touching my boots! I was led upstairs to a single room where I peeled off the rest of my wet clothes, made a warming pot of tea and took a hot shower. There's nothing quite like the feeling of being warm and dry after you have been incredibly cold and incredibly wet!

I ventured back downstairs with my soggy, empty rucksack and this too was taken away to dry out. The owner kindly offered to drive me back down to the village if I wished to have a meal at the pub. When I assured him that I would not be setting foot outside for the rest of the day he very kindly offered to make me a sandwich. Not wanting to be more trouble, I politely refused. In any case I had just found a bar of chocolate at the bottom of my rucksack. The chocolate had not travelled well. It had been in the rucksack since my first evening in Clovelly and with the effects of temperature and the pressure of all my clothes it had reformed into a solid blob. It tasted okay though.

That evening I sat in the spacious lounge, windows on three sides giving excellent views of the haven and the sea beyond. Not that I was able to see very much of the excellent views. The gale hurled rain against the glass. I waited anxiously for the weather forecast for the following day. Guess what! More gales and rain, but it was going to brighten later in the north and east! I knew I should have done the Coast to Coast.

When I had begun to plan the walk I had intended to walk the sixteen and a half miles from Bude to Boscastle in one day. I had changed my mind because I thought two days of walking fifteen or sixteen miles rated as severe and strenuous might be too tiring. How glad I was for my change of mind and how appropriate the word "Haven". On that particular day I had not considered the walking to be especially severe, only the weather.

The storm raged throughout the night. I woke up several times to hear rain lashing against the window and the wind howling.

Sunday 12th July

The weather was unchanged. I lay warm and snug in bed and tried to motivate myself to get up. At breakfast I was able to see the cliffs and the sea in the distance. My clothes were all dry, although my boots were nearly as wet as when I had taken them off the previous afternoon. I was able to borrow an iron and did manage, quite successfully, to boost the waterproof-ness of my jacket. By the time I was ready to depart the rain had eased but not the gale force winds. I decided to implement Plan B.

Down in the centre of Crackington Haven I stocked up on chocolate and phoned my mum. There was no signal on the mobile phone, I don't know if this was due to the weather or just because the area was out of range of the nearest aerial mast. I squeezed into the tiny telephone kiosk and fumbled about for change. When she did answer the phone, I could barely hear her voice for the noise of the wind and the sea.

"It's blowing a gale here." I shouted.

"Pardon?"

"I said it's really windy."

"Don't get blown off a cliff, will you?"

I had one ten pence piece remaining for my call to Roger. He was at work and another member of staff answered the phone. I asked to speak to him and was about to explain that I might run out of money before he picked up the phone and that I was just ringing to say I was okay; but before I could explain anything I was put on hold. My ten pence ran out and the line went dead. Well, at least he would know I was still alive. What I had not counted on was him using 1471 to get the number of the call box and ringing me back. When he did, I was in the nearby toilets and out of sight of the person who answered the call. Roger, apparently, described me and asked if the person could see me, obviously he couldn't. Roger spent the rest of the day worrying about me; his colleague told him I had sounded anxious!

Completely oblivious to all the concern I had inadvertently caused, I stood with a small crowd on the beach, watching with amazement as two surfers paddled out into the waves. The stream running into the sea was a gushing torrent of brown water, carrying with it pebbles, mud and broken branches.

Crackington Haven was in centuries past a port, used for the import of coal and limestone and the export of slate. Watching the waves crashing onto the beach that morning, it seemed impossible that any vessels could ever have come into shore safely in the narrow bay.

Leaving the beach I headed inland: Plan B! With great reluctance, I had decided that for my own safety it would be better not to walk along the coastal path that day. Just south of Crackington Haven was High Cliff. The Cornish man who named it wasn't big on originality: at 731 feet it is the highest cliff in Cornwall. If my guidebook was any judge, I would be missing some spectacular scenery but it was either that or risk getting blown half way to Okehampton, in any event the chances of my actually seeing the scenery through the driving rain were not good.

After consultation with maps, guidebook and mine host at the B&B, I had planned a safe, sheltered inland route to Boscastle. I followed the rushing stream through East Wood along a very, very, very muddy track, before diverting onto a lane by the restored farm of Trevigue, now owned by the National Trust. Unfortunately I diverted the wrong way and began following the single track road back towards Crackington Haven. Fortunately, I soon realised my mistake.

I could have followed footpaths through the wood for another couple of miles but the owner of the B&B had warned me that the farmer who owned that parcel of land did not like walkers. He went to the lengths of moving signs, erecting fences and turning signs round to cause walkers as much difficulty as possible. It seemed folly on his part to do this, as surely the result was that walkers tramped across land not designated as footpaths and spent more time on his property trying to discover where they had gone wrong. In one sense I sympathised with farmers and landowners who have to contend with some walkers who cross their land and treat the countryside like one enormous green litterbin. However, I had found just as much litter which could only have originated from farms, as I had litter that was once wrapping someone's lunch.

In the last few days I had seen many cars displaying out of date stickers urging people to "Support the Countryside March". The march had taken place earlier in the year, the organisers claiming it to be the largest demonstration of public opinion since the CND protests of the early 1980's. I empathised with many of the points that the demonstration highlighted: problems of rural decline, increased road building, loss of habitat, use of greenbelt areas. However, the main objective of the march and the one that the pro-hunt lobby ensured received most publicity, was to protect that ancient "sport" of hunting. It seemed to me that the majority of people on the march cared more about the protecting their way of life and their ability to make money out of rural England than they did about actually preserving the land, the wildlife inhabiting it and the environmental issues involved. While I know that many farmers are struggling to make a living, the ones shouting loudest on the march were the ones with the deepest pockets: it costs money to own and keep a hunter. Or could it be possible that there were a few hypocrites amongst the supporters of the Countryside March? Protecting the countryside way of life is fine – just as long as it is a selective process, preserving certain aspects of country life relevant to them. The long tradition of hunting deserves as much protection and preservation as other ancient country pursuits and customs - serfdom, incest, bear baiting, cock fighting, gallows at cross roads, etc. etc. etc. But then what do I know? I'm only a townie; perhaps deer, foxes and hares aren't really part of the English countryside!

After a rather steep section of road walking I diverted along a bridleway, cutting out a long section of twisting road before eventually returning to the road near Higher Beeny. From there I followed lanes and field paths before eventually reaching St. Julitta Church. The church had undergone some restoration work in the last century, carried out by Thomas Hardy. Better known for his writing, Hardy started his working life as a stone mason in Dorset. He met his first wife whilst working on the church. A Pair of Blue Eyes is a semi-autobiographical account of this period in his life.

By the time I dripped into the little church, my stomach could be heard above the noise of the wind and rain. I think it might have been lunch time. Sheltering in the church porch, I ate a bar of chocolate. I could not set off again without viewing the interior of the church and so I pushed open the heavy oak door and went inside. A notice asked for donations to repair the roof. Another noticed apologised for the absence of brasses: here, miles from anywhere, they had been stolen.

Satisfying my morbid curiosity, I took a quick tour of the graveyard. On the outside of the church, on the walls sheltered from the winds blowing up the valley from the sea, lichen grew, carpeting the stonework.

From there it was a relatively short walk down the valley, along the river Valency and into Boscastle. It was raining hard and had been since entering the wood just beyond Crackington Haven, although there inland, the wind had lost some of its ferocity.

My boots, damp when I had put them on that morning, had quickly reached saturation point. Again, one of my waterproof socks had failed to live up to its name. I squelched when I walked, moisture foamed and bubbled from my boots each time I put my feet down. Had I done the right thing buying these boots in preference to waterproof ones? At that point I was beginning to wonder. Walking with wet feet was unpleasant and depressing. Conversely, wet feet did not prevent me from finishing the walk. With other boots, I would have worried for the fortnight that I might injure my tendon, and an injured tendon would definitely have prevented me from finishing. Wet feet, socks and boots could be dried. My tendon had taken six weeks to heal.

The last part of the walk into Boscastle was lovely despite the wind and rain and wet feet. The swollen stream gushed over its rocky bed and in one place it had swept away part of the path. Leaves and branches littered the ground and a sycamore, a recent victim of the gale, leaned drunkenly, caught in the arms of its fellows.

In Boscastle, I did all the touristy things: visited the visitor centre, the National Trust shop, the craft shops and the toilets. I walked down to the harbour mouth; the waves crashing against the rocks were spectacular, sending plumes of spray high into the air. Seagulls zoomed through the air carried by the wind, before realising they did not want to go where the wind was taking them and then attempting to battle against the wind, getting nowhere for their efforts.

In one of the craft shops, a pottery, I nearly died. Throughout my life I had spent half my holidays inching carefully through narrow aisles in expensive gift shops, terrified of breaking anything. Care was my watchword. All breakages must be paid for, were more of my watchwords. With my rucksack still on my back I wandered down the aisles, keeping a firm grip on my walking pole. After all, I did not want to break anything. CRASH!!! Oh God! I dared not look round. How much of my remaining cash would I have to part with to take home a shattered ornament for Roger to superglue back together?

"I'm so sorry, I'll pay for it of course."

Who said that? Not me! Turning, I saw the shopkeeper hurrying towards a lady standing a few feet away. I could hardly believe it: someone else as gormless and clumsy as I usually was. I smiled with relief and received a glare from the hapless shopper. Time to get out while the going was good.

I left the shopkeeper busy wielding her dustpan and brush and staggered up the hill into old Boscastle to find my B&B. I got lost: there's a deceptively large area of old Boscastle, most of it on a steep hill, to get lost in. I was all set to head back to young Boscastle to the Tourist Information Centre, to ask for directions, when I walked by a house displaying a prominent Bed and Breakfast sign swinging in the wind. It took a few seconds to register the sign I had just read was the name of the B&B I was searching for.

It was in converted stables, very large, very posh and very clean. I was shown to my room, conscious of the trail of wet footprints that I was leaving all over an expensive looking carpet. This was my first en-suite room. It had all the trappings of home but without the dust: double bed, tea making facilities, colour television and, most useful of all, two working radiators and a hairdryer. Not that I was too bothered about drying my hair, but I did want to dry my boots.

I was able to wash out socks, leggings and boots and dry them all with ease. Mind you, the smell of hot sweaty boot wasn't too good (but better than hot sweaty dog!) and I had to keep the window wide open.

I took a long hot shower then went back down into Boscastle for tea. I did a quick recce of the eating establishments, ruling some out on account of them being closed and others on account of them being outside my budget. I settled for a quiet café near the car park and after a rather mediocre chicken and chips, had a rather yummy death by chocolate for dessert. After that I telephoned Roger.

"You've only sent me one postcard," he moaned.

"I posted another one today!" I fibbed trying to pacify him.

I listened to him raving about how worried he had been after my phone call that morning. Then I listened to him raving about the football. It was World Cup Final night; both ITV and BBC were broadcasting the game. If I wanted to relax in my room and watch TV that evening, I had a choice of France v. Brazil, My Fair Lady (seen it before), France v. Brazil or Frank Sinatra. I bought a magazine and a postcard.

While I had been sticking a hairdryer down my boots, the weather had been improving. And by seven o'clock, as I left the newsagent's, the wind had dropped, the rain had long since ceased and the skies were clearing. I walked along the south side of the harbour and up to the headland. The weather had changed so much in fact, that I could just make out the satellite tracking station to the north of Bude. To the south, lay Tintagel, where I would pass through the next day. I fervently hoped I had seen the last of the gales and that I could complete the walk along the coast path.

I made my way back to my B&B, passing on the way the preserved "stitchmeal" open field system, now in the care of the National Trust. The name Boscastle is a shortening of Bottreaux Castle. The castle, built by a French family after the Norman invasion – 1066 and all that – no longer survives. It is impossible to visit Boscastle without being aware of its harbour. This is perhaps one of the best natural harbours in the county, standing as it does at the end of a deep, twisting, narrow inlet where the Valency river flows into the Atlantic. The energy of the pounding waves is expended on the Meachard rock that stands beyond the mouth of the inlet, and the tide washes sedately up the narrow channel to the tiny sheltered harbour.

Boscastle is a very historical little place on the quiet. Roger and I had visited it some years ago, it might have been whilst we were on honeymoon. We had missed the old village, the open field system and the cliff top walks. Mind you, we were having an argument that day! Which, thinking about it, does nothing to distinguish it from dozens of other places.

At 9 p.m. I switched the television on, hoping to see a weather forecast. The football was still being shown. I flicked through the channels: football, musical, football, Sinatra. Hang on, the football was the same: the same match obviously – but even the same camera angles! Had the opposing broadcasting channels not heard of competition and variety? Hard though it might be to comprehend not everyone is a football fan and even the most fanatical fans wouldn't watch the same game on two TVs at the same time! If they did they really were sad.

I never did see the weather forecast that night. As I went to bed, the sun was setting in a fiery blaze. Red sky at night, the harbour's on fire.

Monday 13th July

Would it prove to be unlucky thirteen?

When I got up the sun was shining, the sky had a few clouds but not many and the outlook was good. Ten minutes and one shower later all that had changed, clouds had gathered and a light rain had begun to fall. Oh great! Another day of soggy feet and rustling waterproofs! I had developed two blisters, one on each foot in corresponding places and I was convinced they were the result of wet socks. Until the weather had changed for the worst I had not had one single blister.

I had a choice for breakfast, either continental, full English or smoked fish and scrambled eggs. Continental was out of the question – no chocolate croissants. Smoked fish, I'm sorry but I am not a lover of fish and in my opinion there are only two things you can do with fish; one is batter it, the other is feed it to the cat. I opted for the full English breakfast.

The rain did not last long and by the time I was preparing to leave the weather was sunny once more.

"That's £25 then please," smiled my host.

"£25?" I echoed as calmly as I could, panic causing my voice to rise an octave on the last syllable.

The lowest amount I had paid so far had been £12, the highest £20 at Hartland Quay which did have a bit of a monopoly just there.

"Oh, how much did my wife quote you?"

"Well, when I booked I was quoted £20." I replied staring pointedly at a price list by the door. "Bed and full English breakfast £20" it read.

"Oh, okay, £20 then."

I wrote the cheque, my pulse, breathing and blood pressure returning to normal. When it came to money, I had a real problem – I hated parting with it.

I rejoined the coast path at Forrabury Common. Passing a post box on the way I mailed the postcard to Roger, better late than never! At the Valley of Rocks I detoured inland to see the Bronze Age labyrinth, a rock carving thought to be over 3,500 years old. It made a change to see an artistic carving instead of the usual initials and dates and "Des wos ere". Why is it that vandals are so keen to leave their mark? Like a dog urinating against a lamppost.

Approaching Tintagel I overtook an American couple. They too had walked from Minehead but were planning to finish at Falmouth; if they succeeded they would have walked twice as far as I had. I assumed, wrongly, that they were camping. If they weren't carrying tents, sleeping bags, stoves, pans etc. just what was in their enormous backpacks? A suitcase and hand luggage?

The guidebook said I should be able to see seals and puffins. It lied. There were plenty of rocky coves along this section of the coast and I looked carefully into each of them. Hope of seeing seals and puffins dwindled with each successive cove I passed. Guess what? Yep! I didn't see anything. The fulmars, kittiwakes and herring gulls wheeled in circles around the coves, gliding on the currents of air. But comical little puffins or cuddly seals saw I none.

The American couple had passed me. They were obviously more interested in history than wildlife.

"Geez Martha, take a look at that. Tintagel. Built by King Arthur, honey."

Martha staggered along in her husband's wake, bent double under the weight of her rucksack, eyes glazed. At two feet shorter than her husband, she was at a distinct disadvantage, taking three stumbling steps for each one of his strides. Without waiting for her to catch up he swept onward.

While they diverted into the English Heritage shop at Tintagel, (no doubt where King Arthur went for his milk and papers), I diverted into the toilets.

A lot of legends surround Arthur and his Knights of the Round Table. Some may well be true, who knows? He would have had to be pretty amazing though to build a castle at Tintagel – 700 years after he's thought to have died! The Earl of Cornwall, son of Henry I, in fact built the castle in the twelfth century. Later changes were made and the castle was added to, finally becoming derelict in the sixteenth century. Archaeological finds on the site pre-date the castle, which perhaps explains the origins of some of the myths surrounding Tintagel and King Arthur.

I left the coast path to go into the centre of the village where I bought an ice cream: strawberry flavour with clotted cream on top. As I rejoined the coast path I stopped to read an information sign and soon began chatting with a rather large lady who was perched on a rather small stone.

"You young girls don't eat enough nowadays. Have you had a proper breakfast?"

There was that word again – young!

"Yes, I'm always eating," I replied somewhat bemused.

"I was your size when I was your age you know."

I was not sure what to say to that, tact is not one of my strong points, so I just smiled politely.

"Well, I'm going home for a nice salad," she stated. "You make sure you have proper meals. They say young girls are too thin these days. It's as bad as being fat you know! Goodbye."

"Er, yes, I will, bye."

I was beginning to wonder how old I looked. She was the fifth person who had commented on my age. At Ilfracombe I had been catching up on my diary, beginning now to rival the works of Samuel Pepys. Whilst sat there on a bench, a gentleman had begun chatting to me;

how far was I walking, that sort of thing. Then he had asked me if I was doing it as part of a project for college.

My 31st birthday loomed at the end of the holiday. Did I really look as if I was still a student? I didn't think so. Was I just becoming paranoid? I had begun dropping Roger's name into every conversation.

"My husband and I..." (I sounded like the queen) "came here seven years ago."

I felt that I had to justify being there on my own and that I was old enough to be out unaccompanied. It was getting so bad that I had thought of inventing three teenage sons and a married daughter. People would then have been running off to phone the Guinness Book of Records, no doubt!

I couldn't look that young, I'd been married nine years and was getting the grey hairs to prove it! The only explanation was that a lot of people must be terrible at judging other peoples' ages.

I finished the ice cream and set off southwards. By that time the day had become very warm, it looked as if my feet would be staying dry after all. There had been much slate mined along that section of the coast in previous centuries. Some had been taken directly from the cliff face, leaving spectacular pinnacles and pillars. The flora along that section of the footpath reflected the underlying rock. No more foxgloves, instead rock samphire, wild thyme and lots of thistles. The scent of the thyme was released onto the air as my boots crushed the plants along the path. But everywhere still, the ubiquitous sea pinks, their flowers nearly over. Earlier in the year the cliffs would have been a carpet of pink flowers, now most of the flower heads had dried to a light brown colour.

The wind was still quite strong, nowhere near gale force though and the sun was shining brightly. Families took advantage of the improvement in the weather to enjoy the popular beach at Trebarwith Strand. I lingered at Trebarwith long enough to do two things. First, I used the public toilets to change into shorts and secondly, with the words of the lady at Tintagel ringing in my ears, I bought another ice cream. Well, I didn't want to waste away, did I?

Before coming on the walk, someone had asked me if I wanted to get leaner and fitter. Fitter, yes. Leaner? At 5'6" and nine stone, there wasn't much leaner I could go before I started to look anorexic. I was almost capable of hiding behind lamp posts as it was - my nose stuck out though and spoilt it.

Just after Trebarwith I saw my second adder, again on the path in front of me. Although I had seen one two weeks earlier I was still initially unsure of what it was, presumably because sighting an adder is such a rare experience. I was faster with the camera the second time and managed to capture on film the last two inches of its tail disappearing into the undergrowth!

I was to be lucky for wildlife sightings that afternoon. Two Peregrine falcons soared overhead, (no puffins though). As I climbed a stone stile I spotted a lizard on the other side of the wall, sitting on the bottom step. I froze, not wishing to scare it and was rewarded by seeing a second lizard join the first.

Further on still I disturbed a juvenile herring gull. It had obviously only just enrolled for flying lessons and was having some difficulty with the throttle. At my approach it began running down the path, jumping up into the air and flapping its wings ineffectually. I stopped walking, concerned that it might panic and do something silly. It did. It ran straight for the edge of the cliff, a sheer drop of about 300 feet. It continued to flap its wings but it just couldn't grasp the mechanics of take off. Gulls weren't designed for running; as it got nearer to the edge it stumbled over its webbed feet, tripped, and tumbled over the edge of the cliff.

I gasped in horror but I need not have worried. The wind caught the gull, it instinctively spread its wings and suddenly the clumsy bird was no more. It soared gracefully on the thermals. Then like a child learning to ride a bicycle, who realises dad is no longer holding the saddle, it panicked. The loss of bowel control under extreme stress must be universal across the animal kingdom, I was just glad I wasn't stood underneath. It tried to turn, failed and crash landed on the foot path. Not too bad for a first lesson but it wasn't quite ready to take off the L plates just yet!

A less welcome bit of wildlife was the wasp. One minute I was listening to the crashing of waves, cry of gulls and sigh of the wind through the bracken, then BUZZ!!! A wasp in my hair. Peace and tranquillity, oneness with nature – all deserted me. As soon as I realised what had happened it was my turn to panic.

I don't mind creepy crawlies, mice, bats, spiders in the bath, not even maggots in the fridge (I married a protege of J.R. Hartley) but wasps? Wasps are evil personified, (thank goodness I never went on that 3D bug ride at Disney World), I admit I do have a bit of a phobia when it comes to wasps. It probably stems from an incident that occurred when I was about three years old. My mum was stung when a wasp flew down the front of her dress. Even now, a scream has the effect of bringing me out in a cold sweat.

So, there I was on a cliff top path, with a wasp in my hair. What could I do? An aerosol can of wasp killer had not been on my list of essentials for the trip, you live and learn, it would be next time. With no one in sight to render assistance, I was entirely on my own. Help! What to do? I ran! After a breathless sprint along the path, I regained sufficient of my senses to realise two things. One: I was not in the best place for running, one slip and I would be diving several hundred feet into the sea. Two: I had not put any distance between the wasp, still stuck in my hair and myself – obvious really.

I could not bring myself to pick the wasp out of my hair; that would involve touching it. There was only one thing I could do – beat it senseless with my walking pole until it fell out. I hope nobody saw me. A mad English woman, standing on top of a cliff, beating herself over the head with a long pole. I got it in the end, I was slightly dazed and confused by that time but I did get it. After a while my head stopped spinning, my vision cleared and I was able to continue.

One of the few steep descents and ascents of the afternoon came somewhere between Jacket's Point and the oddly named Crookmoyle Rock. The path dropped almost to sea level to cross a gushing stream. Another descent and another stream were reached before climbing towards Bounds Cliff where erosion presents a real danger to walkers. Thankfully I encountered no more wasps at that point, or who knows what might have happened?

At about 5 p.m. I arrived in Portgaverne, where I was booked into a Christian Guest House, one of several in the little village. I had not been aware of the religious theme when I had made the booking, only finding out when a receipt arrived confirming my deposit. I did not have a problem with the religious bit, but for me faith was a private matter, I hoped I wouldn't be expected to say grace before breakfast. I received a warm friendly welcome from the landlady and, once again, a pot of tea. My room was a small attic room, functional but clean and more than adequate for my single night's stay. The house was what I always imagined when I thought of seaside Bed and Breakfast establishments: tall and narrow, with steep flights of stairs connecting several floors, numerous bedrooms and bathrooms leading off the landings, a pervading mixture of smells – bathroom cleaner, air freshener and fried bacon.

You have probably noticed my tendency to harp on about food. The reason being that eating ranks high on my list of hobbies and interests, I live to eat. In fact, if ever eating becomes an Olympic event, I would be up there on the winner's rostrum, bringing home the bacon (sorry, Freudian slip) the gold medal for Britain.

So, when I ventured out into the twin villages of Portgaverne and Port Isaac that evening I had one thing on my mind: food, specifically fish and chips. A helpful looking street plan, proved to be not quite as helpful when I attempted to find the fish and chip shop. Instead I found the road out of town, lots of fields and, after an about turn, a tiny supermarket. I bought a filled baguette, two packets of crisps, apple, satsuma, yoghurt, milk shake and two bars of chocolate; when I got to the checkout I asked directions for the chippy. The cashier expressed amazement at yet another tourist who had managed to get lost in such a small place and directed me down a side road leading to the harbour.

So toting a carrier with my supper in it, I entered the tiny fish and chip shop. A sign warned customers to expect a slight wait; all the food was apparently cooked to order. I put in my request for chips and mushy peas, foregoing the fish on account of all the food I had just bought. For the next ten minutes I stood and read every single notice, advertisement and for sale sign pinned to the walls. Someone had found a cat; the church was holding a fete to raise money for roof repairs; Tony had a Ford Escort van for sale. By the aged appearance of some of the notices I expected the cat to have died of old age, the roof to have fallen in and the van to have gone to the great scrap yard in the sky. If the food took any longer, it would have to be radio carbon dated to discover its best before date. I was beginning to contemplate eating the baguette, just to prevent me passing out, when the chips and peas were ceremoniously handed over the counter.

I sat on a bench and, with an audience of one lame herring gull, opened the bag of chips. They were worth waiting for, crisp, with no lake of grease surrounding them and delicious. The mushy peas were equally good, although they contained enough colorant to dye all the garments for the next Hollywood remake of Robin Hood.

Expecting to be hyperactive on food additives the next day, I made my way back to the guest house and my second supper course. In the end I did not manage to eat everything I had purchased in the supermarket. I saved a bag of crisps and an apple for the following day.

The view from the rattling sash window in my bedroom overlooked the sea. I knew the noise of the window shaking in the frame would disturb me during the night and so I jammed the chocolate wrapper into the gap between window and frame. It did the trick and with the window open slightly the only thing to disturb my sleep was the party being held on the roof by a crowd of juvenile delinquent herring gulls, drunk on scavenged leftovers and bopping the night away.

As I cleaned my teeth that night, I looked out of the window, taking in the view. I could see the line of coast I had followed that day right around to Tintagel in the distance. King Arthur would just be putting the cat out for the night.

Tuesday 14th July

My last day of walking. Breakfast was served at 8.30, early morning tea at 8.00. I rushed to get down to the lounge, not wishing to miss a cup of tea. This proved to be a mistake as, unbeknown to me, the landlady brought all her guests a cuppa in their rooms. While I was sat watching the breakfast news in the lounge and wondering what had happened to the tea, the landlady was apparently hammering on my bedroom door trying to wake me up, balancing a tray of tea cups on her arm.

A bell summoned all the guests to breakfast, very monastical! I was first to arrive. I've noticed before that if I have a large meal in the evening I am paradoxically very hungry the following morning. All the guests sat around one large table. I could see the cereal on the sideboard but unlike at previous B&Bs, we were not invited to help ourselves.

Much to my embarrassment grace was said. I personally thanked God Chris was not there, she would never have let me off the hook. We were then offered a choice of cornflakes or branflakes. I have noticed that those who talk most about faith and religion and call themselves Christians are often fairly mean with it. It's the quietly religious ones, like my mum, who are generous to a fault. The host - that is the landlord – not a deity, measured out a single small scoopful of cereal before placing the bowls in front of us. Why he used a cereal bowl when an eggcup would have done, I did not know.

The cereal was quickly followed by the cooked breakfast. One runny fried egg (personally I only like the yolk to be runny), one extra small new potato sliced and fried and, for the meat eaters, a rasher of bacon from what could only have been a very poorly pig.

The seven pieces of toast were somehow divided between five guests, like a re-enactment of the loaves and fishes. Conversation turned to holidays and inevitably I explained about my walk.

"Minehead to Padstow, 164 miles in two weeks."

"Why?" This demanded of me in a very puzzled and negative fashion by a lady obviously not keen on exercise.

I could not believe the condemnation in her tone and immediately the devil in me surfaced. I bit back the reply: "That's what God gave us legs for," and settled for: "Because I like walking!"

"Oh," was the last thing she said, before putting in a bid for the remaining piece of toast.

As I have already said, I have nothing against religion, I was Christened and Confirmed in the Church of England but the holier than thou atmosphere was really starting to get to me. Every wall had a framed bible quotation or prayer executed in needlepoint. I had to get out!

On my way to the front door, after paying my bill, I was asked to sign the visitors' book. As I browsed through the pages I was amazed to see that neither the Pope, the Archbishop of Canterbury or Mother Theresa had stayed there, perhaps they didn't like Cornwall!

In fairness, the couple who owned the B&B had been very friendly, even offering to fill my flask (shame I didn't have one) and the hygiene was beyond reproach, no smelly dogs here! But as for value for money, this was one of the more expensive places I had stayed, with the amount of food dispensed they had to be making a nice profit. Portgaverne rated as the worst breakfast of the trip.

The Gods smiled kindly on me that day – my last section of the walk was all in sunshine. Once again the path was busy with walkers and, once again, the scenery was fantastic.

Within five minutes of setting out I walked down to the harbour of Port Isaac, where I passed a bakery. As I walked up from the harbour my view was somewhat impeded by the large cream donut I was shoving in my mouth. I hoped the chicken and mushroom pasty would not get too squashed in the rucksack. Well, I know I had just had breakfast but there had not been much of it and Padstow was twelve miles away!

Portgaverne and its Siamese twin Port Isaac, had grown up around their harbours, little more than inlets in the rugged coastline. The locals had landed pilchards and shipped out slate and that had been pretty much it. If the pilchard harvest failed, the villagers faced starvation. Today, the enormous shoals of pilchards are a thing of the past and most of the slate mines are no more. Slate is still mined at nearby Delabole Quarry but it is transported by road. The pilchard cellars have been converted into holiday homes and tourism has become the mainstay of these tiny communities along with many others like them.

The history of the area was much in evidence along the coast. Old adit mines, donkey tunnels and mine shafts, as well as ancient forts and earthworks seemed to be everywhere along this stretch of the Cornish coast. I was reminded of far more recent history as I passed a building on the cliffs beyond Portquin. I thought I recognised the folly from the television series Poldark. It was not until I was in a bookshop in Taunton the following day, browsing through a book all about the making of Poldark, that I realised my suspicions were correct. In fact many of the locations used in the series had been shot in the area. Portquin itself had been used because it had changed so little in the last two hundred years. The Production Company had painted out the double yellow lines and the tiny port had stepped back in time. Poldark had popularised Cornwall, and a quarter of a century after the drama series had first been broadcast the county was still reaping the benefits of all the free advertising the series had provided. How many tourists chose to holiday in Cornwall, I wondered, influenced by the recently repeated series?

A lot of work had lately been undertaken on parts of the footpath, improving it and often moving it nearer to the coastline in some places, eliminating old detours inland. There were several stiles and kissing gates to negotiate, I felt I had become a good judge of kissing gates, not that I had actually done any kissing over them!

In Devon, I had grown well acquainted with the craftsmanship of Chapeltown Sawmill. They must have won a contract to supply a bulk order of kissing gates. I liked their gates; they were generously proportioned with plenty of room to move around in and had obviously been designed with large rucksacks in mind.

The kissing gates in Cornwall were a different story. Not from the House of Chapeltown, they were small and mean. I would get halfway into a Cornish kissing gate and then get stuck when I tried to move the gate past me. I would be wedged, unable to move because of my rucksack, jammed firmly. There's a limit to how much a person carrying a rucksack can breathe in. Sometimes, after a fight and much wriggling, I would get through. At other times I would be forced to concede defeat and retreat as graciously as possible to shed my rucksack. This was more trouble than it sounds, as each time I put the rucksack back on, I would be reminded of the fact that I had still not fixed the bra fastener.

I had hoped to stop at one of the secret beaches the guidebook kept harping on about, the only trouble was that lots of other people seemed to be in on the secret and had arrived before me. So I eventually stopped for lunch at Com Head. To the north I could see as far as Hartland, the view to the south was inland Cornwall, the view further along the coast being hidden by the headland. The bench I sat on was in the midst of a wildflower meadow. As I sat munching my pasty, holding it by the traditional crust just as the miners used to, I thought back to the variety of plants, butterflies and other little critters I had seen. I had not taken any plant or butterfly identification books with me. Whenever I saw something I was unable to identify, I tried to memorise their appearance and then used books on sale in shops and tourist information centres when I reached civilisation. In this way I had learnt the names of several plants and butterflies I had not known before. I had also left a trail of frustrated shopkeepers wondering whether or not I was going to buy a book!

In the early afternoon I rounded Pentire Point and suddenly there was Padstow! A few yards further on I realised I had been looking at the wrong place, *there* was Padstow! (There was still much room for improvement in my map reading skills). It was nearer than I thought, just visible, peeping around a bend in the Camel estuary. Stretching away towards Newquay and beyond, was the coastline I would walk the next summer with Chris.

At Polzeath the tide was out and I walked along the beach. The surfers were out in force. So were Mr and Mrs British-on-holiday and their horde of children: scream-a-lot, litter-a-lot and throw-pebbles-at-walkers-a-lot. They were easy to identify (for once I did not need an Observers Guide): the kids all shrieked "I want", the mother looked as if it was no holiday for her (one of Chris's favourite sayings) and dad, well, dad was dressed in regulation Jesus sandals and dark socks! Little boys staggered towards the sea, carrying surf boards larger than themselves. Little girls built sandcastles. The family dog cocked his leg against them. The latest craze seemed to be stunt kites. They swooped and soared before crashing violently into the sand. Crossing the beach I ran the risk of being decapitated by kite line!

Surf boards and wet suits were available for hire. I quite fancied a go myself; it looked good fun. Wet suits – weren't they the ones you had to urinate in to keep warm? On second thoughts…

The lifeguards ran down the beach, sticking flags in the sand before going back to their huts to lounge around on deck chairs. I didn't fancy being a lifeguard, it looked a fairly boring job to me, sitting around waiting for someone to need rescuing.

An engraved stone seat overlooking the beach was a poignant reminder of the dangers of the sea. It was in memory of two boys aged nineteen and sixteen. Underneath their names was the inscription "The next wave's for you."

I bought an ice cream and continued along the coast path, down the Camel estuary. From Polzeath it was a short walk around the headland, down the estuary and past the dunes towards Rock.

Nearing Rock the path skirted an imposing bluff named Brea Hill. On any other day I might have considered walking to the top but on this, the last day of my walk, a strange lethargy had overtaken me. I could not find the enthusiasm to climb the hill, although the views from its summit would undoubtedly have been wonderfully panoramic. I was nearly at my journey's end and I just wanted it to be over.

The coast path ended at the ferry point, to continue on the other side of the river Camel at Padstow. There has been a ferry at Rock since the thirteen hundreds, not the same ferry of course, a modern motor launch has superseded the sailing vessels and the original rowing boat. Over the centuries the small riverside port has grown and today boasts several hotels and even a health club! In the nearby churchyard of St. Endoc lie the remains of Sir John Betjeman, giving Rock the almost obligatory famous literary connection. And of course, no self respecting holiday resort, no matter how small, would be complete without a golf course somewhere nearby.

I waited with a small crowd on the beach at Rock as the ferry left Padstow. Within a few minutes it had drawn up on the shingle. I boarded the ferry, paid my money and crossed the river to Padstow. I had done it! Journeys end. How did I feel? Hungry. Oh and I needed a toilet. The euphoria I had experienced on my first glimpse of Padstow had faded. Happiness and a sense of achievement were mingled with the thought that the holiday was coming to an end; tomorrow I would be going home, in two days time I would be back at work. Back to routine, commitment and responsibility. Freedom and solitude shut away until the next time, the next summer and the next section of the South West Coast Path. Back to reality – work, shopping, cooking, home life - the real world. Or was it? Which was most real? As a child I had always returned home after a holiday wondering if the places I had visited and the things I had seen still existed when I was no longer there. They did of course, but the present had a knack of distorting the past, what had been real became just memories, snap shots in the mind to be viewed with happiness and regret for a time lived but gone forever.

The ferry discharged its human cargo slightly down river from the harbour at Padstow due to the low tide. It was a short walk back into the heart of the town. Padstow is the Cornish equivalent of Ilfracombe. Boats lay at anchor in the harbour. Tourists and locals alike dodged the dive-bombing gulls. Gift shops and fish and chip restaurants lined the quayside. The most striking difference between the two resorts was the ice cream, in Padstow it was "real Cornish ice cream" in Ilfracombe it had been "real Devon".

The settlement at Padstow all started in the sixth century when St. Petroc sailed up the river, took a fancy to the area, climbed the hill and built on a monastery on land now thought to be where Prideaux Place stands today. The Prideaux family had much influence in the area and the parish church houses several monuments to them, including four life-size statues of some of the children. Padstow is now famous for its yearly `Obby `Oss festival, (Hobby Horse for those of us who haven't got to grips with the Cornish dialect), a pagan fertility rite held each May Day. So perhaps St. Petroc didn't do quite such a good job of converting the locals to Christianity as he would have liked!

A colleague had suggested I celebrate my arrival in Padstow by dining at a well-known T.V. chef's restaurant. I found the restaurant but decided against a meal there for various reasons. Firstly, it looked expensive. Secondly, it specialised in seafood; my love of seafood stopped at prawns and battered fish. Thirdly, it looked smart; the only item of clothing I had brought that even began to approach smart was a pair of navy blue polka dot knickers. I could not really see myself sat in a restaurant in nothing but a pair of navy blue polka dot knickers. I found a pizza restaurant offering a take away menu; a sign on the door said it would open at 6.30 p.m. As it was not 6.00 p.m. I killed time looking round Padstow, finding the bus stop for Wadebridge and browsing in a tiny, crowded bookshop, where I bought a guidebook for the next quarter of the South West Coast Path.

At a little after half past six, I made my way back to the pizza restaurant. It was a popular place and I waited several minutes before I neared the front of the queue at the take away counter. I had spent some time trying to decide on the pizza toppings; should I go for spicy chicken or vegetable supreme? I was still debating when I overheard the girl behind the counter telling the lady at the front of queue that her order would be ready at 7 o'clock. When it became my turn to order I asked how long the pizza would take and was told forty minutes. I had already waited that length of time for the restaurant to open and I was starving! I could not face another lengthy wait. Instead I settled for fish and chips on the harbour wall and considered myself lucky when someone else's fish and not mine, was stolen by a seagull.

Leaving the centre of the town I passed a corner shop and bought a few nibbles for supper and a magazine for the long train journey home the following day. I sauntered up the steep, narrow streets to the main road, trying to eat an ice lolly whilst reading directions to the Bed and Breakfast.

The Bed and Breakfast that night was a mile or so beyond Padstow, in a lovely bungalow set in an old orchard. I turned off the road into the garden and approached an elderly gentleman busy watering some hanging baskets.

"Hello," I called.

He turned to face me with an enquiring expression.

"I'm Julia Merrifield," I said.

When he still looked puzzled, I felt further explanation was required.

"I made a reservation for bed and breakfast tonight."

"Oh, are you sure? Tonight?"

Several thoughts flew through my mind; I had booked the wrong date, I had got the wrong address, they had no vacancies. Oh, well, I suppose it had to happen; all these nights of pre-booked accommodation, I easily mixed up numbers and dates, I suppose it was inevitable that I would make a mistake at some stage. At least it was the last night.

I stuttered my way through an apology and explanation, thinking of the walk back into Padstow and the search I would have to make for alternative accommodation.

"It's okay, we've no other guests tonight," he said. "Come in, I'll just check the guest diary, maybe I've got the date wrong."

It turned out to be his mistake, not mine. The diary clearly showed that I was booked in on the correct day, he had just forgotten to check it.

The bungalow was as lovely inside as it was outside. I sat in the lounge enjoying a pot of tea and much attention from the family cat. In fact I had trouble evicting it from my room that evening. Not that I minded, it didn't smell, of cat, or dog!

Undressing for bed that night I remembered the bra fastener. As I used my teeth to close the hook further, I thought of all the trouble and discomfort I would have saved myself if I had done this two weeks ago.

Wednesday 15th July

Today I was going home. The breakfast that morning was a good one to finish on; juice, grapefruit, cereal, cooked breakfast with home-made roll, and toast and home-made preserve to finish, washed down with a huge pot of tea. Condemned to end my holiday wanderings, I ate a hearty breakfast.

I had planned to catch the bus from Padstow to Bodmin Parkway railway station. However the couple I was staying with were going to Wadebridge and had kindly offered me a lift. I could spend the morning in Wadebridge before catching a bus from there to the station. I climbed out of the car, thanked the couple for the lift and swung my rucksack onto my shoulders, as I did so my bra came undone.

Wadebridge was yet another town that had lost its railway. The old line had become the Camel trail, not for the Bedouins and their ships of the desert but for the river Camel and a cycleway. If I had had the time and the inclination I could have hired a bike and pedalled back to Padstow or followed the trail in the opposite direction towards Camelford. In fact, cycle hire was big business; outnumbering even surf shops, which made a nice change!

I bought a slice of pizza and a cream cake for lunch from a shop, eating them while I waited for the bus. The pizza made up for the disappointment of the previous evening. The cream cake was another matter; it failed the trades' description act when it came to the cream. In the heart of clotted cream country, I bit into the cake to discover the "cream" was a sickly sweet artificial substitute – yuck! Just as well I had also bought a chocolate fudge slice to take the taste away.

From Bodmin Parkway the train travelled along through Cornwall and into Devon, passing through Plymouth and then along the coastline from Teignmouth. The red sandstone cliffs were familiar from happy childhood holidays, although with the train travelling at seventy miles an hour the cliffs were a bit of a blur.

I changed trains at Taunton in the late afternoon and founding myself with an hour and a half to kill between trains. I decided I might as well take a look around the shops. As I walked down the high street, a bus with "MINEHEAD" in the window passed me, going in the opposite direction. Deja vous. I wondered... could I jump on and start again? No, it would have been impractical: not enough money, not enough holiday entitlement and not enough clean underwear.

In the early evening I was at Bristol Temple Meads and it was here that disaster very nearly struck. With half an hour to wait before my train to Preston I wandered into the newsagent shop. Browsing through a walking magazine I became engrossed in a review of boots which included my own. I foolishly forgot all about the time and when I did check my watch I realised with a shock that my train would be leaving in a matter of minutes. My tickets were not transferable, being only valid for the trains and times printed on them. If I missed the train I would have to buy another ticket for another train. Furthermore, the train I was due to catch was the last one of the day to Preston; miss it and I was faced with an unscheduled overnight stop in Bristol.

And so, at the end of my holiday as at the beginning, I found myself sprinting along in an attempt to catch public transport, but unlike the bus at Taunton I was in time to catch the train. I settled into my seat with seconds to spare and with a long journey ahead I reflected on the holiday.

I had not experienced a single moment of boredom in the entire two weeks. I had lived every mile of the walk, enjoying each day, even the wet and windy ones. I had been lucky as far as the weather was concerned. Of fifteen days of walking, there had been no more than two and a half days of rain, and whilst I had been forced to omit a short section of the coast path, I had been able to find an inland route of equivalent distance. There had been something new to discover with each new day and at the end of the day the diversity of a different guesthouse, and in the morning a breakfast that always varied from the one before.

I could be pleased with my efforts; I had raised some money for charity, I had achieved personal goals I had set myself and walked 164 miles. In fact, with getting lost a couple of times, diversions to points of interest not on the official route and finding my B&Bs I had walked 174 miles according to the pedometer. When I had ventured out in the evenings in search of food and to explore the places I was staying in, I had not worn the pedometer, so in total I estimated I had walked approximately two hundred miles.

When I had announced my intention to do the walk, someone had asked me if I was hoping to find myself. My flippant reply had been that I was hoping not to loose myself. In a way though, may be I had found myself. I had found I could initiate conversations with strangers effortlessly, share a table at breakfast and eat alone in cafes without feeling isolated or self-conscious. I had had ample time to think about all manner of things, to push myself physically, to commune with nature and to be content with my own company. I had always considered myself to be shy, reticent to interact with people I did not know; perhaps that would be different in future.

I had suffered nothing worse than a grazed shin, wet feet and two blisters. My tendon had not let me down and if I had not toned up my leg muscles by now then I never would.

I had walked in some of the most unseasonal weather July could have had and yet I had experienced only two and a half days of rain (but what rain!) I had even, foolishly, got sunburnt. I had seen parts of Somerset, Devon and Cornwall it is impossible to see except on foot. I had watched wildlife varying from the mundane to the poisonous: rabbits, squirrels, mice, shrews, voles, moles, stoats, wild goats, Exmoor ponies, pheasants, Peregrine falcons, jays, cormorants, numerous other birds (except puffins), lizards, slowworms and adders.

The days had fallen into a pattern: breakfast, pay up and set forth, followed by walking, resting, eating, gazing at the scenery, staring at the map, walking, eating and walking some more until finding the B&B and then supper before collapsing into bed exhausted but happy. The pattern had been the same but each day had been different.

I had experienced a range of B&Bs. The best, not just value for money but welcome, food and homeliness was at Combe Martin. The worst, cleanliness is next to Godliness after all, (I read that somewhere recently) was at Bude. The most comfortable bed was at Bideford. The nicest bathroom was at Woolacombe. The best breakfast was in Padstow.

I had lived every day to the full, all my senses heightened. I had lain in the grass and watched the clouds moving across the sky; seen the flora and fauna, the views: around every headland a new cove, a new coastline. I had inhaled the scents of summer – the flowers, the seaweed on the rocky shores, the perfume of sun-warmed grass and bracken. I had tasted the wild bilberries and tiny strawberries growing along the path. I had listened to the sounds of the coast: waves crashing and booming against the cliffs, washing the shingle on the beaches; the wind blowing through the trees and sighing through the fields of corn; the raucous cry of the gulls. I had felt the pain of nettle and the sharp sting of gorse and the warmth of the sun on my face. For two weeks I had not merely existed, I had lived. Happy memories.

Regrets? I had a few, but then again… Well, okay, I would mention them (and no, I honestly did not watch Sinatra at Boscastle). One was that with so many other walks I wanted to do (as well as finishing the South West Coast Path) I might not walk this section of the coast again. I would very much like to be able to share the beauty of Exmoor and the rugged cliffs of Cornwall with Roger. The biggest regret though was that Chris had not been fit in time to walk with me. There had been several occasions where I had imagined her sarcastic comments on situations or people. She would not have thanked me for the smelly dog B&B or the holier than thou one but there would have been much shared laughter at many of the things that had happened. Oh well, there was next year, Padstow to Falmouth – more steep ascents, more wildlife, more B&Bs and more food to enjoy.

I had experienced the best of the south west; its beauty and its heritage and the glorious savagery of its weather. Coming away I left only my footprints on the beach, a transitory reminder that I had ever been.

In the weeks that followed my walk I was unable to settle. Each day I would attempt to relive the experiences of the walk. What had I been doing at this time one week, two, three, four, five weeks previously? The smell of a colleague's fish and chip lunch would transport me to Combe Martin or Porlock. A walk home from work in the pouring rain and I would be once more on the cliff path south of Bude. Strangest of all was the sudden jerk back to the smelly guest house when, whilst walking along a river bank in the Yorkshire Dales, a dog climbed out of the river and trotted past me, shaking the water from its fur.

As the train neared my destination I used the mobile phone to ring Roger.

"Hi! It's me! The train arrives at 10.22. Can you pick me up please?"

"Pick you up?" Echoed Roger's astonished voice.

"Well you don't expect me to walk, do you?"

Padstow to Falmouth

Time is a constant. It is also a cheat. I can think of no other constant that exhibits the characteristics of a variable. Measurable to thousandths of a second, time stretches to infinite lengths and compacts to such an extent that weeks can pass as hours. I spent two weeks walking from Minehead to Padstow; yet did the following two weeks pass so quickly? Did the six months Chris spent with her leg elevated and useless speed by as quickly as the proceeding six months had? A week at work is far longer than a week on holiday. Have I made my point yet? After my walk it seemed an age before I would be back in Cornwall once more, back on the South West Coast Path: the year stretched ahead.

But time is also a healer, cliché though this may be. For Chris the healing process of her calf muscle was a slow one. She had returned to work in September, far from recovered and relying heavily on a stick and a gopher; if I expressed reluctance at any time to be her gopher, I got prodded with the stick! We talked about the next summer and the next section of the South West Coast Path, but always in the back of my mind was the doubt that her recovery to full fitness would take too long. Would I be walking on my own again? Perhaps she was thinking the same, I don't know; we didn't discuss it, to put it into words would have been to admit to a possibility neither of us wished to contemplate – particularly Chris.

By December, a family-free weekend spent at a friend's place in North Wales saw her taking her first tentative steps back to full recovery. And later in the month, while Roger and I spent Christmas in sunny Florida, Chris and her family were staying in snowy Germany. A couple of sessions with a German physiotherapist in a health spa convinced her that exercise would not cause further damage to her leg. She returned to work full of optimism for the year ahead, a different person from the pessimist of 1998. By March, and back in Wales for another weekend, she was back to her old self and we spent an active two days walking twenty miles of the Anglesey coastline. Padstow to Falmouth was becoming a certainty.

We had begun planning for the walk in January, before Chris's fitness was assured, breaking down the distance into daily bite-size chunks, and even taking the gamble of pre-booking the accommodation. We had decided to try and raise money for the Leukaemia Research Fund in memory of Chris's father, and several weeks were spent outlining our fundraising strategy. Little did we know at the time just how this would develop!

Even though we had both done a lot of walking it became apparent that we still needed to buy some equipment for the walk. I needed a new waterproof jacket, in the end I somehow bought two – not that I took them both! Chris needed a new rucksack, amongst other things. She spent a lot of time searching for a particular design that her nephew had shown her. It was arched at the back and supported to form a gap between the back of the wearer and the back of the rucksack. My rucksack lay flush against my back, and as anyone accustomed to wearing a rucksack will know, this can get very hot and sweaty. However, the rucksack Chris was hoping to get was twice as expensive as mine. I could not justify buying a new rucksack, much as I would have like this improved design; and Chris was struggling to justify the price. That is how one Sunday I came to be standing amidst the sale racks in Debenham's shouting into a mobile phone, whilst Chris was sitting on her bicycle on Fleetwood promenade straining to hear a very weak signal on her mobile phone and thinking she was talking to her sister. Of all the things to stumble across in the Debenham's sale I had found the rucksacks Chris had been searching for: at half the normal retail price. So I got Chris the rucksack, saved her a fortune and spent two weeks in July wishing I had got myself one at the same time.

I bought new walking trousers and shorts. Chris thought about buying the type of trousers that the legs zip off to transform into shorts, a sensible and practical design. She thought better of this idea though after I asked what would happen if she lost one of the detached legs. We each bought a new American design of drinking bottle, amazing how the purchase of a simple piece of plastic can be so exciting in the planning stages of a walk! Chris bought a pedometer, lost it on Anglesey whilst... well there's not many toilets on the coast paths on the island; and then bought another one. The second one had a calorie counter, which proved to be absolutely useless. Enter the weight and step length of the walker and then go for a fourteen mile walk, at the end of which the pedometer informs you that you have burnt off the equivalent of a bowl of cornflakes!

In the weeks leading up to the walk we were having a planning evening almost every week. Our husbands were both convinced this was just an excuse to get a takeaway and have a gossip but these evenings were vital to the walk; we wanted to be organised and besides we had to eat something didn't we? Bus timetables were studied – we would have to catch several buses to get back to the car at Padstow. Three Ordnance Survey maps were spread across my lounge carpet and, surrounded by the remnants of chicken korma and pilau rice, hampered by indigestion and a cat that thought maps made a comfortable place to have a nap, we knelt and peered intently at the contour lines, earthworks and blue "PC"s. There didn't seem to be many of the latter!

At one of these planning evenings clothing was discussed. What should we take, what could we send on, would Chris's husband, Mervyn, do the laundry if we posted it back to him? For all but one night's accommodation we would be sharing a room, and a kettle, and a teapot. Not a problem for making cups of tea but how would we dry two pairs of knickers and two pairs of socks?

"We'll have to take it in turns to put our knickers on the teapot to dry." I suggested.

"We'd need a tea urn to dry my knickers on!" objected Chris.

Perhaps a re-think was needed. On a trip to the chemist Chris thought she had found the answer – disposable knickers! She enthused over the advantages of these; I had my reservations.

"Disposable knickers?"

"Yes. They're not like J-cloths you know!"

"What exactly are they like then?" I had visions of saggy, floppy paper things, a cross between trainer nappies and incontinency pads, rustling and crackling with every step.

"They come in different sizes."

"Oh good! Are they patterned or plain?" I still wasn't convinced. How would disposable knickers cope with a hot day of sweating and walking? By the end of the day would they have dissolved to papier-mâché?

"It said 'ideal for travel'" Chris persisted.

"So's an aeroplane."

"Well I think they warrant further investigation," she muttered.

"Feel free, Miss Marple."

When you are undertaking a walk that involves carrying all your own luggage, weight is a key consideration. The temptation is always there to think that one more item will not make that much difference to the weight; the trouble being there is never just one more item. Before you know it the stitching on the rucksack is popping under the pressure and it is necessary to hire a team of Sherpas to carry it. Amazing how a piece of canvas with a capacity of thirty litres is capable of taking half the contents of your wardrobe!

I wanted to reduce the weight of my rucksack from the sixteen pounds it had been the previous year. With two walkers this should be possible, my plan was simple – Chris could carry all the heavy stuff. There were a number of things we could share: toothpaste, shampoo and the like, all taken in small bottles to further reduce the weight. T-shirts and underwear, clothes and footwear for the evenings were all assessed for bulk and weight. We tried to think of everything.

Chris had a tool similar to a Swiss army knife but better and I had been wondering if I would not need to take my nail clippers, which, for their size, were quite heavy. I was not planning to have a manicure every day, in fact I am not at all fussy and feminine about my nails, but I hate long nails and keep mine trimmed very short. Nail clippers were a luxury I did not wish to leave at home unless Chris's little gadget had scissors.

"Does your tool thingy have scissors?" I asked her.

"No; it's got a screw driver, a knife, a corkscrew, a thing for removing stones from horses' hooves," she continued to rhyme off a list of items naming everything apart from scissors, "oh, and a pair of pliers. Would they be any use? Why are you asking?"

"Not much use for what I wanted. I suppose I could use the pliers but I'd rather cut my nails with some scissors than pull them out completely."

"Well you wouldn't need to trim them for a while!"

Suddenly it was May, time had played its tricks again, with only weeks to go it seemed we still had much to organise. Each week brought a new peak of excitement and a frantic bout of planning as everything began to come together. Our employers donated T-shirts, a piece about our walk was published in the staff newsletter, our website was constructed and put on the Internet, and collection tins arrived from the Leukaemia Research Fund.

It was at this stage that we decided to check out Ian Botham's web page. He had done several long distance walks to raise money for the Leukaemia Research Fund and was planning his last John O'Groats to Land's End walk in October. We left our names and phone number in his electronic visitors' book, including details of our puny efforts and thought no more about it. The next day I received a phone call at work. It was the project manager for the Botham walk. His helpful suggestions for fundraising elevated our project onto another plane. Signed photographs and cricket bats were offered for us to auction or raffle, along with space on their web-site and, best of all, the opportunity to present the cheque from our fundraising to Ian himself as he walked through our part of the country on his way to Land's End. Little acorns to mighty oaks!

When I finished speaking to the project manager I was in a daze. It was quite a time before Chris got any sense out of me, which is not unusual.

"It's snowballing!" I said, nearly speechless with excitement.

"Avalanching, more like!" was her amazed response.

But if we were astonished with the developments up to that point what was to follow a couple of weeks later was even more surprising. The College issued a press release and we duly appeared in several of the local papers in a variety of silly poses and sporting ridiculous cheesy grins; newspaper photographers must have a permanent competition running to see who can get the daftest shots. One photo that was published consisted of our walking boots on a table with us leaning our chins on the table and our noses almost in the boots. Just as we were recovering from the indignities of press stardom we received a call from the local radio station and before we knew it were being interviewed live on air. Once the interview was underway our nerves evaporated but oh boy, the sleepless nights we had beforehand!

Actually rattling a collection tin and asking for donations was more tiring and certainly more stressful than completing the walk. Neither of us are any good at badgering people for money and the more people we asked the harder it seemed to become. As we went around college collecting donations the responses we got varied considerably. When we said the magic words "164 miles" a lot of people, students in particular, looked amazed and one girl, who obviously had no concept of distance, asked "in a day?" I could just picture us: fast forward around Cornwall – our legs a blur! People would look at me and a "oh, no she's doing another sponsored walk" expression would creep across their faces. Then they would turn to Chris:

"Is your leg better?" was the first question, closely followed by "how far are you walking each day?" quickly followed by "will you be able to manage that far?" One person even went so far as to say "at your age!" Whilst another colleague asked in amazement: "With your leg?" (Yes, unless someone had a spare one they were willing to donate!)

After the same questions were asked of her by different people she began to worry that perhaps she was being too ambitious.

"Do you think I'm over-estimating my abilities?" she asked me one day as I was doing my regular countdown:

"Seven weeks, two days to go! What? No, 'course you aren't! Why?"

"Well when I tell people how far it is from Padstow to Falmouth and how far we are walking each day, they act like I'm about to climb Everest."

I could see she was serious and sought something sensible to say that would reassure her. "Rubbish! Well, actually, you are in a way. If you were to walk all 630 miles of the coast path, you would climb the equivalent of three times the height of Everest."

Not surprisingly this failed to reassure her, so I tried a different approach.

"Are the people who are exclaiming over the distance the sort of people who drive to the corner shop?" I asked.

"Er, possibly, yes."

"So to them a walk of ooh, say, four miles would be long?"

"Er, yes…"

"But you have always done a lot of walking, not to mention swimming and cycling. Your leg's okay now. You're fitter than half the students at college! And what has age got to do with it? You're only ten years older than I am! I don't intend hanging up my walking boots when I pass the big four oh. Life begins at forty and all that! I did have doubts myself before I went last year but once you actually start walking, there's this adrenaline rush, you're on a high, it's brilliant, fantastic, it's the most incredible experience; better than chocolate!" I gushed on, when I eventually paused to draw breath I noticed her eyes had glazed over, she was humming softly to herself and swaying gently from side to side. Had she listened to a word I'd said?

Friday 2nd July

Well, it was here. The big day had finally arrived. Months of planning and preparation were over and we were about to put those plans into action. The final days before D-Day (departure day) had rushed by.

It had been a busy week at work; the end of term had heralded various meetings, staff training sessions and the annual 'A' Level Biology field course. I was in a state of feverish excitement by Monday afternoon, driving everyone mad with my countdown that was now in days, hours and minutes. Chris had been calmer, subdued would perhaps have been a better word.

"What's up? You're not still having doubts? Aren't you even the least bit excited?" I had asked her.

"Just last minute nerves," she replied, "I think I'm getting cold feet."

"You can't be, I was just the same as you last year. You're committed now and there's no going back. Everything will be fine, you'll see." I laughed, "You're getting cold feet and I'm getting itchy feet!"

At 6.30 a.m. on Friday morning, I picked Chris up. Why so early? To get a good start for the three hundred and fifty mile journey perhaps? No. To go swimming at the early bird session at our local pool. An hour later and we were on the road. Two minutes after that we were at the supermarket, stocking up on food for the journey and filling the car with petrol. Then back on the road again – to Padstow? No. To work.

We had never actually decided what time we would leave work on that Friday. At first we had thought about 1 p.m. but this somehow became 12 p.m. then a bit earlier still, until eventually we were jokingly saying we would leave at half past eight in the morning. Only five minutes after arriving at work we were anxious to be on our way. I was so nervous I spent as much time going to the loo as I did at my desk and Chris wasn't much calmer. We cleared our desks and by 10.45 were on our way.

We left work to a chorus of farewells and good wishes. Colleagues came out to the car park and as we drove away others waved from first floor windows and gave us the thumbs up sign. We had received a lot of support from them and it was touching to see their enthusiasm. (Or were they just glad we were finally going?)

Roger and I have often gone to Devon for our holidays, but neither of us particularly enjoys the long drive down to the south coast from Lancashire. The journey down the M6 and M5 motorways has always been stressful, tiring, usually hot and prolonged by traffic jams. This time, after weeks and months of planning and anticipating the walk, resulting in both Chris and myself being high on excitement, I wondered if the journey to the South-West would be any different.

You see, in my opinion the test of a marriage is not moving house, decorating, having children or trying to get your husband to squeeze the toothpaste tube from the bottom of the tube (be reasonable – do it my way). It is something most people do year after year, you think they would learn! It is going on holiday together. To all the couples with children I say God help you; it is bad enough when there are only two adults (I use that term loosely). After only driving to the end of our street, Roger and I are usually well into our first, and let's be honest here, only argument of the holiday. The fact that we are still rowing as we arrive home at the end of the holiday goes without saying; the argument has never drawn to a close.

During this holiday quarrel every fault, harsh word and forgotten promise for the last ten years has been resurrected to use as ammunition; and I must admit I am the main offender at doing this. (Actually that is because I have fewer faults, speak less harsh words and do not forget promises; Roger may dispute this). The altercation is always at its fiercest when we are driving.

"You've missed that turn off!"

"You're the one who's supposed to be navigating."

"I told you about it earlier."

"You expect me to remember one direction after three hours of driving?!"

"Well why didn't you ask for clarification if you'd forgotten? Turn here! Turn here! Too late! You could have turned round there! You're going out of our way now!"

"Do you want to drive?"

"Well we'd use less petrol!"

We now avoid this type of holiday argument. We fly.

Married couples are not designed to spend a lot of time together. They work apart, have different hobbies, different friends. Sharing a common address, or even name, is not a guarantee of their ability to relate to one another. Thrown together on holiday, they need time to acclimatise and adjust, to rediscover all those annoying habits that each thought they could change in the other when they first met. This period of mutual tolerance is a chance to relearn how to ignore all the faults of both parties, and this learning process does take time – usually a fortnight! Were it not for the huge pile of washing and ironing on the day before returning to work, the couple would have a fair chance of getting along amicably on that final evening.

So when colleagues questioned Chris and me if we would be able to get on with each other for a fortnight, the answer was an easy "yes". We worked together eight hours a day, five days a week, forty odd weeks a year; we have done for the last eight years. This was not the first time we had been away together, although it would be the longest. We were not married to each other, we were tolerant of each other, we had interests in common, we didn't irritate one another (well, Chris is bearable I suppose), we would get along fine – we were friends!

As things turned out when we did get lost, miss a road sign or take the wrong path, it did not result in sulks, cross words or accusations. We did bicker, we always do, but it has always been in jest.

By 6.15 p.m. we were approaching Padstow and Chris was getting nervous. Her cold feet had come back!

78

"Oh! All those ascents and descents! What have I let myself in for? Why did I let you talk me into this? Go left! Turn left!"

I spun my head round to read the sign as we passed.

"That's back the way we've come." I exclaimed and, as another sign came into view, "Look, Padstow two miles."

"Ohhh." She groaned.

It was a good job she was only joking.

She was only joking, wasn't she?

The Bed and Breakfast at Padstow was the same one I had stayed in on my last day of the walk last year. It was just as I remembered but with one exception, no cat. I was tempted to ask where it was but was afraid it may have been run over the day before and that any enquiry might result in the landlady rushing off in floods of tears. As Chris pointed out I excelled at putting my foot in it. I played safe and did not ask.

After a pot of tea and time to freshen up we set off to drive back down the hill into Padstow. The centre of town was busy with tourists and as we fought our way through the milling holidaymakers we found the pizza restaurant that I had been unsuccessful with the previous year. History repeated itself. We were unsuccessful. After standing in the doorway for several minutes, being ignored by numerous passing waiters, we were approached by a waitress. She would attend to us in a moment. Many long moments later (how long is a moment?) she returned. Had we booked? No. She barely failed to conceal a sigh of frustration before telling us there would be a table available in an hour. Our stomachs told us an hour was at least fifty minutes too long to wait.

We found a noisy pub by the harbour and had a meal and a drink, courtesy of my mum who had said she would treat us to our first meal out. It was a lovely gesture and much appreciated. With the first of many good meals digesting in our stomachs, we made our way back to the B&B and hoped for a good night's sleep.

Saturday 3rd July

We were both up early, sorting our clothing and storing what we no longer needed in the car. This was it! The first day of our walk this year. Tonight we would lay down to sleep in a new B&B. And the next night. And the next night. We would keep on walking every day to new B&Bs until we eventually walked off the bus and climbed the hill out of Padstow and walked back into this B&B. That would be two weeks away, in the meantime there were a lot of miles to cover. What we needed was a good breakfast. We got one. Napoleon was right about marching and stomachs, even if he did have bad taste in hats!

We shared a table for breakfast with a family of three. Conversation was stilted; just the sort of embarrassing situation I hate. We mentioned walking. They mentioned camping in Rhodesia when they used to live there. I thought of the name change and white supremacy and kept my mouth shut.

Our hosts wished us well as we set off. We were both glad to be on our way. The other guests watched from the doorway as we hoisted our rucksacks onto our backs. My hopes of having a lighter pack this year had failed, in the days to come it would often weigh more than 18 lbs. because of all the extra water we were forced to carry. I set my cap on my head and pushed my walking pole across the back of the rucksack. It swung round and cracked me on the funny bone. Oh great, here we go again!

As we set off down the drive I took a last look at the car. It would be two weeks before we would be back to collect it. A strange feeling: this was to be journeys end but now it was the beginning. What experiences would we go through? What about laughter? Blisters? Cramp? What scenery would we gaze at with admiration or may be even dismay? What would the accommodation be like? The meals? And would we still be speaking at the end of it all? Would the weather gods be kind to us? Would my walking pole ever become one of the team? Only time would tell.

Padstow was quiet. Many of the gift shops were still closed. There was little sign of the herds of tourists preparing to descend on the tiny fishing port after their full English breakfasts. We found a bakery that was open and bought a pasty each for lunch but entirely forgot about fruit or chocolate. The pasties were put in the top of Chris's rucksack where they steamed gently for most of the morning. Following behind her I occasionally got tempting whiffs of pasty, she smelt delicious.

We found the start of the coast path on this, the west side of the river Camel. This section of the South West Coast Path was 164 miles long, an average walk of twelve miles a day for fourteen days. Old hat for me but for Chris this walk would be kill or cure. She wanted to prove to herself that her leg was finally better. One way or the other she would know by Falmouth. At 9.45 with pedometers reading zero we began to walk to Falmouth.

For the first couple of miles we followed the Camel on its journey to the Atlantic. The first part would have been quite pleasant had it not been for the dog dirt festering on the path but, as we got beyond the range of the Padstow dog owners, we were able to pay less attention to where we placed our feet and more notice of the unfolding scenery. The path stayed close to the banks of the river, running at the sides of fields of wheat and barley and through leafy tunnels. Poppies and scarlet pimpernel coloured the ruts along the edges of the fields. Honeysuckle, foxgloves and cow parsley grew in the hedgerows.

Fastened to the top of Chris's rucksack was her beanie toy (read this bit in a deep commanding voice) Buzz Lightyear: Space Hero. He went everywhere with her apart from work – she did have to retain some credibility I suppose. But on this mission he wasn't going to infinity and beyond, instead Padstow and beyond – Falmouth if he was lucky. As in the film, would he get left behind as we moved on? Would he stay firmly fastened to the rucksack? Or more likely, would Chris lose him somewhere in Cornwall and be in a miserable mood for the rest of the holiday? As we left Padstow a little girl spotted Buzz. I cringed in embarrassment as a forty-two year old woman and a six year old girl had a chat about a stuffed toy.

All around Cornwall he sat on top of that rucksack, smiling smugly (supercilious twit), as if to say "I'm no fool, I'm being carried". To get my own back I prodded him every so often with my walking pole.

"What are you doing?" Chris asked.

"Nothing. Just a creepy crawly on your rucksack."

"Leave Buzz alone!"

"Oh, you knew who I meant then!"

We passed a row of old pilots' cottages and a now disused coastguard station, both testaments to the dangerous waters in the Camel estuary and the surrounding coast. Then we reached Stepper Point where the path turned a corner and we walked onto the Atlantic coast. A stone tower, built in 1832 as a guide to shipping, now stands derelict. Posted notices warned of its unstable structure. As we stood at the base of the tower, two Americans passed us, they were the first of several foreign visitors we were to meet on the path. Liam had also been there recently. Don't ask me who Liam is, all I can tell you is that he's a little vandal. He had had a camp fire, attempted and failed to burn some of his litter and so had left the rest scattered over the grass and as a parting gesture of irresponsibility had carved his name in the turf.

The weather was overcast but dry that morning. We soon warmed up to the point where walking in trousers was uncomfortable and we stopped briefly to change into shorts. Twice it began to rain and twice we debated if it was worth stopping to don waterproofs, we chose not to and very soon the light rain stopped completely. It was perfect walking weather, cool, overcast and with a slight breeze. It was not until that evening that we discovered we had become sunburnt despite the cloud cover. Chris was particularly annoyed as, unlike me, she doesn't tan but just turns bright red. Her neck, face, arms and legs were the colour of boiled lobster; she looked ridiculous and the next day she looked even redder if that were possible.

The coastline was spectacular and the geology was fascinating. Chris had taken geology 'A' Level and I badgered her for information about what we were seeing. We passed folded beds of slate, round holes made by the collapsing roofs of sea caves, and Merope Islands that had been made by erosion of the sea along a geological fault. The guidebook told of a shop selling geology guides but where was the shop? We could not find it.

We stopped for a late lunch overlooking Newtrain Bay. The pasties were still slightly warm and very appetising. Despite the cloudy sky the sea was a deep aquamarine.

"You could use the sea and the surf for a shower gel commercial," said Chris.

"Um," I mumbled through a mouthful of pasty, "or a toilet cleaner commercial."

At Harlyn Bridge it tried to rain again. Hard. We sheltered under some bushes and within minutes the rain stopped. The sudden cloudburst had not deterred the surfers though and why would it? The little bay was crowded with them and the small car park seemed to be overrun with old VW dormobiles. Many of the vehicles had been resprayed bright colours and all seemed to have surfboards, towels or wet suits in them. Every trendy young surfer in Cornwall drove a VW dormobile and the vehicles seemed ideal for their purpose.

In times past, before the coming of dormobiles, there had been an Iron Age cemetery where the Harlyn Inn now stood. The remains of hundreds of crouching skeletons had been unearthed. There was now no sign of them, which was hardly surprising as apparently they had all been moved to a museum in Truro.

In the afternoon we followed the path towards Trevose Head where a lighthouse flashed out its warning to shipping. For days afterwards we could still see the lighthouse and it amazed us to think we had walked so far, eventually it was to disappear around a headland but not before it only became visible through binoculars.

Out towards Trevose Head it was possible to see both sides of the headland. On the western side large breakers rolled onto the beaches. The more sheltered eastern side of the promontory had fewer breakers but no fewer surfers.

As we walked around the headland Chris saw a lizard sitting on a clump of bracken. This was the first time we had seen any wildlife and it seemed to herald a whole series of sightings that day. Later on in the afternoon we watched bullfinches, Peregrine falcons, fulmars and razorbills. Some species we saw more of than others and it seemed that each day we saw lots of wrens flitting along and flying in and out of the bushes.

Past Stinking Cove we walked towards Mackerel Cove and another Round Hole. Someone had been dumping builder's rubble by the track leading to the lighthouse. Worse was to come. I gazed down into Mackerel Cove; my admiration of the crashing sea quickly turning to disgust. A rusting car lay at the bottom of the cove. Mackerel Cove had become Ford Escort Cove.

As the evening approached the clouds cleared and the sun came out. The last mile was walked in sunshine. We were being watched, although we had no idea of this at the time. The lady at the B&B we were booked into watched for all her walking guests. Her house had spectacular views of Porthcothan Bay and when she judged the time of her guests' arrival was close she began to check the coast path using binoculars.

Operation Neptune was launched by the National Trust in a bid to safeguard the British coastline. Through bequests and donations pockets of land around the coast have come under the protection of the National Trust, halting development and ensuring the beauty of the coast is maintained. At Porthcothan the National Trust had purchased a large parcel of land on the north side of the bay. Their ownership was evident by the complete lack of development on that side.

What was not evident was where our B&B was located. It took us ten minutes of increasingly frantic searching through my rucksack before we found the landlady's card. It then took us ten minutes of increasingly weary walking before our tired minds made sense of her confusing map and eventually found the cul de sac leading to her home.

As the bungalow came in sight we caught our first glimpse of the best landlady in Cornwall, possibly Britain, although first sight did nothing to suggest this. Her stooping figure was half buried in shrubbery. Initially all we could see was a pair of feet shod in Jesus sandals and a pair of tanned legs almost completely hidden by a flowing, flower patterned skirt.

Chris and I exchanged an anxious bemused glance. We were both thinking the same thing: an eccentric! What had we let ourselves in for? But we could not have been more wrong.

Our stay at Porthcothan was the thing legends are made of. Her warm greeting made us feel like part of the family. She immediately ushered us into the family lounge and set about serving us tea and cake, three cups and three slices each. The cake was homemade and delicious; the tea was poured from a bone china tea service. She spoilt us rotten, kneeling in front of us pouring more and more cups of tea and insisting on us having just one more piece of cake. She chatted to us and expressed a sincere interest in what we were doing. We told her about the fundraising and, as we prepared to leave the following morning, she generously gave us a donation of £10. It seemed she got as much pleasure from her visitors as they all surely got from staying with her; this was much more a hobby than a business. She took photographs of all her guests, keeping a copy for her own albums and sending them a copy too. Her photograph albums were an interesting history and in every photograph her guests appeared genuinely happy to be there.

After a relaxing bath we headed out in search of supper, walking down the hill and up the other side to the village pub. We ordered our meal then went to sit at one of the outside tables. For such a small village the pub was surprisingly full. At one table a group of surfers were soon joined by the village idiot. It was his birthday and he was intent on celebrating, not that he was likely to remember it the following day. Everyone seemed to be buying him drinks as he staggered from one group of locals to the other. His glass having been refilled by the surfers he headed our way, great! But he was not aiming for us; instead he stopped at another table where four young people and their dogs were lounging. One of the dogs was wearing pink socks, with a little frill round the top. Did that mean it was a bitch, would the socks have been blue if it were male?

After the somewhat overcast day, the sky had cleared and it was a sunny evening. But as the sun went down a chill crept into the air and a little breeze sprang up. We made our way down the hill and back up the other side. Our first day was over. We were staying in an excellent Bed and Breakfast. The weather had been favourable. Twelve miles down, one hundred and fifty-two to go. So far, so good. What would the breakfast be like, I wondered?

Sunday 4th July

I awoke at six o'clock; sunlight was streaming through the curtains. I stretched and turned over and a minute later it was seven o'clock. Chris was just getting up and heading for the kettle, without my glasses on her legs looked a red and white blur. With my glasses on her legs were still a red and white blur. Wind burn, heat rash and areas of skin that had been covered by shorts and socks vied for attention.

We had asked for an early breakfast, and it was as well we had. We chatted with the landlady for nearly an hour between eating vast quantities of food. We were not disappointed, the breakfast was every bit as good as her cakes had been.

The table was draped with a crisp linen tablecloth, the Wedgwood China matched the place mats, a carved wooden ring enwrapped pale green linen serviettes that matched everything else. I hesitantly reached for the teapot, being extra careful not to break or chip anything. Chris was obviously thinking the same thing.

"Be careful." She warned.

I was, but although I did not break anything I still managed to spill milk as I served the tea. On the clean table cloth too!

There was fruit juice and a range of cereals, followed by a huge cooked breakfast that included potatoes and easily four ounces of mushrooms each. Everything was cooked to perfection and not at all greasy. We finished off with toast and a selection of marmalade, jam, honey and marmite. Nothing was too much trouble, I felt that had we asked for something she had not got, her husband would have been sent out to buy it.

When we were finally ready to leave, we said goodbye with some reluctance. I think we both knew that none of the other accommodation would be as good, or the welcomes as warm. In the days to come we compared her to every other host, none of them measured up. We elevated her to the position of a saint. St. Sheila, patron saint of landladies. She was worthy of it.

We retraced our steps down the hill and joined the path on the south side of the little beach. The clouds had come over to hide the sun but this morning we were taking no chances and used sun tan lotion to prevent a repetition of the day before. It was not cold and we were comfortable walking in shorts rather than trousers.

Above Porth Mear (porth is Cornish for cove or harbour) the cliffs were slowly slipping into the pounding waves. The land always lost in the battle to the sea.

As we approached Park Head, donated to the National Trust in the 1960's and one of many such areas of land on the coast path, Newquay hove into view in the distance. The town appeared as a sprawling grey scar on the green countryside. It looked horrendous. The nearer we got, the worse it looked. After only a day of walking we had grown accustomed to the rugged solitude and unspoilt beauty of Cornwall.

By mid morning we were nearing Bedruthan Steps and my bladder was nearing the point of overflowing.

"I need to go to the toilet." I informed Chris.

"Not here, we're approaching a honey pot."

"Not a chamber pot?"

I would have to wait. I tried to think of something else but the sound of the sea did not help!

Bedruthan Steps is a series of large rocks standing in a line along a beach. When we arrived the tide was in and the waves were crashing against them, sending plumes of spray into the air. One of the rocks is called Queen Bess Rock as it is supposed to resemble the lady of the same name. Short of swimming out to sea, we peered from every available angle but were unable to see the similarity to any woman, queen or otherwise. The guidebook said she had now lost her head, perhaps that was why. Or perhaps you needed to be as high on opium as the Victorians who promoted the area as a tourist attraction possibly were!

We went wrong at Bedruthan Steps, took a diversion off the path to a viewing area; looked, photographed, leant our elbows on the fence and in some bird muck, then set off up a dead end and had to retrace our steps back to the main path. That sort of thing always happens when there are a lot of people about!

We decided to make use of the toilets at the National Trust owned information centre nearby and walked up the gravel path to the car park. It appeared that the area was popular not only with people but with cows too. The path was covered in large, fresh cowpats. Had a nearby dairy farm had an annual outing to Bedruthan Steps? Not quite. We overheard a warden explaining to a visitor how a cow had escaped from a nearby field. Well, I suppose cow muck made a change from dog dirt, although there was that too along the path near the car park.

The clouds had been increasing and the threat of rain suddenly became more threatening. We walked on for two minutes, hoping the shower would stop but it seemed to be getting heavier. We hastily began taking off our rucksacks and putting on waterproofs. As I heaved my rucksack back on I felt my bra strap come undone. Oh not again! Not this year as well! I struggled to fasten it without taking off the rucksack, no mean feat!

The rain stopped. Immediately. But we were already wet and began to grow cold as our bodies dried. We kept the kagools on and after a little while the rain came back. It rained on and off all day but only lightly. Not enough to make walking miserable and for much of the day we carried the kagools fastened across the tops of our rucksacks where we could easily get to them quickly.

We bought lunch at Trenance, a pasty for Chris, a pie for me. Climbing the steepest hill so far we stopped to eat the food overlooking Berryl's Point. We did not stop long; we had grown chilly and were quickly on our way towards Beacon Cove. The rocks at this cove were a mixture of slate and shale. The erosion of the sea had produced a beach made of yellow sand, with black sand lying in a band closer to the cliffs. It was strikingly delineated and worthy of a photograph.

As we followed the coastline skylarks called, soaring above us. Stonechats flew across the path, alighting briefly on clumps of gorse before flying off as we drew nearer. This area was believed to be the last nesting place of the Cornish choughs. The last one died over twenty five years ago, another case of wildlife succumbing to loss of habitat. The only chough we saw was on the county's coat of arms. It was to be three years before they were successfully reintroduced.

Iron Age cliff castles were plentiful in this area, unlike the choughs. The guidebook kept highlighting them but, like the choughs, we could not see any, possibly because they were hidden in the rampant bracken.

The path was a tapestry of wild flowers, the majority of which we seemed unable to identify. A few we could put a name to, including the delicate purple orchids that grew in profusion amongst the grass, vetches and trefoils.

The path through the flowers was a narrow dusty track. Hairy caterpillars, beetles, spiders and ants scurried along it. One community of ants had made their own track that crossed the path. A shallow indentation ran from one side of the path to the other and we watched as ants hurried along their eroded route. One ant appeared carrying part of a leaf, holding it above its back like a sail.

At Watergate Bay we walked along the high cliffs for nearly three miles, interrupted by one small descent at the Watergate Bay Hotel. We had to join the road a short way there as it zigzagged down to cross a bridge before climbing back to the cliff tops. We used the toilets at one side of the road then paused to admire the view at the other side of the road as two surfers got changed in the car park.

Erosion on the cliffs here had eaten in to some of the coast path causing it to be redirected away from the edge. The landslide must have been quite recent, as the wooden fence that had been erected was pale and unweathered. Chris stopped, leaning against the fence to remove her boot and extract a stone, and giving me an opportunity to look ahead at the approaching sprawl of Newquay.

Newquay is the largest seaside town in North Cornwall. It was little more than a fishing village for many centuries until, as with many other places, the coming of the railway in the 1870's changed all that. By the beginning of this century it was a busy port, involved in the exporting of China clay. Now the town's money lies in tourism. The surfing capital of Cornwall, it attracts not just surf bums and long haired weirdos but families and retired couples as well. In our opinion, it was the worst place we walked through.

Chris had been dreading Newquay. She had never been before; I had, about ten years ago and thought I knew what to expect. It was even worse than I remembered. There were a lot of tourists, which was to be expected. Coaches, cars and dormobiles rumbled along the busy main road. Noisy, dirty and crowded, it was a scaled down version of Blackpool; hotels lined the main road, greasy spoon cafes and takeaways emitted the rancid odour of burgers and fried food. A few local shops were sandwiched between big national chains on the pedestrianised main shopping street. All town planners, no matter where they are in the country, seem to work to the same rigid idea of how a town centre should be modelled. Layout a ring road, close the main street to traffic, pave it with red and beige coloured bricks arranged in pretty patterns and bolt some plant pots and black iron benches to the ground. Hey presto! You have a characterless town centre that could be anywhere in England.

Where there are humans there are dogs. And where there are dogs there's dog dirt. We walked up a narrow paved path from Porth Beach, much used by locals it seemed. The sun had come out and we stopped to remove our kagools. A bike, that I had not noticed, was approaching rapidly down the path.

"Mind the bike," warned Chris.

I stepped closer towards the side of the path, my rucksack on the ground in front of me.

"Mind the dog dirt," she cautioned, then in an exasperated tone, "just mind!"

I think Newquay was getting to her and we had only just arrived! And we were both becoming mightily fed up of trying to avoid dog dirt. There was no shortage of special dog bins, and notices were stationed on every lamppost. But who enforced the regulations? Was anyone ever fined? It did not seem like it.

After asking directions we had to backtrack for almost a mile along a busy road before reaching the guest house we had booked into. Had we only known it at the time, we could have walked inland from Porth Beach and reached it much sooner. The guest house stood on a road lined with similar houses, many of which were also guest houses. There were no pubs, restaurants or even takeaways on this road and we were faced with a long walk back into the centre of Newquay that evening for something to eat. Before that though we intended to put our feet up, have a bath and a nice cup of tea, write some postcards and generally relax.

As we walked up to the door and rang the bell, a thought struck me, the significance of which I did not realise until later. Both guest houses on either side of ours had several cars parked in the drives; our guest house only had one car, presumably the owners; and this was one of only a few guest houses that we had passed with a "vacancies" sign on display.

The house smelt of chip pans, as if one was left simmering all the time; not pleasant but, remembering Bude, it could have been worse. It was clean which was the main thing but it seemed a complete let down after the fantastic B&Bs of the last two nights. The owner showed us to our room and then took me back downstairs to demonstrate the combination lock on the front door. We had got halfway down the stairs when she asked this year's winner in the most stupid question competition.

"Is it your mother you're walking with?"

I was so shocked I nearly fell downstairs. Had I heard correctly? Perhaps I had mis-heard the Scots accent. I hadn't. May be the question had been her way of trying to establish our relationship.

I refrained from saying, "Don't be ridiculous, she's only ten years older than me!" and settled for a rather terse statement that we worked together.

We had had quite a lot of good natured ribbing from some of the men at work along the lines of two women on holiday together, "nudge, nudge, wink, wink".

"What will people think?" said one.

"We're both married, people can think what they like. What difference does it make anyway? It says more about the bigots making those type of judgements."

"Get T-shirts printed: 'We are... Not gay.'"

"Get lost!"

The joking must have been getting to us though. We had both planned a haircut before we went – but how short was too short? And we had found ourselves subconsciously emphasising Mrs as we booked accommodation. This was ridiculous, at the turn of the millennium ignorance and prejudice was still affecting peoples' lives.

When I arrived at work one morning minus my wedding ring and sporting a naked ring finger (my engagement ring having broken several months previously) Chris latched on to it like a seagull to a holiday maker's fish supper.

"Where's your wedding ring?"

"Oh, we had a bit of a row and I threw it at him." I replied nonchalantly.

"Well where is it?" she persisted.

"I'm not really sure... I heard it ping across the kitchen floor. It was dark you see – we didn't have the light on. It's probably under the fridge freezer."

"Well find it!"

That evening at Newquay was the first time someone had attempted to find out if we were lesbians, sadly it wasn't to be the last. I returned to the room in a state of disbelief. Chris picked up on my mood immediately and when I told her what had happened she too was stupefied. What difference did it make? A guest's sexuality had no bearing on whether they might trash the room, steal the pictures off the walls or leave without paying, which is what would concern me if I was running a guest house! The incident set the tone of our stay in that guest house; we nick-named it Doom Mansion.

The leaflet we had been sent by the owners said that every room had either a sea view or a view of the open countryside. Our room had a view of a very busy main road, a roundabout and a lot of houses. By standing on tip toe and peering through binoculars we could just make out a tiny bit of grey, the size of a cheese spread triangle, which may or may not have been the sea.

"Isn't it peaceful when the traffic stops?" I said during a sudden cessation of traffic noise.

"Yes," replied Chris drolly, "you can hear the television downstairs!"

The room consisted of two beds (that was something I suppose), the usual furniture, tea making facilities and a shower cubicle. The toilet was across the landing, as was a bathroom that was locked. Fine. Okay, that meant we would have to have a shower in the room. I hated P.E. at school because of the showers. Chris assured me that the pattern on the cubicle walls meant you couldn't see in but in any case sat on her bed with her back to the room whilst I went in the shower.

The dials for controlling the temperature were fiddley, the markings on them long since obliterated and I struggled to adjust the water to the correct temperature. It did not seem to matter which way I turned the dials; it had no effect on whether the water was warm or cold. The water suddenly turned scalding hot and I let out a shriek of pain that made Chris turn round to see what was happening. As I frantically turned one of the dials, I heard her remark, "Oh, you can see through the glass!" before quickly averting her gaze.

We had a long walk along the busy roads before reaching the scruffy centre of Newquay and finding a fish and chip shop. Having bought supper we had a choice between sitting outside the chippy at a table with an umbrella (to shield us from seagull muck) or sitting on a bench overlooking Towan beach. We chose the bench with a view but would have been wiser to have gone for the picnic table.

We sat there munching away, watching the surfers and minding our own business. I selected a chip and popped it into my mouth then looked up just in time to see a gull coming in low and fast like a Lancaster on a bombing mission. It wasn't intent on bombing us though, which I suppose is one thing. It was on us before I could open my mouth to warn Chris. Too late! The seagull had landed: on Chris's fish and chips. She was taken completely by surprise and in the battle of human versus scavenger the herring gull won. Her supper landed on the ground and we were immediately inundated with gulls. They came from all directions, some from as far away as Eastbourne. Surely there could not be that many gulls in the whole of Cornwall!

We wasted no time in scurrying out of firing range. The cacophony of their screeching cries deafened us as they fought over the scraps. Within seconds the frantic scrabbling between the gulls was over, only the plastic tray and the paper remained. We liked Newquay even less.

We limped slowly back to the guest house, well Chris did; her sandals were rubbing. Once there, we could not get in. I struggled with the combination lock, pressing the buttons in the sequence the owner had shown me but without success. Chris had a go but we still could not unlock the door. We had to ring the bell and wait to be let in. The landlord, who we had not met before, opened the door. I apologised, explaining that we could not get the lock to work. We had been using the correct combination; it was the same as he proceeded to demonstrate, so why had it not unlocked?

"Do you not have combination locks where you come from?" he insulted us.

The tea making facilities in the room were meagre: two teabags and some powdered milk. The teabags were cheap and nasty, that together with hard water made a rather disgusting cuppa. At least we were moving on the next day.

Monday 5th July

We were both awake early, a result of early morning sunlight and traffic noise. We showered in the creaking, flimsy cubicle, planned a small shopping trip and then went down to breakfast.

We were alone in the dining room, the only guests in this stereotypical seaside boarding house. This morning the smell of chip pans was even stronger. There was no sign of the owners until the serving hatch suddenly opened with a bang, making us both jump. The woman's head popped through and with a brusque "good morning" asked if we wanted cornflakes or bran flakes. We both chose cornflakes and the hatch closed with another bang. Her husband came into the dining room and greeted us, then the hatch crashed open again. Two bowls of cereal were shoved through before the hatch slammed shut once more. This continued throughout breakfast, with the pot of tea (same horrible teabags), the fry up and finally the toast.

The breakfast was heavily fried and we persevered with it, watched over by the landlord. He leaned against the wall and watched us eating self consciously for a few minutes before firing a barrage of questions at us. We breathed a sigh of relief when he left, taking out the dirty plates, but his role of inquisitor was taken over by his wife who appeared in the doorway instead of at the hatch for once.

It seemed they often had walkers staying with them, some even came back for a second visit. Who were these people, we wondered? Were they mad?

We paid the bill and went upstairs to get our things. We were eager to get away from the strange atmosphere. We were half way down the drive when we heard the door opening behind us. Chris said later it was all she could do to stop herself legging it, she had dreamt we had been locked in the house for a week, unable to escape.

"You're leaving then?" said the landlady.

"Er, yes, thank you," we stuttered. Too right we were leaving!

Our shopping trip should have been a fairly straight forward one. We intended sending a pair of sexy knickers to the guys at work as a joke. They had made much of the fact that we would be sending home parcels of dirty clothing and we knew they would get a lot of mileage from some naughty knickers. First, though, we had to buy some.

We went into the post office to get a padded envelope and were confronted by a rather strange sight. Carmen Miranda, Scary Spice and Sid Vicious were serving behind the counter. Hmm, was this normal for Newquay? Then I remembered there was a festival in the town this week. That explained it!

Many of the shops had different themes, with assistants dressing up as famous people or in period costume. We had had difficulty booking a room in the town for just one night; the festival was the reason. When I had first read about the festival I expected we would spend the Sunday evening watching a procession or some type of street carnival but that had not happened. All in all, Newquay had been a let down.

Clutching the envelope we went in search of some knickers to put inside it. There were several likely chain stores on the high street but none of them sold underwear. We went in a number shops before finding what we wanted in Dorothy Perkins. The knickers we got were very, very brief; there was more material in a shoe lace, how anyone could wear them without being cut in half was beyond comprehension. We posted off the parcel, wishing we could see Mark and Phil's faces as they opened it.

We called in at a supermarket for something for lunch then began to head out of Newquay along a busy pavement. I turned to say something to Chris, for a moment not watching where I was putting my feet, and felt my boot make contact with something squishy.

"Oh, sh…"

"Yes, it certainly is," interrupted Chris, "and you've really put your foot in it this time!" She began laughing as I frantically tried to scrape my boot clean on the grass verge.

We soon came to a Huer's hut overlooking Newquay Bay, built probably in the 1300's and used by a hermit, it later became the lookout station for a huer. The word huer comes from "hue and cry" which is what he would do when he sighted shoals of pilchards coming into the bay. Once alerted, fishing boats would go out with nets to surround the shoal. We came across pilchard cellars in many of the fishing ports, where once the whole community was involved in the catching, cleaning and salting process. In previous centuries, many would have starved had it not been for the pilchards. Over-fishing has put an end to the vast shoals. The nearest many of the ports around Cornwall come now to this once vital commodity is in the day trips run for holiday makers to catch not pilchards but mackerel.

The tiny Huer's hut was whitewashed and outside steps climbed the walls to the domed roof; it reminded me of buildings in the Middle East. I stopped for a moment, sitting on the low wall in front of the hut to examine my boot. All the ridges in the sole were caked up with the foul filth. What had that dog been eating? It was revolting.

Wherever we went in Cornwall, we knew when we were nearing civilisation – dog dirt would begin to appear on the path. The closer we came to a car park or a town or village, the more excrement would appear until we were hopping and stepping over stinking piles of the disgusting stuff. As the weather became warmer the problem became worse, at times the stench was nauseating. What is difficult about cleaning up after your dog?

By midday, two hours later, we were still in Newquay; we could not escape. We walked around one headland, looked at the building work being undertaken on extending the pumping station and sewage outfall pipe; watched the way a line of scum was being carried by the tide towards the beach and the waiting surfers, and then turned a corner to see Newquay reappear in front of us. We walked along the back of a beach and up beside a golf course and the town appeared again. We followed the path around yet another headland and still Newquay would not leave us alone. We crossed Pentire Point and there was Newquay! Eventually we descended the hill to the river Gannel and the ferry crossing and, for a time at least the sprawling town was no longer visible.

There are several alternative ways to cross the river, either by following the road inland for several miles, crossing another bridge or using a ferry at a point some way inland. We had elected to use the private summer-only ferry at Fern Pit. Sometimes it is possible to walk across the Gannel at this point on a little wooden jetty, but only at extreme low tide. The bridge was underwater when we arrived.

At the other side of the river we got lost in a car park. The signs for the footpath ran out. Our guidebook and the path description from the South West Way Association contradicted one another and only served to further confuse us. We wandered through the dunes before finding a way down onto Crantock Beach. The beach was relatively quiet compared to those around Newquay. We settled ourselves on a rock at the western end of the beach and had lunch. Once rested and refreshed and congratulating ourselves that we had finally seen the last of Newquay, we smeared on more sun protection, packed up and set off.

We had only got as far as the path leading off the beach when we met two elderly walkers coming the other way. I have often noticed how the uniform of a walker acts almost as an exclusive membership to an elite club. People whom you would walk by in the street at home become a kindred spirit, someone to talk to. This had been very much apparent the previous year when I was walking alone; perhaps it is the fact that someone on their own does need to talk, it matters not who to, just so long as they fulfil their need. I had certainly been guilty of this.

Walkers do tend to strike up conversations with one another and the characters you encounter often form lasting memories, for various reasons. With some walkers it is easy to see why they are on their own, but not so easy to shake them off! Were Chris and I scattering bread for the proverbial lame ducks? One chap we met had been dropped off at a point on the path by his wife and was following the coast path back to his home in Dorset. A clever ploy by his family to get rid of him? Would he trudge wearily up his garden path one day in August to find a different car on his drive, different curtains at his windows and a strange family in his house? Meanwhile his long suffering wife and kids would have moved into a terraced house in Oldham with a trucker. Slowly the significance of Roger's offer to drive us to Padstow began to sink in.

The elderly couple we met at the end of Crantock Beach were very chatty and were genuinely interested in our walk. They had walked the path from Bude to Falmouth the previous year but were unable to walk the next section this year as the woman had injured her knee. She really was a lame duck! They had to be content with short strolls in an area of the country they obviously loved. We talked for a while, Chris sympathising with the woman's plight, before continuing on our way.

A short scramble led us away from the beach and onto a low cliff where the path followed field boundaries around Pentire Point West. Views opened up away to the South West and Godrevy lighthouse. Two donkeys grazed contentedly in one field, accustomed to the views, they concentrated on eating.

"How would you like to walk to Falmouth carrying my rucksack?" Chris asked one of them.

The donkey did not leap over the fence with enthusiasm, so she took this to mean "No!"

At Porth Joke we watched a herd of cows sunning themselves on the beach. We stopped for a drink overlooking the beach, sitting on a grassy slope surrounded by islands of bramble patches. As we sat there eating sweets and taking sips of water we were entertained not just by the cows, which were moving to drink at the stream, but by rabbits. Every so often a rabbit would lollop out of one patch of bramble before seeing us and darting down the nearest rabbit hole.

Refreshment stops were definitely less hassle for two of us. We quickly fell into a routine of sitting with me on Chris's left. That way we could get each other's water bottle from the side pockets of the rucksacks without having to move or to take off the rucksacks.

We kept reading about sea lavender but were unable to find any and thought, disappointedly, that we had missed it. But we found some on Kelsey Head. Rubbing our hands over the tiny leaves and dainty purple flowers released the delicate scent. We saw numerous larger patches of sea lavender as we neared Land's End later in the week, perhaps the granite of that area produced soil more favourable to the plant.

From Holywell, which predictably enough, once had a holy well, the path climbed to skirt around the boundary of an M.o.D. camp. The walk past the perimeter fencing seemed to go on for ages. To one side of the fence were Nissen huts and asphalt roads, to the other side were fenced off mine shafts. An open "umbrella" framework of metal covered all the shafts. We soon discovered why they had not just been boarded over: bats! The abandoned workings were the roost of colonies of bats. The metal umbrellas prevented people from falling down the shafts whilst allowing the bats to come and go freely.

There were mines all over Cornwall, there still are, but like mines all over the country not many of them are working any more. And where there's mines, there's mine shafts. The trouble is, unlike the ones we passed that afternoon, some of the mine shafts are hidden and unfenced, some have become partially filled in or covered by a thin layer of vegetation, or capped by planks of wood which eventually rot. For many of the mine workings, no accurate plans remain and so there are shafts, the locations of which are not known.

I had heard of one pony, busy minding his own business one day, walking across his paddock when the next thing he knows – whoosh! The ground had given way beneath his hooves and the next thing he knows he's stood at the bottom of a thirty foot mine shaft. The pony was rescued the next day after the shaft opening was found by a dog. I know what you're thinking – I've switched from factual account to fairy story – but I swear it's true. The fire brigade was called and after one unsuccessful attempt, the culmination of which was the winch breaking and the pony falling all the way down the shaft for a second time, he was eventually raised to the surface with nothing worse than a few scratches. (Chris only goes to a dance and manages to tear her calf muscle!)

The thought of that pony kept haunting me as we rambled through grassy fields. Suppose we were walking over old mine workings? Chances were we were! I found myself prodding the ground with my walking pole, was it firm enough to walk on? Would we wake up in hospital (if we were lucky) in three days time to find both our legs in traction and a "nil by mouth" sign posted above our heads as we awaited operations to rebuild our shattered limbs? Every time Chris got behind me I kept turning round to check she was still there. Would I hear her screams as she fell headlong into the abandoned workings of Wheal Whatever? More importantly could I have her rucksack if she didn't make it? It was better than mine.

The sun was hot and despite a second generous application of sun screen we were beginning to burn. Chris's calves were mottled with heat rash, and I didn't look much better!

One person was luxuriating in all that U.V.A. and U.V.B. though. He was lying on the northern most end of Perran Beach, a stretch of sand almost two miles long. As we looked down over the edge of the cliffs to the beach one hundred and fifty feet below, we could just make out his recumbent form. He was the only person at that end of the beach, which was just as well, considering he was naked!

"He's no clothes on!" I exclaimed.

"Are you sure?"

"Yes, I think so. I'll just check. Thank goodness we borrowed mum's binoculars."

He was naked, middle aged and bald. Not an Adonis. Chris used the binoculars just to make sure. Then we both double-checked.

Our route at that point went steeply down the cliffs to emerge near to where he was lying. As we got to the bottom of the slope he turned his head and saw us but made no attempt to cover himself. Exhibitionist!

We paddled the length of the beach to Perranporth. Somewhere along the way I managed to zero my pedometer. History repeating itself! We had covered thirty eight miles by that time which, this year at least, did not mean that I did not see the reading go over the one hundred mile mark.

It had been a long day. We had walked fifteen miles and not the twelve we had expected. Most of those miles seemed to have been done trying to escape Newquay. The last two miles along the beach had been especially tiring. For most of the way the soft sand sucked at our feet as we walked. On the firmer stretches our feet pounded painfully over uneven crests and dips left by the receding tide. We were tired and collapsed in a heap on the soft dry sand at the end of the beach. It took us ages to summon the energy to stagger to our feet, and getting up with our rucksacks on was as time consuming as putting our boots and socks back on.

The Bed and Breakfast was only a short way inland. Although it was a bit shabby it did not have the Twilight Zone atmosphere as the one at Newquay had, that one had been more like Bate's Motel!

After a bit of sock washing and a freshen up we walked down into the little town for some supper. We sat on a bench in the park enjoying a takeaway pizza. Around us the local youths skateboarded along the road. I wonder how many got run over each year? We bought some fudge from a little gift shop and ate it as we sat on the quay, watching the sunset. How romantic! Then we made our way back to the B&B where I attempted to wash a grease stain out of my trousers, made when I slopped pizza down them. It refused to wash out and was in a very embarrassing place. I had to slop at the beginning of the holiday didn't I?

Tuesday 6th July

Before breakfast that morning we did two things. The first was to pack up our dirty clothes to send home. We had sent two parcels of clean clothes to Perranporth. We would have to wash them all once, as the next convenient place to send another parcel was at The Lizard, almost a week later. It was lovely to open those parcels; the fresh clothes smelt of fabric conditioner, the same could not be said for the clothes we were posting home!

As we were up quite early that morning we went out for a short walk before breakfast to explore the little town. Perranporth is rather quaint. One side of the town is dominated by the towering dunes, whilst at the other side the cliffs rise away from the beach. A clear, trout filled stream flows through the centre of the town before emptying into the sea. Built around this stream is a small park. Further inland a wooded path follows the course of the stream. We walked along this path for a little way before returning for breakfast.

For the first time, we were not the only guests. Another walker had spent the night there. He was walking to Portreath that day like ourselves, although we were not to see him on the path at all, as we had some shopping to do before we could set off.

As we were stood in a steadily growing queue outside the post office at five minutes to nine a few spots of rain began to fall. Fifteen minutes later as we were leaving the grocers, loaded with fruit and pasties, the rain had stopped.

The path climbed to Cligga Head passing old mine workings, much of the scenery that morning was to be influenced by the once busy industry. We walked over a colourful spoil heap, the recent rain had acted on some of the spoil and we could smell the odour of iron sulphide. Less than two decades ago the mine there had been reopened but found to be unprofitable. The result was a variety of ores scattered across the slopes and although ugly to look at in one sense, it was also strangely beautiful with the yellow, pink, white and greys of the various ores.

Chris kept stopping to search for interesting rocks. I kept stopping too, but I was searching for something completely different: a secluded spot. Women's bodies have a definite design fault. As I may have highlighted already, there is a paucity of public toilets scattered along the coast path. The few there are tend to be in towns and villages, with the odd one or two to be found at car parks located near remote but sandy beaches. So it is almost inevitable that when your bladder contents build up to the point where there is only one thing you can concentrate on, there are no toilets in a four mile radius.

So far this year we had been fortunate. Due to the prolific numbers of surfing beaches between Padstow and Newquay, we had passed many conveniently located toilets. After leaving Perranporth though, all that changed and by mid morning I was becoming desperate and was forced to make the first al fresco toilet stop of the holiday. I could not have managed another step, let alone the two miles to the nearest toilets shown on the map at Trevaunance Cove.

Chris's daughter, Clare, amazes me by her capacity to retain water. She could shame a camel! I've been on walks with her that have lasted hours between toilets and never once has she darted behind a fallen tree or ducked under a bush, to emerge minutes later with a look of blissful relief on her face. How does she do it? It must be an effort. Several hours into a walk

95

she goes quiet and seems to go into her own little world but the one place she does not go is to the toilet.

The problem for women which men do not have to worry over quite so much is the obvious one of convenience. For men, it is a simple matter but for women half the time is taken up with belts, buttons and tucking your clothes back in afterwards.

It was as I was crouched behind a spoil heap only yards from the path, praying no one would come along for the foreseeable future and concentrating on (a) not getting my feet wet and (b) not impaling my behind on a thistle or clump of gorse, that I was reminded of the African elephant. Would the fate of female walkers be the same as that of the elephant? Due to the poaching of elephants for their tusks, the gene pool has altered. Elephants breeding in Africa are now exhibiting smaller and sometimes no tusks. It is a process of natural selection; survival of the fittest, in this case elephants with smaller tusks are at a lower risk of being shot than their tuskier kindred, and it is these that live long enough to produce several offspring. Would, I pondered, women hikers die out due to lack of public toilets, higher risk of discovery and embarrassment and a general unwillingness to partially remove their clothing during cold weather? The tough, brazen-it-out-with-a-gorse-patch kind of woman would cease to exist as fewer women took up the challenge of walking in areas deplete of restrooms. As a result this would leave the gene pool to become concentrated with high-heel clad shop-a-holics.

I am undecided whether it is a simpler process when there are two of you, as there were this year, or if it is better when you are alone. Chris could stand guard for me and vice versa, which is useful to distract other walkers.

"Hello! Gosh, look up there, it that a Peregrine?" Thus the sound of running water at the other side of the hedge is obscured and dignity retained intact.

However, when there are two of you the problem of suggestion arises. The words "Can you see anywhere convenient for a toilet stop?" often had the effect of making whichever one of us was being asked also need to make a stop. And when both of you need to go it takes twice as long, increasing the risk of encountering other walkers. Team building or what?

Further along on Cligga Head we came across the abandoned remains of the processing works of an old tungsten and tin mine. This was one of the last mines in Cornwall to close, surviving until 1945 when the end of the war brought an abrupt halt to the demand for tungsten which was used in armour piercing shells. Little now remains of the nearby factory owned by the Noble Explosives Company, just a scattered collection of derelict buildings and wind-blown rubble.

We zigzagged along a wide, stony track passing more mine shafts and workings. Clumps of purple heather grew all along the cliff tops. It was turning into a very peaceful, warm, sunny morning.

A kestrel flew overhead and stopped little more than ten feet from us to hover gracefully. As the currents of air moved its body, it adjusted with a faint movement of its wings, keeping its head perfectly still. We watched for a while, fascinated at this display of control. Although so close it seemed totally unconcerned at our presence, turning its head just once to look at us before returning its searching gaze to the ground. Eventually, having found no sign of any prey, it glided quietly away to hunt a little further along the cliffs.

We turned our attention to reading a paragraph in the guidebook and almost immediately the kestrel flew over us. We looked up, at once thrilled and disappointed. Thrilled to see it was carrying in its talons a slowworm; disappointed that we had not seen it strike.

We did not see it again but a little further along the path we watched three buzzards. These birds were considerably larger than the kestrel but lacked none of its grace in the air. Soaring in the thermals they looked magnificent. Small wonder people tried to emulate flight! The gliding club just inland from this point was obviously popular; we watched a number of gliders being towed up into the clear skies to finally be released to glide silently back to earth. It looked a fantastic experience.

At Trevellas Porth the path descended into a narrow valley taking us down almost to sea level. More ruined mine buildings were strung out inland, following the course of the tiny stream. Someone still made a living from the products of the mines; a sign advertised tin brooches and other souvenirs for sales. Had the souvenirs been made of lighter material, say plastic for example, I might have been tempted but my rucksack was heavy enough already!

We joined a steep rutted track, apparently used each year for the London to Land's End motor trials. I felt sorry for anyone trying to ride a motorbike along that track, walking was bad enough.

Once at the top of the hill the path soon began to descend to Trevaunance Cove. We stopped here, first for toilets and then to buy the first ice cream of the holiday. After loosing a bet I owed Chris an ice cream with clotted cream on top. The problem was, the shop had run out of clotted cream, well that got me off the hook! (For the time being at least.) So we settled for just a plain old cornet. My first choice was lemon meringue flavour but they had run out of that as well. Okay, I could live with Belgian chocolate flavour if I had to!

The ice cream gave us a boost to climb once again almost from sea level to the top of the cliffs. Here we could see St Agnes Beacon peeping over the cliffs ahead of us. Turning we looked back to see a white glint of the lighthouse at Trevose Head. Each time we rounded a headland it would appear again. Unlike Saunton Sands Hotel the lighthouse was not an unpleasant sight but an acceptable part of the scenery. Like an acquaintance almost, we would turn to look back and there it would be, fancy seeing you again!

Then Newquay reared its ugly head. A grey blot still visible.

"Oh God!" groaned Chris.

We quickly averted our gaze and did not look back for quite some time after that.

The ice cream kept us going for quite a while and it was not until almost two in the afternoon that we stopped for lunch. At Newdown's Head we settled at the side of the path to eat our pasties. Within minutes of sitting down, people began to appear from all sides. Our quiet picnic became like a stop on Blackpool promenade. Each time we had a mouthful of pasty more walkers would materialise with a cheery "hello!" and we struggled not to spray pastry over them as we replied.

Typically, as we finished eating, the sudden stream of walkers stopped. Chris laid back and closed her eyes, she later admitting to falling asleep. I sat there and vegetated for a bit before deciding to have another sip of water. At that point several things happened simultaneously. I raised the bottle to my lips to take a drink. A walker appeared with a cheery greeting. Chris began struggling to sit up, dazzled by the sun she failed to see my elbow sticking out and whacked her head against it. The bottle tilted violently and I inhaled most of the water I had been trying to drink. As I sat coughing and gasping for breath, Chris sat rubbing her head and the walker passed us, barely able to control his laughter.

From St Agnes Head the path took a sharp left hand turn and began following the coastline in a southerly direction. For the first time we were treated to views of Godrevy Island with St Ives across the bay behind it.

As the afternoon drew on we passed increasing amounts of dog dirt and realised we must be getting near to either a town, a car park or a tourist trap. It may be biodegradable but I find it equally offensive and unsightly as litter and cigarette ends. Sadly it was to be a reliable but detestable indication of approaching civilisation for the entire walk.

The magnet for all the dog walkers was Wheal Coates. The ruins of the engine house stood majestically right next to the path. Chris and Buzz posed for a photograph, dwarfed by the enormous building and its tall chimney. Curiously, although built of stone, the tip of the chimney was topped with bricks. This was common, apparently, for many of the chimneys although we never discovered why.

Tin was commonly mined throughout Cornwall; some mines also mined copper, bismuth, arsenic, tungsten and silver. Few of the mines remain except as ruins or museums. As the mines closed the miners moved on, some went as far afield as Australia and North America, seeking their fortunes in the gold rush.

The mining industry has left a legacy of not just spoil heaps and abandoned workings but technology too. At Hayle, Harvey's foundry made engines that were used not just in the mines but all over the world. Richard Trevithick improved on Watt's design for the steam engine, first using it to pump water out of the mines. Necessity being the mother of invention indeed!

Into Porthtowan we staggered and stumbled our way down a very precipitous, rough path. Whether it was because I was feeling particularly tired by that stage I do not know, but I found Porthtowan to be a grey, ugly place. A line of horrible modern shops led inland from the beach. They were square, unsightly concrete structures, far more offensive to the eye than the spoil heaps or mine ruins. The architect responsible should have been made to live in the small community.

Portreath did not seem to be getting any nearer. We climbed down and then up some incredibly steep granite steps at Sally's Bottom. Chris later described them as being like a roller coaster. By the time we reached the top our legs were shaking.

Past the second airfield of the day the path seemed to go on and on following tall wire fencing. The monotony was broken when Chris suddenly stopped dead in her tracks and whispered "Look!"

I had been looking out to sea at that moment and, unaware she had stopped, walked right into her. The handle of her walking pole fastened to the back of her rucksack nearly poked my eye out and I squashed Buzz, putting his nose out of joint literally!

"What have you stopped for?" I snapped.

"Sshh!"

Peering over her shoulder I followed her pointing finger. Lying on the narrow path was a slowworm. It seemed to be trying to catch the ants as they scurried across the path as fast as their six little legs could carry them. We watched for a while and then took a photograph before stepping carefully over it and moving on. It was the first time either of us had seen a live slowworm. They are fascinating creatures, not as their name implies a worm, nor as their appearance suggests a snake. They are actually legless lizards and unusually for reptiles they give birth to live young rather than laying eggs. The eggs are retained in the body until they hatch when the mother then gives birth.

Whilst the camera was still handy we took a photograph of the parasitic dodder covering the gorse. Its bright pink filament-like strands shining in the sunlight.

As early evening approached we arrived in Portreath. The B&B was on a circular road with an illogical numbering system. We were warmly welcomed and shown to our en-suite room, a pleasant surprise, as we were not expecting en-suite. We immediately dubbed the room Flanders. The theme was poppies. Poppy wallpaper, poppy duvets, poppy light shade, poppy crockery, poppy curtains, poppy chair, poppy light pull, poppy picture. Someone in the household obviously liked poppies! They also liked running a B&B and knew what appealed to tired walkers; it was clean and comfortable and hospitable.

Revived by a shower and a drink we made our way to the nearby pub, The Basset Arms, taking its name from the local lords of the manor. The Bassets gained much of their wealth from mining and Portreath developed as a port handling the ores from their mines. An incline of the now defunct Hayle railway can still be seen leading down to the harbour. By the harbour, where once stood a coal yard there are now maisonettes. They were not particularly in keeping with the older buildings, but I suppose they were an improvement on the industrial remains.

From being one of the most powerful families in Cornwall, the Basset family fortunes suffered with the decline of the mining industry (and a lot of help from one family member gambling on the wrong horses). Their ancestral home is now a hospital and the grounds a country park.

The Bassets may have lost their money but the pub named after them must have been making a fortune. In such a tiny place as Portreath on a Tuesday evening in early July, the large pub was packed with people. We saw more people in the pub that evening than we had seen on the path all day. Most of them were dining and we struggled to find a vacant table. Once our meal arrived we understood why the pub was so popular; the food was excellent; well cooked, reasonably priced and the portions were huge. We both agreed it was a superb end to the day.

Wednesday 7th July

Breakfast was at eight thirty, half an hour later than we would have liked. We were awake early and had some time to occupy. Chris wrote a postcard to her mum. She was sending one each day as a record of our walk. I checked on the clothes we had washed the night before. Most of the socks and underwear were dry but our T-shirts were still damp so we fastened them to our rucksacks to finish drying during the day.

We were part way through breakfast that morning when a fellow guest joined us. An elderly man, he was staying there while his daughter was on holiday and he was obviously being treated like one of the family. He began chatting about Warwickshire, a common interest for him and Chris.

"I'm partially sighted," he explained as he peered into the hot water jug.

The landlady appeared with his toast and saw what he was doing.

"That's your hot water jug, Bill."

"Oh, I thought you had forgotten to put the teabag in!" he laughed.

Sleeping in a different place every night gave us an insight into the lives of other people. Sometimes, as at Newquay, it was an insight we could well have done without. We had some very pleasant and some very unpleasant accommodation. The best B&Bs were the ones such as Porthcothan and Portreath where we made to feel welcome; a guest in someone's home, not just a paying visitor. Unfortunately not everyone put the needs of the guests over their own desire to make money. We had some very uncomfortable beds, surly welcomes and unappetising breakfasts. The lady at Porthcothan enjoyed what she did and had expressed amazement that at some places we would be paying more than £15 a night. She would doubtless have been shocked by some of the places we stayed.

It was overcast when we left that morning and we quickly bundled our damp T-shirts into the rucksacks to prevent them getting any wetter. Checking the notes we had made in the planning stages, we realised there would be nowhere convenient to buy lunch later in the day and so headed for the local shop.

Leaving Portreath we started the day's walking with a steep climb to the top of Western Hill. This was quickly followed by another steep descent and ascent as we crossed the stream flowing into the sea at Porth-cadjack Cove. It had been a misty start, with visibility much reduced as the low clouds flowed over the cliffs. The sounds of a fishing boat and, inland, a tractor travelled to us sounding muffled and ghostly in the damp foggy air. We sweated inside our kagools as we toiled up the steep slopes to the top of the cliffs. After less than an hour the weather improved, the mist clearing to reveal the fields and woods stretching away inland. We thankfully removed our kagools. We were not to need them again for over a week.

The path hugged the cliff edge along Reskajeage Downs. Two hundred and fifty feet below us the sea pounded the bottom of the cliffs. Rock pipits and meadow pipits flitted amongst the maritime buckthorn and gorse bushes growing by the path. Then for a short while the path clung to the roadside before veering away to run along the top of the cliff once more to the eerily named Deadman's Cove. The cove earned its rather grim name due to the nature of the currents along that stretch of coast. Many drowned mariners were washed ashore there.

At Hudder Down we were able to look across the breadth of Cornwall. Clearly visible to the naked eye was St. Michael's Mount. Just east of Penzance and with its feet splashing in the English Channel, it was nine miles directly south west from us. It would be another four days before we saw it at close range.

And so, to the lighthouse, to quote Virginia Woolf. Godrevy Lighthouse that is, which featured in her book. I had tried to borrow a copy of 'To the Lighthouse' from the library before we came down to Cornwall but had been unsuccessful. The best I could manage was 'Orlando' and, having read it, can appreciate the fact that Mrs Woolf was "bad with her nerves". Suffering from depression that had troubled her all her life and fearing another breakdown, she committed suicide in 1941.

Rounding Godrevy Point the whole of St. Ives Bay opened up before us. It was a panoramic view. We sat down to eat lunch above the beach at Magow Rocks, looking across the bay to St. Ives.

Spreading our kagools on the springy turf we began to eat, sharing a whole roast chicken and some chocolate. It is astounding how two competent adults can make such a mess of eating a cooked chicken: grease on Gore-Tex, grease on shorts, T-shirts, rucksacks, even socks. When we had finished we realised we had nothing to wipe our sticky hands on. All our tissues were in our rucksacks, trying to reach them would result in transferring grease to even more of our belongings!

After wiping our hands on the grass to get rid of the majority of the sticky mess, we packed up and set off towards Gwithian. Although we passed a car park and a café there did not seem to be any litter bins. In the growing heat of the afternoon I carried the remains of the chicken several miles until we finally found some toilets and litter bins.

We walked through the dunes and then down onto the beach. The beach was three miles long. It looked like six. It felt like nine. It was even longer than Perran Beach and seemed to stretch on and on and on. After we had been walking an hour I turned to look back, then wished I hadn't. We did not seem to have covered half the length of the beach. We plodded on, inching slowly nearer to the speck in the distance that was the coast guard hut. A life guard on a quad bike sped up the beach towards us, seemingly on a pointless quest. He turned before reaching us and drove back to the hut, shrinking to a tiny black dot.

"He could have offered us a lift," muttered Chris.

As we got closer to the far end of the beach, the sands became increasingly crowded with holiday makers. Beach tents seemed to be in vogue. Every family had marked out their territory with wind breaks, towels or colourful plastic tents. Children shrieked, seagulls cried and dogs barked. And I watched where I was putting my feet.

The caravans of summer camp Colditz stood in regimented lines along the top of the dunes overlooking the bay. Their inhabitants let out for good behaviour to enjoy the late afternoon sunshine. The POW feel was reinforced by the pill box nearby.

The day had brightened considerably from the mist of the early morning. The sky was cloudless and the sun shone warmly. A little too warmly for us. Frequent applications of sun screen had little noticeable effect on our already burnt calves. Each time we stopped, the skin on the backs of our legs seemed to tighten and shrink, burning painfully; it felt better to just keep walking. My ears had become sunburnt and I fidgeted with my cap trying to stop it aggravating the pain further. As the holiday went on and my ears got redder, our bright scarlet Leukaemia Research Fund caps faded with the sun to a dull pale red. The sun reflected off the white sand and clear turquoise sea, dazzling us. The unpredictable English weather was steeling itself for a long hot spell.

We stopped briefly for Chris to swap her ordinary glasses for sunglasses. My photochromic lenses had already gone as dark as they could. Peering over the top of them I saw a much brighter, if more blurred, view of the beach.

Where we had thought we were supposed to leave the beach was, in fact, across the Hayle estuary. With the tide out and the heat haze shimmering over the sand it was impossible to pick out the river. We studied the map, Chris complaining she could not see properly because of her dark lenses.

"What's that red line there?" she asked.

"A black line!" I laughed.

"Oh, it's these glasses!"

We found the correct route with a signpost pointing up the steep shifting sands of a tall dune. The arduous climb drained all our energy and we stopped at the summit for a drink but our water supply was almost gone. We were running on empty. Chris felt faint, a result of too little water and her burnt calves. We needed a rest, but just as importantly we needed a drink. Fortunately a refreshment hut was close by. Leaving Chris sprawled out on a bench I went to buy several litres of lemonade. We both felt better after a long drink but what we really needed was to find some shade.

Looking back now after completing the walk and knowing what awaited us in the coming days, it is astonishing that we achieved what we did. On that first Wednesday afternoon we thought the heat unbearable, somehow we later learnt to accept the hotter temperatures. That day had been a fairly easy walk of just over twelve miles on good paths. It is fortunate that we travel through life unaware of what lies in store, otherwise many more people might do the same as Virginia Woolf!

The last section of the walk that day took us past some pretty awful chalets before dropping down to the riverside to pass a derelict power station and industrial grot spots. We crossed a swing bridge, with the tide out the muddy channel below was exposed to the hot sun. The pungent aroma of rotting seaweed was enough to put even me off any thoughts of food. Crossing a busy road we entered the small but once busy industrial town of Hayle. The footpath followed the main road right to the door of our B&B.

The view from our room at the front of the house looked across the harbour, the river and the mud flats towards a builders merchants. It does not sound like a particularly nice view but it was not too unsightly; in the distance was open countryside and almost opposite our window we could see the tower of the church at Lelant.

I volunteered to do the washing, leaving Chris napping on the bed. I spent ages in the bathroom, first washing out all the clothes then having a cool shower (anything too hot and I could not endure the pain from my ears and calves). When I first entered the bathroom I had noticed there seemed to be a film of red dust on the sink and floor. I discovered the cause of this as I dried myself on the soft fluffy burgundy coloured towel. The towels were new. And moulting. My entire body was coated in red fluff. It transferred itself onto my clothes and no amount of brushing and shaking could remove it completely. Weeks later I was able to identify underwear that I had worn at Hayle because of the tiny specks of red fluff still clinging to it! At least I did not have the awesome task of trying to keep the bathroom clean! The landlady must have bitterly regretted buying those towels.

Tea consisted of a picnic made up of various goodies from the local shop. Sitting on the grassy gardens by the river we watched the sun go down. I turned to look along the row of terraced houses.

"Which is our room then?" I asked sarcastically.

"The one with all the smalls hanging up in the window!" retorted Chris.

Our room was easy to pick out. Along the entire row, only one window was festooned with two bras, two pairs of knickers, two T-shirts, a pair of trousers and four pairs of socks!

Getting ready for bed that night we coated our sunburnt limbs and faces in calamine lotion that we had purchased from the shop. Would it ease our throbbing skin?

Thursday 8th July

Another walker had stayed that night and we all shared a table at breakfast. He was walking in the other direction along the path. We asked him what it was like towards Land's End and he answered rather vaguely about privet bushes and staying in Pendeen the previous night. He had walked a total of nineteen miles to reach Hayle in one day; we would be stopping after thirteen miles when we reached Zennor that evening. What we found more astonishing was the fact that this was his first long distance walk after recovering from a double knee operation earlier in the year. He was in his sixties, undeterred by a set back that for many people would have put an end to long walks. This walk was a test for him; his aim was to walk from Land's End to John O'Groats once fully fit. He made our efforts seem puny in comparison. Over the next two days we came to discover why his reply about the walk towards Land's End had been ambiguous and our admiration for him increased.

It was hot that morning as we set out around the mud flats of the estuary towards Lelant. The Hayle estuary is a nature reserve owned by the R.S.P.B., so of course we saw nothing! The first mile along the road was almost enjoyable after the seemingly endless beach of the previous afternoon. Soon we were walking along an attractive wooded suburban lane down the other side of the estuary towards Lelant. A bird flew past us along the lane.

"What was that?" said Chris.

"A bird."

"I know that. What sort of bird?"

I knew but infuriatingly could not remember its name; my mum had a picture of one on a tablemat. The answer evaded me but when I stopped trying to recall the name it suddenly came to me.

"Waxwing!" I blurted.

"Pardon?"

"That bird we saw, it was a waxwing."

"That was ages ago."

"I know, the name just hit me then. I'm surprised you didn't see the light bulb appear above my head!"

The church at Lelant marks the start of St. Michael's Way, a path that picks its way across the skinny bit of Cornwall to finish at St. Michael's Mount. If only we had turned left there we could have spared ourselves a lot of hard, difficult miles!

We were keen to take a look in the church but as we neared the porch, we could hear voices coming from inside. I crept to the doorway to listen.

"Oh God! There's a service on." I whispered.

"Great choice of words, Julia!"

We were both disappointed but we could hardly go inspecting the inside of the church during a service. We had to be content with looking round the graveyard and reading the church notice board. Ironically, there was only one mid week service held there each month and we had arrived on that one day!

Crossing under the railway line we emerged onto more sand dunes. Soon the path began to climb diagonally up the cliffs away from the beach. We had not gone far before my boot found some more dog dirt. Typical! Why was it always me and not Chris?

"Because your feet are so big, you're more likely to step in something!" Chris replied to my grumbling.

I suppose that made sense.

We walked through a tunnel of sycamore, privet and honeysuckle; passing many other walkers, most simply out for a morning stroll. The vegetation provided shade from the hot sun but added to the humidity. The perspiration rolled down our faces, our clothes stuck to us and the brims of our caps became wet with sweat. Drops of moisture collected on my chin and on Chris's nose, we were constantly flicking our heads or wiping the backs of our hands across our faces to wipe the sweat away.

At Carbis Bay we stopped for a drink and to use the toilets. It was a relief to be in a cool building. Actually going to the toilet was not easy, my clothes were sticking to me and the cloth belt of my shorts seemed to be acting like capillary matting, drawing moisture from my back around towards the front.

Back in the full sun once more, we climbed a gentle hill, crossing the railway for the third time and emerging onto a private road. Large, luxurious houses were set well back from the road in beautiful landscaped gardens. The views from their windows across the bay must have been spectacular.

After our experiences of Newquay we were dreading St. Ives. Neither of us had been there before. Virgin territory, undiscovered country. Mum and Dad had spent a day here on a BC (before child) holiday. I knew it to be popular with artists – excellent light quality, don't you know!

But St. Ives had stuck in Mum's mind for another reason – one particular restaurant. The restaurant had obviously been suffering from delusions of grandeur. After a mediocre main course with a pretentious name, both Mum and Dad plumped for the Hawaiian Delight dessert. Hawaiian Surprise would have been a more suitable name. Both my parents were certainly surprised by the unexpected dish of pineapple rings.

As we dropped down to the obviously popular Porthminster Beach we were surprised to discover we liked what we saw. We did not like the crowds of tourists flocking along the pavements or lying in rows on the beach, they did tend to spoil things a bit. But the buildings were clean and freshly painted and the parks and gardens were well manicured with colourful flower beds.

"This is rather nice!" We chorused in astonishment.

From there a short walk took us round to the harbour. The more we saw of St. Ives, the more we liked it. It was quaint. A definite improvement on Newquay. Yes, there were cafes and ice cream vans, but everything seemed so much cleaner. A maze of steep streets lined with tiny shops and cottages led away from the waterfront. We stopped at a little gift shop selling, amongst other things, ice cream with clotted cream on top; and at last I was able to pay off my bet with Chris. We walked slowly along the harbour, looking for somewhere to sit to eat the ice cream but people were everywhere and there was not a vacant seat to be had.

Fishermen vied for customers, shouting about their boat trips.

"Want to visit seal island?" one bellowed in my ear as we passed.

I was sceptical. "The guidebook kept mentioning seals all last year," I told Chris, "and I never saw one!"

We strolled on passing a row of benches. I was still thinking about seals when Chris nudged me. She was grinning.

"Look at those people on that bench."

I turned and looked and immediately understood why she was grinning. An elderly couple sat there, both wearing knotted handkerchiefs on their heads. They did look silly. But they were right to protect their heads from the sun. Would they have not been better with a hat though? Less likely to blow away for one thing and what happened when they wanted to blow their noses?

We made our way through the narrow streets of the town, searching for somewhere to buy lunch and for a cash machine. The rucksacks proved a definite hindrance when it came to squeezing through crowds of people. I kept a tight hold of my walking pole, mindful of the damage it could inflict. Chris left me outside as she went into a bakery, then abandoned me once more at a greengrocers whilst she bought fruit. Loading up her rucksack with the food we hunted out a bank and then a little supermarket. We needed more liquids. The water at the B&B at Hayle tasted awful; so having bought two litres of spring water, we filled our water bottles then shared a two litre bottle of orangeade. We were determined not to run low on liquids again.

As we left the supermarket, Chris drew my attention to a headline in one newspaper. It announced the Government was having a rethink on its scheme to cull thousands of badgers to see if they were responsible for the incidence of tuberculosis in cattle. I fervently hoped they would abandon the ridiculous scheme. It brought to mind the witch trials. Throw someone believed to be a witch into a lake, if she floated she was guilty, if she drowned she was innocent. Shame she had had to die but at least everyone knew she was not a witch! That seemed to be the cockeyed logic behind the badger cull. Thousands of badgers could die to prove they were not responsible for bovine TB. Badgers would be eliminated from entire areas of the country and the question of how cattle contract tuberculosis would remain unanswered. Many of the urban areas of Lancashire had high incidences of TB. You don't see many badgers there, could it be spitting that was a main contributory factor? Because that's something you do see a lot of! If the health authorities were to cull everyone found spitting in public, would the number of cases of TB decline?

We carried our lunch out to St. Ives Head which was marginally less crowded than the rest of the town, passing a tiny stretch of beach on the way. The sand was hidden under masses of red bodies.

"They all look like boiled lobsters," I commented.

"Coming from you that's the pot calling the kettle red!" replied Chris.

Some of the sun worshippers were exposing more than others. As I peered over the railings a 36C peered back at me. Hell, I bet sunburn there would be painful! Nearby, one young man lay on his back his eyes closed, the sun glinted off something metallic on his chest: a nipple ring. The heat conduction on that little piece of shiny metal did not bear thinking about!

One person on the beach was doing something more constructive than just lying and cooking. He was making a large sand sculpture. It was incredible watching him as he scooped up handfuls of sand and smoothed them into shape creating a life-sized model of a galloping horse.

On top of the hill on St. Ives Head there stands a small chapel. We found an unoccupied bench in the shade of its north facing wall and stopped for lunch. We eased off our rucksacks and slumped down onto the beautifully cold stone seat. Chris took off her boots and socks and lined them all up in the sun to dry. The people at the next bench got up and left.

Fed and rested we prepared to leave. Chris put her socks and boots back on and I dumped our litter in a bin. It was two in the afternoon and the walk to Zennor was less than seven miles, we had plenty of time. Next time I say anything like that, just hit me over the head will you? We stepped out of the shade. For the next three days we would be walking in constant, unrelieved, glaring sunshine.

We left the last of the town's periphery along the back of Porthmeor Beach, passing the Tate Gallery. According to the guidebook the gallery stands on the former site of the old gas works. Hmm, I contemplated whether, aesthetically, this newer building was an improvement or not. A modern building housing modern art. Not my cup of tea.

The first part of the path from St. Ives was surprisingly boggy, stone sets had been laid in some areas. The compensation was the variation in plant life that the wet conditions favoured. Soon we left the marshy ground and the receding view of bustling St. Ives to follow a beautiful stretch of coastline.

The coast from just beyond St. Ives all the way to Cape Cornwall, a distance of some seventeen miles, has been designated a Site of Special Scientific Interest and it was easy to see why. Countless rocky headlands rolled away to the west, with jagged cliffs of varying heights falling down to the clear waters of the Atlantic. A variety of flora coloured the cliff tops with their flowers and leaves. For the first time we saw the distinctive royal fern, a rarity outside Cornwall. The purple flowers of orchids and sea lavender contrasting with the delicate white bell-shaped flowers of sea campion. The map showed a tiny patchwork quilt of old fields, the fields were small in real life too!

A nearby campsite had erected information boards at intervals along the path and, although we saw no one from the campsite, we read the boards with interest. One urged the reader to keep a watchful eye out for basking sharks and seals. I was still sceptical of seeing any wildlife that we were informed of. We did look for sea life but we failed to see any sharks. The seals proved to be another matter.

For much of the afternoon we heard the put-put-put of boats laden with tourists heading along the coast to The Carracks; a group of rocky islands just beyond Carn Naun Point. The rocks are a favourite haunt of seals and obviously provide a nice little money spinner for the local boatmen. So, with Chris full of anticipation and me full of doubt, we settled down on the cliff tops overlooking the rocks to have a drink, a biscuit and to enjoy a bit of seal watching.

"Look, there's one!" pointed Chris.

"Where? Where?"

"Bobbing in the waves. There's just its head visible."

I peered through the binoculars but could see nothing. Chris took a turn with the binoculars, but the seal had gone. We scanned the rocks but could see none basking in the sun. Then suddenly I spotted one in the water!

"Look, look!! There's one really close to the shore!" I squealed.

Chris trained the binoculars on the area I was pointing.

"I can't see anything."

I took a turn with the binoculars and suddenly found what I had been looking at. Through binoculars the 'seal' appeared to have a short pole sticking out of its head with a flag on top. My 'seal' was a buoy!

We overtook two people walking together. The young man had stopped to remove his T-shirt, which seemed rather foolish as he was carrying a rucksack. It was sure to rub. Later on they passed us as we sat having a drink. He was still topless and looking very red by that time.

Another couple passed us further along. They were obviously husband and wife: colour co-ordinated and with the man striding out leaving his wife to trip hurriedly along behind. They both carried equally huge rucksacks, no regard had been given to the woman, and whilst her husband looked easily capable of walking at a rapid pace with such a heavy pack, his wife was most noticeably struggling with her burden and the pace. Neither of them wore hats and their water bottles, carried on the outside of their rucksacks, could not possibly have provided them with sufficient liquid in that heat. The woman looked dehydrated and extremely weary. We saw them the following day, the man once again setting a blistering pace and the woman plodding along behind. That was the last we saw of them but Chris must have frequently thought of them because a week later she suddenly mentioned them saying: "I wonder where that couple are by now?"

"Well, I don't know about the man but I suspect his wife is in a hospital somewhere suffering from heat exhaustion!"

In the early evening the character of the path changed. Granite forced its brutal influence on the landscape; the cliffs suddenly became more precipitous; inland, granite tors dominated the skyline making the landscape look harsh and bleak. The path, which had been following the contours, changed from a dusty track to a very rocky, uneven and snaking trail. The vegetation changed; the flowering plants replaced by great walls of bracken, with the occasional foxglove rearing its purple head beside the path. There was no let up in the temperatures; the sun continued burning down as afternoon slipped into evening. As the sun began to sink towards the horizon, we were as hot as ever.

We stumbled over rocks in the path, kicking up dust as we went. Our pace had slowed to less than one mile an hour. I checked my watch: seven o'clock. Looking at the map, Zennor Head still seemed hours away. The vegetation was getting worse, now nettles and buckthorn had joined the bracken to obscure the path. The undergrowth was taller – taller than we were in some places. I remember walking (walking? Stumbling!) up a quite gentle slope and turning to see where Chris was. I could not see her. Not even her red cap was visible. She was completely drowned by foliage. Only the movement of the bracken fronds revealed her location.

Every few yards we stopped to wipe the sweat from our faces and flap our caps to create a breeze. Our skin would dry, salt encrusted, before we continued on our way and the sweat flowed again. I began going over my first aid training for heat stroke and heat exhaustion, but found I could not remember the symptoms or the treatment for either. I knew the treatment for one was different from the treatment for the other. Chris would know. I asked her but hardly had the energy to listen to her response. I think my query caused her some concern, it was the first indication I had given about how tired I had become, and was the first time I had spoken for over an hour.

I was kept going by the thought of the farmhouse we were staying at that night. We had discussed what we imagined it to be like, but Chris thought I was heading for a big disappointment, that my expectations were too great. I had never stayed in a farmhouse. I imagined being greeted by a matronly farmer's wife, hair in a bun, with sleeves rolled up to reveal arms the size of hams, still dusty with flour from her recent baking. I pictured us being ushered into a homely kitchen, with a stone tiled floor, beamed ceiling from which hung bunches of drying herbs, and a huge Aga sitting in an enormous stone fireplace. The air would be filled with the delicious smells of baking. And in the centre of the room I visualised a huge oak table, groaning under the weight of a vast array of home-produced fayre. Great loaves of bread fresh from the oven, scones, cakes and fruit loaves. A massive round cheese, a side of ham, another of home-cured bacon, fresh free-range eggs. Jacket potatoes dug that morning, steaming tureens of garden vegetables, steaming bowls of home made soup, a gigantic pie with crisp golden pastry. Dishes of freshly picked raspberries and strawberries, jars of home-made jam and chutney. Apples, pears and damsons straight from the orchard. Jugs of milk straight from the dairy, glasses of elderflower cordial and farmhouse cider and, finally, a teapot of tea. My mouth watered, my stomach rumbled and my fevered brain thought of more and more appetising foods. These gluttonous daydreams were the carrot to the tired donkey.

The coast path should have followed the curve of Zennor Head but we arrived on the far side of the headland without having walked around it. We had seen no path turning off the one we had followed and could only assume it had become entirely overgrown, which was hardly a

109

surprise! We cursed the National Trust for not clearing the paths and for the absence of signposts.

The tiny hamlet of Zennor was less than a mile inland along a lane. As we entered the hamlet at the side of a farm, we came to the church. It was unlocked and we quietly entered. The cool interior swallowed us and quenched our heated bodies. The shock was like diving into a cold pool and the perspiration immediately dried. To my amazement I began to shiver.

I find a peacefulness in old country churches that I fail to find in urban ones. It must be the history and the atmosphere, the sense of timelessness, centuries of tradition unchanged, the closeness to nature that only exists in a rural community. The church at Zennor is different from any other church and famous for one thing. A mermaid.

Carved into the end of one of the benches in the church is the Mermaid of Zennor. A legend tells of a mermaid who, enchanted by the voice of one of the choristers, used to sit in the church and listen to him sing. He fell in love with her and was lured to the sea. He was never seen again but can be often heard singing in the depths of the sea.

Leaving the church we passed the pub and decided it would be a good idea to find out when they stopped serving food. Having found out, and also asked directions to the farmhouse, we set off up the road.

We arrived at the farmhouse, a long thatched, white-washed building on the edge of the village, to the strains of the Eastenders theme tune floating through an open window. It was eight o'clock. No wonder we felt tired, we had been walking since nine that morning with little more than a thirty minute break for lunch and a few stops of five minutes for sips of water.

I have to say though, Chris was right and I was wrong. The farmhouse of my dreams might exist somewhere but not there, not that night. It was an old building, much built on over the centuries to produce a thick walled, rambling structure of low ceilings, oddly shaped rooms and twisting corridors. In that respect, at least, I was not disappointed. But only in that respect. It was clean and there was a bath, there's nothing quite like relaxing in a bath after a long day spent walking, but that was about it. Our room even had tea making facilities, such a shame it did not have any decent tea bags.

We freshened up and an hour later were standing in the pub waiting to be served. We were not waiting because there was a queue, we were waiting because there was no barman. The pub seemed to have been left completely unattended and we were just contemplating serving ourselves when someone appeared. He took our order for drinks and then began to get slightly confused as we placed an order for food. The maths of four items was beyond both him and the till. Eventually we paid for all four separately, which they both seemed able to cope with.

As we made our way to the beer garden I asked Chris if she knew the name of the pub; I had not seen a sign as we approached.

"I think it was something to do with fish," she replied confidently.

The next morning I saw the pub's sign. It was nothing to do with fish: the Tinners' Arms.

The garden at the rear of the pub was quite busy. A number of white plastic picnic tables and chairs had been set out and we chose one with an unimpeded view of the setting sun. As we waited for our meal we watched the sun sinking slowly towards the horizon, turning the sky a multi-coloured canvas of pinks, oranges and reds. As the sun touched the water it appeared to be sucked into the ocean. If you listened carefully you could just hear the hiss as it cooled and a jet of steam was given off – very similar to the hiss produce when my feet were immersed in a cool bath!

Our meal arrived and we pounced on the food ravenously. A ploughman's for Chris and chicken and mushroom pie and salad for me. It was delicious and went some way towards making amends for my disappointment at the farmhouse. The trouble was, when we had finished we were still hungry. Apple pie and clotted cream would help to assuage that, so I went inside to order two helpings.

Ten minutes later and we were still waiting for dessert. We sat in the cooling twilight, eavesdropping on conversations at other tables and people-watching as we waited for our pie.

"Mount's Bay does nothing for me, darhling, absolutely nothing." Piped up a woman at a neighbouring table. The accent was pure Etonian. The stereotypical English upper class voice.

"Oh yes, I agree Daphne. It's dead, isn't it? Quite, quite dead!" Replied her equally plumy companion.

I nearly choked on my cider. When I eventually dared to look at Chris she was bright red from the effort of stifling her giggles. We were recovering from our hysteria when a voice from the depths of the pub bellowed out, shattering the peaceful evening.

"Oi zay ee'z a loyur."

This time, in contrast, the accent was pure Cornish. And this time we could not help but erupt into laughter.

"A loyur, oi zay!"

"What's a loyur?" I squeaked.

"Liar." Blubbered Chris as the tears welled from her eyes.

"Ee'z a loyur!" Echoed again from within the pub.

Then suddenly the barman appeared and began walking towards our table. It had obviously taken him all that time to come to the conclusion that there was only one piece of apple pie and to manage an angry exchange with who ever was in the pub with him. Looking very apologetic he explained there was a piece of pecan pie, would that be acceptable? Yes it would. So, some time after beginning our meal we got our desserts and very good they were too! The wait had been worth it.

The evening had grown chilly, the midges had come out of wherever it is midges hide when they are not busy biting people, and we were tired. We strolled up the quiet lane toward the farmhouse and bed. The farmhouse might not have been all I had expected but I looked forward to a peaceful night in the country and an uninterrupted sleep.

We laid in bed at 11 p.m. listening to the sound of a tractor haymaking in the next field. I woke some time later to the sound of a dog barking. At 3 a.m. a donkey began braying and a wild animal snuffled in the grass below the bedroom window. At 3.30 a.m. a cockerel started to herald in the new day. Half an hour later someone used the bathroom next to our bedroom; they could not get the toilet to flush properly and seemed ignorant of the skill needed to close doors quietly. At 4.45 a.m. another dog began to bark somewhere on the farm. I had just gone to sleep again only to be awakened fifteen minutes later by the chatter of magpies on the roof above our open window. What if they stole our knickers that were hanging from the handle of the window? Chris got up and moved the underwear, just in case! At ten minutes to six, having just drifted back to sleep for the umpteenth time, a cow went into labour and began mooing her little bovine head off. You probably will not be too astonished to learn that we were unable to sleep after that. By 6.45 we were getting up.

Friday 9th July

Breakfast at Zennor was the most meagre of the holiday. Yet another knock to my vivid imaginings! We sat alone in a dining room crammed full of ornaments and family photographs, it would be hell to dust. It did not take us long to eat the breakfast, accompanied throughout by a radio in the kitchen playing 'Amazing Grace' and 'Jesus Wants Me For A Sunbeam'. As we munched the cold toast and commercially produced marmalade we were entertained by the voice of the farmer coming from the kitchen as he tried to place a telephone order.

"Oi want a lead fur moy bull. Strongust you arve."

There was a brief pause, followed by: "Oi've got the ring! Oi just need a lead. Thick mind ee! Ee'z a big un. Lead'll arva b'strong."

Listening to this one-sided conversation we spluttered and choked and giggled our way to the bottom of the teapot. And I think I've got a silly accent!

We collected our packed lunch, paid up, packed up and set off. It was fifteen minutes to nine and red hot already. On the lane back to the coast we passed the Wayside Museum, it was reputed to house an interesting array of exhibits of country life and mining artefacts. We would both have liked to spend some time browsing there but, like the museum at Hartland Quay, it did not open until mid morning. Too late for us energetic, keen walkers! One more place on our list of "must visits – one day".

By 9 a.m. we were on our way to Botallack. It was as hot as ever. We were very much aware of the complete absence of any refreshment facilities on this stretch of the path. There would be no toilets, no shops, no tea rooms or pubs, not even an ice cream van at the one car park we passed. Between Zennor and our stop that night we would have to rely on the food and water we were carrying, and we were walking on one of the hottest July days in years. As we were to discover, there was one other thing completely lacking on the path that day: shade.

Just after Zennor we passed a badgers' sett. The earth and bedding cleared from the sett spilled down onto the path. I have never seen a badger, not alive at least. I was unlikely to see one there unless I dallied for fifteen hours and waited for these nocturnal animals to surface. As that was a little impractical (we did have a timetable to stick to) I had to be content with the thought that these badgers might live to see another year thanks to a rethink by the Government.

With us constantly that day was the sound of the crickets, a perpetual background noise, ceasing at our approach and continuing once again as our footsteps carried us away from them. No breeze stirred the undergrowth or helped to cool us. The soothing sound of the waves on the shoreline came to us briefly now and then as the path carried us closer to the edge of the cliffs and frequently down to almost sea level to cross the tiny gushing streams. For the most part the sea was virtually silent; it really was as flat as a mill pond.

We crossed the occasional streams on little wooden bridges. The refreshing, soothing sound of the water tumbling over rocks gave a brief, if false, impression of coolness. The course of the streams was plotted down the hillside by a corridor of lush Balsam, a non native species that was quickly colonising the area. It grew in thick succulent stands, the large pink flowers attracting fat furry bumble bees and other insects. So rapidly did it grow that its stems crowded onto the footbridges as they crossed the virtually hidden water courses. Nearer the edge of the streams grew ferns, musk, lush dark green mosses and shiny liverworts.

On we hiked around Gurnard's Head, and around countless cliffs and headlands all with rugged granite faces. Never far away inland loomed the tors, often scarred with the visible history of Cornwall's past: mining. Mines were to dominate the landscape later in the day.

Bosigran Cliff is a favourite of climbers and we stopped on the other side of the cove to watch. The climbers were little bigger than ants, scaling up the sheer face of the cliff in their brightly coloured clothing. Climbing did not appeal to me, too far to fall but I admired the skill involved.

With our caps providing the only shade we sweated constantly. Springs and tributaries of perspiration ran together forming rivers of sweat that poured down our faces, arms and legs. Our hair stuck to our heads. My back was a lake of moisture. With her new rucksack Chris was faring a little better.

"Feel my back it's bone dry!" she bragged as I twisted about trying to prise my T-shirt away from my skin.

She was right. The material of her T-shirt was completely dry. I felt my own back. The fabric was saturated and could have been wrung out.

"Feel my back." I invited.

She did. "Ugh! That's disgusting!"

"Don't I know it!"

One consolation of all the sweating was that our bladders remained empty. On such an exposed part of the path, totally devoid of any cover and with no facilities, car parks or any sign of civilisation, this was perhaps fortunate.

The path was once again very overgrown. We waded through seas of stinging nettle, stabbing gorse, scratching bramble and prickling thistle. It was impossible to dodge these tortuous weapons and our legs became blistered with nettle rash and badly scratched. The occasional giant hogweed towered in isolation over all the other plants and where these evil, triffid-like monsters grew by the path we battled determinedly to avoid brushing against them. In some areas, steps are taken to eliminate this horrible plant. The sap, if in contact with the skin, can react with sunlight to produce an unpleasant chemical burn. We were suffering quite enough, thank you very much, without that added discomfort. Where our limbs had been cut and the flesh torn, the sweat stung the sores making them itch painfully.

As midday approached we began looking for a convenient spot to stop for lunch. There were no grassy mounds, benches or even dry stone walls to perch on; the path was just too overgrown and narrow. Not exactly spoilt for choice, we finally threw ourselves down on a large granite boulder at the edge of the path. We could not bear to rest there for too long, as we were fully exposed to the sun. By unspoken consent we both just wanted to get to the

B&B at Botallack and get out of the sun. So our lunch stop, as with all the other stops that day, was just long enough to refuel and no longer.

Shrugging out of our rucksacks we placed them on the path in front of us and opened them to get out our packed lunch. The food was warm but that did not matter, we were too hungry to care. The sandwiches were cheese and pickle, and they shared a plastic bag with cake and fruit. The only problem was that all the food had been put in the plastic bag without being wrapped individually. Cheese and pickle sandwiches were followed by fruit cake and pickle, cherry cake and pickle and apple and pickle. Slightly messy! I gobbled down the sandwiches and cake, pickle and all. The apple was a large, juicy Braeburn. I bit hungrily into mine, the juice running down my fingers and chin (it made a change from sweat!)

"Oh no!" Chris shouted and began swearing.

"What's up? What have you done?"

"I don't bloody believe it!"

"What?" I asked exasperatedly.

"My apple! Oh! I was looking forward to that!"

She wasn't making any sense and I was beginning to think she'd been out in the sun too long.

"What about your apple? Have you dropped it in some dog muck?" That seemed the most likely possibility.

"No, I've lost it! Down that hole."

"Hole? What hole? I can't see any holes!" (Had a mine shaft opened up and swallowed her apple?) "Never mind, you can have half of mine," I said magnanimously.

"Thanks, but I don't want half of yours, I want mine," she muttered sulkily. "That hole." Pointing, she drew my attention to a hole at the base of the boulder we were sitting on. When we sat down we had failed to see the hole as it was obscured by grass growing in front of the rock.

Getting off the rock I knelt on the path and peered down the hole. I could not see anything it was far too dark, I waited while my eyes became accustomed to the dimness and until the photochromic lenses in my glasses grew lighter, then I looked again. The only thing I could see was a large cavity under the boulder.

"I can't see your apple!"

"Well may be you could feel it!"

"If you think I'm putting my arm under this rock, you can think again! There could be an adder having a siesta or, or, anything. Or a wasps' nest!" I said, aghast at the thought of jamming my hand into a papery mass of vicious angry insects.

"But your arm's longer than mine, if the apple's there you'd be able to reach it. I would have a go but it'd be pointless."

She sounded so pathetic that pity overcame common sense. So I shoved my arm into the hole and began to feel tentatively about. Unable to feel anything except soil, I came up for air, my arm covered in dirt. Chris sat dejectedly watching my futile efforts.

"One last go, then you'll have to share mine or go hungry," I muttered.

Kneeling on the path with my head to the ground and my bum in the air I must have looked like I was praying religiously. I was, praying that nothing would attack my arm and drag me under the rock! I waited for my eyes and spectacles to adjust to the low light levels and then looked into the hole once more. I could see something! But it didn't look like an apple; it looked like a plastic bag. Aha!

"Is your apple still in the bag?"

"Yes," responded Chris eagerly, "can you see it?"

"Yes."

"Can you reach it?"

"No."

"Oh."

I withdrew my arm, rolled the sleeve of the T-shirt up to my shoulder and laid across the path. In that position my fingertips were just able to touch the plastic bag. Next moment, I was triumphantly brandishing the apple.

"Oh you're wonderful. I take back everything I ever said about gorilla arms."

"Gee, thanks."

I stood up and began to brush soil from my arm and vegetation from my clothing. Chris began chomping happily on her apple.

"The things I do for you! Just watch where you're putting things next time. I'm not doing that again!"

"Well, what a stupid place to have a hole."

"Write to Cornwall County Council or the National Trust and complain, perhaps they could send a cement lorry out to fill it in!" I said sarcastically, but I could not help laughing. "Don't feel too bad, you're not the only idiot to loose something under this rock. There's a white paper bag with some sandwiches in down there!"

Just when we were beginning to think we would never see our feet again under all the vegetation, the path improved. The gorse and heath had been managed and the land cleared of bracken. It was a sudden and welcome improvement to the path. Now, instead of wading and battling through dense vegetation we walked along an open grassy path that wound between low growing gorse and heather. The heather displayed its purple flowers in full bloom; in contrast the gorse flowers were almost over, a few yellow flowers still remained but the majority had already seeded. The heat caused the seed heads to burst open with a popping sound which we could clearly hear.

We walked along the outside edge of a field where lichen grew thickly on the granite boulders of the dry stone wall and turned a corner to see, lying on the path sunning himself, a slowworm. He began to move slowly along the path, burying his head into the short grass until he was partially hidden. As we stood watching, some walkers approached and, concerned that they might inadvertently stand on the slowworm, we remained standing in the middle of the path to prevent this.

Seeing us staring at the ground the man asked if we had lost something.

"No, we're just watching this slowworm," replied Chris.

"Oh," he said disinterestedly. His wife caught up with him, looked at us, looked at the ground and saw the slowworm.

"Ugh, a grass snake!" she shrieked and hurried away.

In the late afternoon we reached Pendeen Cliff, visible for miles, which was just as well as it played host to a lighthouse. The day was getting hotter and we were slowly melting. Actually no, we were rapidly melting. Our water supply, of which we had had several litres at the beginning of the day, was dwindling. From Zennor to Botallack there is nowhere near the path for refreshments. In fact, the section of path from St. Ives to Sennen Cove, a distance of twenty-two miles, is possibly the longest, most isolated part of the entire coast path.

We stopped at Pendeen Watch for a drink and a biscuit and read with disgust a sign nailed to the gates of a large house. It informed walkers not to knock because they would not provide toilets or water and that refreshments were available inland at Pendeen village. No toilets: okay, fair enough. I would not want all the walkers on the coast path knocking on my door requesting to use the bathroom. You would end up with bits of mud, grass, bracken and may be dog dirt all over the carpet. But water? Water! To refuse anyone a drink, particularly someone walking, usually with a heavy pack and possibly in hot weather, was disgusting, uncharitable and contemptible in the extreme. Yes, some walkers might, through lack of experience or pure irresponsibility fail to carry enough water; but in the type of heat we had been experiencing and particularly on that stretch of difficult path even experienced walkers might find themselves running low on liquids.

Only minutes along the path from that house of miserliness we passed a second house. On the gate were fastened bird feeders, a bird table sat in the middle of a neat lawn and outside the gate was a large washing up bowl, full of water and with the word "DOGS" written on the side. The differences between the owners of this house and its near neighbour were remarkable. We wondered how many thirsty walkers had been tempted to share in the dogs' provender.

Beyond there we looked along the coast, to chimneys, engine houses and the winding gear of Geevor, now a living museum. Nearer to the coast and right beside the path is Levant, where, thanks to members of the Trevithick Society, a beam engine has been restored. Had we arrived in time – which surprise, surprise, we didn't – we could have been taken on a tour and seen it working. We arrived as the last tour of the day was drawing to a close and watched a group of Japanese tourists, with heavy looking Nikons worth £400 slung around their necks, head back to their hired Ford Mondeos after taking one final photograph of the chimneys and slag heaps. Next stop Land's End. Then up to Stratford, no doubt. Britain in a week. Europe in a fortnight.

At the Crowns Shaft near Botallack, two restored engine houses are all that remain of the mine there. The workings extended under the seabed and miners could hear rocks rolling along above their heads as they worked! Not a job for the nervous! Many mines were flooded when the sea broke through, this happened at Levant, fortunately the mine had closed down prior to this, although this was not always the case. Using our disposable fun camera worth £4.99, we took a moment to photograph the twin engine houses, rather an appealing scene with the cliffs dropping steeply into the sea below the buildings.

Shortly after we came to two chimneys and a mile or so inland from the path at that point we emerged onto a road leading into Botallack. Our accommodation for that night was only yards away and for once we did not need to ask for directions.

The B&B was full. Of women. As we arrived tea and scones were just being served in the lounge and we gratefully slumped into the chairs and tucked in to the refreshments. There's something about a pot of tea. One lady was having an evening meal there and she went into the dining room, leaving her pot of tea unfinished. We were thirsty, so having emptied our teapot, we finished hers as well.

As we drained the last of the tea, the landlady reappeared. "Did she leave her glasses in here?" she asked, referring to the guest now having her evening meal.

"No," I replied, "she was carrying them when she left the room."

The landlady disappeared only to immediately reappear tutting and rolling her eyes.

"She hasn't got them now!"

Somehow, as the dotty guest had walked from one room into the adjacent dining room, she had lost a pair of glasses. The search continued and we listened with amusement as the guest and the landlady tried to track down the miscreant spectacles by a process of elimination, their voices drifting to us from the other room.

"Did you bring them into the dining room?"

"No. Well I might have. But I don't remember doing."

"Well when did you last have them?"

"I'm not sure. Perhaps I've left them in the bathroom!"

"The ladies remember you carrying them out of the lounge."

"Do they? Are they sure?"

Grinning to ourselves, we went upstairs to unpack, shower and change. Our room was a family room at the front of the house. A clean, airy room not at all cramped as the one at Zennor had been. A bowl of pot pourri stood on the dressing table, immediately making Chris sneeze.

"Oh, no I'll be sneezing all night now," she groaned.

"No you won't!" I said and opened a drawer of the dressing table, put the pot pourri into it and closed the drawer.

"Good thinking. We must remember to take it out before we go though, or the landlady will think we've stolen her pot pourri!"

"What would two walkers want with a bowl of pot pourri?"

With the window wide open the scent soon faded. But we never did remember to put the bowl back on the dressing table before we left the next morning. I wonder if its absence was noticed? Would the next people to stay in that room yank open the drawer to find it scattered with dried petals?

The bathroom was a large room with a shower cubicle and a bath. I started filling the bath and began to undress, removing my glasses as I did so. Mm, strange, the floor, the sink and the toilet seat seemed to be covered in white flakes. Chris had used the bathroom first, surely her skin wasn't peeling so much? I put my glasses back on and looked at the flakes more closely.

Well, the dotty guest might not have left her specs in the bathroom but she had left half of Sennen Cove in there! The white flakes were sand and lots of it. She had said she came to Cornwall for the beaches and the swimming, she never said she liked to take most of the beach away with her!

Removing my glasses, I climbed into the bath and stretched out. Which was a painful mistake, 'Dotty' had been in the bath before me and left a lot of sand behind! The grains abraded my sunburnt legs and scratched my backside as I moved.

As there was no sink in our room and no tea making facilities Chris had decided to ask if there was somewhere we could wash and dry our clothes, I think she was hoping to be offered use of the washing machine. If she was, her little plan didn't work. I came downstairs after my bath to find her stood at the kitchen sink washing our clothes in the washing up bowl. Instead of soap powder she was using liquid soap from our tiny shampoo bottle which she had refilled from the bottle of liquid soap in the bathroom. (Our supplies of conditioner and shampoo having run out a couple of days earlier.) We hung our clothes on the washing line to dry then with our chores done we set out for some food.

Our evening meal that night came from a rather busy pub in the nearby village of St. Just. A room upstairs had been converted into a family dining area and we ate our meal to the accompaniment of screaming children, shouting parents and the music of a jukebox emanating from downstairs. After the peace of the coast path, the noise was an assault on the eardrums but the food was good and we left feeling full.

St. Just is the largest town, if it merits the title, west of Penzance, the largest collection of shops and houses in that most westerly point of England. Friday evenings, St. Just is a Mecca for the inhabitants of all the surrounding farms and villages. All the pubs seemed to be overflowing with revellers, gangs of youths hung around the market square as they seemed to do in all the places we travelled through on our walk and in one large house on the edge of the community, a party was in full swing. For the young, the not so young, the trendy and the dowdy, for anyone in that part of Cornwall who breathed, it seemed St. Just was the place to go on Friday evenings. We probably fell into the categories of dowdy and breathing; so we went, we ate and we came away. We arrived back at the B&B just in time for a pot of tea in the lounge. Dotty was there again (now reunited with her glasses), as were the other guests – a grandmother and her granddaughter. Dotty hogged the conversation to the exclusion of everyone else. Grandma escaped first, quickly followed by granddaughter and me but Chris was trapped having just accepted another cup of tea which she was finding too hot to drink.

Fifteen minutes later, Chris appeared in the bedroom as I was deep into writing my diary.

"You swine!"

"What?" I asked, putting down my pen and grinning. "Was it my fault you had another cup of tea? I was beginning to think you'd never get away."

"I haven't! She wants the address of the B&B at Porthcothan, I've just come to get it." She began hunting for our accommodation list, found it, made a quick note of the address and hurried back downstairs.

Fifteen minutes later, Chris appeared once more, I was even deeper into writing my diary having given up all hope of seeing Chris again before breakfast.

"You swine!"

"I know, you've told me once!"

"I couldn't get away, she just kept wittering on and on and on and..."

"I know. Why do you think I made that excuse about phoning Roger and scarpered?"

"Because you're a heartless, uncaring, selfish... swine."

"You're only jealous!" I said laughing. "You're the heartless one, giving her the address of the Porthcothan B&B, fancy inflicting Dotty on such a nice landlady!"

We got undressed and Chris slipped out to the bathroom, hoping to avoid meeting Dotty on the way. I waited until she returned, spending the time smothering myself in calamine lotion, but as soon as Chris was back someone else went into the bathroom and I had to wait. Listening, I heard a door open and close and decided to make a dash for the bathroom before anyone beat me to it a second time.

As I began to open the bedroom door, I heard a movement on the landing.

"Great!" I muttered, "Dotty's probably gone in now!"

Dotty hadn't, but she was standing at the end of the darkened landing with her hand on the knob of the bathroom door, and had probably heard every word I had said! I stood in the bedroom doorway feeling very embarrassed and foolish; backlit by the bedside lamp I must have looked very ghostly in my thin nightie and with white smears of calamine all over my face, arms and legs.

Dotty might have been absentminded and a chatterbox but she was also considerate. Realising we would be having an earlier breakfast she offered to let me use the bathroom first. I accepted gratefully, feeling very small for my churlish behaviour.

In bed at last, I turned off the lamp and snuggled down. Something crackled under the sheet as I moved. There seemed to be a ridge down the centre of the mattress and as I adjusted my position, trying to get comfortable, the crackling continued. I endured the ridge and the crackling until I could bear it no longer. Leaping out of bed I began to smooth out the sheets but the plastic mattress cover, responsible for the ridge and the crackling, refused all attempts to be flattened. I dragged the bed away from the wall and began stripping off the sheets. By this time Chris was sitting up in bed and switching the light on. She watched as I continued to battle with the bedding, becoming more and more frustrated.

Chris started to laugh and was soon laughing uncontrollably. I became even more irritated until I eventually snapped, "what's so funny? If you think it's funny why don't we swap beds, you come and sleep in this one. Then we'll see if you still think it's funny!"

She continued laughing, the tears rolling down her cheeks. She finally managed to splutter that she was laughing at my appearance. Red from my exertions and with white smears across my face and over my ears where the calamine had dried in streaks, I looked like a barber's pole. I saw the funny side of it and soon we were both laughing hysterically. What the other guests must have thought we were doing, is anyone's guess.

Neither of us slept particularly well that night. It was too hot for sleeping comfortably and the plastic mattress cover made things worse. It was the second night of broken sleep in a row and was to affect us physically the following day.

Saturday 10th July

The day started off badly. In the shower that morning, my elbow hit the door of the cubicle, knocking it open, although I did not immediately notice. By the time I did turn around and see the open shower door, my nightie, which I had dropped on the floor next to the cubicle, was soaking wet. Socks and T-shirts tied to the back of a rucksack to dry are one thing, but a nightie?

We had an early breakfast, hoping to avoid Dotty. Once in conversation with her we thought we would never get away; and today we had over twelve miles to walk. If the path was the same as on the previous two days, we knew those twelve miles would be difficult.

Breakfast was good and for the first time since Padstow there was bread on the table. The toast came at the end of the cooked breakfast, which meant it would be hot – delicious. Unfortunately, the landlady had forgotten the butter, by the time she remembered the toast had cooled.

We set off just after eight thirty, feeling cheered by the overcast sky. This was better we told ourselves, a nice cool day. Oh, would we never learn? The first two hours were cool and pleasant but by mid morning the sun had broken through the cloud and the day grew steadily hotter until the temperature was pushing into the thirties once again.

Fifteen minutes after setting off that morning, my bladder was full. Chris waited as I performed the necessary functions, this time crouching precariously on what I realised (when I had gone beyond the point of no return) was a capped mine shaft. Fortunately, the cap did not give way under my weight, or that really would have been an embarrassing rescue!

A short walk led us along the cliff tops, dipping down into a lush valley to cross a stream before heading along the coastline towards Cape Cornwall. This is England's only cape and was once thought to be the most westerly point in the country until, that is, the Ordnance Survey came along and decreed it wasn't; that distinction now goes to Land's End (and so do all the crowds). Like an elderly dowager stripped of her status and usurped by a young upstart, Cape Cornwall sits facing the westering sun, stretching her toes out into the Atlantic Ocean, her glory days now just a distant memory.

Unlike many headlands, Cape Cornwall is easy to identify from a distance, due to the chimney crowning its low summit. The mine, of which the chimney was once a part, was last worked in 1878. Over a century later, in 1987, the land was donated to the National Trust by the then owners H J Heinz Limited, although what a company made famous by the humble haricot bean was doing owning the Cape in the first place I don't know!

We detoured off the path to visit the remains of the tiny chapel dedicated to St. Helen, which shelters to the landward side of the low hill on Cape Cornwall. A single grave lies near to the wall of the chapel but this is not the only grave on the cape. Climbing towards the summit we found a second grave. This one brought a lump to both our throats. It was the recent grave of a young boy, lying just inside the consecrated ground of the chapel and sheltered by a low boundary wall. The grave was marked with a small, simple headstone set in a circle marked out with pebbles. Planted in this circle was a young shrub and around it and amongst its leaves were the child's favourite toys.

Silently we walked up to the summit and sat looking south and slightly west to Land's End, now visible for the first time. I could understand why the parents had chosen that spot as their son's last resting place.

The path from there to Sennen Cove was relatively easy walking for the majority of the way, at first cutting down into a narrow valley where once tin streaming had taken place. The ruins of the works were now very overgrown with rowan trees and the ever-present bracken. The luxuriant fronds of green bracken would soon fade to brown with the passing of summer. The younger leaves were gently uncurling from their coiled position, the larger leaves releasing cancer-causing spores. Of more immediate concern to me however, was the possibility of sheep ticks lurking in the bracken.

One of my cats had recently played host to a tick picnic (much to my disgust) and now that I had seen a tick in the flesh (literally) I was not keen to see any more.

Chris had obtained a leaflet all about what to look for and what to do if you were unlucky enough to find a tick attached and feeding. The leaflet suggested checking your companion and getting them to do the same for you. "Ticks like warm moist areas of the body, search in creases of skin and on the legs. DO NOT pull ticks off if you find any!" read the leaflet.

"There is no way I am searching warm moist areas of your body for ticks!" stated Chris.

"Me neither. How are you supposed to remove them, does it say?"

"Rubbing alcohol."

"Have we packed any?"

"No and I wouldn't rub you down with any if we had!"

"We'll just have to be sucked dry then. I can picture the headlines – Dried Husks of Women Walkers' Bodies Found."

Beyond the valley the path wound across the low lying cliffs. The vegetation was walker friendly and to our joy was dominated by sea lavender. Despite the heat, it was a pleasant stretch of walking with the sound of the sea, the beautiful colours of the waves and breakers and the heavenly scent of the lavender. Colonies of ants swarmed amongst the lavender, what was the attraction for them I wondered? It was a busy part of the path and we often had to squeeze to one side to allow other walkers to pass. Each time we did so we were standing on the lavender and this released more of its perfume.

The only difficulty on that stretch of our walk was the granite boulders that at one point loomed across the path bisecting the worn dusty track. There was no way round them except climbing or swimming, the path seemed to stop at one side and continue on the other. We had no choice but to do what every other walker must do – climb and crawl up one side and slither on our bottoms down the next.

It was easier for me with seven inches more leg than it was for Chris, but difficult nonetheless and the situation was made worse by thoughts of a steep drop down the rocky hillside to the sea should we loose our balance or our footing. Once on the far side we both had dusty shorts and grazes on our knees and palms. It was time for a break and a good excuse to have a fruit Shrewsbury and a drink!

The beach at the aptly named Whitesand Bay stretched towards the small village of Sennen Cove and was crowded with people sunbathing, swimming and surfing. Trying to walk along the beach would have added to the distance, as we would be required to dodge between hundreds of prostrate forms. Instead we walked along the back of the beach, into the car park and then along the road to the village.

We squeezed between badly parked cars in the busy car park to reach the toilets, pitying anyone in a wheel chair attempting to get to the disabled facilities. With one bodily function satisfied we then headed for the ice cream van to satisfy another. Slumped sideways on a bench (a necessary position if one wanted to sit down whilst wearing a rucksack) we ate our ice creams with clotted cream on top and gulped thirstily at cans of pop, desperate to replace lost fluids.

As we sat there I scanned the people on the beach. How could they bear to lie there all day in that heat? No nudists, but this time a 36B flaunted itself.

It was a short walk from there to Land's End and it seemed a lot of people had chosen to park at Sennen Cove and walk rather than pay the inflated entrance and car parking fees. The path was busy and much eroded by the numbers of tourists opting for this money saving alternative.

Chris had anticipated Land's End with apprehension, imagining it to be completely spoilt by the theme park and all its trappings. I had been before and knew what to expect, although on my previous visit the scenery was blotted out by a heavy fog. When we arrived she declared it was not as bad as she had expected, seeming impressed by the American style of queuing and exhibits. There were of course the expected gift shops and photo opportunity with the signposts indicating miles as the crow flies to various cities and countries and, for a less than small fee, your own town complete with a souvenir photograph. We avoided all that with the exception of a fudge shop, then sat down to write some postcards and eat some more biscuits. Whilst we were busy licking stamps a group of elderly Brits walked by.

"Is that The Needles?" asked one lady pointing towards the lighthouse.

"No dear," muttered her long suffering husband, "The Needles are at the Isle of Wight!"

It seems incongruous that some far pinnacle of England should merit a theme park. What was wrong with just coming, looking and going away? Twentieth century commercialism had covered the most westerly point of mainland Britain with tarmac, signposts and white-painted buildings. Instead of seagulls and ocean waves all you could hear was the sound of high heels on tarmac and the buzz of air conditioning units. The seeds for all this exploitation were sown last century when the First and Last House was opened as a tea room; from such humble beginnings has grown one of the most popular tourist attractions in the country!

Land's End is where English Channel meets Atlantic Ocean and even on such a calm day as it was when we were there the sea foams and churns below the rocky cliffs. The Scilly Isles, twenty five miles away, are visible from there on a clear day but the heat haze prevented us from seeing them.

A tiny farm recreated to represent the traditional way of life in Cornwall marked the end of the theme park for us and we rejoined the path at the back of a pigsty to continue on our way to Porthcurno. It was four o'clock, we had five miles to walk to reach Porthcurno, and looking at the map the path did not look too difficult. Once again we were being optimistic in our expectations.

Land's End was psychologically, if not geographically, the half way point for us. We had viewed it as such ever since the planning stages of the walk, and therefore it should be metaphorically downhill all the way from there. But our walk was to become harder before it began to get easier.

A rough path continued along the line of the cliff tops. The sun continued to blaze down. We continued to wilt and burn. We had several unexpected valleys to climb that had a disproportionately negative effect on our morale. The cumulative effects of days of difficult walking and high temperatures, combined with two nights of broken sleep, was beginning to take its toll on us.

The ice cream at Sennen Cove seemed like days ago, and breakfast was another lifetime. The path dragged on, so did the heat and the long, tiring day. Chris kept saying to herself "one foot in front of the other". My mantra was "just around the next headland". But like Chris's footsteps, the headlands just kept on coming; as we reached the pinnacle of one headland, a series of more would come into view. Our tired minds and bodies could not focus the concentration needed to map read; we had no idea how far we were from Porthcurno. Neither mantra was soothing or relaxing. They only served to remind us of our ant-like progress across the map of Cornwall.

Late in the evening we arrived at the Minack Theatre on the cliffs above Porthcurno. We were hot, dirty and fatigued but there was something we had to do before going down into the village to our guest house. With mixed emotions and low spirits we paid the nominal entrance fee and went into the Minack.

This theatre was the one place of all the places on our walk that we had desperately wanted to visit. Our guest house offered the option of theatre suppers consisting of picnic hampers, rugs and cushions to any guest who watched a play at the theatre. As we planned our walk, we visualised sitting on cushions, a rug spread across our knees and a picnic hamper at our feet enjoying one of the plays performed by various theatre companies who visited the Minack. We searched the Internet for information on the theatre and the plays that would be performed there: a different play each week throughout the summer. And it was at this point we began to realise that a trip to the theatre would not be the simple affair we had imagined.

Plays ran from Monday to Friday with no performances at the weekends in order to allow the various companies to change over. Problem number one: we were staying at Porthcurno on a Saturday. Okay. We would travel on another day to watch a performance, either on the Friday from Botallack or on the following Monday from Porthleven. Problem number two: public transport – the buses were infrequent and did not run in the late evening, we could get there but would we be able to get back? We telephoned the Minack theatre. Did they run or know of anyone who ran a minibus service to the performances? No, but if we got there, they were sure there would be someone willing to give us a lift afterwards. Problem number three: what if there wasn't? Perhaps we should consider a taxi! Problem number four: cost, £12 each way from Botallack to be precise. We had to make a decision, to ensure a seat we would have to book in advance and there was one other thing to consider. Problem number five: what if, after buying our tickets, booking a taxi and building ourselves up for an unforgettable experience at a unique theatre, we arrived late at the B&B? We could only estimate how long each day's walk would take, if we misjudged our timing we would be too late to go to the Minack and our tickets would be wasted. Reluctantly we made the disappointing decision to abandon all hope of watching a play. We comforted ourselves with the knowledge that we would still be able to look around the Minack, and with that we had to be content.

By the time we arrived on that Saturday evening, the guided tours were over. With two other latecomers we walked down the terraced rows of seats to view the stage. Taking a seat on one of the terraces, we gazed in awe at the magnificent theatre. The atmosphere was almost surreal; a paved stage, balconies, lighting, gates leading off stage where actors would run down steeply staired paths to gain access to the dressing rooms and other stage entrances. Terraces of seating, seemly carved into the granite, but in reality formed from decorated concrete, subtle lights illuminating the way for the audience to reach their seats and, as a backdrop to it all, the placid deep blue sea and the dusky sky, with the setting sun colouring the cliffs across the narrow bay in a golden glow.

Modelled on an amphitheatre, the Minack is unique because of its history. In 1935 a middle aged woman named Rowena Cade, living in a house above the cliffs, began work to transform what was a natural amphitheatre in the rocky cliff face into an open air theatre. Her love of literature and drama spurred her on to accomplish her amazing task with the help of just one local labourer. It took them many years before the Minack Theatre was finally completed. Towards the end of her life Rowena Cade was pushed in a wheel barrow to the theatre to watch the performances. An incredible lady.

We reluctantly left the theatre, overwhelmed by what we had seen and dejected by what we had been unable to watch. We stumbled down the steeply stepped path to the head of the narrow bay and walked slowly up the single road leading through the linear village of Porthcurno. As we passed the only pub, noisy with the sounds of revelry and karaoke, we realised that supper that night would be little more than biscuits and chocolate; I had already suspected as much and taken advantage of the gift shop at the theatre to buy some chocolate and flapjacks.

Our guest house was half way up the road. That last hill of the day was pure hell.

Sunday 11th July

The previous evening we had not been in a particularly receptive state to appreciate our accommodation but after a good night's sleep we took in our surroundings with fresh eyes. The twin bedded room had an en-suite shower room, tea and coffee making facilities and a view of the sea! It was comfortably furnished, clean and welcoming, with a menu detailing bounteous breakfast choices and café-style light teas, which we had been too late to take advantage of the previous night.

We went down to breakfast with my stomach rumbling in anticipation. We were not the only guests enjoying this superb guest house. A middle aged couple sat at one table and on his own, by the window, sat a real life Thespian, (luvey, darling). Complete with beret and shooting stick and Minack T-shirt, he orated an account of his previous experiences at the Minack Theatre. He was a well-built individual, who would no doubt take full advantage of all his breakfasts at this guest house, and I wondered how he would cope with the physical requirements demanded of any actor at the Minack.

The landlord came to take our order from a large choice of various cooked items and invited us to help ourselves to "cereals, fruit etc. etc." The sideboard was laden with expensive cereals, fruits, juices, yoghurt and plenty of et ceteras. I goggled at the choice! Whilst I was stood there with my mouth open trying to decide what to have, Chris was busy ladling various fruits onto a bowl already full of muesli and yoghurt.

As I picked up a bowl and began to pour in cereal, Chris muttered, "Don't take all the grapefruit segments!"

Was I never going to live that slight faux pas down? You eat one catering-size tin of grapefruit segments and it's with you for the rest of your life!

By nine o'clock we were standing in the road, struggling into our rucksacks, with me battling to let out the waist harness so that it would fasten over my breakfast. The weather was already scorching hot and sweat was standing out on our faces as we walked down the road, passing the Museum of Submarine Telegraphy and the old Cable and Wireless building.

This seemingly insignificant little bay marks the landfall for numerous Trans Atlantic telegraph cables, including the first ever to be laid and a fibre optic cable that is the longest undersea cable in the world, running all the way to Japan. Impressive! But still not as impressive as the Minack Theatre.

The path zigzagged out of Porthcurno to the cliff tops, passing numerous little coves. I looked down into each cove in turn to see seals in three of the coves, one swimming only yards away from a man, much to his obvious delight.

Moving away from the edge of the cliffs, the path wove along between hedges of hawthorn and honeysuckle, cutting off two large headlands and for a while the views were restricted. With no views to look at I walked along with my head down, watching the path. Which is how I managed, just, to avoid stepping on a sleeping adder. The path was a narrow strip of eroded soil between the hedges and the adder was curled up in the precise spot that my right boot was about to occupy. I hopped awkwardly over the reptile, landing heavily on one foot, the resulting earth tremor waking the adder. Judging by its size, it was a she. She slowly uncurled, lifting her head and tasting the air with her flicking tongue. I turned to look for Chris; she was not in sight, hidden behind the turn of the hedge. It was the first adder of the holiday and I wanted to share it with her. But the adder slithered fluidly into the hedge before she arrived.

At Cribba Head we got our first glimpse of Tater Du lighthouse before dropping down into Penberth Cove. This tiny fishing hamlet is a gem, totally unspoilt it nestles in a narrow valley, shyly unaware of its charm. We stood and watched a fishing boat being winched up the stone-paved slipway using the old capstan. Once a donkey was probably employed to operate the capstan, today a generator hidden in an unobtrusive shed does the work. Two cats sat on the slipway in the sunshine, pretending nonchalance at the prospect of fish scraps, busily washing themselves on the warm cobbles. The fisherman walked slowly behind his boat, his bright yellow wellies seemed out of place in this period setting.

Walking out of a living piece of history we continued toward St. Loy. The path descended into what the guidebook described as a semi tropical woodland, a description which would have better fitted the entire county at the time, crossed a narrow brook and continued beyond hidden houses to the coast. That tiny section of the walk stands out in my mind because of the vegetation and the complete contrast to the character of the path on either side of it. The humid shade of the woodland, the sound of the babbling stream rattling over pebbles, the houses screened by trees and the profusion of massive blue flower heads of hydrangea bushes, as well as all the other colourful plants and flowers. The path emerged from the undergrowth onto the back of a rocky beach. We walked at sea level, striding across the huge boulders with the woodland on our left and the flat calm sea on our right.

The sea tempted me. I just wanted to take off my rucksack and boots and wade into it. My clothes were so wet, that a little bit of English Channel would not have made any difference. In the heat of mid morning the blue sea looked so cool and inviting, it was easy to forget that in reality it would be cold enough to make you gasp for breath at the initial plunge.

During the planning stages of the walk we had considered the possibility of going swimming, either in the sea or at local pools. There were leisure pools at Newquay and Falmouth, which if given the opportunity, we had decided to visit. As events transpired we were not given the opportunity, but at least we went prepared.

With weight in mind once again, we had cut our normal swimming paraphernalia to a minimum – a costume. No goggles, no towels, no rubber rings and no arm bands. As a concession we did take a mini towel each, these incredible little scraps of cotton came vacuum packed into a solid block no bigger than a match box and when unfolded measured thirty centimetres by thirty centimetres. Once opened they would never be as tiny again! Incredible though they were, and yes it was possible to get thoroughly dried using one, they would not be much good when it came to attempting to hide underneath one on a beach whilst getting changed! We might as well try to hide behind a tissue.

Much as I would have liked to go for a swim that morning, the voice of reason and the voice of Chris talked me out of it. On our past record of late arrivals and long days we could not spare the time for the luxury of a swim. If we had learnt one thing so far, it was that no matter what the maps looked like and no matter how far the mileage remaining to be walked, it was impossible to judge how long it would take us. Another factor to consider was sunburn. The sun was so intense and the water so clear that swimming for only a few minutes would probably result in very sunburnt necks and shoulders. As the sun lotion had not proved particularly effective so far we dare not risk swimming without a T-shirt and, joking apart, it would be troublesome to dry. So it was with some regret that we continued, passing a young woman in a bikini and sarong and obviously about to go for a swim.

As we approached Tater Du lighthouse we passed a couple clutching a map and looking very lost. They were trying to find the home of author and broadcaster Derek Tangye, who had written many books about the area. They sought our help, which they no doubt later regretted, as we sent them off in the wrong direction; half an hour after we left them I found the house on our map, it was in the opposite direction to which the couple had taken. Oops!

The lighthouse was located down a steep track leading off the main track that we were following. By Cornish standards, Tater Du is a baby, not built until 1965. That area of the coast was known as 'fishing boat graveyard' having suffered a higher than usual number of wrecks. It took a further eleven lives before the lighthouse was finally built.

A more recent death just along the coast near Lamorna had occurred only two weeks before we walked there. A holiday maker walking up from the village had slipped on the rocky path, lost his footing and fallen to his death. A wilted bunch of flowers at the side of the path marked the tragedy. It was not an especially high section of cliff, a fall into the sea from that height would have been survivable but numerous outcroppings of rock had proved fatal. Our landlord at Porthcurno had told us about the tragedy and warned us to be careful.

A yacht was moored in Lamorna Cove, people were diving into the sea from its decks and others were swimming out to it. Closer in to the minute harbour someone was scuba diving. The whole scene, with the sun burning down and the clear blue sea was very Mediterranean.

The café at Lamorna was a welcome sight. We went into the cool interior, chose a table away from the other diners where the smell of our sweaty little bodies wouldn't put them off their filled baguettes, and shed our rucksacks with sighs of relief. Across the seat of both our shorts was a darker line of damp where the perspiration had been greatest due to the waist straps of our rucksacks. We must have looked a sight!

Two cold cans each and lemon meringue pie and Bakewell tart consumed in the shady cool of a tea room did much to revive us. This was what had been missing on previous days! We emerged feeling ready for anything the path could throw at us, well, perhaps not quite anything, but we did feel fresher.

Lamorna was once the sight of a busy quarry; the scars are still visible today. Granite from here was shipped all over the country to be used on the Thames embankment and various Cornish lighthouses amongst other things. The quarry is now no more than yet another silenced reminder of Cornwall's industrial past. But dare I say Lamorna is a nicer place without it. Despite its size, the village was busy with holiday makers bringing much needed business to the local community.

Rounding the next headland from Lamorna we got our first glimpse of St. Michael's Mount in the distance across Mount's Bay. Behind it the land stretched away to the south towards The Lizard, the view becoming gradually fainter in the haze until it was impossible to differentiate land, sea or sky.

The path wound between hedges and through a nature reserve owned by the Cornish Wildlife Trust. The area had once been bulbfields, now it was colonised by coniferous woodland. I had never before been in a nature reserve where the dead trees out-numbered the living trees. Their dead branches, stripped of bark and bleached by the sun, stretched skywards like skeletal hands from the grave.

Butterflies fluttered along, resting briefly on flowers before resuming their haphazard flight as we drew near. The woodland groundcover offered a different variety of plants to the ones on other areas of the coast. Wood sorrel and wood anemone grew close to the ground in the open glades, and ragged robin and red campion lined the hedges. It must be a colourful sight in the spring with the daffodils and bluebells covering the woodland floor.

As we passed into and out of the kaleidoscope of light and shade on the path, I began to vary my pace, taking advantage of the cooler shade and almost sprinting through the sunlit patches.

Chris immediately realised what I was doing. "Stop dawdling in the shade!" she chastised as she stood in a triangle of sunlight with sweat pouring down her face, frantically fanning herself with the guidebook.

We met a number of people on that part of the path. Mainly families and young couples, they seemed to be in search of the quieter coves along the coast away from the popular tourist spots, to spend a peaceful relaxing day in the sunshine. As we passed with cheery (or in our case weary) 'hellos' we could smell their deodorants and perfumes. They smelt so clean and every one of them looked fresh and cool. I wonder what they thought of us in comparison. Each time we passed someone their appearance and odour was an indication of how far they had walked. None of the people we met smelt as if they had been walking for miles and if they did carry rucksacks these were small and could only have contained sandwiches and swimming costumes.

The path joined a track passing isolated houses and well tended gardens. Someone was having a bonfire, the smoke filled the path and we choked our way through it, hardly able to see where we were going, our eyes stinging. The track joined a metalled lane and snaked down into Mousehole passing quaint thatched cottages festooned with colourful hanging baskets. From the top of the lane we looked straight down on the tiny harbour, the tide was in; fishing boats bobbed at anchor and hordes of tourists lined the quay.

At the bottom of the hill we squeeze into a gift shop to avoid a sudden surge of traffic. The narrow road was barely wide enough for two cars to pass, impossible if two walkers with two large rucksacks were standing in the gutter!

The shop sold fudge, sweets, postcards and a range of souvenir items, most popular of which seemed to be books and ornaments of the Mousehole cat. The Mousehole cat is a bit of a local hero, the story goes that during a severe winter the weather was so bad that the fishing boats could not leave the harbour. The cat and his aged master risked their lives, going out into the tempestuous sea to bring back fish for the starving villagers. The Mousehole cat tamed the old wild cat of the storm by singing to him and so the fishing boat returned safely to port with a full catch. The villagers celebrated with a feast of fish dishes to shame Rick Stein. Every Christmas the feast is re-enacted and villagers parade through streets decorated with coloured Christmas lights, before stuffing themselves with seafood, most popular of which seems to be Stargazy Pie. That's the one with the fish heads sticking up through the crust! I think I'll just stick to fish and chips.

Browsing in the gift shop whilst wearing a rucksack was not something that could be done without careful, calculated movement; one inch in the wrong direction and considerable damage could be inflicted on a number of ornaments without even trying.

"Mind your rucksack Clare!" instructed Chris absentmindedly as she selected a postcard.

"Yes mum!" I replied shaking my head; the heat must have got to her brain.

"Oh, sorry," she laughed, "it's habit."

"Nagging or calling everyone Clare?"

She avoided that question with a tactical one of her own: "Do you fancy sharing some saffron buns?"

Food!

"Oh yes please!"

We sat on an already crowded bench on the quayside and cooled off with an ice cream with clotted cream on top. How many was that now? I'd lost count. Trying to remember induced a headache that threatened to blow the top of my head off. It started suddenly and was soon pounding like a steam hammer behind my temples.

Chris, oblivious to my headache, inadvertently made it ten times worse by pointing out a Pavorotti look-a-like on the harbour wall. Laughing made the pain worse. Leaving me holding my head, Chris went into a nearby shop to buy a cold drink. When she emerged fifteen minutes later (busy shop obviously!) I was fumbling in my first aid kit for some heavy duty painkillers. I got the foil packet and pushed a tablet out into the palm of my hand, then I dropped it. We watched as the little white tablet bounced off my knee, hit the pavement, rolled into the road and dodged passing cars and tourists before rolling over the edge of the harbour wall and plopping into the sea. We exchanged a glance; Chris took the packet from me and dispensed the tablets into my carefully waiting hand. The tablets did the trick! The headache seemed to go almost as quickly as it had come.

We set off through a car park at the back of the beach to climb some stone steps (as per instructions in the guidebook) and found ourselves in someone's back garden.

"This can't be right," I said.

Chris checked the guidebook, looked along the beach and began walking back down the steps. "Wrong set of steps," she muttered sheepishly.

At the correct set of steps we rejoined the road. From here until Marazion was nearly all road walking but the majority was not unpleasant, the views were good and for once we did not have to worry about where we were putting our feet. Perhaps I should qualify that by saying we were less likely to twist an ankle, although the chances of stepping in dog dirt were increased on this populated section of our walk.

The route took us directly past the Penlee Lifeboat Station and its commemorative garden, a tribute to the crew of The Solomon Browne, the lifeboat that set out in December 1981 to rescue the crew and passengers of the stricken coaster Union Star. The coaster had been swept ashore beyond Tater Du lighthouse and Penlee was the nearest lifeboat station, the crew being from Mousehole. Both vessels were lost with all hands. The tragedy touched everyone in the small community; nearly every family had lost a father, husband, son, brother or friend. A plaque in the garden reads 'Service not self'. The tragedy spawned research into safer designs of lifeboats. The lifeboat at Penlee Point was never replaced. A new larger replacement lifeboat is now stationed at nearby Newlyn.

In no time at all we were in Newlyn, a busy port since mediaeval times and boasting three quays. On this summer Sunday afternoon there was little activity around the harbour, and unlike Mousehole, Newlyn was not a magnet for the tourists. Above the harbour we found a curious memorial to a maid who died in 1917. The inscription informed us what a pious, hardworking girl Miss MacTrigor had been but, frustratingly, did not tell us how she died. We had to speculate: was the cause of her death a particularly nasty case of housemaid's knee? Or was she poisoned by years of black-leading the range? Choked to death after a vigorous session of carpet beating? Was it Anaphalatic shock brought on by an allergy to dust mites whilst changing the bedding? Had a drunken master beaten her to death? Did she fall off a ladder whilst cleaning the chandeliers? We will never know.

From Newlyn harbour we turned a corner, passed a car showroom and were in Penzance. This is the only town in Cornwall with a promenade and we strolled along it at a little after four in the afternoon, we had reached our stop for that night well ahead of schedule and we still felt relatively fresh.

Penzance was the only place we met responsible dog owners. Walking towards us along the promenade was a small woman with a Yorkshire terrier on a lead. She carried a small plastic bag with something brown and tubular inside which she deposited in a red bin with a picture of a dog on the front. Shortly behind her came a much larger woman with an Old English sheepdog. She too was carrying a plastic bag, much larger than the other woman's and with more in it. I suppose it makes sense: the bigger the dog, the more it eats, the more...

Chris interrupted my exercise in logic to ask if I knew where our B&B was. We rummaged in our rucksacks for the receipt and, having found it, asked for directions at a nearby filling station. We were in luck; the B&B was just down the next side street, only fifty yards from the promenade.

The house was similar to the one at Portgaverne, tall and narrow with rooms leading off the main staircase. We followed the silent landlady up the dark stairs to our room at the back of the house. A new en-suite shower room had recently been installed which, she informed us, she would not be charging us for. It was so new in fact that it still had that characteristic smell of tile grout and fresh paint. It was the fourth en-suite room and by far the best. The shower cubicle was enormous and for once I was not constantly banging my elbows on the walls. The spray from the power shower almost pinned you against the tiles. The rest of the bedroom was clean and the bedding and towels smelt of fabric conditioner, although a spot of dusting would not have gone amiss.

We relaxed with a cup of tea and a shower, Chris wrote some postcards, I read the next chapter in the guidebook and before we realised it was seven o'clock. We had been sprawled on the beds taking it easy for two hours! My stomach let out a bellowing rumble of protest and we decided to find somewhere to have supper.

Our B&B was in a residential area of the town; there were one or two noisy pubs nearby but a shortage of tea rooms, restaurants or cafes. We found a popular fish and chip shop down a side street just off the promenade and decided fish and chips were just what we both fancied.

Ten minutes later we were sitting on the promenade, eating fish and chips and fending off seagulls. Fortunately, Penzance has a nicer, more ethical class of gull than Newquay. We were allowed to eat all of our meal without being mugged. I had not asked about skin or bones in the fish, remembering with embarrassment the episode at Bude, and so it was with relief that I only found a couple of bones and not even one scale of skin. The fish and chips were actually very good but made us both rather thirsty.

As we were finishing our meal, Chris's mobile phone began to ring. It was Clare, just arrived home from a holiday in France with Chris's sister and her family.

"Hello!" she shrieked down the phone loud enough for people passing by to hear. "How's the walk going? Have you got any blisters yet?"

The next few minutes were spent with mother and daughter gossiping and laughing together. Thank goodness I wasn't paying the phone bill!

"She sounds to have enjoyed herself in France," I said as Chris finally ended the call.

"She has," replied Chris attempting to wipe grease off her phone, "but I wish I wasn't paying the phone bill!"

The shop near our B&B had closed so I volunteered to go in search of a pint of milk to supplement the little tubs of UHT provided in our room. I set off, leaving Chris to return to the B&B, and took a direction that I hoped would take me towards the town centre.

Penzance is not a particularly large town. An invasion of Spaniards in 1595 destroyed the town and little remains from before that time. It has a history of commerce and sea faring; it is still a busy port and today runs a regular helicopter service to the Scilly Isles. In common with many other towns along the south coast, the mild climate resulted in Penzance becoming a popular resort for gentle folk. Its popularity was increased after 1866 with the coming of the railway from points east and Paddington. The commercial eastern side of the town with the heliport, docks, harbour and railway terminus seems unattached from the tranquil suburbs of the western side.

If last year's stretch of the coast path had been thick with literary connections, this year we could not get away from founding discoveries in science and technology. The Cornish mining industry had led to many inventions to improve safety and production. You could not move in Porthcurno without metaphorically tripping over telegraph and fibre optic communication cables. Marconi had used a site on the coast of The Lizard to conduct his experiments with radio. And one of Penzance's most famous sons was Humphrey Davy.

Davy was born in the town in 1778, son of a woodcarver. He was apprenticed to a surgeon-apothecary and his reading led him to develop an interest in chemistry. After serving his apprenticeship he moved to Bristol where his studies into chemistry began in earnest. In 1801 he was appointed as a lecturer at the Royal Institution in London. The then unknown Michael Faraday attended the lectures and after much persistence became Davy's assistant.

Knighted in 1812, Sir Humphrey Davy was responsible for many important discoveries in chemistry, although he is perhaps most famous for inventing the miner's safety lamp. The lamp was of use, not to the Cornish miners, but to the coal miners in other areas of the country. Coal mines produce methane, and many miners were killed each year in explosions when their candles ignited this gas sometimes known as 'firedamp'. Unfortunately for Davy he failed to patent his safety lamp which led to claims from some chap called George Stephenson that he and not Davy had first invented the lamp!

Health and Safety and COSHH were not an issue at the beginning of the nineteenth century. In 1829 Davy died after a serious illness thought to have been caused by inhalation of harmful gases.

Having said Penzance is not a large town I was finding it increasingly difficult to find a shop, and was at risk of dying of inhalation of exhaust fumes as I wandered along residential streets. I walked up one street; then another very similar looking street, past rows of neat stone houses with pretty front gardens. I passed a cat washing himself on a wall. Ten minutes later I passed the same cat on what I thought was a different street. How had he got in front of me? Did he know a short cut? Or was I going round in circles? I tried to look purposeful as I strode up a cul de sac, only to do a one hundred and eighty degree turn at the top and walk back down again, passing two men on the way.

Lots of people seemed to be lost as well as me. Lost Germans. Lost French. Lost Italians. Lost Americans. The United Nations must be having a conference in Penzance; would any of the delegates find their way to the convention in time?

Walking down a narrow alley I suddenly found the town centre. It was full of banks, building societies and clothes shops. The only shop that was open was an off license. I asked but they didn't sell milk, hardly surprising!

This was becoming a challenge. I grew increasingly determined not to be cheated of a pint of milk. I would not give up my quest.

I was about to give up when I crawled past a Spar. Were my eyes playing tricks? Had my fevered brain conjured a mirage of a Spar out of the empty window of a jeweller's perhaps? I crawled back for a second look. No, this was no mirage; it really was a Spar. Yippee! I got the milk and a bar of chocolate (just in case I could not find my way back and was out all night) and set off back.

I found the alley I had come along earlier and there, on the corner at the head of the alley, was a Co-op. Open. Somehow I had walked past it twenty minutes earlier without even seeing it!

I found a different way back to the B&B via a park. The park was well kept, clean, free from vandalism, with a range of semi tropical plants growing in the mild climate, and totally different to parks where I come from. The small museum and art gallery in the park had been highly recommended by the guidebook, although of course the building was closed when I trudged past.

I had been able to hear music for some time and as I walked through a narrow path between overhanging branches of ornamental trees, I discovered where the music was coming from. A band concert was taking place; the Penzance Silver Band was seated in the bandstand, playing to a large crowd arranged on the grass and the benches around them. The path I had been following had led me right to the concert. Feeling rather self conscious and clutching my cold slippery bottle of milk, I walked between the band and the audience toward the park gates.

Despite my embarrassing emergence on to the scene, I found the whole event rather pastoral. It was a beautiful summer Sunday evening and young families and old people alike had turned out to enjoy the music and to support their local band. The music carried through the park to the surrounding streets. I had already concluded that I liked Penzance, its architecture and leafy suburbs. Had she been with me, Chris too would have been impressed by the park and the suburban streets around it. As with St. Ives, Penzance was another pleasant example of a Cornish seaside resort and another contrast to Newquay.

Forty minutes after setting out, I arrived back at the B&B. I was hot and sweaty and my legs were beginning to ache. I stumbled up the stairs, almost blind in the darkness after the bright evening outside, my spectacle lenses slow to adjust to the reduced light level. I could hardly see the door knob in the dim light filtering through a dirt encrusted skylight in the ceiling and almost fell into the room as I twisted the knob and the door swung open.

Chris was lying on her bed reading a magazine, looking fresh and relaxed, the antithesis of how I felt. I plonked the milk down next to the kettle on her bedside table and collapsed onto my bed.

"You've been a long time!" said Chris, glancing up from her reading. "Where have you been?"

"I don't know. Stop asking difficult questions!" I replied as I pushed my trainers off and began removing my socks.

I stood up and moved over to Chris's bedside table to switch on the kettle.

"Pooh! God! Your feet stink!" she cried flapping her hand in front of her nose.

Forty minutes. All that walking. Getting lost. All so she can have fresh milk in her tea. And what does she say? Does she express concern for my welfare? Fear that I might have got lost? Worry that I might tire myself out after a day of walking?

No.

After all I had done for her, all that effort and she tells me my feet stink!

I moved back over to my bed and began sniffing my socks. Hmm, she was right. I was just about to see if my trainers smelt as bad when Chris compounded the insult by saying,

135

"You've put the milk bottle against my socks, the condensation's getting them wet, they had almost dried on the kettle."

I got up, knowing now that Chris was deliberately winding me up, it was a game we frequently played, usually with me losing – but this time I had the trump card and I was prepared to play it. As I reached her bedside and began to move the milk bottle and make the tea, the odour of my feet came with me.

"Oh, yuck! For God's sake! Go away will you!"

"I thought you wanted me to move the milk bottle?"

"Oh, poor Roger! How does he put up with your feet?" she asked, now flapping both hands and a magazine in the air.

Having poured boiling water onto the teabags I moved back to my own bed. Chris went back to her magazine. Two minutes later I was back at her side, adding milk to the tea. She immediately started to complain.

"I can't make you a nice cup of tea from the other side of the room, can I?" I said with pseudo innocence and a hurt expression as I carefully put the milk bottle against her socks.

I took my tea and sat down on my bed. Chris cast aside her magazine and turned to reach for her cup.

"You've put the bottle against my socks again!"

"Oh, sorry!" I stood up. "I'll move it."

"No! Stay over there! I'll do it."

"I think I'll give my feet a quick wash."

"Good idea!" muttered Chris.

I stood up; it was time to play my trump card.

"Mind you, these are the socks I'm supposed to be wearing tomorrow. They're pretty smelly as well." With that I picked up a sock and hurled it at her. Bull's eye! It landed right on her nose.

"Oh! Yuck! You little sod!"

I was safely in the bathroom before she could retaliate.

Monday 12th July

The silent landlady served breakfast to us and the other guests in a large, many tabled dining room. Her conversation ran to 'tea or coffee?' 'white or brown toast?' and 'cooked breakfast?'

I had never seen any of the cereals before; they were cheap own-brand products from a southern chain of supermarkets I had never even heard of. The brown scraps of cardboard masquerading as bran flakes were tasteless and, on contact with milk, immediately dissolved to form something similar to the stuff dentists use to take impressions. But the cooked breakfast was good and the toast, when it finally arrived, was hot, and to my joy the teapot was huge.

"If you drink all that tea you'll be needing a toilet within half an hour," warned Chris prophetically.

"I know but there's bound to be some on the way out of town."

We were both right. By the time we had passed the harbour and reached the far end of Penzance (with me pointing out the distance I had walked the previous evening) my bladder was full and a pictogram on the wall of the Tourist Information Centre pointed the way to the toilets.

"Good morning ladies," said the attendant on duty.

"Morning," I replied reading the notice on the wall in the entrance. "However, I'm not that desperate. Good bye."

We had walked over a hundred miles and in bustling, affluent Penzance tourists were being charged to spend a penny. Only, with inflation it was no longer a penny but ten pennies.

"Well, that was embarrassing," chastised Chris. "You're now going to walk goodness knows how far wanting to go to the loo rather than spend ten pence. You skinflint!"

"It's the principle of the thing! Ten pee! It's as bad as Blackpool!"

We walked on with me slackening the waist strap on the rucksack to ease the pressure against my abdomen.

The first three miles that day were along the busy A30 Trunk Road, then along the railway line and finally along the beach. We had rejoined St Michael's Way near the end of its journey. Juggernauts and coaches thundered by along the road, the draught from one blowing my cap off my head and into a nearby flowerbed. As we walked along a raised embankment between the beach and the railway, the smells of the bakeries in first Tesco and then Safeway supermarkets wafted across to tantalise us. Unfortunately we could not shop at either unless we were prepared to scramble over the railway line and climb a couple of fences to reach them. I offered to hold Chris's rucksack if she wanted to make this sacrifice for our team but she did not seem too keen. Really! And after all I had done for her!

Much to my relief there was a toilet block just before the path diverted onto the beach, these toilets were clean, well maintained with paper and soap and, best of all were free! What extras did you get for your ten pence at Penzance I wondered?

We descended steps to the beach, well known for its agates and other semi precious stones. As we walked along we were both intent on the pebbles at our feet.

"What's an agate look like?" I asked.

"I'm not sure."

I began passing stones to Chris for her opinion.

"No. No. No."

Every pebble was given a cursory glance before being tossed away. Neither of us had a clue what we were looking for but the beach combing was fun. I began to select larger and obviously more inappropriate pebbles for her examination.

"What about this one?" I asked heaving at a large chunk of red brick.

"No."

"This one then?" I handed her a piece of glass worn smooth by the action of the sea.

She glanced at it briefly before it too was thrown back onto the beach.

And so we came to the historic little town of Marazion overlooking St. Michael's Mount. At low water it is possible to walk to the Mount from Marazion along a causeway. The history of both places is long and fascinating.

The National Trust now owns St. Michael's Mount and the buildings on it. But it has been a Benedictine Priory, a port for the export of tin and copper, was once owned by the Basset family (they do keep cropping up!) and a fort. It is thought to have been a port as far back as the Bronze Age when Phoenicians visited it to trade in tin. If legends are to be believed St. Michael's Mount was built by Cormoran, the one-eyed giant.

Marazion once had two markets and one school of thought is that its name derives from old Cornish for two markets. The other theory is that the name comes from 'market Jew'; the town once being the ancient home of Jews who smelted tin to trade with the Phoenicians. Today there might not be any tin smelting or even Jews but, amazingly for such a tiny settlement, Marazion has its own Mayor and Town Council. Thankfully it now also has a by-pass. Having seen at first hand the volume of traffic using the A30, it is frightening to imagine how the twisting narrow main street of Marazion ever coped with the vehicles.

We viewed St. Michael's Mount from a vantage point at Marazion. People scurried across the causeway like so many sunburnt ants. I wondered if the incoming tide ever trapped anyone.

Sitting there squinting into the sun and looking at the silhouette of the Mount we were unaware that we would be watching that same view again in a matter of weeks. The BBC

138

broadcast live coverage of the eclipse the following month showing the lunar action taking place over Mount's Bay, with a temporary studio set up in a hotel in the town and interviews with astronomers on the beach. Watching the programme, sitting in the staff room at work, Chris and I bored everyone with our squeals of "we were there five weeks ago!" and "we walked along that beach!" more interested in where we had been than the drama unfolding on the screen.

Cornwall was the only part of the country from where it would be possible to view a total eclipse and the whole county seemed to have gone eclipse crazy. Every gift shop sold postcards of the Cornish eclipse, which were blatantly not the Cornish eclipse but some other eclipse – how could it be, when the event had not yet taken place? Every grocers and newsagents we went in were selling eclipse viewers. Every B&B had leaflets about the eclipse. One landlady told us that after an initial mad rush to book accommodation during the week of the eclipse, there had been a sudden rush of cancellations as everyone began to realise how congested the roads would be. Booking was starting to pick up again in July, although it was apparent by then that the eclipse was not going to be the enormous money spinner that many hoteliers and tradesmen had predicted.

By the time I witnessed the partial eclipse in Lancashire I was heartily sick of all the hype. The light levels did not fall as much as I had expected, it goes darker before a bit of a storm! And when you consider that eclipses take place fairly regularly somewhere in the world, for me at least, it made the whole occasion rather insignificant.

Before leaving Marazion we got some refreshments at a corner shop and found a shady bench in front of a small church where we sat drinking lemonade and eating ice creams. A seagull paraded along the pavement watching us eat, eager to snatch any proffered scraps. After several minutes he realised that we fell into the category of mean walker instead of generous holiday maker, and so decided it was time to beg elsewhere. However, his timing and method of departure were an excellent example of how not to make an exit. Was he the same gull I had encountered last year struggling to grasp the mechanics of flying? He ran down the pavement, making no effort to use his wings, and suddenly veered out into the road and the path of an oncoming car. The car screeched to a halt, throwing both occupants hard against their seat belts.

"Stupid seagull!" bellowed the driver, retrieving his glasses from the end of his nose before driving off to curious glances from passers by.

Chris and I chuckled with amusement and continued watching the gull who was still making rather a fool of himself. The screeching of brakes and, no doubt, the sight of a radiator grill bearing down on him, had given him a bit of a fright. And he was now employing both legs and wings to propel himself across the road. Having reached the far pavement he finally succeeded in becoming airborne and flapped up to the top of the church porch where he settled unsteadily on a copper orb. Gulls feet are not designed for gripping, especially a slippery smooth circular object. He balanced on the orb, first slipping with one foot and then the other, trying to find purchase on the impossible perch. He stayed up there, continuing to lose his footing, and flapping his wings to correct his balance, peering at the pavement far below him and looking far too frightened to fly down. A small crowd of people had gathered to watch his antics as we heaved on our rucksacks and continued on our way. For all I know he could still be there, doomed by his own terror to spend the rest of his life slipping on that ball!

We continued to Perranuthnoe and our next toilet stop following an easy path through fields, along low cliffs and cutting across the backs of beaches. As we climbed a stile behind one beach we looked down onto a nudist. He was sitting quite unconcernedly on the rocky beach only a hundred yards from where a little old lady was exercising her Yorkshire terrier. The path cut behind a line of bushes hiding our view of the beach and so we could only surmise what happened next.

There was a high pitched cry, some excited yapping and then the voice of the old lady shrill with panic.

"Jake! Come back! Put that down! Drop! Bad dog!"

The yapping continued.

Chris and I looked at one another; I raised a quizzical eyebrow. We were both thinking the same thing: just what had taken Jake's fancy?

Just before Perranuthnoe we made an unscheduled stop in order to attend to the first blister of the walk. Of all the places you might expect to get a blister this one was unusually located on the top of Chris's little toe. It was a result of wet feet caused by sweating and a tiny crease in her sock that had rubbed the softened skin. A couple of minutes spent applying a special blister dressing and we were on our way again.

Just beyond Perran Sands the beach gave way to rocky inlets. Looking down we could see the pattern of rocks jutting out into the sea below the water line, granite fingers stretching away under water. Between these fingers the dark turquoise of the sea indicated how deep the water was so close to the cliffs. The inlets were ideal places for swimming and several young men were plunging from the rocks into the inviting water. Only a short distance from where these friends were swimming and diving, was our second nudist of the day. He emerged from the sea and strolled over the rocks to his clothes. This one was more fortunate than the last; there were no dogs to bother him but we noticed with amusement that a seal was watching him!

We didn't need the binoculars to see that he was old, bald, overweight and very wrinkled. Why were the only nudists we saw old men? It wasn't fair! Was it the hot weather bringing them out? Too much sun?

The South West Coast Path started life as a route trod by revenue men. And so by necessity the path was close to the shore, hugging headlands and inlets so that diligent watch could be kept for smuggling. Centuries of use, first by the revenue men and later by coast guards, created the miles of path which today make up the longest National Trail in the country.

We were very much aware of the smuggling that had taken place on a considerable scale throughout Devon and Cornwall in past centuries. With the innumerable secluded inlets and the proximity to France, the area was well suited to this illegal and often dangerous trade. However, it was not until we reached the area around Prussia Cove that we were able to see visible evidence of smuggling, in the form of ruts across the rocky beach at Bessy's Cove, where the contraband was landed. Brandy landed here would then be transported to neighbouring Piskies Cove where it was stored in caves.

The Carter family ran a highly lucrative smuggling business here in the eighteenth century – Prussia Cove being named after The King of Prussia Inn that they kept. While one brother was in charge of the smuggling operations the other brother collected the brandy in his heavily armed ships. The organisation and secrecy involved must have been incredible.

The next two miles to Praa Sands seemed to drag on. The heat was once again to blame; it sapped our energy. By mutual consent we decided that that afternoon would be an ideal time to sample our first cream tea. Perhaps it was the thought of the scones, jam and cream, the refreshing tea and a chance to sit and unwind in the shade that made those two miles seem so long!

We wilted in the heat, climbing what at any other time we would have considered quite gentle slopes, as if we were making an ascent of Kilimanjaro. Staggering to the top of one incline we threw ourselves to the ground. I could hear the blood rushing in my ears and felt my heart pounding against my ribcage. Once again I found myself wondering how fell runners coped, supreme fitness and a total lack of fear regarding injuries, I assumed, not to mention no heavy rucksack.

I lay in the grass, fragrant with the scents of summer. Breathing and heart rate slowed to normal. The muscles in my legs tingled with their recent exertions and the perspiration evaporated from my brow. My eyes closed, I watched the sun dance patterns of scarlet and amber across the inside of my eyelids; kaleidoscopic, hallucinating, restful. The breeze stirred the grass and bracken and lifted my hair. So quiet, just the cry of the gulls. Had I been the type of person who can fall asleep anywhere and at any time, I might have done just that. So restful, so peaceful, so tranquil...

"Wake up!"

"Uh, what?"

"You were asleep."

"It may have appeared that I was asleep but I was not, as a matter of fact I was resting my eyelids," I countered; deeply affronted that Chris could even think such a thing.

"And snoring!"

"Ah!" I knew I was in a hole, so I stopped digging.

Lying there, gazing up into the sky I saw a cloud. Wow! Hadn't seen one of them for days! Then I saw a second one. Two clouds! Joy. Did this herald a change in the weather and a return to cooler temperatures? Probably not, the clouds were pathetically tiny, wispy things – if someone sneezed in Plymouth they would probably be blown all the way to France!

Hunger and discomfort finally forced us to regain our feet; it's not really comfortable lying on your back when you are still wearing a rucksack! We set off again with butterflies dancing along in front of us. I felt like Uncle Remus in Song of the South. Zip a dee doo dah, zip a dee hey, my oh my, what a scorching hot day!

There was one particular species of butterfly that I had seen several times in the last few days but had been unable to identify. And searching through identification guides in the few bookshops we found had proved futile. Had I imagined them? Had I not remembered the wing patterns correctly? Or, had I discovered a new species? If that was the case I could call it anything I wished. Perhaps a combination of our surnames in honour of the walk! The Ashfield Flutterer. The Merriford. No, no, that sounded more like a drug and alcohol rehabilitation clinic!

As we reached Praa Sands the path carried us right past a café. A sign advertised clotted cream teas. It was fate. As one we turned sharp left and through the gate. Ah, food, drink and cool, cool shade!

"I assume we're going inside?" I asked.

"No," replied Chris, "I'd rather sit at one of the picnic tables."

Had the sun finally got to her? Was she going mad? We'd spent all day in the sun, here we were within feet of blissful shade and she was saying she wanted to sit outside! Heat stroke – that was it – she had heat stroke!

"But it'll be cooler inside, out of the sun," I explained patiently, adopting my most sympathetic first aider voice.

"Yes, I know, but we can sit at that picnic table with the parasol. We'll be in the shade then." With that, she headed for the table and began shrugging off her rucksack.

Reluctantly I followed, groping for a handkerchief to wipe perspiration from my face, as if to emphasise just how hot I was feeling. I dumped my rucksack by the side of the table and went inside to order two cream teas. When, a short while later, I came out into the searing heat of mid afternoon, I realised why Chris had been so insistent about staying outside.

She was sitting at the picnic bench, her little legs swinging, her bare feet hardly reaching the ground. Arranged in a line along the adjacent wall were two pairs of socks and her walking boots. Not the sort of thing you could do inside a café!

The cream tea was pure nectar. Looking back, I think it was these almost daily stops at cafes and tea rooms in the second week that contributed to the latter half of the walk seeming less arduous. Compared to the first week, the path was generally easier but the daily miles were greater and the weather for most of the last week was equally hot. I felt I had become accustomed to the heat, or as much as one could become accustomed to it when carrying a rucksack all day, although whether Chris felt the same is another matter. But our diversions into shady tea rooms provided us not only with an energy boost in the form of some delicious food, they also gave us a chance to rest in comfort, out of the sun: an important factor that we had failed to benefit from during the first week.

We set out feeling much refreshed and slightly queasy after all the clotted cream. Praa Sands was, unsurprisingly, full of people. We elected to walk along the green behind the beach rather than trying to pick our way through the crowds on the beach. Automatic sprinklers were watering the grass and we delighted in walking directly through the cooling spray of water.

That afternoon we said goodbye to granite for the last time and stepped onto slate. The Lizard peninsular is geologically unique in Britain and over the next few days the rocks we walked over were to change several times.

I can remember very little about the nature of the path from Praa Sands to Porthleven, which disappoints me; if I have forgotten that, what other details can I not recall? I do remember the pair of Peregrine falcons which soared in the thermals above the cliffs and how we stood and watched their aerobatics with awe, the way they turned so gracefully and swooped to drop below the edge of the cliffs so that we were looking down on them.

I remember our careful progress along the diverted paths around recent landslides where the slate cliffs had fallen into the sea. The old line of the path could be seen finishing at sheer drops where fences and walls came to an abrupt end. Wide cracks in the ground threatened more landslides to come. The fields at that point sloped quite steeply toward the cliff edge; the erosion and landslides a constant threat to the stock that grazed there.

Another nudist emerged from the sea at a tiny cove just before Bullion Cliff. It seemed a strange time to be bathing, the sea was almost at high tide and the beach was almost covered. We thought at first he was another middle aged man but he was actually quite young with a shaved head. We had only gone a little further before we became aware he was following us. It was probably just coincidence, Porthleven was not too far away, but his behaviour made us a little uneasy. He was striding out at a brisk pace and rapidly shortening the distance between us. Every so often he would stand perilously close to the cliff edge and hurl stones into the sea below. He caught up with us just as we met a couple walking from Porthleven and as we stood exchanging greetings he hurried on along the path. We breathed a sigh of relief and continued toward Porthleven without seeing him again.

The accommodation at Porthleven sounded wonderful. The leaflet we had been sent showed a picture of the fishing village with the B&B clearly visible. As the path emerged above the harbour we stood looking across to the houses rising up the hillside on the opposite side of the valley and found we could easily pick out the one we were booked into. We descended the narrow street, walked around the harbour and began climbing a steep street to reach the B&B. We arrived hot and sweaty but not too tired.

We were booked into the loft room and so followed the landlady up a very narrow staircase to the top of the house. As I brought up the rear I squeezed myself and my rucksack round a bend in the stairs, almost sending a picture crashing to the floor.

"We had two German walkers here the other day and their rucksacks were huge. They had to take them off to get them up here!" laughed the landlady, entering the loft. "The ceiling's not too low for you is it?"

Chris's reply was drowned out by the sound of my forehead connecting sharply with a beam as I reached the top of the stairs and entered the loft. I was back in Song of the South but this time there were birds, not butterflies, flying around my head!

"I'll make you a pot of tea and leave it in the lounge," said the landlady and disappeared back down the stairs.

"Hmm, a nice cup of tea and a headache tablet are just what I need," I muttered, ducking low to cross to one of the beds.

"For once being five feet two inches is an advantage," said Chris.

"Oh don't make me laugh, I've got a headache!"

Five minutes later we were sat in the lounge on a very plush sofa. It was soft and comfortable but neither of us dared to lean back and relax into the cushions because our clothes were wet with sweat. We perched on the edge of the seat, sipping tea and listening to the weather forecast. When clouds were predicted for the following day we both cheered.

After a shower in the tiniest bathroom I have ever seen in my life, (walk in, put your foot down the toilet, step out of the toilet and into the shower cubicle), we strolled down the hill to the harbour-side pub for an evening meal. Garlic chicken and chips were followed by apple crumble and clotted cream: delicious.

From our loft room we watched a glorious sunset over Mount's Bay. As the sun disappeared below the horizon, the night descended and we could see the lights of Penzance, Newlyn and Mousehole across the water. Tater Du lighthouse flashed out its warning. Over the sea we watched red and green lights flashing in the darkness. What was their source? They were moving too quickly for ships. Then, Chris came up with the answer: helicopters. The Royal Naval Air Station at Culdrose, the training base for new pilots was not far away on The Lizard. A fact we were to be constantly reminded of for the rest of the week.

I leaned over the tiny sink under the eaves cleaning my teeth as Chris continued to watch the dancing lights. As I moved to reach for a towel, a loose floor board farted.

"That wasn't me," I said hastily as Chris turned to look at me.

Mistaking her silence for disbelief I began stamping on the floor trying to make the floor board repeat itself. My attempts were not successful, the more I shuffled around flexing my feet on the floor, the more Chris laughed.

Shaking her head she said, "It wasn't the floor."

"Stop laughing. It *was* the floor, not me! If I can just find the right board I can prove it!"

Gasping for breath and holding her sides, Chris finally managed to blurt out, "It was me!"

Really! She could have admitted to it sooner and saved me all the effort.

"Well, that's just charming!" I said with mock disgust. "I hope you're not going to be doing that all night. I think we'll leave the windows open, I'd rather run the risk of being attacked by an insomniac seagull than be gassed to death!"

"Sorry," said Chris, sounding anything but, "It's all the eggs, and the swede in the Cornish pasties! Don't tell me you aren't suffering too."

"I don't think I need to answer that. I am not the one polluting the atmosphere at the moment! At least our beds are at opposite ends of the room," I said as I climbed under the duvet.

"Julia?"

"Yes?"

"You haven't turned the light out."

I got up, crossed the room to the light switch, turned off the light, turned back towards my bed and walked straight into a beam.

Tuesday 13th July

Up at 6.30 a.m., showered and dressed, I left Chris still in bed and headed down to the beach. For me to be first to get up was extremely unusual, it's Chris that is the morning person not me, but the call of an empty beach and the chance to enjoy a paddle were more than I could resist.

The streets were deserted as I made my way down to the shore. The tide sucked at the beach and with every step my feet sank into the wet shingle. I spent half an hour walking in the slowly receding tide along the beach with nothing but the sound of the surf and the occasional cry of a gull to break the peace of the early morning. Mentally, the exercise may have been beneficial, but my feet suffered on the sharp pebbles, my soles ached dully for the rest of the day. As eight o'clock approached, imagining I could smell bacon frying, I made my way back for breakfast.

The meal was served in the sun lounge at the front of the house overlooking the sea and the harbour. As we ate breakfast the clouds began to gather over Mount's Bay, the forecast had been correct, that day the walking would be in cooler, fresher conditions – thank goodness! If the wind was picking up outside, it also seemed to be freshening under our table.

"Don't look at me!" said Chris as I eyed her suspiciously.

"Well it certainly wasn't me."

The sound of escaping gas was repeated, quickly followed by a low groan. Holding our breath, we both peered under the table. The flatulent culprit was fast asleep, stretched out at our feet: a dog!

An American couple were staying at the B&B. We had not met them the previous evening as they had gone to the theatre; "the Minack" the landlady had elucidated, watching as we both turned green and began groaning. They seemed to be packing a lot into their stay in Cornwall and would not be joining us for breakfast, as they were booked on a mackerel fishing trip.

We were just on to our second helping of cereal when the Americans appeared, dressed for action in yachting caps and deck shoes. They bid us a hasty good morning on their way out. The woman looked a lot like Sandra Dickinson and her squeaky high pitched voice, as she tripped over the door mat and almost fell through the doorway, was identical as she gasped "oh, I do that every time!"

How was she going to cope onboard a small fishing boat, tossing about on the sea, with dead and dying mackerel flapping at her feet, I wondered, when she couldn't even walk through a room without mishap?

With breakfast over I waited for Chris to settle the bill, standing in the hallway and looking with interest at a gallery of old framed photographs depicting storms battering Porthleven. Many of the photos illustrated the clock tower, part of the old town council building on the harbour wall, with high seas crashing over the roof and covering the tower with spray. The photographs varied in age, all were titled 'Great Storm' and a date. Porthleven has a lot of storms; it faces south-west and gales and high seas are not uncommon. It is a credit to the craftsmen who built the tower that it still stands despite the onslaught.

The guidebook told us the distance to The Lizard was thirteen and a half miles, it also told us the walking was relatively easy along cliff top paths with a few steep climbs to cross coves. For once the guidebook was right. The walking that day was not taxing and we were to arrive after only eight hours covering the greatest daily distance of the walk that year.

We were heading south, following the undulating line of the coast towards the most southerly point of mainland Britain. It would have been another day of little shade had the weather remained the same but fortunately the clouds continued to gather throughout the day and we were spared the discomfort of a hot day spent walking into the sun. We were both dressed in shorts, revelling in the cooler temperatures and almost potty with glee as we watched the first goose bumps form on our thighs as the afternoon advanced.

The morning was spent in intermittent sunshine as the growing clouds battled to gain dominance of the sky. We walked downhill from the southern end of the town passing tiny fishermen's cottages to emerge on the beach at the northern end of Loe Bar, a sand bank now effectively damming the river which flows down from Helston and creating the largest natural fresh water lake in Cornwall. We crossed Loe Bar, walking between clumps of sea holly before climbing briefly to the cliff tops.

We made an unintentional detour inland to the village of Gunwalloe, having got lost, before returning to the coast path and Gunwalloe Fishing Cove along a narrow lane. Here we negotiated our way around a JCB and an open-backed lorry parked on the narrow strip of beach and almost blocking access to the footpath. Gravel is extracted from the beach at Gunwalloe and, judging by the vehicles present, the operation is not exactly small scale.

Only a short walk from there we passed Halzephron Cove, where extensive landslides have resulted in re-routing not only of the footpath but even the road. The sight of a stretch of tarmac ending at a cliff edge is quite unforgettable.

Gunwalloe Church is not in Gunwalloe as you might expect but a little further down the coast. The tiny church shelters in the lee of the low cliffs at the northern end of Church Cove. Frequently damaged during stormy weather and out in the middle of nowhere it seems a really stupid place to build a church. No doubt there was some logic employed when it was built hundreds of years ago, perhaps its location is due in part to the nearby Saxon Royal manor.

We explored the tiny church and then wandered around the graveyard. I find graveyards fascinating and yet at the same time depressing. Row upon row of names, unknown lives, for the most part forgotten. But yet a solemn reminder of our own mortality. One day we too will be forgotten. Until then, the carved headstones and silent tombs act as catalysts, urging us to achieve and experience all we can, sooner rather than later.

Many of the graves were hundreds of years old, the engravings made almost illegible over time by erosion and the growth of moss and lichens. But two more recent gravestones caught our attention not merely because of their poignant message but their ironic link to one another. The first was a simple headstone marking the grave of a Luftwaffe pilot shot down over The Lizard. The second was that of a young evacuee killed by an unmarked mine whilst playing on the beach with his friend. Would he have survived had he remained in London? Probably not. The engraving also remembered his parents – killed in the Blitz.

May be there is such a thing as fate. May be we are all walking a path that has already been marked out for us; if we stray off the path then may be it is because we are meant to, the diversion will rejoin the main path, the destination is always the same. May be. I hope not. I do not like to think we have no real choices in life. I prefer to believe in chance and coincidence. But who knows?

Leaving the church behind we crossed the almost deserted beach. The lack of tourists compared with other beaches on other hotter days was striking. The empty beach, the wet sand and the lowering clouds hinted at an out-of-season Cornwall, the real Cornwall when the holiday makers have all gone home. The Lizard is not as tourist orientated as other parts of Cornwall and is all the better for it.

Climbing wooden steps, dodging dog dirt (yes, there was a car park nearby) and passing a golf course we reached another quiet sandy beach. Leading from the beach the path followed the drive of what was once a grand hotel perched on the headland and is now a nursing home. At the top of the drive we got lost. Why does that always happen in unlikely places? It's always in a car park or an urban street, never deep in the wilds of rural Cornwall miles from civilisation! We spent some minutes walking around the rear of the building and through the car park, unable to find any indication of where the footpath might be. Reading and re-reading the map and guidebook failed to show us where we had gone wrong and eventually we walked brazenly around the side of the building towards the cliffs.

We passed windows looking in onto rooms where elderly occupants sat watching television or knitting. It was lunch time and on the T.V. in one room, I could just make out a weather map. I paused outside the window, staring in, unable to hear what the weatherman was saying but easily able to see the symbols on the weather map: grey clouds with three drops of rain falling from each one of them. Was it actually going to rain?

I turned and hurried after Chris, eager to tell her the good news. She had some of her own; she had found the path. There was only one problem – we could not get to it. Between the path and us was a white painted wooden fence trimmed with barbed wire. It was too high to stride over and we could hardly begin to climb it in full view of the nursing home. I had been uneasy as we walked around the building, expecting all the time to be chased off the property by a Gestapo-trained matron or orderly, what might happen to us if we were caught climbing the fence was too frightening to contemplate! We followed the fence along until we came to a gate. Chris lifted the latch and pushed. Nothing happened. She pulled. Nothing happened.

"Here, let me try," I said and began pushing and pulling at the gate. Still nothing happened.

"Perhaps it's sticking," said Chris.

I was beginning to get frustrated and, eager to leave the property before we were seen, I kicked the gate. It didn't budge. And that's when we saw the nail. The gate had been nailed shut. (Presumably to prevent residents escaping or trying to throw themselves off the cliff).

"That's it!" I muttered angrily. "If we're seen it's just too bad."

I moved down the fence to where it dipped a little bit and standing on tip toe managed to stride over the top rail without snagging my shorts on the barbed wire.

"Oh, fine! What am I supposed to do?" asked Chris. "My legs aren't long enough to stride over."

"Well crawl underneath. If I hold the barbed wire up you could get under just here."

Chris took off her rucksack and handed it over the fence. Then she got down on her hands and knees and I pulled the lowest strand of barbed wire up as high as it would go.

I have played the following scene out in my mind hundreds of times since then and I still don't know what happened, it's almost as if a few frames are missing, the tape has been badly edited and some of the action has been lost.

Chris began crawling under the fence. She went under head first. And came out bum first! I do not know how she did it. It's not like she was pot-holing and had plenty of space to turn round in; she was only going under a single strand of barbed wire! At what point did she execute a one hundred and eighty degree turn?

"How did you do that?" I asked as she got to her feet.

"Do what?"

"You went in head first and the first thing to come out at this side was your bum!"

"Was it?"

"Yes!"

"Oh!"

Our escape from Colditz successfully completed we set off along the path. A man walking his dog was coming towards us, he wished us a cheery 'hello' before leaping the fence and crossing towards the nursing home. The dog followed him. They both made it look easy!

Immediately behind the former hotel stands a monument erected to Marconi. He conducted many experiments in radio communications from this headland and in 1901 he sent out a signal from here that was heard across the Atlantic in Newfoundland. Engraved on the monument was a potted history of his work. The only thing it did not explain was why he chose that particular spot.

At Mullion Cove we stopped to buy lunch. We confused the rather slow witted shop assistant by asking what type of pasties were available. She went away to find out and it was several minutes before she came back. Chris added to her confusion by asking for a cheese and onion pasty. The girl disappeared again and came back with a pasty suffering third degree burns to seventy percent of its surface.

"It's a bit burnt," she understated. "It's our last cheese and onion pasty. We can knock you some money off if you like."

"Er, no thanks," said Chris "I'll have a traditional Cornish pasty instead please."

The girl once more left the counter, going into the back of the shop to get Chris's pasty. When she returned Chris asked for some chocolate and a can of lemonade and then really confused the poor girl by asking to send some clotted cream by post.

Looking very flustered the girl grabbed a bar of chocolate, totally forgot about the lemonade, looked round dizzily for some clotted cream and then retreated into the rear of the premises, from where we could hear her yelling "Does anyone know how to send clotted cream by post?"

Within seconds she was being ushered back into the shop by an older woman who looked as if she might have a grasp of the retail trade. The older woman began taking Chris's order for clotted cream and the girl turned her attention to me.

I ordered a pasty, a bar of chocolate and said that I too would like to send some clotted cream by post.

"What sort of pasty do you want? We've got traditional, veg or cheese and onion."

The cheese and onion? I wondered.

"Veg, please and a Snickers bar."

The pasty was plonked on the counter, grease already staining the paper bag and steam rising from it. The girl then put a Snickers bar on top of the bag. I moved the chocolate bar onto the counter where it would not melt.

"Do you want to pay for those now and pay for the cream separately?" she asked, putting the Snickers bar back on top of the pasty.

"No, I'll pay for them altogether," I said handing her the correct amount of money and moving the chocolate back onto the counter.

Meanwhile Chris was filling in the order form for her clotted cream. The girl handed me an order form and a pen and I began writing my parent's address on the form.

"Are you paying for all the clotted cream?" the girl asked me as she picked up my Snickers bar and put it back on top of the steaming pasty.

Some dispute exists between Chris and I regarding my response at that point. Chris maintains I snapped. I do not think I did, it's not in my placid nature to snap, I have been known to shout occasionally – but snap, never! Chris would have you believe that my tone of voice was so harsh that her pen jerked across the order form and she momentarily forgot her sister's address. I would say that if I was a little abrupt it was unintentional but oh, for goodness sake the girl was an idiot!

I stood, pen poised, watching the steam ebbing around the bar of chocolate as it lay on top of the pasty.

"No," I replied to the girls query, "and I don't want my chocolate melting!"

I reached out and moved the chocolate once more. After a brief pause Chris resumed filling in her form.

With the cream ordered and our food paid for we crossed the stream and climbed the far side of the cove to Mullion Cliff where we stopped for lunch.

"That poor girl!" said Chris.

"What?"

"She'll probably never work in a shop again after the way you snapped at her!"

"I didn't snap," I objected.

"Yes you did. 'I don't want my chocolate melting!'" imitated Chris.

"I never said it like that."

"Oh yes you did! I couldn't believe it. I forgot my sister's address, I was so shocked!"

"I didn't mean to snap. Are you sure I said it like that?"

"Yes, of course I'm sure. I bet she throws away those order forms now just to get even, that clotted cream will never be posted. Snapping at her like that! It's not her fault she's an idiot, it's probably inbreeding."

"Well, she was an idiot! Three times she put my chocolate on top of the pasty. Three times! And three times I moved it!"

The pasties were not worth the effort of eating them; greasy and heavy they sat in our stomachs giving us both indigestion, the fat from them coated the insides of our mouths. Not even a bar of partially melted chocolate could take the taste away.

"You said you were going to phone your mum today," Chris reminded me.

"Oh, yes." I took out my mobile phone and began tapping in her number.

As the phone began ringing a helicopter appeared on the horizon. It came rapidly toward us, the thud thud thud of its rotors cutting through the peaceful afternoon. It was directly overhead when mum answered the phone.

"Hi mum, it's me!" I shouted into the instrument.

"What's that racket?"

I explained, adding, as the helicopter moved out to sea, that we were on The Lizard having lunch. Mum told me she was defrosting the fridge. I told her we had seen an adder. She worried and told us to be careful. Then she asked about the heat and worried some more. The helicopter was coming back, making conversation almost impossible and so we said our farewells and disconnected.

I cannot describe our days of walking on The Lizard as peaceful. Each day from ten in the morning to five in the afternoon the sound of helicopters was with us constantly. Sometimes they were a background noise, far away in land or out at sea. More often they swept the skies above us, occasionally singly but usually in formation. When one disappeared and silence descended another would fly over almost instantly to fill the peaceful void.

We were sick of the sound of them. They appeared from all angles; everywhere we looked to admire the view a helicopter would be present even if it was only a minute speck on the horizon. Public toilets were in short supply but we never dared to nip behind a rock or a bush for fear a helicopter would fly over as we were crouched there. They kept coming back to haunt us, and weeks after returning from the walk, Chris was startled by the sound of a helicopter and for a brief second she was back on The Lizard.

We had grown quite chilled as we sat eating lunch but decided against putting on our kagools before setting off, we would soon warm up we told ourselves. I think we walked at least ten yards before deciding that perhaps we would put our kagools on after all. We did warm up after a while and before long were carrying the kagools across our rucksacks.

Serpentine rock is found in Britain only on The Lizard and it supports unique plant species. In an effort to protect these plants English Nature have introduced Soay sheep and Exmoor ponies on some of the land south of Mullion Cliff. The animals eat brambles and gorse which, without this conservation grazing, would smother many of the rarer plants. We did not see any ponies but we did see some Soay sheep that afternoon much to our delight. The Soay is an old breed, rare now and quite tiny compared to the modern breeds everyone is accustomed to. Their presence on The Lizard has a two-fold use, helping to conserve the breed as well as controlling the vegetation.

For much of the afternoon we walked along the cliff tops, the weather gradually deteriorating all the time. Just before the path descended to Kynance Cove the guidebook informed us we should be able to see the two towers of The Lizard lighthouse. But the clouds came down, the kagools went on and we could not see a thing.

By the time we reached the bottom of Kynance Cove we were both very much in need of a toilet stop. Neither of us had been since the late morning and with the ever present helicopters and without the hot sun to make us sweat, we were reaching desperation point. There had to be a toilet somewhere nearby. There had to be! The numbers of tourists crowding the tiny cove had to go somewhere. But where?

The map indicated the toilets were some way inland adjacent to the car park. A short cut led up from the far side of the beach and along a gravel path. The short cut was only possible when the tide was out. The tide was in. So we took the long route, fairly racing up a long winding track which eventually reached the car park. We were so desperate by that time that all the interesting geology and flora of the cove and the surrounding heathland were ignored. Kynance Cove is (apparently) full of the beautifully marbled serpentine rock and the track up from it passes (apparently) a rich variety of rare plants including (apparently) Cornish heath, thyme broomrape, bell heather and bloody cranesbill. We were heedless of all that; sod the bloody cranesbill, where were the bloody toilets?

We arrived at the top of the track leading into the car park. A wooden building at the far side of this large expanse of gravel had to be the toilets, it had to be! We rushed across the car park, collecting a few peculiar looks from the car loads of holiday makers. I suppose we did look pretty crazy: two walkers with bright red legs disappearing into flapping kagools, staggering rapidly uphill under the weight of heavy rucksacks and then almost knocking one another to the floor in a battle to squeeze simultaneously through the door of the toilets.

Nothing can quite compare to that blissful feeling of relief. Nothing. With that over-riding need fulfilled we were able to concentrate on other things, so we had some sweets.

It was beginning to rain, a delicate but persistent drizzle as we rejoined the coast path. Silly as it may sound, we welcomed that rain; if you have ever had to walk in hot weather you will know how we felt.

Without warning the lighthouse suddenly appeared, its whitewashed walls and flashing light seeming ethereal in the misty afternoon. We were almost there! Britain's most southerly point. Another landmark on our walk.

Heads down, we rounded Lizard Point to turn east. I was in the lead and as I reached the top of the rise I lifted my head to take in the view. And what a view!

Turning to Chris as she breasted the rise I said, "Look up, look up now!"

She did and gasped as I had done. Laid out in front of us was a bay with a rocky outcrop stretching out into the pounding sea, huddled against the cliffs was a boat house, its slipway reaching down into the green sea and rising up behind was the lighthouse. I think that had to be one of the most spectacular views of the entire walk, worthy of a photograph.

But we did not take a photograph, not that afternoon at least: we had used all the exposures on the fun camera. Typical!

This was one night's stay we had been particularly looking forward to. The most southerly point in England! And we had joked about staying in the most southerly bedroom, eating the most southerly breakfast and flushing the most southerly toilet; if not 'the most' then at least one of the most southerly at any rate.

Julia's Law: eager anticipation always leads to disappointment.

We walked up the garden path of the B&B, enchanted by the numerous wild rabbits that ran for cover in the hedge. The rabbits were the only enchanting element of that place! The house, a dormer bungalow, was approximately sixty years old. The decoration and furnishings were approximately seventy years old. A faint odour of dog tainted the air but, fortunately, it was in no way as pungent as it had been at Bude.

The view from our upstairs room looked down towards the rocky cliffs, and as we stood at the window a lifeboat sailed into view. As we were to find out later, it was taking part in a charity event and began sending out bright orange flares. It was as we stood watching this free entertainment that a squall replaced the drizzle. The rain lashed against the window and a sudden wind whipped up the sea and battered the plants in the garden. The cast of Watership Down bolted for cover, their white tails bobbing. It was a timely display by nature to coincide with that by the lifeboat. Standing watching the lifeboat being tossed about on the waves, I felt nothing but deep admiration for the courage of the volunteer lifeboat crews who risk their lives, often in weather far worse than that.

Summoned by a shout from the landlady we went downstairs to the dining room for a pot of tea. The room was full of plants, ornaments and, much to our surprise, two stuffed foxes. I had begun to pour the tea, making rather a mess of things, when we were both disturbed by a scuffling sound coming from behind a closed door at the far side of the room. The door burst open and we both jumped, the landlady seemed to propel herself into the room and hastily shut the door behind her. The scuffling increased. What was causing it?

The landlady was friendly but quite eccentric. Standing with her back to us, gazing out of the window and dressed entirely in leopard skin patterned Lycra (an unusual choice for someone in their seventies) she proceeded to hold a conversation with us. We found out she was married, although we never saw her husband, and that there was another guest staying that night, although we never saw him either. We were later to hear the sound of a television from the adjoining bedroom, and at one stage someone other than us was in the bathroom. But we never saw anyone else. Most peculiarly, all the doors in the house had locks, which she was always careful to lock behind her. Was she just extra cautious? Did we look untrustworthy? Or did she keep her husband locked in the house? Was it him we heard, trying to escape from the kitchen? We could only speculate.

Back in the bedroom, ignoring the copious notes of does and don'ts, I elected to wash the socks whilst Chris went for a shower. Our two parcels of clean T-shirts, underwear and toiletries had arrived and Chris unpacked them and repacked our dirty garments as I took my turn in the bathroom.

What can I say about the bathroom? The toilet, once flushed, took hours to refill. The toilet paper appeared to be a roll of kitchen towel sawn in half. There were more notes in the bathroom than in the bedroom, which believe me was some achievement! The primrose yellow bathtub was old but, unbelievably, was a spar bath. Oh, to relax in an effervescing bath of hot, scented, bubbling water! Luxury! Just a second… what was that note pinned above the bath taps? Putting my glasses back on, I bent down to read it: 'showers only please'. ****!!

Chris later said she did not have any difficulty taking a shower. I did. The shower consisted of an attachment leading up from the bath taps to a spray head mounted four feet up the tiled wall. While I cannot complain about the water pressure – plenty of that, I can complain about where the water hit me – my stomach. I have never had a shower bent double before.

The phone began ringing as I was just climbing out of the pathetic excuse for a shower. It was sometime later, however, when we were both in the bedroom that the landlady knocked on the door to tell us that Merv had telephoned, wanting to know if everything was okay with the parcels.

"There's a pay phone in the hall if you wish to return his call," she added.

We didn't need the pay phone, we had our mobiles, but the landlady did not know this. Perhaps she hoped to make some money from us using her phone; if she did, it backfired.

Carrying the parcels we walked into the centre of Lizard village intending to call Merv from there if we had a signal. As we left the B&B, each hugging a parcel, we bumped into the landlady. I wonder what she thought of those parcels? They were important enough to warrant a call to ensure they had arrived, we took them with us when we went out for an evening meal and (as things turned out) brought them back with us at the end of the evening.

"She told me you were both in the shower when I telephoned!" Merv exclaimed when Chris called him.

"Julia was, but I wasn't! I had quite enough of that at Newquay!"

In the centre of the village, some distance from the B&B, we discovered our careful plans had come unstuck. The post office was closed, our parcels were too big to fit through the letter box and to return when the post office was open in the morning would considerably delay our start. We would have been wiser to send these parcels to Coverack for the following night. All that careful planning and we had overlooked one simple point – post offices are not open late!

We wandered round the village, passing several workshops displaying ornaments carved from serpentine. The Victorians popularised the rock using it for fireplaces, lamp stands and numerous other decorations. Worked and polished it can be very beautiful, with its marbling effect of red, green and black. Popular serpentine ornaments in today's market seemed to be barometers, lamps and lighthouses. The runways at Culdrose airfield are even made of serpentine!

The options for our evening meal were restricted to the local takeaway, which seemed overrun with adolescents, a common occurrence at every place we had stayed, and a pub. The latter looked promising, if somewhat busy. After some discussion we opted for the pub.

The pub was busy. Chris headed for the bar, whilst I headed off in search of a table. I am no expert when it comes to pubs, but I don't think too many will have a one way system in operation: enter the dining room through one archway and exit through another. Following the signs, I found a vacant table and shrugging off my kagool, dumped the parcels on one of the chairs and settled down to peruse the menu.

Chris seemed to be a long time. If I leant back I could just see the bar. There she was, right at the front, waving her purse in the air and jumping up and down! She was not getting served though. People kept coming up behind her, they would get served, but not Chris. The bar staff were height-ist!

I continued to sit, reading and rereading the menu, admiring the framed paintings on the walls and watching the dining room gradually filling with people. Still Chris had not been served. I was just contemplating reading the menu for a third time when the landlady appeared at my shoulder.

"How many are in your party?" she snapped.

"Two," I replied.

"This is a table for four. You'll have to move to a table for two, I have a large party coming in."

This was one pub that would not win awards for its customer care! Grudgingly, I moved to the only vacant table for two. It was behind the kitchen door. I spent the rest of the evening sat in a draft, with the door banging into me every time a waitress charged through carrying steaming plates of food. If I did not get knocked off my chair, I would surely end up wearing someone's meal by the end of the evening.

Chris finally appeared carrying two drinks and coming into the dining room through the exit archway.

"You've come in the wrong way!" I exclaimed. "You'll get shouted at."

"What?"

I explained the one way system.

"God, what a pub! You can go to order the food. They might serve you – you're taller!"

Four inches obviously do make all the difference. I was served almost as soon as I reached the bar. Two minutes after going to place our order I was back in the dining room.

"Told you!" said Chris.

"I notice they are sitting at a table for four," I indicated a middle aged couple across the room. "Why didn't she order them to move?"

It was not the best of evenings. We waited forty minutes for our meal. By the time it arrived I was almost asleep. The food was good and although tempted by a dessert, the possibility of another forty minute wait put us off. We returned to the B&B for tea and biscuits in our room (ignoring the notice banning eating in the rooms) but the tea bags were foul.

Settling down under the horrible nylon sheets, I commented on the trapdoor above my bed: was someone locked behind that as well? Creepy, creepy!

Perhaps I should not have made that comment. It put Chris on edge, thinking about the scuffling noises, the locked doors, the unseen husband and the mysterious other guest. She was still awake an hour later, when I shouted myself awake from a nightmare in which I had swallowed a wasp.

Wednesday 14th July

Neither of us could say we had a comfortable night. Every movement between the nylon sheets caused discharges of static electricity that lit up the room. It was like sleeping in a thunder cloud. I was the first to get up, stumbling around the bedroom, tripping over rucksacks and boots, to put the kettle on. But remembering how awful the teabags were, I changed my mind about a cup of tea and made my way to the window to check out the weather. It was overcast but fine, good walking weather as far as we were concerned.

The freckled, sunburnt, bleary-eyed face that stared back at me from the mirror shocked me awake. My lips were dry and cracked, my hair stood up on end and the skin on my neck and ears was beginning to peel. I felt like a worn out Chesterfield. I looked like one too! I tentatively tugged at a flake of skin on my ear lobe: a piece of ear came away in my fingers.

Leaving Chris to take a shower, I went out with the new fun camera that had arrived in the parcel, to take the snapshot we had been unable to take the day before. I retraced our route along the cliff top, enjoying the early morning peace, before hurrying back in time for breakfast.

Returning to the house I entered the garden, scattering rabbits in all directions, and followed the gravel path around the house to the main door. Rounding the corner of the house, I stopped dead in my tracks. A huge Alsatian was standing just beyond the doorway. Neither of us moved; for fixed seconds we stared at one another. I was clutching the door key in my sweaty palm but I knew that I could not reach the door before the dog. Oh, to get so far – nearly at the end of our walk – only to be mauled to death by this ferocious beast, before I had even had my breakfast!

I gulped involuntarily and quakily stuttered, "N-n-nice goddy, th-th-there's a bood goy."

The dog's reaction was immediate. His mouth lolled open, his tongue dangled out, strings of saliva dripped to the ground and he charged straight towards me scattering loose gravel with his enormous paws!

I was still deciding on the three courses of action open to me – faint, wet myself or run like hell – when he reached me. Nearly knocking me off my feet, he pranced around me, his tail wagging and slobbered all over my hands as he greeted me enthusiastically. Never, ever, have I been so pleased to be covered in dog saliva!

I won't dwell too much on the breakfast we ate that morning, let me just say it was one of those extremely rare occasions when I was glad there wasn't a lot of it! Our hostess was resplendent in Lycra leopard skin again; she held another conversation with her back to us between darting in and out of the kitchen. At least now we knew what was scuffling and banging against the door!

The landlady asked where we were staying that night and, when we told her, explained she knew the owner of our next B&B through their mutual guests. A lot of walkers stayed at one B&B before spending the next night at the following one. The landladies often chatted on the telephone although they had never met!

"My guests tell me all about her," she added, "She has an old cottage with a big fireplace and beamed ceilings. I'm sure you will enjoy your stay there."

It was Chris's turn to pay the bill that morning, and while she wrote out a cheque, I used the loo. Then we were off, another early start but a shorter day of only eleven miles.

We had gone less than a mile before Chris muttered something about needing to go to the loo.

"Why didn't you go before we came out?" I demanded.

"Because you beat me to the toilet and I wouldn't have been able to flush it because it takes ages to fill up!"

"Well, pop behind a bush," I said.

The words were no sooner spoken than we heard the all too familiar sounds of an approaching helicopter. Chris would just have to wait!

Our route took us past Lizard Lighthouse and at the most southerly point, Bumble Rock, we turned north. Numerous footpaths left the coast path heading inland, all were sign posted for Lizard village and from several points that morning we were able to look across to the easily visible tower of St Wynwallow's church in the tiny village of Landewednack. This church can claim to be the most southerly in England and the geology of the surrounding area is reflected in its architecture, the tower is made of granite and serpentine. The pulpit too is serpentine and the last sermon preached in Cornish there was in 1678.

We had been grappling with the remnants of the language ever since Padstow. Although conversational Cornish is not something you hear, the language still exists in place names. Ynys was easy, it means the same in Welsh: island, and we had both been to Anglesey often enough to remember it. Wheal is mine. Hayle apparently means estuary, rather confusing when you think of the Hayle estuary! Carn is quite straightforward too, as it means rock or crag. But as for pen, pol, tre, bre, chi, los and all the other three letter prefixes, we got totally confused!

We had seen a lot of one particular plant growing along the path, which we had failed to identify, a trailing succulent it had pretty pink flowers and reminded us a little of Livingstone daisies. The guidebook provided enlightenment.

"Oh, that plant we couldn't identify," I exclaimed, "it's Hottentot fig!"

"Hot and cold food?" queried Chris, not really paying attention.

"Hottentot fig! Do you need a hearing aid?"

"No, a toilet!"

A little further on I found another strange looking plant with very distinctive leaves, I had never seen it before and asked Chris if she knew what it was.

"Cannabis."

"!"

"How do you know that?"

"Because it has very characteristic leaves."

Kilcobben Cove is now the home of the lifeboat that was once stationed in the old lifeboat house on the southern tip of The Lizard. The decision to move it was a common sense one, Kilcobben Cove being much more sheltered. We took a short break there, sitting on a conveniently placed bench, looking down into the cove below.

Like many benches we had sat on (or sprawled on) during our walk, this one was dedicated to someone's memory. Most of the benches bore epitaphs of the "this was a place they loved" ilk, but the inscription on this particular bench was refreshingly different and we both appreciated the humour as we read "in memory of (a man's name and a date) he always was in trouble."

Memorial benches were a nice way of commemorating someone's passing; we discussed what we would like inscribing on ours.

"Yours should read 'she was always bad tempered'!" laughed Chris.

"Thanks very much! After all I've done for you! Trudging the streets of Penzance for your milk, and all you could say was 'your feet stink'. And who's carrying both the parcels this morning, may I ask?" I whinged.

"Oh, God, she's off again!" muttered Chris with mock exasperation.

Before reaching Cadgwith (and toilets!) we skirted the edge of the Devil's Frying Pan, another collapsed sea cave. We stopped for a quick photo before hurrying on, following the path between gardens and down into Cadgwith. Our plan was to post the parcels and then visit the toilets.

Cadgwith is yet another lovely, mostly unspoilt, little fishing village. And it has everything one would expect of such: thatched cottages with colourful hanging baskets, narrow winding streets, lobster pots, fishermen in yellow waders and woolly hats, a tiny sheltered cove with fishing boats drawn up on the shingle. The one thing it did not have was a post office! It used to have one (hence the "PO" marked on our out of date map) but it had closed. Oh well, I guess I would be carrying the parcels for the rest of the day; I just hoped that the post office at Coverack was still open!

Walking through the little village we came across a tea room in what had once been an old pilchard cellar. No discussion was needed. Chris zoomed off in the direction of the ladies, while I settled down at a table to study the menu. A few minutes later and looking considerably happier, Chris reappeared closely followed by a waitress.

"Hello!" she greeted us. "We have fresh scones straight from the oven and freshly cooked donuts. What can I get you?"

We could smell the baking and it smelt delicious. We both opted for donuts, strawberry jam and clotted cream, washed down by hot chocolate with whipped cream on top. Those donuts were every bit as good as they smelt. Ah, memories are made of this!

The path from Cadgwith climbed to the cliff tops and we followed it as it wound in and out and up and down, hugging the jagged coastline and dipping down to sea level. Kennack Sands is a popular beach with holiday makers from the nearby caravan sites. The clearing skies, promising a warm and sunny afternoon, were drawing the happy campers down onto the beach. Of more interest to us, was the geology at the southern end of the beach where gneiss, talc, gabro, serpentine and even asbestos is all visible.

The worst part of the path that day wasn't the slippery serpentine stiles that seemed to be modelled more on cattle grids than conventional stiles, (one slip and you could break your ankle!) but a few metres of path before the promontory at Lankidden. The path skirted a fenced garden, dropping steeply to cross a stream. At the point where the path descended was a smooth slab of bare rock, the gradient was too steep to walk down and there was nothing to hold on to. Even with walking poles, we would struggle to get down; in fact my walking pole would probably be more of a hindrance. Some serious assessment was called for. So we sat down at the top of the rock and ate some chocolate. In the end, we went down the only way possible – on our backsides.

We were now heading east but at Black Head the path turned north and views towards Falmouth opened up. It seemed like a good point to have a little break and a biscuit or three. As we shrugged back into our rucksacks, I checked the time.

"Three o'clock. That gives us two hours to reach the post office at Coverack before it closes."

I adjusted my rucksack, checked my pedometer and put on my cap. Then I looked round for Chris. She had disappeared! There was nowhere she could have gone. Mine shafts sprang to mind, but there were none around here. She must have set off whilst I was checking our mileage, so I set off along the path and climbed a stile. From my vantage point at the top of the stile I had a good view of the path winding between banks of bramble, and there, about fifty yards in front of me was Chris.

I scrambled off the stile and hurried on to catch up with her. Why was she going so quickly? She was almost jogging!

"Wait up!" I gasped staggering along under the weight of my over-laden rucksack; those parcels seemed to be getting heavier by the second. Was this how the Marines felt when they were on exercise on Dartmoor?

Hearing my pounding feet and ragged breathing, Chris turned and waited for me.

"What's the sudden rush?" I asked.

"You said we only had two hours, I thought you were hinting for me to speed up."

"No, we should be okay for time, there's only a couple of miles to go," I replied. "I've never seen you move so fast; your little legs were a blur – you looked like Benny Hill on fast forward!"

After that we resumed our normal, leisurely pace. Thank goodness.

When we were not hiking to a post office we were walking for the pleasure, a chance to take in the scenery, to see areas of Cornwall you would not see in a car – except perhaps as a passing blur at fifty miles an hour. Walking was a means of escape if you like, the opportunity to interact with a Britain that had changed little in hundreds of years; we had literally walked away from suburbia: the dirt, the noise, the rush of modern living. When we did encounter civilisation it was but a short walk back into Cornwall's natural retreat.

Many of the people walking the coast path were, like us, escaping a nine to five routine in a town. The physical exertion a recharging of mental batteries, just being there was an opportunity to experience nature without intruding on it. Not everyone walking around Cornwall though was intent on taking in the scenery. Several individuals marched along, heads down, their eyes never wavering from the path at their feet. Were they perhaps researching a Ph.D. in gravel path construction? Alternatively could they be inordinately proud of their new state of the art footwear? Whatever their interest, they all had one common denominator – their speed.

A back packer sped by us like a thirty tonne truck, sweeping us along in his slipstream. Tornadoes of dust rose from the path and vegetation danced in the air currents as he passed. Walking for walking's sake. Would he get home and boast of the distance he had covered in a limited time span? Would he be able to recall visions of his route? Would he have enjoyed it? The honest answer to all three might well be "yes"; but by charging head down around Cornwall he was missing so much.

One thing he could not have failed to miss was the smell that assaulted our nostrils at Chynhalls Cliff. We could smell the pig farm there long before we reached it. According to our map and guidebook, the path crossed the yard. Except that it didn't! Someone had been moving a few signposts! Thanks to that someone we wandered around, exposed to the foul smell for longer than necessary, trying to pick out the correct route. Emerging from some bushes completely confused we took a wrong turning and followed a path for a few hundred yards before realising our mistake and retracing our steps. When we did find the correct route we were faced with 'Private Property' signs. What a walker-friendly place this was turning out to be!

We arrived in Coverack with time to spare, the post office was open and I was finally able to rid my rucksack of the parcels. Once free of the parcels I turned my attention to other things, namely ice cream. The guidebook recommended the ice cream makers at Coverack, whose emblem was a dancing cow. So at the sign of the dancing cow, us two silly ones headed for the shop. We too, can recommend the ice cream! I wonder if they do mail order?

Coverack, lying on the eastern side of The Lizard peninsular, is quite remote and remains relatively unspoilt. It is nearer to France than it is to Bristol and because of its secluded location has been the base for much smuggling activity over the centuries. Locals would row the one hundred miles to France before returning with their illegal cargoes of silk, tobacco and brandy. Would it not have been easier to sail? Surely they could have afforded to stick a sail in their boats!

A public house stood at the southern end of the harbour and thatched cottages lined the sea wall. The general store was a hotch potch of food, ironmongery and haberdashery; it took us ten minutes to find a pint of milk in the tiny, overstocked interior. Seed potatoes shared a shelf with biscuits and writing paper. I am sure that had we searched long enough we would have uncovered tallow candles and first editions of The Beano on the cluttered shelves. The shop also seemed to act as the local estate agent, yellowing notices pinned in cobweb trimmed display cabinets outside the shop advertised farms, cottages and fishing boats for sail.

We found our B&B near the path and yes, it was an old cottage and yes, it did have beams but no, we did not enjoy our stay there. We very quickly dubbed it Cobweb Cottage. The only new, clean item was the tall front gate; so new in fact that it had not been treated and did not even have a latch. It was fastened shut with a loop of string that was at the top of the gate and beyond Chris's reach. We walked up the garden path, full of anticipation of a nice pot of tea, a comfortable room and a relaxing bath.

What we got was another eccentric but welcoming landlady and a great deal of confusion over our rooms. She had two other guests staying, but only room for three guests in total. She had been unable to persuade the other guests to leave, despite the fact that we had pre-booked our accommodation there. Would one of us mind having the tiny bedroom? With a distinct lack of alternative accommodation in the village, we had little choice but to agree.

She showed us upstairs and ushered Chris into the tiny bedroom, there was only just room in there for the bed which, as Chris was to find out to her cost, was hard, lumpy and impossible to sleep in. My room was a little bit bigger. It contained a creaky old bed, a chair that had a bad case of woodworm, a rickety chest of drawers and a prehistoric dressing table with a pitted mirror behind it. Arranged on the dressing table were tea making facilities and a kettle. We later examined the kettle, it was an electrician's nightmare; the flex had been extended by joining it to a longer length of flex with a piece of insulation tape, this then snaked across the floor, under the bed and to the only socket in the room on the far wall. The tea bags turned out to be even worse than ones on the previous night and the teapot contained so much tannin that it really needed a re-bore. A surprisingly modern television sat in one of the deep window recesses and a scrawled note on top, written on the back of a torn up Christmas card, warned guests not to open the window behind it. I wondered why, would the window pane fall out?

Everything in the house was covered in a thick layer of dust and the carpet in Chris's bedroom was thick with hair.

The bathroom was larger than both our bedrooms combined and contained another ancient dressing table, a shower cubicle with no door that stood clear of the wall at an angle, an old enamel bath (complete with stains) and a toilet with a seat that had surely been on the original privy in the back garden! The cork tiled floor was uneven and sloped violently to the right, so much so that on walking across the floor I actually staggered sideways. The wooden door did not fit in the frame and even when shut it was still possible to see into the bathroom.

The landlady demonstrated how to operate the shower but when she failed to make any mention of the bath, Chris, in desperation, was forced to ask if we were allowed a bath.

"Well, I have no objection to you having a bath but the cold water tap doesn't work. All the hot water comes from the Aga, so it would be too hot," explained the landlady. Seeing our disappointment she added, "But it is a very good shower!"

She went back downstairs leaving us to unpack. I tentatively switched on the kettle and Chris carried her rucksack into her room, then carried it back into my room.

"Do you mind if I leave this in here?" she asked.

"'Course not, your room is a bit small."

"It's not that, I just don't want to put it on the floor."

"Hmm, it's not what you might call clean, is it?" I replied. "Who are these other guests who don't want to leave? Escaped lunatics?"

I flopped down on the bed, leaving Chris to pour the tea, and rested my chin on my arms. I could smell something unpleasant, yet vaguely familiar but I couldn't quite identify it. Was it coming from the room? The bed?

"Have you stepped in something?" I asked Chris as I began examining my boots.

"No."

Then I realised what it was. Pig muck! My arm smelt of pig muck!

"It's pig muck. I must have brushed against some bushes near that pig farm. Do they spray it on the fields?"

We both spent the next few minutes sniffing ourselves, our clothes, our boots and our rucksacks. Everything smelt of pig muck. How delightful!

We took our turns in the shower and came out smelling fresher if somewhat dizzy. It is not easy taking a shower in a cubicle that slopes dangerously to one side and with only a flimsy curtain instead of the usual door!

The meal we had that evening in the local pasta restaurant was superb. Garlic mushrooms in a rich creamy sauce with an endless supply of crusty bread was followed by lemon chicken pasta and then, tempted by the desserts, Chris had chocolate mousse while I had treacle tart and clotted cream. And whilst Chris indulged in a glass of wine I drank the best apple juice I have ever tasted, it came as no surprise to learn it was another product of the local ice cream makers.

We could barely walk after such a splendid feast and strolled back along the sea front to our B&B. I entered the door first, to be greeted by a sight that threatened to bring my meal rushing back. Backlit by a lamp, the landlady was stood in the hallway, chatting into the telephone, dressed only in a very thin, transparent nightie. I quickly averted my gaze but too late to avoid seeing more than I wanted to. Cutting short her conversation, she disconnected and began asking if we had had a nice meal. I mumbled that we had, all the time looking in any direction except at the landlady.

"Where did you go?" she enquired.

"The pasta restaurant," replied Chris, unable to see as I was blocking her view, and wondering why I was suddenly acting so strangely.

"Oh yes. It's very good; a lot of my guests eat there. Well, if you'll excuse me I'm going back upstairs to David Attenborough. He's wonderful isn't he?"

She began climbing the uneven stairs treating Chris to the sight I was still trying to forget.

Chris did not sleep at all that night and was frequently heard to mention granite pillows when later describing our experiences in that B&B to friends and colleagues. I spent some time trying to get to sleep, my rucksack had made my shoulders ache and I tossed and turned trying to find a comfortable position. The return of the other guests and the sound of their ablutions in the adjoining bedroom disturbed me. Water gushed from a tap and air trapped in the pipe banged and echoed through the plumbing, a loose sink knocked against the wall.

All went quiet eventually and I breathed a premature sigh of relief. Then heavy footsteps thumped across the floor and the music of the pipes began again. Someone began gargling. Then there came the sound of a glass being filled and then I heard a plop, clink that sounded very much like someone putting their dentures in a glass of water!

Thursday 15th July

I had been awake for some time when my bedroom door creaked open and Chris shuffled in. Her hair was tussled and the dark circles under her eyes suggested she had either not slept or had been involved in a punch up. Her first words confirmed it was the former.

"That bed kept me awake all night, it was like lying on a rock. For the last eight hours I've listened to the sea washing up on the beach. I'm tired, I ache all over, the floor's filthy and I want a bath. What will we do if tonight's B&B is as bad? I can't stay in another grotty place. I want a bath, what if there's no bath?"

I had been thinking pretty much the same. The accommodation for our stay at Helford was on a farm, some way inland from Helford itself. The arrangement was that we would telephone the landlady when we arrived at Helford, where she would meet us and then drive us to the farmhouse. If, having been taxied to the farm we found it was dirty and substandard, what could we do? We would be miles from anywhere! We had put up with two unpleasant places; a third consecutive night of poor accommodation was more than we could tolerate.

"Well now we know why people who have stayed here told the lady at The Lizard guest house about the beams and the fireplace!" I said. "They were the only positive things they could find to say about this place."

"I wonder what the breakfast will be like?" mused Chris dejectedly as she handed me a cup of tea.

"Don't! Please don't! I dread to think."

We took it in turn to brave the gradients of the bathroom floor and have a shower. As I stood in the bathroom, arranging my towel and deodorant on the dressing table, a sudden movement on the front of my nightie caught my attention. Blurred and out of focus without my glasses on, the hairy spider seemed huge. Eeeck! I flapped crazily at my nightie until the spider dropped onto the floor and rolled away down the slope. I don't dislike spiders but I would rather not have one running up my nightie, especially when I'm still wearing it!

The dining room was as sparsely furnished as the rest of the cottage, but equally thickly endowed with dust. We seated ourselves at the only table in front of a begrimed window. My chair was too far from the table and so grasping the arms I tried to inch it closer but one of the arms lifted off in my hand. Chris tried to control her semi-hysterical laughter and I hastily fought to replace the arm before my vandalism was discovered.

Over breakfast the landlady chatted about Tourist Board inspectors, telling us of their last visit. It must have been many years ago or she would surely have been closed down! Most of the crockery was old and mismatched, which would have been quite acceptable had it been clean. It wasn't. The rim of the milk jug was stained orange. The cutlery was smeared and the pot of marmalade was encrusted with hardened lumps of orange peel. The cooked breakfast had a decidedly fishy flavour and the scrambled egg was crunchy. On the positive side the toast was hot.

The landlady was friendly enough but her hygiene standards left much to be desired. As she stood talking to us she kept bobbing into the kitchen to continue the washing up and would appear every few minutes with a plate or a cup which she would dry using a grey tea towel.

We could not wait to get out and into the sunshine. I had dreadful visions of nausea, stomach pains and worse as a result of the food we had just eaten. For the first mile I walked along trying to think of anything other than food. Fortunately there was plenty to attract my attention. The path ran along the low cliffs just feet above the beach until it reached Dean Quarries. The scrubby vegetation of pineapple plant, grasses and camomile were covered in fine dust from the quarry. The path actually skirted the outer workings of the quarry, passing under conveyor belts and beside huge vehicles before finally leaving the quarry boundaries.

Out to sea lie The Manacles, an infamous group of rocks that have been the cause of many shipwrecks. On that peaceful sunny morning in mid July, the waves lapped placidly against the rocks. At high tide however, the rocks are submerged and lie on the route into Falmouth; it was easy to see how, in rough weather, they had claimed so many vessels. A map in the pub at Coverack records twenty eight wrecks on the rocks between 1787 and 1915.

Once again the weather was cooler, although still fine and sunny, and walking was much more enjoyable. On earlier days I had been sweating so much that my clothes were stuck to me. Trench knickers had been as much a possibility as trench foot!

A plane appeared towing an advert. Then helicopters were crowding the skies. Were we never to be free of them? Three appeared in formation over Falmouth Bay. The whirring of their rotors becoming louder as they drew nearer. It was like a scene from M.A.S.H.

From Leggan Point the South West Coast Path became a bit of a paradox. It ceased to follow the coast and headed inland for quite a distance before returning to the coast some miles to the north. The inland route followed fields and hedge bound country lanes. It was pleasant walking and an enjoyable variation after so many miles of cliff-hugging paths. We discovered hidden farmhouses, delightful cottages and the odd eye-sore.

As I was quick to note on the first part of the walk last year, the majority of the junk in the countryside seems to be generated by farmers. As we were leaning on a five bar gate gazing down at one farmhouse, I wondered why farmyards always looked so scruffy! This dwelling would never find its way onto the front of a box of clotted cream fudge. A mountain of old tyres rose against the wall of an out building, a muck spreader festered outside a barn, the stripped carcass of a decaying Ford Anglia rotted in a mass of nettles and in an adjoining field an ancient caravan with greying curtains at the windows and moss on the roof sagged on four piles of bricks. I could imagine the smell inside – damp, mildew and old socks – a bit like my rucksack really.

"Why do all farms have a clapped out caravan stuck in the corner of a field?" I pondered.

"So that they can fleece an unsuspecting holiday maker into booking a fortnights holiday in it!" replied Chris. (The bitter voice of experience?)

At Porthoustock we had a choice – official route or unofficial route. The sign post on the unofficial route indicated that it was a permissive path. Just what is a permissive path I wondered? Something, I think, to do with it not being a right of way but there by the permission of the land owner.

Chris had a strange encounter once on a permissive path. She was working as a Countryside Ranger at a local Country Park at the time and one of her duties was early morning litter picking. So there she was, early one morning, walking along looking for litter. What she found was slightly more than she bargained for.

With litter picker in one hand and rubbish bag in the other, she rounded a corner of the path and almost fell over the recumbent forms of two lovers, trousers at half mast and white buttocks shining in the early morning sunlight.

A lesser woman might have tried to exit the scene quietly and pretend never to have noticed the lovers; (that's what I would have done anyway). But what if a family with young children had been walking along the path instead of Chris? Fired with righteous indignation and not sparing any time to consider how to phrase a reprimand, she stood her ground and rebuked: "Excuse me! This is a permissive path you know!"

Quite!

We chose the official route, not for fear of what we might meet on the alternative but because the official route would carry us past a vineyard and, according to a leaflet we had seen, the vineyard offered free tastings. We weren't solely interested in free samples, you understand, we were hoping to buy refreshments as well.

But it began to look as if we were not even going to find the vineyard. The path skirted around it but although we saw orchards and the roof of a building, we could not find the entrance. With a hedge on one side and a barbed wire fence on the other, we squeezed along a very narrow path, climbed a stile and were suddenly in a herb garden. The door of a nearby barn stood open and inside were displayed a collection of cider presses dating back over the centuries.

We had found the vineyard. And for the first time during our walk an attraction we wished to visit was actually open! We admired the herbs, read the blurb about the presses, chatted to the owner and sampled the samples. Then we left without buying anything. I know that sounds tight-fisted but we could hardly carry our rucksacks, never mind bottles of cider, apple juice, wine, cherry brandy and sloe gin! The hoped for refreshments were not available, there was no café or tea room attached to the vineyard.

We descended the hill into the quiet coastal village of Porthallow, passing a sign for an award winning tea room. Refreshments! Bread and butter pudding for Chris and a mountain of meringues, fresh raspberries and clotted cream for me. The owner of the tea room was keen to know where we were staying that night, and when I told her it was on a farm near Manaccan she immediately named the farmer's wife, explaining they were friends; further highlighting how close knit and isolated that rural area of Cornwall was – everyone seemed to know everyone else. Perhaps the farmer's wife would have the same high standards as her friend the tea room owner! We could but hope.

Porthallow was where the coast path rejoined the coast and we crossed the beach, pausing to watch a thatcher at work, before climbing through bracken to the cliff top fields. After five cups of tea at the tea room I was in dire need of a toilet stop but there were no public conveniences and I would have been all too visible from the air! I would just have to wait.

The field we were walking through was huge, perhaps not huge compared to the scale of American prairies, or even East Anglian wheat fields, but for Cornwall it was big. And it offered nothing in the way of concealment for someone with a full bladder. In the middle stood a lone telegraph pole. We had entered by a stile and in the normal course of events we would leave by one. I say this because what followed was the most terrifying experience of the walk. We were almost half way across the field when we spotted a herd of cattle, bullocks to you, in an adjoining field. At about the same time, they spotted us. Then we discovered that a gate into their field was open, wide open – and the bullocks knew it! How fast can bullocks run? We found out. One minute they were in the other field, the next minute they were stampeding towards us, fast. It was like something out of a Western: the Indians charging down on the hapless wagon train, I kept expecting Jimmy Stewart to appear and order us to form a circle.

The bullocks skidded to a halt ten feet from us. We tried our best to form a circle and look brave and unintimidated – not easy when there are only two of you! At one point I remember being back to back with Chris and clinging to a strap of her rucksack, but that was no good though as I had my back to the animals.

We whispered "shoo" and "go away" and flapped our arms ineffectually. Could we climb the telegraph pole? To do what? Spend the next day and night waiting for a farmer to come and rescue us? Use our mobile phones to ring for the coast guard? Chris had a thing about the TV programme "999", we would be the first people to re-enact a RAF helicopter rescue from the top of a telegraph pole in the middle of a field! That was it! We could flag down a helicopter! But just like buses, there's never one about when you need one.

We tried inching sideways towards the stile just visible in the distance. The bullocks inched sideways too. One moved a step nearer.

We were face to face with approximately thirty bullocks, not cute little things but big, beefy things: walking, snorting sirloin. If they decided to rub shoulders with us, we would be the ones with the crushed toes and the cracked ribs. We could think of two people at work who had both come off the worst against some cattle; one, a student, had received a broken arm.

"That one's a nice colour," I said faintly. Fear causes you to do and say the daftest things doesn't it?

"Don't you run off and leave me on my own!" ordered Chris, clutching hold of my sleeve.

"I won't!" I replied, deeply offended that she could even think I would. Had I wanted to I doubt if my legs would have moved.

The bullocks were getting restless at all this talking and no action, they started swaying and pawing the ground.

In a tone of voice I've never heard her use before, and doing a fair impression of a boy soprano Chris squeaked "Shoo!" and slapped a hand against the guidebook. Whether it was the high pitched voice or the sound of skin on paper we will never know. One bullock shied at the noise, frightening the rest and the next moment the entire herd were stampeding for the safety of the gateway. We stood watching their departing bums, tails swinging madly in their haste to escape the Aled Jones sound-a-like.

"Right, come on, let's go and find you a toilet!" said Chris with relief.

"I don't need one anymore!"

Before reaching the Helford River we had to cross Gillan Creek, a muddy tidal estuary that, in the guidebook at least, did not appear too intimidating. If the tide was in we could catch a water taxi. If the tide was out we could use the stepping stones. The tide was midway between in and out. We could not find the water taxi and the stepping stones were partly submerged.

As we stood pondering our next move, two German girls marched past us and headed down some steps onto the mudflats. We watched as they shed boots and socks and proceeded to wade across the creek, slipping and sliding, the sticky mud pulling at their feet with every step. They finally made it to the far side of the creek, each now sporting a pair of black, mud socks that reached almost to their knees.

Chris and I looked at one another, then at the Germans (who were now attempting to wipe the mud from their feet and legs with bits of grass), then at the muddy creek, then at the map. Then we turned and headed away from the river, taking the two mile diversion that would lead us to a bridge over the stream further inland. An extra two miles was preferable to a possible mud bath!

Judging by the nettles spilling out over the path at one point on the diversion, we were amongst the minority of walkers who chose the inland route. We walked up a winding lane, passing quaint cottages, their gardens colourful with flowers, the heavy massed heads of blue hydrangeas, the purple horns of buddleiah and the bright orange blossoms of monbretia. Then following the footpath sign we clambered over a stile and walked through fields to join another lane that eventually crossed the stream and ran down the far bank of the river towards Dennis Head. Our diversionary route added two miles and one hour to our walk but it was an enjoyable alternative. Walking along the road we watched wading birds feeding on the mud flats, and listened to the cry of the curlews and oyster catchers.

We left the road by the church of St. Anthony in Meneage, stopping in the church yard to have some chocolate and a drink. The church is thought to stand on one of the earliest Christian sites in Cornwall. Like so many country churches, this one was open, but we could not go in; scaffolding ringed the building and the sound of a stone mason at work echoed from inside.

Regretfully leaving the church unexplored, we crossed the road and entered a field, climbing the gentle slopes to emerge on Dennis Head. Directly in front of us was the mouth of the Helford River where yachts lay at anchor. Across the water of Falmouth Bay a panorama of inlets and coastline beyond Pendennis Point and Carrick Roads stretched to the horizon. The port of Falmouth embraced Pendennis Point. After thirteen days of walking we could see our goal, one more day and we would have succeeded.

169

We lingered for a while admiring the view before Chris spotted some birds on the rocks below us. The waves lapped over the rocks and some of the birds hopped into the sea as others waddled further up the seaweed covered rocks. We were too far away to distinguish the species; they were dark and seemed rather comical, could they be puffins?

I quickly freed the binoculars from the case on my belt and fumbled to focus them on the rocky shore, thankful once again that I had decided to bring them. When mum had offered to lend us her binoculars I readily agreed, although they were likely to be one of those items you take on holiday and never use. They were a small lightweight pair and with them fastened to my belt it would have been a pity not to have them with us just in case. And with them so easily accessible we had in fact used them quite a bit. But how many people, I wonder, often struggle to adjust binoculars properly?

Still unable to identify the birds, I handed the binoculars to Chris who began hurriedly trying to locate the mystery birds through the lenses.

"Can you tell what they are?" I asked, still watching the antics of the birds.

"No. I can't even see them!"

"I think you'll find the magnifying properties can best be appreciated if you turn them round and look through the other end!" I advised, staring at her in disbelief.

Even looking through the correct end of the binoculars we were still unable to identify the birds. After some consideration we decided they were more likely to be razorbills than puffins.

With the binoculars, Falmouth seemed very near indeed. It was amazing to think we were almost there. Before journey's end, however, was the prospect of the farmhouse at Manaccan. What awaited us there?

"What are we going to do if it's filthy like last night?" asked Chris.

"Realistically, how bad can it be?" I replied.

"Awful!"

I had to admit Chris was right. I am often told that I am a pessimist and it is probably true but I work on the principle that pessimists are rarely disappointed – a bit of reverse psychology on Julia's Law! So when Chris began muttering about dirty accommodation and no baths, I decided that if we imagined the worst possible scenario, reality might not be too bad. We walked along trying to imagine the most terrible things possible and soon our accommodation was beginning to sound similar to Jamaica Inn, all it lacked was a smuggler!

"Cobwebs festooned across the doorway," I suggested.

"Earth floors and scattered straw everywhere!" responded Chris.

"Broken windows, hanging in their frames."

170

"Chickens running round the kitchen and roosting in sagging armchairs."

"Damp, mildewed walls and peeling wall paper revealed in the dim glow cast by a paraffin lantern swinging from the ceiling!"

"The stench of tom cats and wet dog."

"The farmer's wife will have BO, bad breath and greasy hair."

"Don't forget the cigarette end dangling from her lips, ash dropping into the frying pan and overflowing ashtrays everywhere!"

"Will they even bother with ashtrays?" I queried.

"We'll be given a tiny room under the eaves, with a hole in the ceiling where it rains in and the view from the window will overlook the pig sty," groaned Chris becoming almost suicidal.

"The beds will be made of rusty cast iron and the thin, greasy mattresses will be full of ticks and fleas!"

"Oh, shut up, shut up!"

I shut up. The drawback with my philosophy on pessimism is that you tend to have a rotten time waiting for the outcome!

The path along the south bank of the Helford River ran through woodland and into secluded coves harbouring small (and not so small) yachts and dinghies. It was all very Swallows and Amazons-ish. One of the tributaries of the Helford River is Frenchman's Creek, the second Daphne du Maurier connection of the day. In the past the river has been the haunt of pirates and smugglers, and oysters have been harvested from the river since before the Roman invasion.

In one cove a game of football was in progress, the players coming from somewhere like Henley-on-Thames judging by their accents.

"To me Alex!"

"Oh good shot Peter!"

Richard's, Peter's, Alex's and Laura's. No Gary's, Steve's or Sharon's. I wondered if they found Mount's Bay as dead as the couple at Zennor had?

I had opened my mouth and put my foot in it before I saw one of their party sitting within earshot. Oops, too late! Chris cringed with embarrassment and hurried on. I turned bright red and hurried after her.

Walking through the trees we saw occasional glimpses of the river before the path twisted or dipped and our view was obscured. At one point I paused, leaning my hand against a tree trunk. The path dropped away to my left, Chris was twenty yards ahead and unaware that I had halted. I made a conscious decision to remember as much of that cameo moment as I could, and now, although time has cast its veiled curtain over some parts of the walk, I can recall every detail of those minutes quite clearly. The deep furrows of the trunk and the texture of the rough bark under my palm. The buzz of insects and rustle of leaves, the snap of a twig under Chris's boot as she continued down the path. The view through the mosaic of leaves to the blue water and the sound of rigging striking the masts of the boats as they moved with the rising tide. The brown skin on the back of my hand accentuated by the paler band of skin exposed where my signet ring had slipped around my finger. The dull ache across my shoulders and the weight of the rucksack on my back. The sun-dappled ground and the patchwork of shadows cast by the moving canopy of leaves. The scent of the hot dusty earth under my feet and the sharp odour of the dying wild garlic. The exposed, gnarled roots straddling the path as it sloped away to my left and the beetle scurrying over the earth near my boot.

Chris was out of sight and it was time to move on. Very soon we came to Helford: a small collection of typical Cornish cottages lining a narrow lane running down to the ferry point on the banks of the river. It is very picturesque and popular with tourists and sailors alike, for the broad river provides safe anchorage for the expensive yachts of the holiday makers and the less expensive rowing boats and dinghies of the locals. Accommodation seems to be none existent in the village and facilities are limited to a post office and a pub. Tourists arriving in cars, as opposed to boats, are required to park in the large car park at the entrance to the village.

The path skirted behind a fence at the rear of the car park and it was almost impossible to wander off the path at that point due to the high bank on our left. A large bay horse stood blocking the path half way along. Cropping the grass he ignored our approach and refused to move when we reached him.

"You're good with animals," said Chris, looking nervous, "get him to move!"

"Walk on!" I ordered.

"Not while he's there!"

"Not you! I was talking to the horse."

But the horse pretended he hadn't heard.

"Here you are, some nice grass!" I said, picking a handful and offering it to him.

He feigned indifference. I put a hand to his shoulder and pushed. Nothing happened. I put a hand to his rump and heaved. Something happened! He turned his head, reached around and grabbed hold of the walking pole that was hanging from my rucksack. He determinedly chomped away at my pole, saliva running in strands all down the shiny blue metal and chips of paint flaking off. Chris found all this highly amusing and was still laughing as she scrambled up the bank on all fours and skirted around the horse before rejoining the path further on. Meanwhile I was left to rescue my pole and duck under the horse's neck to continue along the path. In over three hundred miles, that horse was the only thing that got the better of my walking pole!

Reaching the post office we saw a sign illustrating a dancing cow: ice cream! Half an hour and two ice creams later we decided we were ready to face our fate, well actually we weren't ready but we had little choice, and so we telephoned the landlady of the farmhouse. We waited in the car park for her arrival, dreading what the next few minutes would reveal. After ten minutes, a battered old Peugeot estate car shot into the car park, slewed across the gravel and screeched to a halt next to us.

A woman in her mid thirties jumped out, threw open the boot and told us to dump our rucksacks in. Asking how our walk had been and telling us that she did this all the time for walkers, she ushered us into the car and set off out of the car park to a wail of tyres and scattering of gravel. What followed was possibly the most frightening ten minutes of my life. We hurtled along narrow country lanes, zooming round blind bends with barely a break in speed; the only concession the driver made to the possibility of other vehicles was a heavy and prolonged leaning on the horn at the approach to any sharp bends, of which there were plenty! Outside the car gravel and straw from the recent passage of a farm tractor were thrown up against the bodywork. Inside the car, Chris and I were thrown from side to side and against the restraining safety belts, desperately clinging on to door handles and the edges of our seats. The driver, who was not belted in, seemed oblivious to the violent motion of the car and chatted happily throughout the journey.

We arrived at the farm in a very nervous state and shakily climbed out of the car. First impressions seemed hopeful. The farmyard was immaculate; there was not even a wisp of straw out of place! But the inside of the car had been filthy; what if the house was the same? On one side of the yard stood a large open barn, on the other side was a long modern bungalow and at the top of the yard sat an old white-washed farmhouse. It was peaceful, no dogs barked, no cows mooed and no donkeys brayed. I felt hope growing inside me. Then a chicken appeared.

The landlady spotted the chicken in the garden of the bungalow and began chasing it. Oh no! Was this to be our evening meal? Was she about to wring its neck in front of us, before plucking and dressing it? The chicken squawked, the landlady clucked and what followed was pure slapstick.

The chicken ran around the garden and over flowerbeds, the landlady chasing it, making clucking noises and clapping her hands. Chris and I watched with growing amusement. Would the chicken be caught? Would the landlady have a coronary? Would there be anything left in the garden by the time one pair of feet and one pair of claws had chased one another for ten minutes?

Breathing heavily, the landlady finally succeeded in shooing the chicken out of the gate and into the yard. "She scratches up my plants!" she explained, gasping for breath as she led us into the bungalow.

We followed her down a short hall, on one side was a kitchen and on the other a large dining room and combined lounge; turning right she walked down a corridor stretching the length of the bungalow, passing a bathroom before reaching our bedroom.

"That's your private bathroom," she indicated. "I'll make a pot of tea and leave it in the lounge for you. I won't give you anything to eat though because I'll be serving your evening meal in an hour if that's convenient."

We thanked her and she left us standing in an immaculate twin-bedded room. Her driving might have been scary but her house keeping was beyond reproach. All that day we had been dreading what we might find, but the accommodation was wonderful and we were delirious with relief.

The pot of tea refreshed us, the deep warm bath relaxed us and the enormous three course evening meal of soup, cold meat salad and banana split filled us. The landlady offered to run us to the pub and pick us up later in the evening but we were content with a gentle stroll along the lane to a post box that we had passed as a blur of red on our ride to the farm.

Returning from posting a card to Chris's Mum we went into the lounge, where we were sipping cups of tea when two more guests arrived. Like us they were walkers and had been collected from Helford by the landlady.

Lying in the comfortable beds that night we quickly fell asleep. I awoke in the middle of the night with a full bladder. It was pitch dark; no light came from outside and there were no subdued night lights to guide the visitor to the bathroom. I was reluctant to fumble my way to the toilet in the dark, fearful of making a noise and waking everyone. But could I wait until morning? That was doubtful, I might be forced to make an emergency trip before then and for me, full bladder equals total loss of concentration. In short, putting it off could be disastrous.

I laid in bed wondering what to do and heard Chris moving in her bed.

"You awake?" I whispered.

"Yes."

"I need to go to the loo."

"Oh no, you'll wake the entire household. I know what you're like."

"I know, but I've got to go."

I began groping my way to the door then out onto the dark corridor. Chris's voice drifted out to me: "Don't forget the first door is the airing cupboard!"

I reached the second door and opened it. A piercing shriek filled the corridor. What had I done? I panicked. Had I stumbled into the little girl's bedroom, or perhaps worse still, her parents? But the shriek was not human. The door handle needed oiling.

Mission accomplished I retraced my steps. The noise of the door handle now barely audible, drowned out by the sounds of the flushing toilet and the gurgling pipes. Whilst the household was still awake, Chris decided she too could use the bathroom and so the whole process was repeated, with the added fun of Chris feeling her way around my bed to the door and nearly yanking my foot off as she collided with my bed.

As dawn brightened the room I was woken by a thud. I raised myself onto one elbow and peered around the room trying to locate the source of the noise. I was just in time to see a fluffy black tail passing the foot of my bed and disappearing through the partly open bedroom door. Just like a cartoon skunk! But it was no skunk, it was the family cat and a few seconds later it was back, meowing noisily. Getting up I picked up the cat and carried it to the open window, no doubt where it had got in, and put it back out. But I had not expected it to be so heavy, it was a much larger cat than any of mine, and I almost overbalanced onto Chris's bed as I struggled to lift the squirming animal onto the windowsill. Chris slept through that bit of nocturnal excitement but we were both woken some time later by a cockerel crowing lustily. Well, you can't expect total peace when you stay on a farm, can you?

Friday 16th July

We were looking forward to breakfast that morning, if it was half as good as the evening meal had been, then we were in for a treat. We were not disappointed! The dining table was placed under the window and we munched our way through cereal, watching the chicken scratching up the flower beds.

The other guests arrived fifteen minutes late for breakfast. Seating himself at the other end of the table, the man barely answered our cheery good morning. His wife ignored us completely. This was even more embarrassing than breakfast at Braunton the previous year; at least there had been a bit of conversation on that occasion. She refused cereal and ate only a small piece of potato from her cooked breakfast before pushing the plate aside. Then, reaching across the table, her sleeve nearly dipping into Chris's cup of tea, she snatched a piece of toast from our toast rack and began munching on it.

Exchanging 'can you believe it?' glances, Chris and I continued chatting to each other as normal. The other guests spoke to one another in whispers, utterly ridiculous and extremely rude when sharing a table.

The landlady came in to remove our empty and their full plates, rolling her eyes when she noticed the toast thief! Two minutes later she returned from the kitchen with a rack of steaming toast for the other guests, as she reached the table she removed a piece of toast and put it in our rack. The man noticed this and had the grace to blush slightly.

The late arrival to breakfast of the other guests had resulted in the landlady running behind schedule for taking her daughter to school in Manaccan. As she hurried in with yet more toast she offered us a lift if we could be ready in ten minutes. We gratefully accepted and I began hurrying to drink the last cup of tea. While I waited for the tea to cool I became increasingly tempted to recommend the B&Bs at Coverack and The Lizard to the other guests. They were walking the path in the opposite direction and from earlier conversation with the landlady we had discovered that they did not have pre-booked accommodation. They were so rude, not only to us but to the landlady, they deserved a couple of awful nights! I did not say anything, my nerve failed me; I wish it hadn't.

We were dropped off where we had been picked up the afternoon before, in the car park, and after sincere thanks to the landlady, strolled down the lane into Helford. A family of swans were standing just before the wooden footbridge over the creek that bisects the village. I stopped to admire the proud parents and their three grey cygnets.

"What about a photograph?" I asked Chris.

"I'll take one from this side!" she called back to me, scurrying over the footbridge.

I was about to say that the swans would appear too small photographed from across the creek, when one of the parents suddenly lunged at me hissing furiously. My legs were carrying me over the footbridge before my brain had time to register what was happening. I joined Chris on the other side of the creek where she was laughing.

"That's why I decided to take a photo from over here!" she grinned.

The ferry across the Helford River runs once an hour, we arrived with ten minutes to spare for the first ferry of the day. Fine drizzle began to fall as the boat came into view, weaving a course between the yachts moored in the river. We climbed down into the boat and began the slow journey across the river to Passage Cove, a crossing that has been undertaken here by travellers for over five hundred years.

On the north side of the river the weather was fine and the day soon brightened as the breeze chased the clouds away. We walked eastwards back towards the sea, sometimes through fields, sometimes along lanes, keeping close to the river and climbing to reach the top of low cliffs. We passed the boundary of Glendurgan Gardens, now owned by the National Trust and on the rising ground in front of us, silhouetted against the skyline stood a group of Monterey pines. Chris was enthralled by them.

"I've seen these growing in Monterey."

We stood under the towering pines, leaning back and gazing up into their branches.

Above Parson's Beach, where the Helford flowed into the sea, we turned to look back. Behind us was a beautiful view of the Helford River winding between wooded banks, the boats on the river now appearing as little colourful dots. Ahead was Falmouth, hidden from sight as yet. To the right the scrubby heath and bracken covered slopes fell away to low rocky cliffs with the sea beyond.

Chris was some way behind as I stopped to admire the view out to sea. But my attention immediately focused on the fox standing on the edge of the cliff some thirty feet away. I stood frozen, staring at him as he scanned the cliffs. Risking a look back the way I had come, I saw Chris appear around a bend in the path. Seeing my frantic gestures she hurried to reach me and together we watched the fox. The breeze carried our scent to him and he turned, looking directly at us. For seconds none of us moved, then he shook his head and moved unhurriedly away, remaining in view before hesitating on the edge of the cliff and finally disappearing down the steep slope.

Hedge bordered fields lined the path to Maenporth. The wild roses and brambles in the hedgerows were in flower. We were surprised to see some of the brambles were already producing ripening fruit and one patch bore fat, dark blackberries, two months earlier than we would have expected. The blackberries tasted delicious!

The sheltered sandy cove at Maenporth had a tea room at one end, a hotel in the middle and some public toilets and a snack van at the farther side. It was the most deserted beach we had found. We bought cups of tea and bars of chocolate at the snack van, sitting on picnic benches to consume them. I expect we were their only customers that day!

Near the entrance to the cove is the rusting wreck of a trawler that foundered during a gale in 1978. Further out in the bay was anchored the rusty hulk of a container ship that looked as if it should have sunk. It had been visible to us after rounding Rosemullion Head when we had a view of its port side. As we walked along the winding coastal path our view of the ship had changed until, leaving Maenporth, we looked across the water to the starboard side of the vessel. The ship didn't have a good side: it was ugly from all angles!

We skirted a golf course to Pennance Point where a monument commemorates the efforts of Falmouth's Home Guards. The wide track from there down towards Swanpool Beach was obviously popular with dog walkers. We reached the outskirts of Falmouth at Swanpool Beach, from there it was all road walking for the final few miles. The pool at Swanpool has had a mixed past, at one time it was the site of a silver and lead mine, swans were bred there and now the lake is a S.S.S.I. and nature reserve. According to the information board the rare trembling sea mat can be found here.

"What's a rare trembling sea mat?"

"I don't know but it sounds rather cute. Maybe it's a bit like a timid hamster, only flatter!"

Whatever it was, we didn't see one.

We walked along the pavement towards Pendennis Point, passing numerous posh hotels. Parked at the side of the road was an ice cream van, a board on the side of the van advertised a fantastic sounding concoction for only one pound. Tempted, I passed the guidebook to Chris and ordered an ice cream.

"Are you having anything?" I asked.

"No, I don't fancy an ice cream."

The double cornet came with two chocolate flakes, smothered with whipped cream and loaded with chocolate sauce. The ice cream seller had run out of chopped nuts and so had put extra chocolate sauce on.

As I struggled to put my purse back into my pocket, the whipped cream began to slip off the ice cream. I jerked my hand, attempting to counteract the sliding but only succeeded in making matters worse. The whipped cream and chocolate sauce were catapulted off the cornet and landed with a splat on Chris's arm, I was left holding a double cornet with two flakes and nothing else in a hand that was dripping with chocolate sauce. We both burst out laughing, and Chris began flicking whipped cream onto the pavement.

"I thought I told you I didn't want anything!" she scolded sarcastically.

The ice cream man stopped laughing long enough to hand us some kitchen towel to mop up the mess, then kindly offered to replenish the cream and sauce. Chris kept her distance as we walked along the pavement, with me licking frantically at the melting ice cream.

The walk around Pendennis Point was one and a half miles long, taking us in a loop to the docks at Falmouth only a few hundred yards from the beginning of the loop on the other side of the point. Pendennis Castle was built in the 1540's by order of Henry VIII and further defences were added by his daughter Elizabeth I. The castle was to become the last Royalist stronghold during the Civil War, withstanding a siege lasting five months. The Victorians added a barracks, which is now a Youth Hostel, and in this century the castle had been manned throughout both World Wars.

Crossing the road to get a better view of Zone Point Lighthouse across the water, we were almost run over by the tourist train, the Dotto, which runs tours around Pendennis Point and through Falmouth in the summer. Our close-shave did have one consolation, we overheard the commentary from the driver and learnt the lighthouse was the setting for the children's television programme Fraggle Rock.

Having climbed almost to the summit of Pendennis Point the road descended towards the town with grandstand views down into the busy docks. A huge tanker sat in the dry dock undergoing renovation work. It was difficult to appreciate the scale of the ship until we spotted a group of men standing under the hull; they were dwarfed by the immense size of the vessel.

We stood with our feet resting on the bottom railing of the fence and looked across the expanse of water to St. Mawes. Neither of us spoke for some time. That would be our starting point next year, if we decided to continue walking the South West Coast Path. Nothing was certain. At that time our plans for the following year were just dreams. We had lived one dream for the last fourteen days and counted ourselves fortunate to have reached our goal safely and without injury. The previous year I had set myself a challenge and completed it. This year the walk had been Chris's. After a year marred by her calf injury that was seemingly unwilling to heal, she had been determined to fulfil her ambition. For her the walk had been a watershed and, until she completed it, she had refused to take her fitness for granted.

Turning to Chris I grinned and said, "We've done it!"

"Not quite. We have to get to the Prince of Wales Quay."

The temperature seemed to drop as we walked into the bustling streets of Falmouth. The town is a busy working port as well as a holiday resort. The roads were crowded with cars, pedestrians thronged the pavements and the noise and the smell and the dirt were alien to us after so many days in the peaceful countryside. We used the public toilets at a harbour car park but they were horrible and smelly, just like the ones in Padstow. The toilets in towns seemed unable to cope with the high demand from tourists, unlike the ones we had found in quiet coves along the way where paper, soap and cleanliness were standard.

Outside the toilets was a Tourist Information notice board, detailing things to do, places to visit and urging the holiday makers to enjoy getting in touch with nature in Cornwall.

"Have you got in touch with nature, Chris?" I asked with mock seriousness.

"Yes, several times," she responded, "whenever there were no public toilets!"

We continued through the busy streets, passing shops selling food, books, souvenirs and outdoor clothing. In one shop window was a display of walking gear, including boots identical to my own.

"Look you can buy yourself some new boots," said Chris. One of mine had developed a split in the suede upper during the second week that had expanded to a hole one inch long.

"Those are ten pounds more expensive than the price I paid!" I exclaimed as I read the price tag. "I think, if I'm careful, these boots might just last out for another half mile!"

We continued pushing through the crowds until our attention was captured by the smell of Cornish pasties. By that time it was approaching four in the afternoon and we had eaten little all day. Ten minutes later we were sitting on a bench on the Prince of Wales Quay eating Cornish pasties and nectarines.

We had made it. Our walk was completed.

In ebullient mood, Chris got out her mobile phone and rang her daughter. There was no answer. She phoned her husband: no answer.

"I want to tell someone we've made it and no one's answering!"

She keyed in her Mum's number and eventually got an answer. As she chatted away I decided I would ring Roger. No answer! But my Mum was sure to be in and so I decided to phone her. I was just tapping in her phone number when the batteries ran out and my phone died. But, good friend that she is, Chris let me borrow her phone when she finished speaking to her Mum.

One thing remained to be done before we could set off to find our B&B – a photograph. We looked around for someone who looked capable of operating a camera but there wasn't anyone fitting that requirement, so we asked an eccentric looking middle aged couple if they would mind.

"Oh, I'm no good with cameras," said the man. "Ask my wife."

We did and she reluctantly took the camera from us. Leaning against the railing we posed for the photo. The woman dithered with the camera, first putting her fingers over the lens, then pushing the wrong button before she finally held the camera at a forty-five degree angle and took the photograph. Both of us expected the shot to look as if we were leaning into the wind but when we got the film developed it had come out surprisingly well.

We asked for directions to our B&B in the Tourist Information Centre and climbed a steep hill towards the residential area of Falmouth. The B&B was in a row of Victorian terraced houses, down a side street overlooking a playground. We had already decided that if this accommodation was of a poor standard then we would go elsewhere, there would be no shortage of alternative accommodation to choose from in Falmouth. We walked past the B&B, looking into the open doorway as we went by. From the outside it did not look too bad but then neither had cobweb cottage! Chris was not keen but I persuaded her to at least view the interior and against her better judgement we walked down the garden path and rang the door bell.

A young woman answered the door and led us inside and up the stairs. As soon as we entered the house I noticed the dirty carpets and began to regret ringing the bell. The landlady gave us a key, told us breakfast was at eight o'clock and left us standing in a bedroom at the front of the house. Walking into that room was like stepping from Oz into Kansas – monochrome – everything was grey. The dusty net curtains filtered dull light into the room. The cacophony of cries and screams from children in the playground bounced off the walls and reverberated around the room.

We stood looking around in despair at yet another awful guest house. Still wearing her rucksack Chris sank down onto one of the beds and an ominous twang of doom reverberated from one of the springs. What were we going to do? If we stayed neither of us would be happy but how could we leave now? What would we say? Why had I talked Chris into coming in?

"What do we do now?" she asked dejectedly.

"I don't know."

"Do you think we could find somewhere else to stay? There seems to be a lot of holiday makers in Falmouth!"

"I don't know. It might not be as easy as we thought."

"We've paid a deposit here."

"How much?" I asked.

"Ten pounds."

We were faced with a decision and neither of us could decide. Leave, loose our deposit and risk being unable to find alternative accommodation. Stay and be miserable.

I moved over to the sink and examined one of the minuscule grey towels hanging over a radiator. The towel had not started life grey, the fabric was plucked and thin in places, and worst of all there was something resembling dried snot sticking to it.

"That's it," I exclaimed, "we're leaving!"

"But how? We can't just walk out. I can't say anything, you'll have to!"

"You amaze me. You can chair meetings at work, stand up and talk in front of a room full of people, discipline people, do all that and more but you can't tell this landlady that the accommodation we are paying for is crap!"

"Will you do it?"

"Yes," I sighed, "I suppose I'll have to."

"What are you going to say? Don't loose your temper!"

"This is me you're talking to."

"Exactly," replied Chris. "Which is why I'm telling you not to loose your temper."

"Don't worry. Here's what we are going to do. We go downstairs and you walk out into the street. I will go and find the landlady and simply tell her that we do not find it acceptable. Then I will leave and meet you outside."

"Okay," mumbled Chris looking anxious.

We put the plan into action; at the bottom of the stairs Chris shot into the street as if she was on roller skates and I turned in the direction of the kitchen. The landlady met me in the doorway. I reached out and handed her back the keys. So far so good!

"I'm sorry but it's not acceptable," I said calmly and began turning to leave.

"Well good riddance!" shrieked the landlady (obviously an ancestor was a fishwife!)

Had she not said that I would not have lost my temper, but she did, and I had to have the last word.

"Well try using a vacuum cleaner!" I bellowed, enraged by her response.

Chris had heard me shouting and as I walked outside I half expected her to be part way to Plymouth. She was waiting at the top of the street and we retraced our steps to the Tourist Information Centre, feeling very pleased with ourselves. We had lost our deposit but we had not lost our principles. This was the end of our walk and it would have been marred by a night spent in that grotty place.

The lady at the Tourist Information Centre told us the B&B was not registered with them and so there was nothing they could do about the poor standards. Which I suppose means that anyone can offer Bed and Breakfast without being regulated in any way, and some poor suckers could find themselves staying in a dump! There was plenty of alternative accommodation available and so we found ourselves booking into a two star hotel overlooking a quiet park in a very nice area of the town.

When we entered the hotel looking hot, weary and dishevelled the owner greeted us warmly, immediately making us feel welcome and, ignoring our dusty boots tramping across his vacuumed carpets, he showed us to a second floor room. It was a typical family run hotel, with a friendly atmosphere. The en-suite room was light and airy and everything was clean and smelt fresh. We slumped down onto the beds, no springs twanged. Bliss.

"We deserve this luxury."

"Yep, you're right. We've earned this. What an excellent way to finish the walk."

"I think we should see what the menu is like for evening meals here."

"Good idea."

"So nip downstairs and ask to borrow one would you?"

"Me? It was your idea. If it wasn't for me we would be stuck in that awful Bed and Breakfast!"

"If it had been up to me we would never have gone in in the first place!"

I left Chris making a pot of tea whilst I went to investigate the possibility of an evening meal. I found we were just in time to book a meal and had an hour before dinner time. Borrowing a menu, I raced back upstairs, not realising the stairs were not the same ones I had come down. The hotel had originally been two houses, now converted into one. I was lost. I found our room quite by chance after several abortive attempts along the wrong corridors.

The evening meal was delicious and afterwards we spent some time relaxing in the lounge before going out in search of a post box. We took the opportunity to locate the bus station and confirm times for our first leg of the journey back to Padstow the following morning.

Neither of us wanted to go immediately to sleep that night. To fall asleep would put an end to our walk. Long after we went to bed both of us were still awake thinking over events of the past fortnight and it was quite a while before either of us realised the other was awake. When we did we began chatting, reliving the good, the bad and the hilarious moments of the walk. There had been difficult sections, when our morale slumped but overall the experienced had been enjoyable. We had had fun.

Saturday 17th July

Our journey back to Padstow that day was relatively uneventful. Four changes of bus were needed to carry us across the county. We sat squashed together on the seats, our rucksacks jammed on our laps in the surprisingly crowded buses, bouncing over rutted lanes linking peaceful rural villages and slaloming through bustling markets towns.

In the middle of the afternoon we disembarked at a supermarket on the outskirts of Bodmin. With thirty minutes to wait before our connecting bus arrived, we passed the time browsing in the store. In good time for catching the bus, we stood outside the supermarket at the bus stop. The bus entered the car park, sped past lines of parked cars and swooped towards the bus stop. We moved to the edge of the pavement and I stuck my arm out to flag down the bus. The driver looked at us and carried on going.

We stood in disbelief watching the departing bus. A driver from a second bus that was parked nearby, apparently killing time until he was due to leave, had seen what had happened and approached us asking where we wanted to go. When we explained that we were travelling to Padstow, he shook his head and told us that bus did not go to Padstow.

"It had 'Padstow' on the front!" I said.

"No, that bus does not go to Padstow."

"According to this timetable it does," said Chris brandishing the timetable.

"That must be an old timetable."

"It is this summer's timetable. I know what I'm talking about!" Chris was beginning to loose her temper.

"No, it can't be," insisted the driver. "That bus doesn't go to Padstow. In fact no buses leave here for Padstow."

Now it was my turn to loose my temper. "Well, why did the bus have 'Padstow' on the front and why is it printed in this timetable?"

"Uh, I don't know," he muttered and wandered back to his own bus.

"In-bred idiot!"

We checked the timetable, the next bus to Padstow would be along in forty-five minutes. What could we do while we waited? The café in the supermarket had an offer on cream teas – what a good idea!

Sometime later we were once again standing at the bus stop, this time determined not to let the bus drive by without stopping. As the bus came in sight, we edged nearer to the curb. This time I was quite prepared to throw Chris in front of it if it did not look likely to stop! There was no need for such drastic measures, the bus stopped.

After a brief stop in Wadebridge the bus continued to Padstow. Surprise, surprise. We disembarked and headed for the shops strung out around the harbour. Chris bought her final postcard to send to her Mum, she chose one showing a sunset over Padstow harbour. It was an appropriate choice, the sunset closing the day and that day closing our walk.

We walked up the hill away from the town and along the country road to our B&B. A battered tennis ball, denuded of its lime green felt, lay in the gutter. We had noticed it two weeks previously as we set out on our walk, now our walk was over but the tennis ball was still there. A reminder perhaps that no matter what you are doing or where you are, life continues as normal? Enough of all this claptrap! I kicked the ball and it bounced along the road hitting the back of Chris's boot. She turned and kicked it back to me. We continued on our way, kicking and dribbling the tennis ball as we went, until a car came along and squashed it. Now *that's* more representative of life: just when you're enjoying yourself something comes along and stuffs things up!

A nice surprise was awaiting us at the B&B, two nice surprises in fact: champagne from one husband and flowers from the other. The landlord had made a huge pot of tea and ushered us into the lounge, asking us to tell him all about the walk. He was the first of many to express such a keen interest and in the next few days, on our return to home and work, we were to tell our travellers tales many, many times.

The champagne troubled Chris; she was wondering when we could drink it. She knew what I was like after a couple of drinks and did not relish the prospect of me getting drunk.

"I'm not going to get drunk after a couple of glasses of champagne," I assured her.

I was right; I didn't get drunk after two glasses. It was the third one that did it!

"Oh great! I knew this would happen!" moaned Chris.

"Stop worrying, I'm okay," I giggled.

I persuaded her that I just needed a little fresh air and I would be fine and so we began walking back to Padstow in search of an evening meal. The surface of the narrow country lane was bumpier than I remembered it; matters were not helped by Chris who seemed to keep colliding with me, although she insisted I was colliding with her. I decided to phone Roger and began fumbling with my mobile phone.

"What are you doing?"

"I'm going to telephone my husband."

"Not here you're not! Wait until we get on that grass verge."

I ignored Chris and carried on dialling.

"Julia! You're in the middle of the road." She grabbed my arm and dragged me into the gutter.

"I was not in the middle of the road. I may have been in the middle of this half of the road but I was not in the middle of the road."

"Yes you were. Now leave the phone until we reach the grass!"

When we left the tarmac and stepped onto the verge I immediately began dialling. Roger answered and laughed when he realised I had been drinking. I babbled on about the walk and then explained that Chris was worried about me.

"Tell her I'm okay," I ordered him and handed the phone to Chris.

They spoke for a few seconds before disconnecting.

"Now, are you reassured?" I asked her.

"No. He told me you throw up when you're drunk!"

"The liar! I do not. Well I might have once. I'm not going to throw up, okay?"

I was right, I didn't throw up, much to Chris's relief. We sat on a bench by the harbour until my head stopped spinning, the world came into focus and I regained full control of my legs. Then we went to a pub for the last meal of the holiday but I don't remember what I ate.

Autumn 1999

After spending months of planning and preparation for our walk, that fortnight at the beginning of July seemed to pass all too quickly. We both felt strangely desolate in the weeks that followed.

Before setting off we had hounded people at work for donations, hoping to raise £500 for the Leukaemia Research Fund. Some colleagues had expressed astonishment at what we were about to do, many wished us well and donated generously to our cause. A few had done the walk themselves, one such commenting on the gradients, "I pity you all the ups and downs!" The gradients had not really been a problem for us but the heat and the uneven, overgrown, boulder-strewn paths certainly had!

As I had packed waterproof clothing in my rucksack the day before we were due to leave, I had worried about the weather conditions we might have to endure. The two days of gales and torrential rain of the previous year's walk had alarmed me, and I was concerned that we would spend a fortnight buffeted by winds and wrapped in Gore-Tex. Never, for one second, had I considered we would suffer because of the heat. On the first weekend, whilst we were being burnt under overcast skies, the majority of the country had been experiencing heavy rain. Flash flooding in Chris's village had resulted in many houses in the centre being under several feet of water. Who, I wondered, was the sage who observed that Britain does not have a climate, it just has weather?

On our return our fundraising for Leukaemia Research continued in the form of a raffle and although there were high points with that as our total continued to rise, we still talked wistfully of our walk. Friends and colleagues quickly tired of hearing us recounting our adventures over and over. The drama and the humour and the low points lost something in the telling. We would laugh hysterically at incidents we recalled, only to look round and notice the bemused and slightly bored expressions on the faces of those around us. Perhaps you had to have been there!

But the shared memories were special and precious. With Chris's companionship the walk that year had been even more enjoyable than the previous year. We had experienced not just laughter and fun but perhaps more importantly, difficult periods which we had struggled mentally and physically to overcome. We had both been spurred on by accounts from colleagues whose relatives had died of Leukaemia: someone's niece who lost a long battle with the illness at the age of sixteen; the dying stonemason, determined to finish his last commission, completing a carving of praying hands on a gravestone the day before he died; and of course, Chris's Dad. Chris had gained strength from memories of her Dad and confided that she had felt his presence on several difficult occasions during the walk, a moving statement from someone not at all fanciful or melodramatic.

The seasons changed, warm wet days of late summer succumbing to sharp frosts and misty mornings of autumn. The routine of work replaced the excitement of our walk. Ian Botham began his last great walk, leaving John O'Groats, travelling south, passing through Lancashire on his way to Land's End. On a dull morning at the beginning of November, Chris and I travelled to meet him and present the cheque, now totalling over £1700. We had been amazed by the support of family, friends and colleagues and it was thanks to them that we raised such an amount. For us, it was over, for Ian, walking an average of twenty-five miles a day for five weeks, there was still some way to go. The difficulties he had to endure on that epic road walk and the sums he raised made our efforts seem puny.

Feeling particularly low at work one morning and wishing I was back on the coast path, it did not matter which part of it – even the rough, difficult section west of Zennor – I was dragged from my melancholy by Chris.

Bursting into the room she grinned foolishly.

"Well you're in a good mood," I muttered grumpily.

"I have just been speaking to a member of staff who I've not seen for ages."

"Very nice."

"We were talking about the walk and he asked me how my leg was." She was still grinning and I was beginning to find her ebullient mood infectious.

"And what did you say?"

"Something I've never been able to truthfully say before."

"Which is…?" I prompted.

"Better."

And perhaps that was the most significant achievement of all.

Falmouth to Torbay

The South West Coast Path rolls, wiggles and kinks its way along the coast from Minehead in Somerset to Poole Harbour in Dorset. 630 miles-worth of ups, downs, ins, outs, cliffs, beaches, cream tea establishments, B&Bs, sewage outfalls and dog dirt. And roughly halfway along Britain's longest long distance path is Falmouth. Travelling from Minehead to Poole, the next place on from Falmouth is Place (original name, eh?) But there is one slight problem: Carrick Roads. This great big wet expanse of river mouth blocks the path for all but the most divine walker, and probably explains why in the series of guide books we were using, one book ended at Falmouth and the next began at Place. Which is where Chris and I were beginning this year's walk. This diary is an account not just of walking but of the adventures, the accommodation, the food – oh yes, definitely the food – and all the silly things that two friends can get up to when they are left to their own devices for two weeks without family to control them!

On reaching Falmouth the previous year we had stood clutching the railings above the dry dock and looked across Carrick Roads to Place.

"Next year we'll be walking along that headland!"

"Yeah, it seems ages away."

It wasn't.

Once again it was spring; the weeks had passed turning the hazy hot days of the previous summer into a chill, damp winter and now with the approach of another summer came the torrential rain that seemed to typify late May and early June. Chris and I were stuffing our faces with Chinese takeaway at our penultimate planning evening. The accommodation was booked, the transport organised, the parcels packed and awaiting posting. Everything was finalised. So why the hell were we having another planning evening, our husbands wanted to know!

All the planning had gone worryingly well this year with the exception of one B&B that had cashed our deposit cheque and ignored repeated requests, both by mail and telephone, for directions. As this particular B&B was located somewhere in Cornwall and nowhere near anywhere we were rather concerned about ever finding it. When directions were finally forthcoming we were even more concerned. The handwriting was dreadful and the information was even worse. The handwriting from both B&B owners at The Lizard and Coverack had been terrible, and the accommodation there had been disgusting. Was there a pattern emerging here? We worried, but there was little we could do.

As there was no point in worrying about something we could do little about I turned my attention to other matters.

"We need a gimmick!"

"Grumph!" responded Chris battling to eat a salt and pepper spare rib.

"Well, think about it – last year we were raising money. Everyone could see why we were walking, they only needed to look at our Leukaemia Research Fund hats."

"Umm."

"A microwave. We need a microwave."

"I thought you just bought one?"

"I did, but that's no good, it's too heavy."

"What?" asked Chris. "No, never mind, I don't want to know. Now what were you saying about a gimmick?"

"The microwave – that's the gimmick! You've read 'Round Ireland with a Fridge'. Well we can go round Cornwall with a microwave!"

"You're mad," was Chris's considered response as she began tackling another rib.

"Not as mad as you'll be if that rib brings your crown off again," I muttered.

It's quite painful, being hit on the nose by a carefully aimed rib. However, when it came to teeth, Chris had the last laughed – I lost a cap from my front tooth the week before we went away!

In hindsight a tumble drier would have been a more appropriate choice of gimmicky kitchen appliance. However, with or without a gimmick, this year we were doing the walk for our own enjoyment and that alone. No fundraising. No appearing on the Internet, or in the press, or on the radio. No tin rattling. No sponsorship. No college T-shirts provided by our employer, or Leukaemia Research Fund caps. No raffles. Just Chris, her Beanie toy Buzz Lightyear and me and possibly Eeyore, if he didn't weigh too much.

Three days before we were due to leave we had our final planning evening, this was to ensure that what we had both packed in our rucksacks was correct – if one of us had forgotten something the other would notice. That was the idea anyway! It was also an opportunity to divide between ourselves the items we would be sharing, things like the fun cameras, toothpaste, and shampoo. It sounded easy didn't it? But the toiletries had caused us considerable aggravation.

Some months ago we had treated ourselves to miniature bottles of luxury shampoos, conditioners, moisturisers and bubble baths with the intention of carrying some and posting the rest to various B&Bs along our route. On the afternoon we bought them we were already loaded down with carriers full of shopping and the assistant in the shop suggested we might like to leave all our purchases behind the counter until we had finished the rest of our shopping. We were only too eager to take her up on the offer.

It was some two months later and the date of the walk only a few weeks away, when we discovered neither of us actually had the toiletries. I thought Chris had taken them and she assumed I had got them. A frantic search of both homes revealed nothing. There was only one explanation – we had left them behind the counter and failed to notice because of the number of bags we had accumulated.

I had volunteered Chris to telephone the shop to check if our goods had been found. The assistant checked behind the counter but, not surprisingly after two months, our carrier bag of toiletries was no longer there. She suggested Chris telephone the following day when the manageress would be in, and might be able to help. And so the next day Chris found herself relating the tale once more, growing red with embarrassment as she explained that it had been two months since we had purchased the goods. The manageress was unable to help us, no unclaimed items had been found despite a search by two members of staff.

We kicked ourselves for loosing the toiletries and wasting our money, now we would have to buy some more. But we didn't have to shop for more miniature bottles of "smelly stuff" as my husband liked to call them. Chris arrived at work one morning looking cheerful – which is a rare enough phenomenon to be noteworthy – and clutching a bag, the bag, of toiletries!

"I knew you had them!" I exclaimed with the benefit of hindsight. "Where did you find them?"

"In the bathroom cupboard!"

"Oh, well, no wonder you lost them. I mean fancy putting toiletries in the bathroom cupboard, that would be the last place anyone would think to look!"

"There's no need to get sarcastic. I would not have put them there in the first place. The main thing is that we do not need to buy any more, saving *you* money, which being so tight-fisted you should be happy about!"

"Charming! I am not tight-fisted," I objected.

"Oh yes you are!" chorused a roomful of colleagues.

So with our bags packed and the moths stuffed firmly in my purse we eagerly awaited the day of departure.

Friday 30th June

Isn't it funny how you don't mind getting up early if you are going on holiday? Asked to wake up for an extra early morning appointment with the dentist and you would probably baulk at the prospect, but on that Friday morning I positively sprang out of bed, showered and dressed and awaited Chris's arrival at 6 a.m.

Our starting point of the walk was Falmouth but we were not going there that day, instead we were travelling to Porthcurno only a few miles from Land's End. After our disappointment at missing a production at the Minack Theatre the previous year, we had decided to fit a visit into our schedule. Therefore we had booked a room at the same B&B in Porthcurno where we had stayed before and purchased two tickets to see the evening performance at the Minack. Our plan was to travel down on the Friday, watch a play and drive to Falmouth on the Saturday morning, where we would leave the car at a pre-arranged hotel to be collected on our last day, and then take the ferries to Place to begin our walk. It would mean an early start and a long journey but we felt the chance to actually experience the thrill of a performance at this unique theatre would be worthwhile. It was whilst we were discussing the Minack at work that one colleague asked what we were going to see.

"David Copperfield," I replied.

"Is he going to make Land's End disappear?" asked another colleague.

"Not that David Copperfield!" I responded with exasperation, "Dickens!"

The four hundred miles from our homes in Lancashire to almost the tip of Cornwall passed uneventfully. For once the motorways seemed to lack road works and the traffic was free moving, not even a single contra-flow to slow our progress! We arrived in the small village of Porthcurno and had checked into our accommodation by mid afternoon, giving us plenty of time before the play.

With a few free hours and sun shining the sea looked very inviting and we hurried down to the relatively uncrowded beach for a swim. We slipped our costumes on in the public toilets and were just about set off down the track to the beach when we spotted a rather prominent notice posted nearby. It warned of the hazards of phosphorus canisters that might have been washed up by the tide; it was a sign we were to see several times during the first part of the walk. 'DO NOT TOUCH! WHITE PHOSPHORUS BURNS FIERCELY!' I'll say it does, we had recently disposed of all our stocks of phosphorus at work, and we both cringed at the possible consequences to anyone who was daft enough to tamper with a canister of the stuff. Whether a diligent search had been made by the authorities we were not to know, but phosphorus was not to feature on our spotters' list.

Funny how a blue sky, aquamarine sea, golden sand and blazing sun can fool you into thinking the sea temperature is actually going to be warm! Chris took the plunge first, well, up to her ankles anyway, and squealed at the cold. Slowly she paddled further out, teeth chattering with every step. I was tempted to return to our pile of clothes and get changed but swimming in the sea had been something I had promised myself this year. I figured that the best thing to do would be to just charge straight in and begin swimming, so that is what I did. And it was freezing!

"Whose daft idea was this?" asked Chris through chattering teeth.

"Start swimming and you soon warm up," I suggested, following my own advice but not really believing it. "Funny how no one else is swimming."

"They've got more sense!"

However, some people did leave the warmth of the beach and enter the water, no doubt encouraged by our example and unable to see our goose bumps.

As I was swimming about I began to notice lots of little critters swimming about with me. What were they? I stopped and tried to catch one, eventually managing to.

"What have you found a phosphorus canister?" enquired Chris swimming over.

"No, nothing quite that dangerous, I hope. Is it a tiny shrimp?"

Chris peered at it before finally agreeing that it was a crustacean of some kind.

Following the swim we made our way to the nearby gift shop for postcards. Chris was intending to send both her Mum and mine a postcard everyday. She had done this for her Mum last year and had decided to do the same for my Mum because Mum had bought her a sun hat. I had been looking for a new hat for some time before the walk and when I eventually found some I thought were suitable Mum offered to buy one for me. It was made of cotton, a lightweight material with a snazzy blue and white checked pattern. The big floppy brim covered my ears, my neck and even my nose! I modelled it in a variety of poses: brim up, brim down, brim half up and half down, on the back of my head, pulled down over my eyebrows and at a jaunty angle across one ear. Some of the poses made me look ridiculous. Some made me look incredibly ridiculous. But my ears would be protected, and that was the main thing!

Chris fell about laughing when I first put it on, until I told her that Mum had wanted to get her one as well. Initially she blanched but after some consideration decided it would be a good idea and gratefully accepted my Mum's gift. And hence every evening whilst I was catching up with my diary, Chris would begin her postcard writing session.

As we stood outside the shop, clutching postcards and some flapjack that had looked too delicious to ignore, we had a good view down into the bay. Chris was the first to notice something breaking the surface of the water a hundred yards from the beach.

"What's that?" she asked.

"A phosphorus canister," I replied flippantly, glancing in the general direction of her pointing finger.

"Is it a fin?"

"A fin? Where?"

I looked properly and yes, it was a fin. Shark!! SHARK!!! But no one on the beach looked too concerned. The lifeguards did not seem perturbed. No swimmers splashed frantically to shore. No threatening music played in the background. No one screamed. No surfers were dragged bloodily under the water. Nothing happened. Bit disappointing really. Well actually it wasn't at all disappointing because we were watching our first basking shark! We had heard about them the previous year but never been lucky enough to see one. We watched it for some time, slowly cruising in the bay, obviously attracted by the crustaceans we had seen earlier. This year we didn't see any seals, and after several years of walking the coast path I have still not seen a dolphin, but watching that shark was quite incredible.

In the early evening we set off for the Minack Theatre carrying a promisingly heavy picnic hamper and a bag provided by the B&B. The bag contained two cushions and a rug that would ensure we were comfortable for the three hour performance. Our host advised us of a footpath to the theatre which would avoid the road. It seemed sensible to take the path because hundreds of cars would soon be squeezing along the narrow lane to the theatre. But what should have been a simple stroll across a field and through a farm yard resulted in us forgetting his directions and getting lost. It did not bode well for the coming walk!

When we arrived at the theatre, a queue was forming and marshals were busy directing cars. Because of the large capacity of the theatre compared to the relatively small entrance, it takes quite some time for the theatre to fill up; hence the audience is allowed in an hour before the performance starts. In arriving early we were lucky to get seats only a few rows from the stage and spent the time before the play began eating our picnic tea. Nearly everyone around us had taken a picnic. Tupperware popped, foil scrunched and in some cases wine glasses clinked and cutlery rang off china plates.

It is always much nicer to eat food someone else has prepared, especially when it was as delicious as the hamper we shared that evening and in those surroundings. The food was superb: melon, salad, pastries, fresh bread rolls and finally strawberries, raspberries and fresh clotted cream. And the atmosphere of the amphitheatre created an unforgettable backdrop to the meal. The sun was beginning its slow descent into the sea, turning the water into liquid gold and reflecting off the cliffs across the bay. In the fading light a line of cormorants skimmed low across the waves. Just before the stage lighting came on and the play began, a soft drizzle began to fall. Seven hundred and fifty people stood up in unison and the gentle sound of the waves was drowned out by the mass rustle of Gore-Tex, Sympa-Tex, Hydro-Dry, Aqua-Dry, Gaberdine, Neoprene and even bin bags, as the entire audience shrugged themselves into waterproof clothing.

We sat huddled under our cagoules and with our legs wrapped in the blanket throughout the play. But rain could not spoil the wonderful experience of watching a play performed in that unique theatre. The clouds and rain meant we did not see the sunset but as darkness fell we could pick out the flashing light of The Lizard lighthouse far away across Mount's Bay. The amateur theatre company performing that night was superb, the production well adapted and the whole evening was totally unforgettable. What a fantastic start to our holiday!

Saturday 1st July

We had booked into a hotel at Falmouth for the last night of the holiday and that hotel was where we had arranged to leave the car for the fortnight. Arriving in Falmouth the following morning we parked the car at the hotel and set off on the short walk to Falmouth waterfront from where we were to catch the ferry firstly to St. Mawes and then take a second ferry to Place.

The ferry from Falmouth was to be the first of many before we reached Paignton, our finishing point for this year. I quite liked ferries – all the scrambling in and out, all the bobbing about, the smell of the sea, the rush of wind in your hair, spray on your face. Chris didn't share my enthusiasm; she hated boats – all the scrambling in and out, all the bobbing about, the smell of the sea, the rush of wind in your hair, spray on your face – but especially the bobbing about.

She had not been looking forward to the many river crossings to come, and after my having to drag her quivering form out of the ferry at Helford River the previous year, I was not particularly looking forward to them either.

But this year, Chris informed me, she had a secret weapon! I was expecting her to produce a jet powered rocket suit capable of folding down small enough to fit into a side pocket of her rucksack, yet powerful enough to enable her to fly over all the estuaries. The last thing I was expecting was an acupressure wristband.

"What the hell's that?" I snapped, when she first showed it to me.

"It's an acupressure wristband."

"It looks like one of those bands that hospitals put on patients in case they mix them up – you know 'Oh, dear, we've just performed a lobotomy on the wrong patient! That would never have happened if he'd been wearing one of those things that look like an acupressure wristband!'"

"You can laugh, but this is the answer to all my ferry worries!" replied Chris.

"Ferry nice."

I may have laughed, and indeed I did, I stopped laughing however, as I pictured the possible scenario which might arise if the wristband failed to work. The ferry might travel no more than a few yards from the dock at Falmouth, before Chris turned green and threatened to throw up on my new walking boots! Until that possibility occurred to me I had not considered that there could be worse things on your boots than dog dirt. Nevertheless the wristband seemed to work and getting Chris onto a ferry was to prove less irksome than I had imagined. The first ferry docked in St. Mawes and we disembarked slightly wetter than when we had set off from Falmouth. Carrick Roads could best be described as choppy and Chris had survived that ferry crossing, surely none of the others could be any worse?

St. Mawes sold itself in the brochures as an affluent and select community, stuffed full of millionaires. When we had been trying to find accommodation our first idea had been to drive directly to the resort and leave the car there. The problem was none of the few hotels and guest houses were prepared to put up with smelly walkers or to look after their car for two weeks and so we had to adapt our plans accordingly. Perhaps our accommodation difficulties had coloured our view of St. Mawes, but we thought it was a bit of a dump compared to some of the other delightful small communities along the Cornish coast. The waterfront seemed a little dilapidated, the gaily-painted houses were flaking in the sunshine and several of the commercial premises were closed down. We passed an old garage with servicing facilities tucked behind two ancient petrol pumps. The white pumps were rusting, the yellow shell emblems on top faded. But the most telling clue to the time when it had last sold petrol, was the price displayed in the windows of the pumps: "3s 2d". Was the last person to buy petrol there still alive? And had he ever imagined that a gallon of petrol would one day cost over £4?

We took the small ferry to Place, disembarking onto a seaweed covered jetty and carefully making our way across the smelly weed to dry land. Place isn't much of a place. Set back slightly from the tiny bay is a rather grand, imposing house, which likes its privacy and hence the footpath weaves around the back of it. However, if it were not for this then we would have missed the old church and its curious churchyard. The church, St. Anthony-in-Roseland, dates from Norman times and is now maintained by a charitable church organisation but no longer used for worship. We quietly entered the hushed stillness of the church, marvelling at the solid aged door. Dust motes danced in the light coming through the stained glass. We might have been the only human presence in there for centuries, but the visitors book gave proof that the church had been visited quite recently; Chris picked up a pen and bent to enter our names. Returning to the churchyard the sudden sunlight momentarily dazzled us. The graveyard was somewhat overgrown but appealingly so, many of the gravestones covered with moss and lichen, and a robin hopped from one crusty monument to another.

We followed a quiet lane before climbing slightly along a footpath. Views across Carrick Roads opened up and as we rounded a headland the freshening wind threatened to blow our hats into the fields of barley. We had barely gone a mile before we got lost. It was our own fault, the guidebook told us to descend the field, what a pity we had failed to read that bit before striding out confidently along the field boundary at the top of the slope! We retraced our steps feeling rather foolish.

The path climbed behind the lighthouse on St. Anthony Head to arrive at a former fort and World War II gun emplacement. It was to be the first of several reminders of how seriously the Government of the time took the threat of German invasion. Some of the buildings were open, although the fort itself was closed and the former officers' quarters are now holiday cottages. A bird hide had been constructed overlooking a narrow cove and we walked down to it, expecting to be confronted with a cliff face crowded with gulls and guano. The guano was there but as for the birds well, they seemed to have flown! A couple of herring gulls nested on the cliffs but we could not see any other birds. Chris began scanning the cliff through binoculars not holding out much hope of seeing anything exciting and that was when she spotted a Peregrine falcon sitting quietly on a ledge. We watched for several minutes, taking advantage of the cool interior of the hide but we saw nothing else and the Peregrine remained firmly rooted to his perch, he was probably stuffed and put there to fool visitors!

We ate our packed lunch sitting on a bench on the top of Zone Point. It had been provided by the B&B that morning and we were very much looking forward to it (the packed lunch, not the bench, the bench had been provided by friends of Mildred who had 'loved this place'). We were not disappointed; the lunch was every bit as delicious as the theatre hamper had been, and the bench was quite comfy too! While we sat there munching sandwiches and dipping into a bag of salad, two walkers approached along the path.

"Sharks on your left," said one of them, and looking out to sea we saw our second and third (and last) basking sharks of the holiday.

"Thank you!" we chorused through mouthfuls of tuna and cucumber sandwich, it had been nice of the walker to draw our attention to the sharks. We ate the remainder of our lunch watching the sharks and it was with some effort that we dragged ourselves away to continue our walk.

Peregrines soared, skylarks sang and the sun shone down, the forecast rain never materialised. At Porthmellin Head we could see across the fields inland, towards St. Mawes and the Percuil River, less than a mile away over the peninsular but three miles away as we had walked.

An elderly lady and her corgi were strolling along the path in front of us. She looked a lot like the Queen from behind. It couldn't be – could it? No, she didn't have a handbag. The corgi looked hot, his low-slung belly scraping along the sandy path with every step. He turned baleful bulging eyes up to us as we passed.

The path ran along the edges of fields in which a farmer was practising crop rotation. In one, barley trimmed with the occasional red poppy, swayed gently in the breeze. In another field was a ripening crop of peas, this one sharing the soil with the delicate flowers of scarlet pimpernel. A third field was a sea of pale blue and we were puzzled to identify the stitchwort-like plant with the delicate flowers, it was not until later with the help of a botany text that Chris was able to triumphantly declare the mystery crop to be flax.

An ominous crunch drew our attention to the snail on the path, now a squashed mess thanks to Chris's foot. As the afternoon wore on she seemed to be getting very good at squashing snails.

"Do you know what I could just eat?" I asked visualising ice cream with clotted cream on top.

Crunch!

"A snail?" said Chris, lifting her foot to reveal the fourth squashed mollusc of the day.

We walked in silence for some time around Greeb Point. Nare Head came into view looking steep and far away. In reality it was less than one day away, we would walk over it the following morning. The sun shone, reflecting off the blue sea, giving false promise of the weather to come.

"My bra's too tight," muttered Chris after fidgeting suddenly.

"Unfasten it a bit then."

"I can't until I've had an antihistamine."

"What? I didn't know there was an allergic reaction to putting your arms behind your back! 'Oh geez, I break out in hives every time I take my bra off!'"

"There isn't. Unless you're a hypochondriac!"

"Well what's the problem then?" I asked. "Are you allergic to your bra?"

"No! Just the metal clasp."

Ah! Good old nickel!

We walked six miles to Portscatho that afternoon – it was a gentle introduction to the walk – arriving at half past four. We sat for a while overlooking the small breakwater in this small backwater. It was very peaceful and a different world from the bustling streets of Falmouth we had left that morning.

Our Bed and Breakfast at Portscatho was the cheapest of all the ones we stayed in that year, which is not to say it was poor. Set back from the square, it was a large double fronted house, painted a delicate shade of pink. We were greeted by the owner, who took our rucksacks and beckoned us to follow him as he staggered upstairs, saying, "Oh, yes, it's a double room isn't it?"

"No!" we both squeaked in panic.

"Sorry, I mean twin," he replied, obviously sensing our joint anxiety.

Our room overlooked a small kitchen garden and was furnished with two brass beds, wardrobe, hand basin and a very useful ceiling fan. Ranged on a cabinet by the sink were the usual tea and coffee making facilities, then the more unusual drinking chocolate, chocolates, bag of salted peanuts and bottle of orange squash, then the even more unusual generously filled biscuit barrel, and finally something which neither of us have ever found in a bedroom at a B&B before.

"There's sherry!" squealed Chris in amazement.

This was one establishment that knew how to look after weary walkers!

Before we could relax with a glass of sherry, there were certain things we had to do. It was a routine familiar to us from the previous year and one that we carried out every evening on arrival at our accommodation. Firstly, we put the kettle on and made a cup of tea. Then we had a bath or more often a shower. We unpacked our rucksacks, extracting clothes for the evening; these consisted of one pair of trousers (which we wore only in the evenings and not for walking) and clean tops and underwear that we alternated every day. The dirty tops, underwear and socks we took in turns to wash each evening, these would then be clean for us to wear the following evening. The washing was a chore but it meant our pack weight was kept to a minimum. After two years of long distance walking we had refined our luggage and now considered ourselves quite expert in packing only essentials but still maintaining cleanliness and comfort.

We sat on the beds with our rucksack contents scattered around the room, each nominating the other to be laundry maid. As a ploy to divert attention from the dirty washing I commented on the heat rash on Chris's legs, "It looks really silly! Is it itching?"

"Yes it is," replied Chris and began scratching as if to demonstrate just how itchy it was.

"Don't scratch, that will make it look even worse."

"At least I am not sporting Mount Vesuvius on the side of my nose!" she said tartly.

This remark sent me scuttling to the bathroom where I examined the offending pustule in the mirror, before performing a little open-face surgery with my fingernail – I wanted this to be a blemish-free holiday. By morning Chris's heat rash had gone, the same could not be said of my zit; it went a day or so later, never to return, the same could not be said of Chris's heat rash.

Chris wanted a sherry but that would have to wait, I wanted some food. We strolled down to the tiny harbour, little more than a corner of the sea protected by a short concrete breakwater. A wet-suited father and his similarly clad little girl were running across the jetty and leaping into the sea. For the dad this was obviously an enjoyable pastime. For the little girl, it looked nothing short of torture as she hung back reluctantly before being dragged off the jetty and into the deep water by the momentum of her insensate father. As they climbed out and repeated the process, I half expected the girl's arm to come off, leaving the father in the sea clutching a severed arm and wondering about shark attacks.

A lone seagull stood hopefully watching as we ate our fish and chip supper. After the incident at Newquay the previous year we were particularly on our guard. A blackbird and several sparrows picked at scraps under the nearby tables, we watched as one family of sparrows fed their youngster tiny pieces of potato. Sparrows have much nicer table manners than gulls!

Having only walked six miles that day we were quite tired, probably a result of the long journey and the late night of the day before. By half past nine we were in bed, Chris with a glass of sherry, me with a cup of tea and the tin of biscuits. It began a pattern of early nights we were to maintain for the remainder of the holiday, although regrettably the sherry and biscuits did not feature much in this pattern.

Sunday 2nd July

The night before I had promised myself I would go for a swim before breakfast but I woke too late. We hurried down to breakfast, the only guests there at that time, and feasted on cereal, fruit and yoghurt, followed by a cooked breakfast and toast, all served on expensive China at an elegant dining table with a Lazy Susan on which a variety of expensive looking condiments and preserves were arranged. I spun Susan, waiting for a particular jam to come within reach, but my enthusiastic spin threatened to send jars, pepper pots and mustard dishes flying across the room in all directions. Chris dived for cover under the table as I hastily put a hand out to slow the centrifugal effects!

Before we could begin the walk that morning we had to shop for our supper. Our destination that evening was a farm in an isolated spot with nowhere to have a meal, so we had planned to buy supper and carry it with us. Portscatho had one shop, which fortunately for us opened early on Sunday. Half the population of the village seemed to be in there buying their milk and papers, and we squeezed between the tiny aisles being very careful with our rucksacks. We had to be frugal in our shopping without stinting on quantity, we needed food that would not perish in the heat nor be too heavy to carry all day. We settled for flapjacks, bananas, a packet of biscuits and a couple of packets of instant pasta meals – a variation on a theme of Pot Noodle. I was an unashamed Pot Noodle virgin and was not over keen to find out what they were like but they would provide warm nourishment (of a sort) and be light to carry. I viewed Pot Noodle in much the same way as you might view an endoscopy – an alien, novel experience but one that you were reluctant to try and unlikely ever to wish to repeat. Suitably provisioned we joined the queue at the checkout.

We had barely left Portscatho behind before there was a familiar crunch, crunch noise as my boots came down on two unfortunate snails.

"Two nil," sighed Chris.

"Oh, we're starting from scratch are we, not aggregate?" I asked.

"Yes because you would forget!"

"Me forget?"

"Yes. You know you're no good with numbers."

The weather was warm and humid but soon a breeze sprang up to chase away the humidity and brought with it wet but not too heavy rain. We reluctantly put on our cagoules. The drizzle soon stopped and we thankfully removed our waterproofs, fastening them to our rucksacks to dry. Had we known what was to come we would have done well to keep them on; they would have offered us some protection, not against rain but vegetation!

We entered National Trust land and our problems began. The path was signposted up and around the top of a field, although an obvious route, (probably made by more sensible walkers than us!) led directly down the field and up the other side in a straight line. However, we decided to follow the designated route; so being the good little walkers that we are, we ignored the obvious path and began staggering up to the top of the field. What a shame the National Trust had failed to maintain the path! On the way down the far side of the field the path was completely overgrown and we battled our way through gorse, buckthorn and encroaching nettles down a precipitous slope to the bottom of the field, cursing all the way. Our bare arms and legs were scratched and covered in nettle rash, unfortunately not for the last time.

Twice that morning our route veered inland to skirt the perimeters of exclusive hotels. We walked up the high-banked lane around the first hotel noticing the abundance of one particular plant with tiny pink flowers, these must be the pink purslane mentioned in the guidebook. At the second hotel we sweated our way past an immaculate croquet lawn and around a car park stuffed with Jaguars and four wheel drive vehicles. The smell of Sunday roast was tantalising until we saw a menu posted outside the gates; the price of a three course meal was more than double what we were paying for some of the B&Bs! The fence and the prices were obviously there to deter any sweaty hikers – can't let the riff raff mix with their betters you know! Shame really, the croquet lawn would have made an excellent place for any backpackers wishing to pitch their tent.

The day brightened as we approached Nare Head and the afternoon became quite warm and humid once more. The path began its familiar rollercoaster of steep ascents and descents, made all the more difficult for us with the rising humidity. The path climbed steeply to Nare Head and as we rounded the headland turning north east two things came into view. The first and most obvious one was The Dodman, a fat finger of land sticking out into the sea across Veryan Bay. The second was dog dirt, which indicated to us a car park was not too far away. As in previous years, we still had to watch where we were walking for fear of putting our foot in it. There were plenty of dog-poop bins but unfortunately the majority of dog owners seemed to spurn them. I don't know why this was so, it was not as if the special bins were difficult to notice – they were bright red and about five feet high and sited with pleasing regularity along various parts of the coast path particularly in the towns and villages we passed through. We saw as many of these bins, in fact, as we did post boxes. And come to think of it, for the short-sighted or absent minded dog owners, the two could quite easily be confused, especially as in many places the bins and the boxes seemed to be located dangerously close to one another! Imagine popping out to post a letter whilst taking the dog for a walk at the same time. Pity the poor postman!

The path entered a belt of trees below the National Trust property of Broom Parc, used in the filming of a television drama series. It was not your typical NT property with guided tours and that sort of thing. A notice on the gate advertised it for holiday lets and, strangely we thought, for out of the way parties. It seemed odd that the National Trust should be encouraging people to have wild parties there!

From Manare Point the path descended gradually in the direction of Portloe. As we began the final steeper descent into the village we were faced with two paths and no signposts. I don't suppose you will be surprised to hear we chose the wrong path, skidding rapidly through undergrowth to emerge in the village behind someone's garden before following an alley to find ourselves standing beside a tearoom. At which point we congratulated ourselves on choosing the wrong path!

Apparently the tearooms at Portloe, situated in the same building as a tiny post office, are renowned for the quality of their food. It was three o'clock in the afternoon, we had not really had any lunch other than a few biscuits and so the decision to indulge in a cream tea was not a particularly difficult one. The Cornish cream tea was excellent but the owner of the tearooms was certainly not Cornish. She spoke with a Home Counties accent, nothing like the local dialect, but she could certainly cook!

Portloe was probably one of the nicest villages we passed through. Its charm lay in the lack of pretension and the absence of tourist tat that was to be found in abundance at the larger villages and towns along the coast. No amusement arcades or garish cafes, restaurants and shops. The car park and toilets were small and obscure. And although some tourists must visit the village (for how else could the tearooms survive?) the place retained an atmosphere of peace, a seemingly untouched backwater whose character was retained. A collection of tiny boats were anchored in the cove, small fishermen's cottages lined the lanes leading away from the shore, the whole village being squeezed between the wooded hillsides lining the valley. Bigger resorts exhibited some evidence of poverty but Portloe appeared well cared for, a small community surviving long after the traditional pilchard fishing had ceased.

It was a steep climb out of Portloe, made all the more difficult because of an excess of clotted cream. As we crossed the road I noticed a tiny black thing on the ground, it was a toy cat moulded out of rubber and no bigger than my thumbnail. I could not say what made me pick it up and put it into my pocket, perhaps because black cats are supposed to be lucky, if you believe in all that.

We passed yet another ruined coastguard lookout station to follow the rocky, cliff-hugging path towards West Portholland. The path dipped and rose between mixed hedges of sea buckthorn and gorse, coloured and scented with the yellow and pink flowers of honeysuckle.

In order to save jarring on our knees we began using our walking poles on the steep parts of the path. Chris extended hers easily but mine was proving difficult once again. This was my third year with the pole and my third year of difficulty. It should have been simple – unscrew the two sections and extend to the desired length, before screwing the telescopic sections secure. It would have been a simple process if only I had stripped and cleaned the pole before coming on holiday. I hadn't and as a result dirt and corrosion in the mechanism were the cause of the problem. After some tugging and cursing I managed to adjust the pole to a useful length; however, when I no longer needed it I had further difficulty trying to collapse the pole. Chris tutted and rolled her eyes and watched me struggle, until I finally succeeded.

After a particularly steep ascent just before West Portholland, we sat down for a drink and to recuperate. A family passed us and then stopped to chat to us as one little boy was curious about the spike thing on the back of my rucksack. Eeyore was tied to my rucksack, but this little boy was more interested in my walking pole! The perverseness of children!

There is not a lot at West Portholland but a step away is East Portholland and toilets! And having drunk the teapot dry at Portloe I was in need of some. Chris headed for the beach whilst I headed for the loos. The sink in the toilets was one of those 3-in-1 hole-in-the-wall affairs. Push a button and soap is dispensed, push another button and water is dispensed, or not in my case. I ended up with a handful of soap and nothing to wash it off with. I never even got as far as the hot air of button number three!

From East Portholland it was a short if somewhat steep ascent over the cliffs to Porthluney Cove and the impressive Caerhays Castle. We walked down a lane made dark by the overhanging branches, with cars passing us as families made their way home after a day spent on the beach. Caerhays Castle came into view with the lake and marsh in front, highland cattle grazing and a large, orange earthmover parked just behind the boundary wall. The castle and the cattle set in the wooded valley looked as if they had been there for centuries. The JCB just looked out of place. In fact neither the cattle nor the castle have been there all that long. The castle was actually built in 1808 and owes its design to the same man who was responsible for Buckingham Palace, John Nash.

Across the road from the castle is the awarding winning beach at Porthluney Cove and just behind the beach a large car park. We had hoped for the beach to ourselves, visualising a peaceful swim the falling dusk and maybe a picnic tea on the beach. But the car park was still quite busy and further events were to conspire to thwart our plans.

Of all our nights accommodation it was this one that I was concerned about. We had been unable to find anything conveniently near to the coast in any brochures and our stay on a farm near Caerhays had been the result of a suggestion from a campsite owner in the locality. As we got nearer to the farm my anxiety increased; I had had a bad feeling about this one ever since we had booked it back in February. We found the farm without difficulty, although finding the door was a bit more challenging. We wandered through the farmyard cluttered with decaying cars and scrawny chickens until we came to a path leading into an old orchard and around to the front door. The place seemed deserted and after ringing the door bell the door was finally opened by a young man in scruffy jeans. I launched into my introductory routine, which seemed to confuse him.

"You'd better come in," he responded. "I'm staying here with my brother. I don't know where the owner is. Is she expecting you?"

I explained how we had booked a room for the night and he led us into the dining room. His brother appeared and seemed surprised that we were staying.

"I didn't know they had another room to let!" he exclaimed. "We are here for the week, we came last year as well."

Once again I explained about our booking. This was beginning to get embarrassing. The brothers conferred before eventually deciding they would go to look for the owner, one of them switched on the kettle, suggesting we make a cup of tea, then leaving us alone in the house, they disappeared outside. Left in the dimly lit dining room we slumped down onto a sagging sofa and looked at one another.

"I told you I had a bad feeling about this place," I said.

Chris was just about to reply when the kettle emitted a loud crackling noise and we both jumped. We decided against a cup of tea, preferring to go thirsty rather than risk electrocution. We sat there for some time, contemplating our options if the B&B was indeed double booked. Actually there did not appear to be many options; miles from the nearest seaside town there were not enough hours of daylight left to walk further along the coast to find accommodation even if we had the energy, which we didn't.

The brothers came back from their search and began chatting. They had been unable to find the owner but a few minutes later she arrived carrying a young child. She seemed embarrassed to find us there and at first asked if we had got the correct day. We had and were able to show her the letter of confirmation she had sent us.

"I don't know what to say," she said. "I don't have another room. I'm gutted." But her reaction seemed staged. It had occurred to both of us by that time that the woman had deliberately accepted the longer booking of the two brothers because she would make more money. After all, what was a little embarrassment on her part compared with an increased revenue of over £200?

We sat, saying nothing, feeling numb, dejected and disbelieving that this could be happening. If we were going to be let down why did it have to be here, in the middle of nowhere? Why couldn't it have been in a town with lots of alternative accommodation?

"I could get our room ready for you, I suppose. If you can give me two hours?"

Two hours? Our room? We didn't want to wait two hours. What state was it in that preparation would take two hours? So much for that lucky black cat! What could we do? I was beginning to panic. Why tonight? Why here? Why us? I turned to Chris for inspiration. She was completely calm. What was wrong with her? Why wasn't she panicking?

"Is there anywhere else nearby that do Bed and Breakfast?" she asked.

"Er, a few," said the woman and disappeared to return a minute later with a telephone directory.

While she was gone Chris muttered, "She can give us lift after all this inconvenience!"

"We could try the youth hostel, that's not too far away," I suggested feebly.

Chris found the number in the directory but our mobile phones were out of signal range. Reluctantly the woman produced a telephone. The youth hostel was full, the manager suggested somewhere nearby that might have vacancies but he did not know the telephone number.

"I'm gutted," said the woman for the nth time.

If I could have found my Swiss Army knife at that moment she might well have been!

Sensing our growing rancour the woman produced a leaflet of attractions in the area, with a few B&Bs listed. She indicated one that was about a mile away and reluctantly offered us a lift if we needed it.

Chris rang the number, leaving it ringing out for some time. It was not looking hopeful and I was beginning to contemplate a search for my knife so that I could end it all. Just as Chris was about to hang up the phone was answered and yes, yippee, they had a twin room available for that night!

"I can give you a lift there but only one at a time because it would have to be in my van," offered the woman. She seemed to be eager to be rid of us now our problems were resolved.

"You go in the van with the rucksacks and I'll begin walking," I suggested to Chris. I did not want to have to listen to any more insincere apologies.

Chris and the woman set off in the ancient van and I began walking up the lane after them. The lane seemed very long and I began to hurry, half running in the hope that I would be almost at the B&B before the woman returned in her van. I was still some distance from the B&B when I heard the van coming down the lane. With a crunching of gears she turned it in a driveway and I reluctantly climbed in. The first thing I noticed as I got in was that there was no door lock – obviously there was a very low crime rate around these parts – either that or the lock had been stolen! I shut the door, or rather I heaved it in the direction of the car, but it had failed to shut.

"You have to slam it," instructed the woman.

Taking her advise, I threw the door open as wide as I could and slammed it violently shut; the window shook threateningly, the car rocked on its worn out suspension and the door handle nearly came off in my hand. I perched in my seat, my feet resting on a wide assortment of tools, rags, jump leads, empty cola cans and something that looked suspiciously like a nappy: used, I wondered? Reaching for the seat belt I had problems 'clunk-clicking' myself in securely as the belt seemed to be missing its buckle; I was still trying to find it when we drew up at our new B&B.

"I'm gutted!" she said as I got out of the van.

Then I remembered where my knife was: in the side pocket of my rucksack! But she had turned the van and was driving away before I could get to it!

The lady at our new B&B welcomed us and took us up to a lovely airy room that stretched the width of the house. Windows at both ends of the room overlooked the fields to the sea in one direction and the cottage garden to the rear. I was relieved to have our problems finally resolved but Chris still seemed to be angry.

"The stupid woman asked if you were my daughter!"

It was a question we had been asked twice the year before and an obvious pattern had emerged – the people asking the question were invariably idiots.

"Never mind, it's all worked out okay. I doubt if the accommodation at the farm would have been as nice as this," I said.

"Did she leave her toddler alone in the house while she gave us a lift?" asked Chris.

"I suppose she must have done, those two brothers had gone out. The poor kid might have been electrocuted by that kettle by the time his mother got home!"

We relaxed with a much-needed cup of tea and Chris began reading literature about the place we were staying in, that she had found on the bedside table. I laid back and thought of Pot Noodles, did I really want one for tea? The day had been challenging enough already. But as a great writer once said, all's well that ends well, and it really was very pleasant here I thought, listening to the hens and ducks clucking and quacking in the garden.

Chris looked up from the brochure she was reading and said, "This place is described as a rural retreat. They have weekends dedicated to yoga, aromatherapy and holistic healing. I could come away a new woman!"

"Merv would be pleased."

We showered and changed and did the laundry, then the dreaded moment could be put off no longer. It was Pot Noodle time. I was pleasantly surprised, the food was rather tasty; followed by flapjack and biscuits it was quite a good meal. Things had turned out rather well in the end I thought, reaching into my pocket for a handkerchief. As I removed the hanky out fell the tiny model cat. Now didn't I say black cats were lucky?

Monday 3rd July

The crowing cockerel woke us both up at 4 a.m. He seemed to have an inbuilt snooze facility like my alarm clock, because he let us sleep for three hours and then he woke us up again.

We had another excellent breakfast, this time organic, with Chris opting for the porridge rather than the cooked breakfast. The couple who owned the small holding and B&B were very pleasant, asking us all about the walk and chatting about the wonderful attraction, The Lost Gardens of Heligan, which we would walk quite close by that day. Although we would not have time to visit it then we decided to spend some time there on our last day before driving home, and it really was a beautiful and fascinating place to visit; acres of gardens restored after years of neglect, growing traditional plants and produce.

We walked two miles down the lane to pick up the coast path at Porthluney Cove then climbed above Lambsowden Cove on another overgrown path belonging to the National Trust, tramping through nettles and bracken. We paused to get our breath back, watching our first kestrel of the holiday. We left National Trust property only to re-enter at the land of Penare Farm, where we encountered a herd of Dartmoor ponies. As with the Soay sheep we had met the previous year, the ponies were an environmentally friendly way of controlling the vegetation. The only problem was no one had told them they were allowed to stray off the path! And although horse manure is not as offensive as dog dirt, it is more difficult to step over when it is totally covering the footpath.

In the warm, humid morning a steep climb brought us to the stone cross on the pinnacle of Dodman Point. The cross was placed there in 1896, to act as a daymark for shipping, although it has not been entirely successful in preventing several wrecks. Not without good reason is the point called the Dodman, it literally means dead men! We sat on the base of the cross, shared some chocolate and admired the panorama. Low cloud was building up on the horizon and it reduced the visibility. Very often we would see black clouds amassing, sometimes they seemed to travel away from us but more often we seemed to be walking towards them. Hopefully the clouds that morning were heading away from us.

I slopped on some sun block, we donned our rucksacks and set off towards Gorran Haven and suddenly it was raining hard! Chris blamed me for the change in weather – I should have risked sunburn, then it would not have rained. We hastened into our cagoules but it looked like the rain would soon blow over and so we shunned our waterproof leggings. As we walked our legs became wetter, rain started wicking up into our shorts and running down our calves into our socks and boots. But on this coast the moods are so very changeable and within one mile the rain had stopped, a fresh wind sprang up and the sun came out.

By the time we were sat on a bench at Gorran Haven eating Cornish pasties, our legs were dry and our shorts nearly so. We changed our wet socks for dry ones and set off again. Eeyore was the last thing to dry out and his paws dripped water down my rucksack for the remainder of the day. Before leaving Gorran Haven I retraced my footsteps to the pasty shop which doubled as the general store and which sold Cornish clotted cream ice cream. I ordered one made with Malteasers in and then asked for clotted cream on top.

"My God!" exclaimed the rather dishy young man serving me, "is there not enough in there already?"

"I've got to make the most of it while I am on holiday," I explained, adding: "You might as well stick a flake in the top while you're at it please."

We left Gorran Haven by a steep road. (Why is there always a steep, strenuous bit just after you have had something to eat?) The older part of the village is quite nice, but as with many places on the coast there has been an influx in recent years of retired people and the increased demand for housing has resulted in some less than traditional bungalows sprouting fungi-like on the fringes of the village. We were to encounter more urban expansion later in the day.

We followed field paths out towards Turbot Point, passing an unseen earthwork and climbing the headland before stopping for a drink and to admire the views. We always made a point of admiring the views after we had climbed to the top of a cliff and, if the climb was particularly steep or prolonged, we would stop several times during the ascent again on the pretext of admiring the views.

"Just admiring the view," one of us would gasp as we gulped in air.

The view from above Turbot Point scored double points. Across Mevagissey Bay the sea stretched away towards Black Head and beyond into St. Austell Bay; further over to the northeast we were able to identify the red and white striped daymark on Gribbin Head. It seemed very far away and inconceivable that we would actually walk beyond it the following day. What was far easier to believe was that we would very shortly walk past the houses on nearby Chapel Point. The three houses were built in the 1930's of local materials but their architecture is pure Spanish. With the sun now shining strongly, the sea a deep blue and the houses with their clustering of pine trees it was easy to imagine you were looking down on a Mediterranean scene.

We crossed an open field of short-cropped grass, interspersed with daisies and birds foot trefoil. A track led across the field, the only access to the beautiful and remote Spanish houses. It was a short low level walk from Chapel Point along the coast to Portmellon and from there up the road into Mevagissey, which for some strange reason I always want to pronounce Megavissey! New building work was in progress, spoiling the hillside above the town and adding to the expansion of what had once been no more than a small but thriving fishing community. Unlike many of the coastal towns and villages in Cornwall Mevagissey's fishing industry has survived, the town is still one of the leading fishing ports in Britain and seems to have prospered when others have floundered, possibly due to its two harbours. The town also exists as a honey pot, drawing in the visitors. But at what point did small and quaint become sprawled, bustling, crowded and well, spoiled? Areas of the resort had a neglected feel to them and we were only passing through!

As we walked down into Mevagissey Chris commented on a piece of carpet lying in a heap outside a house. A little further down the hill and we noticed a discarded curtain against a wall. Next we saw half a velvet curtain in a bedraggled heap. What was with all the home furnishings? Had there been a flood? It seemed unlikely with the gradient of the hill! We had heard on the news at breakfast time that parts of Falmouth had been flooded after heavy rain; would the car still be there or had it been washed out to sea? Would we step off the coach in Falmouth to be surrounded by flood damaged carpets and curtains?

Stepping over shag-pile and velvet we found our way to the toilets on the harbour. They were fairly typical of those usually found in a busy tourist spot, that is, awful. Chris muttered something derogatory as we entered and then all words were swallowed up by the sounds of several cisterns flushing in unison. As I emerged from a cubicle a little girl, clutching a cuddly rabbit between her knees, was using the automatic hole-in-the-wall washing facilities. Hoping that on this occasion I would get more than just a handful of liquid soap, I joined her at the adjoining machine, clutching the guidebook between my knees. I don't know how long she had been stood there but it was obviously too long for her irate mother who was waiting outside.

A strident, posh voice shrieked into the toilets: "Lydia, how many times are you washing your hands?"

Anticipating an impending domestic incident, I abandoned the hot air and hastily left the toilets.

As I stood outside a shop, bulging at the wall ties with tourist tat, and waited for Chris to buy some postcards, I recognised a family we had seen in Portmellon little more than half an hour previously. They glanced at me standing there with muddy boots and scratched legs and their expressions seemed to suggest I must be crackers. I glanced at them in their designer chinos and deck shoes and thought of how much they were missing by driving from one coastal resort to the next. They were not walkers and, already becoming possessive of "our" path and mode of transport, we disdained their choice of holiday – resort hopping, as we saw it, by car. Seeing Cornwall but not really seeing it; concentrating on the tourist centres but missing out on the best parts, the unspoilt parts, the parts which epitomised the real Cornwall – the wild, rugged landscape of sea, cliffs and coves. Cornwall in a day, as Chris said. Oh well, each to their own. And it was to our advantage that the majority of tourists did prefer to concentrate their holiday in the towns and resorts. Imagine all of them clambering over the stiles and marching along the coast path – erosion, pollution, litter, noise, environmental damage, not to mention the dog dirt. We would have to go to the towns to avoid the crowds!

Authorities in Mevagissey actually seemed to be winning a battle against dog dirt, if somewhat slowly. Dog bins abounded, as did notices displaying severe financial consequences for any offending dog owners. The cliffs had fallen on the northern outskirts of the town and a diversion notice directed walkers along a temporary path through hotel grounds (a big thank you to the hotel owners for their liberal attitude – we were saved a longer diversion). The council had taken the opportunity at this point to once again remind dog owners of their responsibilities but we were sad to see that the warnings were not always heeded. We were not the only ones who felt this way; someone had written on the sign 'some dog owners cannot read!' It seemed particularly irresponsible of dog owners to allow fouling on that part of the path, had I been the hotel owner it would have given me second thoughts about allowing access. As I have commented before the coast path was always "dog dirtier" near car parks, and particularly worse in towns where locals use the path for exercising their pets. I have no objection to this but why do some owners think it acceptable not to remove the excrement? In Mevagissey someone had even taken offence at the 'clean-up' signs and gone so far as to deface many of them!

From Mevagissey the path climbed and then dropped to climb again before reaching Penare Point. Walking with heads down to avoid the tall bracken fronds we spotted a lizard sunning itself on the path. But it didn't look quite right! The sun was, at that moment, behind a cloud and the lizard was lying on its back displaying its orange belly.

"It's dead!" announced Chris stating the obvious.

"What a silly place to die!"

"Some large footed walker probably trod on it."

Throughout the walk we saw numerous shrews flattened on the path, so I suppose if it could happen to a shrew, not to mention a snail, it could happen to a lizard.

Continuing on our way we heard the song of a skylark, a sound that was to mark our progress over the coming days. Rabbits dashed across the path, darting into the neighbouring fields, their white scuts flashing in the sunshine. It was a beautiful afternoon, the kind of walking that drew a person closer to nature, all that existed were ourselves, the path, the plants and animals and the sound of the waves on the shore. And then suddenly, climbing a rise, views towards Pentewan opened up.

"Oh! Look at that view," exclaimed Chris with such awe that at first I missed the honeyed sarcasm entirely.

I looked and I saw and I said, "Urgh!"

The whole length of Pentewan beach was backed by a large, sprawling caravan site. It was our first big holiday park of the walk that year, and I am particularly allergic to caravan parks. My legs came out in a rash – although Chris maintained the rash was already there and due to the heat and humidity, not the caravan site! The coast path joined the road and dropped down to the entrance to the caravan park, where I reluctantly admitted that, for a caravan site, it wasn't too bad. We were not seeing it as it would be at the height of the summer season, crowded with tents and towing caravans but in fact it was rather nice. Beautiful flowerbeds lined a neat drive into the site and all the static caravans looked in good condition. The whole site was laid out in an orderly fashion, with plenty of green stuff in the shape of shrubs and well-tended grass, and even some brown stuff in the shape of rabbits, (you expected me to say dog dirt then, didn't you?) The scene spoke of investment and prosperity, and so it should, as we were to later discover the company that owned the site owned the beach and a considerable amount of land and some property in the area. Facilities on the beach, for those people staying at the caravan site were plentiful, varied and well organised. And if, as we suspected, the company also owned the local pub then that too was a reflection on their management and quality.

The village of Pentewan itself was only tiny, and the majority of that too seemed to be owned by the caravan site. A cycle route led inland from behind the village, with bicycles for hire, (it was closed when we arrived, or who knows, we might have been tempted?) The harbour provides refuge for a family of swans, although before it silted up it had been used to relieve some of the congestion at Charlestown harbour further along the coast. The history of the harbour at Pentewan is a familiar one: someone thought 'I know we'll build a harbour there!' Someone advised against it, saying it would silt up. And so in the 1820's they built a harbour. And guess what? It kept silting up, until finally this century it silted up entirely and was abandoned.

We found our B&B along a quiet lane, a very pleasant and scrupulously clean place overlooking a stream. So scrupulously clean in fact, that the owner eyed our wet boots with foreboding. We performed our tea, bath and laundry ritual, and I even dismantled and cleaned my walking pole, and then we headed off to the one and only pub for a delicious meal culminating in apricot crumble and the obligatory clotted cream.

It rained hard during the night, waking us both. I lay in bed listening to water gurgling in the downspout and bouncing off the patio, thankful that I was not walking on the coast path.

Tuesday 4th July

In the morning the rain had gone, leaving puddles and mud along the route and the vegetation heavy with moisture. Our boots and washing had been drying overnight next to the boiler in the garage and, planning ahead, we wore our waterproof socks to ward off any wetness from the undergrowth.

We left Pentewan climbing the road to double back and pass a row of houses and a church along an unmade road called The Terrace. In the quiet of early morning a workman's hammering was the only sound to disturb the peace. He emerged from a house as we passed and greeted us cheerfully, covered in plaster dust and wearing an old pair of work-worn jeans and very little else, he looked as if he had spent the night there sleeping on a bag of cement. We climbed field paths hugging close to cliff tops, dipping down to sea level at the beautiful wooded Vans and on towards Black Head, passing badger setts along the way.

Numbers of rabbit corpses in various stages of smelly decay caused us to wonder about the local foxes. But the answer sat alone in a field close to the edge of the path. As we drew nearer the rabbit lolloped about oblivious to our approach. From where we stood watching him he appeared normal but through the binoculars the reason for his seeming disregard for our presence and the possible danger we might present, and for the countless rabbit corpses, became apparent. Myxomatosis. Further along the path, near to the corner of the field, we disturbed three younger and much healthier rabbits. They ran from us, disappearing into the hedge at the bottom of the field. But chances were they too would eventually get this horrendous and lingering fatal disease.

Right out to Black Head we were still stepping over dead rabbits. The bulbous promontory of Black Head sticks out into the sea at the end of a thin arm of land, like an ovary floating at the end of a Fallopian tube. At the tip of the headland Iron Age man built a hill fort, although little evidence of it now remains, and greater imagination than mine is needed to visualise the fort from the scant clues of the banks now buried under vegetation. But only a fool could miss the more recent addition to Black Head, a huge monolith of carved granite planted upright at the point where the path divided. Its carved inscription commemorated a local historian. Sadly a vandal had been at work, obliterating some of the lengthy inscription by chiselling out a random selection of letters. Who would trouble to do such a thing and why? There was no arguing that it was a fine monument, if a little large, but Chris and I could not help feeling it would have been better appreciated, certainly by walkers, had it been turned on end and used as a bench! As we kept finding, there was never a commemorative bench when you most needed one – so, no flowers at my funeral please – have a whip round and buy a bench and stick it at the top of one of those nasty, strenuous ascents on the South West Coast Path. But! Be warned! I shall come back and haunt anyone who defaces my bench, drops litter behind it or allows their dog to use it as a urinal!

Just after Black Head the rain came down and we stopped and put on the full Monty of Gore-Tex. Not wanting Eeyore to get another soaking I removed him from the back of my rucksack and sat him inside my hood, giving him a view of where we were going to instead of where we were coming from, which I am sure he appreciated. Two minutes later we met a couple of women hiking up the hillside and we exchanged greetings, I received strange looks when they spotted Eeyore!

"Do you think they were mother and daughter?" asked Chris bitterly.

"No, I don't think so. Despite the preconceptions some idiots seem to have, it is possible for two women of whatever ages, not related to one another and not having a relationship with one another, to be friends. And if any other morons ask us I shall tell them so in no uncertain terms!"

"No you won't."

"No, you're right, I won't. But I'll wish I had the nerve to."

The wet grass was slippery and treacherous on the steep slopes and walking poles seemed like a sensible idea. Chris had hers extended in no time but once again I was battling with mine. Why was it being awkward, for goodness sake? I had cleaned it only the night before! Chris tugged at one end and I tugged at the other until we eventually forced it to a reasonable length. What it needed was a little WD40 to lubricate it and to repel any moisture. I wondered if I could borrow a squirt or two from somewhere.

The sun came out from behind the black clouds and patches of blue sky over the sea began to spread and coalesce, pushing the clouds inland. We sat on the sea wall overlooking Porthpean Bay and shared some biscuits and a drink, watching the steam rise from our waterproofs and boots. We didn't trust the rain not to return and so kept our waterproof clothing on for a while longer.

An inconvenient landslip at Carrickowel Point added over a mile to our route. A signpost explained the cause of the footpath closure and mapped out a diversionary route that had come into effect only four days earlier. Very frustrating! We removed our waterproofs, stowing them under the flaps of our rucksacks to dry and began to trudge up a quiet road in a wide loop which would finally join another road and bring us back to the coast path at Charlestown. A shorter diversion would have been possible through a private holiday park but negotiations were still taking place between the Council and the owners of the park. We remembered with gratitude the hotel in Mevagissey that had allowed the path to be re-routed through its grounds.

As we entered Charlestown we passed a small, tasteful development of new housing and then an older building near to the harbour. At one time this building must have been a boat builders but now it was a workshop. The huge doors were rolled back to reveal a man working at a bench, fiddling about with some part of a car's innards.

"I wonder if he's got any WD40?"

"Go and ask him."

But he had disappeared before I could pluck up the courage.

Charlestown is only small but has an impressive harbour filled with a collection of old sailing ships. It is still used for the export of China clay and more glamorously has been used as the location of several films and television drama series. The village started off life with a different name until the early nineteenth century when a local businessman, Charles Rashleigh, invested considerable money to develop it for the export of copper and china clay from his mines; a story familiar to many small fishing ports around Cornwall.

We had estimated the walk from Pentewan to Fowey to be thirteen miles and considered it a practicable distance to cover in a day. But at Charlestown we realised with horror that we had miscalculated by several miles. It was probably my mistake, I am notoriously bad at maths, I had probably forgotten to carry the decimal or something! It was one o'clock when we arrived in Charlestown and we had walked less than five miles only to discover that instead of another eight we had another ten miles to walk that day! The walking should be easier from Charlestown around the head of St. Austell Bay where the path followed a level route but with half the day gone and only a third of the distance covered we felt dejected. We considered catching a bus to the other side of Par, which would cut out a section of road walking but as it transpired buses were not as prolific as rabbits in that part of the world. We had no choice but to walk the full distance but we still had plenty of time, the last ferry across the river from Fowey to Bodinnick and our B&B was not until 10 p.m., it said so in the guidebook. And the guidebook is always correct. Isn't it?

We hurried past the Carlyon Bay Hotel, it looked ultra stylish and very exclusive, leaving us feeling ultra dowdy. The path dipped towards a car park and then crossed the seaward side of a large golf course, passing above the Cornwall Coliseum, apparently *the* nightspot of Cornwall. It was an eyesore, a huge car park and semi derelict waste ground surrounded a dull orange hanger-like structure that appeared to be more like a DIY superstore than a trendy nightclub.

"That has got to be the ugliest sight we have seen since Newquay," said Chris.

"How did it ever get planning permission?" I wondered.

"Probably because it is hidden from view. Unless, that is, you're walking the coast path!"

On we hurried alongside the golf links, constantly on the lookout for a golf cart we could hijack to cut down the miles. The golf course was an undulating expanse of sterile short cut grass, hemmed in between the low cliffs on the seaward side, and on the inland boundary by a thin hedge of hawthorn and a railway line serving St. Austell and the china clay works. We both heard a high-pitched squealing noise and turned, expecting to see a golf cart or perhaps a bird. What we did see was a rather more startling and much rarer sight. A petrified rabbit was racing over the ninth hole, closely pursued by a weasel. The weasel caught the rabbit, tumbling with it over the grass and after a brief but futile struggle the rabbit was killed. Unfortunately for the weasel four golfers appeared at that point, disturbing him before he could carry off his dinner. Unfortunately for the rabbit they had not appeared soon enough. The weasel ran to the edge of the course, hiding in the long grass, every few seconds he would dart out hoping to retrieve the rabbit but would be frightened back into cover at the approach of other golfers or walkers. The golfers tutted at the corpse littering their fairway before continuing to the green.

At Par, the path turned inland (just before the sewage outfall pipe), running along an enclosed route that wound through the china clay works and over a footbridge. The china clay works dominated the area, the plume of steam from the chimneys could be seen from several miles away. Everything was coated in a fine patina of white dust: the plants, the fence, the path, and our boots, even the rabbits that lived inside the boundary of the complex seemed whiter than normal. Our boots were wet, would we not end up with plaster casts on our feet?

At a confluence of two paths our route turned under the railway line and joined the busy main road leading into the town of Par. It was nearly four o'clock and we had had no lunch. Par seemed like a convenient place to grab a bite to eat. Entering the small town I noticed a sign advertising baby Guinea pigs for sale.

"Can we get one?" I asked excitedly, "they are supposed to taste just like chicken."

"We've nothing to cook them on," replied Chris practically.

We spotted a sign for a tearoom up ahead but when we got there it was obvious that the tearoom had served its last cup of tea some time ago. Instead we headed for the post office and general store, Chris left me outside to guard the rucksacks and went in to buy some food. She appeared several minutes later with a bulging carrier bag and we set off down the road in the hope of finding a convenient bench upon which to eat our snack. The road didn't seem to have any convenient benches and we continued until we came to the local car park and recycling centre.

We sat on the low wall of the car park and watched the cars pass by whilst we shared saffron buns, bananas, chocolate and two pints of milk. Two walkers sitting on a wall eating are obviously quite a rare sight in Par. We received curious glances from every car and passer-by.

"Maybe they are looking at your moustache," I laughed as Chris handed me the carton of milk.

"What? Oh, shut up!" she said, wiping the milk from her top lip.

I took a swig from the carton and I too got a matching white moustache.

"At least I don't have a beard as well!" retorted Chris with amusement as a dribble of milk ran down my chin.

But as we continued with our 'afternoon tea' it seemed like everyone was looking, every car going past had children in the back, every child stared. I felt like waving, Chris did, at which point I decided it was time to make tracks.

The path left the road at Polmear, turning south and passing through Polkerris before continuing out towards the Gribbin with its prominent red and white daymark. We got lost in Polkerris, unable to find the path out, quite an achievement considering how tiny the village is! When we did eventually find the path and followed it into a small sycamore wood we got lost again! We wandered under the cool canopy of the trees, and realising we were going in the wrong direction were forced to retrace our steps until we found the correct path. A little accurate signposting would not have gone amiss!

The guidebook described the next section of path as pleasant and easy. And for a while there we actually began to believe it. The vegetation along this part of the path had been very recently trimmed, for which we were most grateful.

"We will probably catch up with a man wielding a strimmer in a bit," said Chris half in jest.

She spoke too soon, shortly after leaving the wood the man must have knocked off for the day! We waded for one and a half miles out to Gribbin Head through thigh deep vegetation that seemed to be mainly composed of nettles, thistles and an alarming amount of giant hogweed. By the time we emerged onto the close-cropped grass at the daymark, our legs were wet with moisture from the vegetation, and cut, red and stinging. The nasty hogweed had been unavoidable and several blisters were beginning to form on my legs where the sap had come into contact with my skin. It was several days before the fluid filled blisters finally burst and several weeks before the wounds healed and the scars began to fade. Chris had faired slightly better, her legs were shorter than mine and her shorts were longer than mine and had offered more protection, even so, she too looked as if she were suffering from a bad case of measles!

The daymark was built in 1832 and stands prominently on Gribbin Head, reaching eighty-four feet into the air, a clear warning to shipping enabling them to identify the headland from other peninsulas along the coast. There were apparently excellent views from the top and, according to our literature, it was possible to climb up inside the tower. Feeling refreshed and refuelled after our 'high tea' I was tempted to see the views from the top.

"I think I might go up," I said to Chris and leaving her to find a convenient al fresco toilet spot I made my way to the door at the base of the tower. It was locked. Yes, you could climb to the top, but only on Sundays, this was Tuesday!

I had to be content with the views from the ground and the views were still good even from that lower altitude. We could see across St. Austell Bay, and were able to track the shape of the Roseland Peninsular trailing away far to the south as a hazy line on the horizon. Across the wooded slopes of the Gribbin we looked to the north and down into Polridmouth Cove with its enclosed lake beyond. This was Daphne du Maurier country, she lived nearby for many years at Menabilly, the 'Manderley' of Rebecca. I had read Rebecca some years ago and promised myself that I would renew my acquaintance with Mrs de Winter again soon. That scene, across the sloping fields of Gribbin Head, looking down into the small cove and the turquoise sea, with the lake and the wooded slopes beyond, is one of my favourite views on the coast. It is not a vast panorama, of which there are so many along the coast, with majestic headlands, sheer cliffs and open bays; and so in that respect it is not representative of the path as a whole. I think perhaps its appeal for me is in the seclusion, the romance of the place and the secretive, hidden nature of that tiny cove with its sheltering of deciduous woodland climbing the slopes behind. It was an area that Daphne du Maurier had loved; reluctant ever to leave her Cornish paradise she was evidently a reclusive figure and shunned much of the outside world, becoming something of a hermit and an eccentric in later life.

We dropped down the slope in the evening sunshine and crossed in front of the lake with its families of swans, coots and moorhens. The path climbed steeply for a short section through a narrow belt of woodland to enter National Trust land at Lankelly Cliff. We passed two men out jogging and exchanged greetings, later on they overtook us on their way back to Fowey.

"Where have you walked from?" asked one.

"Pentewan."

"Is that all?" he joked before sprinting off to catch up with his friend. It was all right for him – he wasn't carrying a rucksack!

The last part of the day, the walk into Fowey, did not look far on the map. Deceptive things, maps. From Southground Cliffs the path dipped and rose and dipped and rose and dipped again before passing St. Catherine's Point and dipping for the last time down into Fowey. Even when we had reached the town we still had a lengthy walk through the winding streets to the ferry point at the far end of the long meandering main road.

Fowey seemed rather upmarket, catering for yachting types, it reminded me very much of Cowes. We were looking for a takeaway, having decided that due to our late arrival (it was nearly 8 p.m.) we would have supper before crossing the river to our B&B. Fowey only seemed to have one takeaway and we collapsed at one of the pavement tables outside, grateful for the rest, before realising that one of us had better go in and buy some food. I ordered fish and chips and waited and waited and waited whilst the food was cooked to order, the organisation seemed poor but we had another two hours before the last ferry of the day, there was no rush.

Having eaten our supper we dragged ourselves to our feet, shrugged on our rucksacks (were they really that heavy when we took them off?) and shuffled along the road to the ferry point. Suddenly we heard a blaring siren getting nearer and presuming it was the ferry we broke into a staggering run, keen not to miss it and be forced to wait for the next one. Our tired legs carried us in a haphazard jog trot along the narrow road, earning odd glances from passers by. Our view of the river was blocked by a long row of cottages and it was not until we arrived at the car park by the ferry point that we realised the horn had come from another vessel moving slowly up river. We did not have to wait very long for the 8.30 ferry to carry us across to Bodinnick. We got off the ferry to find ourselves standing at the foot of a long steep hill.

"Where's the B&B?"

"Our farm is at the top of the hill," quoted Chris, reading from the directions we had been sent.

"Oh good!"

We looked at one another and began walking slowly up the hill. Ten minutes later and we found the B&B. It was a fabulous farmhouse occupying the sight of a former Elizabethan manor house: the manor having not survived the Civil War due to a bad choice of sides by the owner. The farmhouse was L-shaped, climbing roses covered the mellowed stone and the numerous chimneys cast long shadows across the lawn, an old King Charles spaniel tottered down the path looking as if he too had just run for the ferry! As we turned in at the gate and walked down the garden path, the front door was thrown open and a lady came out to greet us. Her first words made us realise how well timed our arrival had been.

"Hello there! I was beginning to get worried about you. The last ferry is at 8.45!"

The guidebook had got it wrong – we had been fortunate and had unwittingly caught the pen-ultimate ferry of the day! It was hard to believe how close we had come to being marooned on the wrong side of the river.

The inside of the farmhouse was every bit as beautiful as the outside. The guest rooms took up one branch of the L-shape, each bedroom having en suite facilities, whilst downstairs a single large lounge and dining room stretched the length of the wing. We followed our host into the cool interior, marvelling at the inglenook fireplace that dominated one end of the room, at the beamed ceiling, the polished oak floor and the huge refectory style dining table that promised much of the breakfast to come. We were led up the open plan staircase to our room on the upper floor, treading carefully but still leaving clumps of mud behind, feeling very guilty we collected them up later! The bedroom was under the eaves and with the windows thrown open to let in the fading daylight we could hear the birds in the garden and smell the delicate scent of the climbing roses.

We shed our rucksacks, boots and socks and returned downstairs for a pot of tea and plate of biscuits. In our bare feet we browsed the bookshelves and admired the framed before and after photographs of the transformation of this part of the house from a ruin to its present glory. The owners had worked hard to make it into a beautiful home and continued to work hard to provide warm and friendly accommodation. The bare floorboards felt wonderfully cool under our hot, tired feet but we soon sank down into the deep cushioned sofa to drink the tea, it had been a very long day and there was a limit to how much longer our legs could hold us up!

Our room that night was the first of many that had zipped together beds, these were a clever and versatile way of providing flexibility for the B&B, converting a double into a twin room in a matter of minutes. Our beds were unzipped, obviously, but pulled only a few inches apart. I settled down to sleep that night, clutching Eeyore in one hand, but as I began to nod off I turned over, flinging my arm out and across onto Chris's bed.

"Get that donkey off my pillow!" she shrieked, waking me up.

"Uh?" I mumbled.

"Your arm and that donkey are on my bed."

"Oh, sorry." I withdrew my arm but dropped Eeyore in the process. Where had he gone? I sat up in bed and began myopically scanning the bed. In the dim light and without my glasses I could not see him. I shook the duvet then I began to feel down the gap between the beds.

"What on earth are you doing now?" came Chris's sleepy voice.

"I've lost Eeyore."

"Good."

"That's not very nice. I wouldn't say that if you had lost Buzz."

"I don't take Buzz to bed with me!"

At that moment my groping fingers found Eeyore. I pulled him back into bed, rearranging the duvet and plumping up the pillows and settled down, clutching Eeyore firmly by the paw.

"Poor Roger, how does he put up with you?"

"It's the other way round! He snores and grinds his teeth all night."

218

"So do you!"

"I do not."

"Yes you do and this morning you were gargling in your own saliva!"

"Was I?"

"Yes. And you mutter."

Some discussions you know you're just not going to win, so I went to sleep.

Wednesday 5th July

The breakfast was every bit as good as we had been expecting, a huge loaf of homemade bread sat in the middle of the table and Chris and I consumed vast quantities of it that morning along with the cereals, cooked breakfast and homemade jams and marmalades. Some places you just don't want to leave, and that was one of them. But we had to and so we settled our bill, heaved on our rucksacks and descended the hill to the ferry point.

The coast path starts on the eastern side of the river at Polruan. We had been staying on the eastern side of the river but at Bodinnick further up the river. Therefore we had to take a ferry across to Fowey and then the lower ferry from Fowey back across the river to Polruan.

Fowey is a picturesque small town, with pastel painted houses lining the river and climbing the hillside above the town. It is unusual in that it occupies a position on a narrow deep-water inlet. So deep is the river at this point that cruise ships visit the port, and the docks, concealed further up river, are used for the export of china clay.

As we waited for the ferry a tug appeared towing a huge freighter towards the docks, sailors standing on the deck were dwarfed by the size of the vessel. The massive bulk of the ship hid much of Fowey from view and delayed the arrival of the ferry.

Whilst we were waiting, amongst a growing crowd of cars and pedestrians, I decided to try to collapse my walking pole to its shortest length, I had grown tired of carrying it all the time and preferred to have it fastened to my rucksack. The pole had been stuck at a length of about three feet, too short to use to walk with and too long to fit comfortably on my rucksack. I attempted to unscrew the sections but they refused to move more than a fraction, so I put the point of the stick on the ground and forced my whole weight onto the handle until, with a sudden rush, the pole telescoped to its shortest length and I collapsed on top of it. From a distance I must have looked like a Samurai throwing himself onto his sword!

"I don't know why you just don't buy yourself a new one," commented Chris as she fastened it to my rucksack.

"I just need to fix it, that's all. A squirt of WD40 and it will be fine."

She gave me that 'exasperated mother' look which mothers are so good at, but I was spared further comment by the arrival of the ferry. We crossed to Fowey amongst an assortment of school-run cars, workman's vans, shoppers and a postman.

"You've got sunburnt," said one old man pointing to the welts covering my legs.

I felt like telling him it wasn't sunburn but the result of nasty vegetation, but I did not think he would have understood my accent. That morning my legs were still red and angry from the stings and scratches, and the blisters caused by the giant hogweed were swollen with clear fluid. Chris's legs in comparison were pale and unmarked, yet we had walked through the same vegetation, why were mine so red?

We stocked up with chocolate and cakes at Fowey, once we left Polruan there would be no opportunities for refreshments until we reached Polperro seven miles away along a section of path that was graded as strenuous.

The second ferry dropped us off onto a slippery jetty at Polruan from where we walked up the village through steep narrow streets to the top of the hill and the remains of an ancient chapel. The path turned away from civilisation and dropped slightly, heading east towards Blackbottle Rock.

Most of the path on the South West Coast Path is not as you might imagine a clearly defined broad sward, level and well trodden. For the most part it is often a narrow channel of earth between thick vegetation, wide enough for only one foot; or a rough, rocky path strewn with loose stones, protruding roots and hidden holes; or sometimes just bare rock that must be scrambled over and negotiated with care whilst balancing and reaching for hand holes in order to climb large boulders. It is the difficult nature of the path combined with the steepness of the ascents and descents that make many experienced walkers consider this long distance trail to be the hardest in the country. And in the section of path to Polperro, every difficult trait was represented in fair measure.

This is not to say that we did not enjoy our walk that morning because we did; the scenery was spectacular, the sea a deep inviting blue and the weather was kind. The air was full of the scent of sweet smelling delicate white flowers of ladies bedstraw; red campion grew in abundance, its bright pink flowers contrasting with the yellow flowers of hawkweed and the blue scabious, and a profusion of marguerite daisies attracted fat bumble bees. Buzzards floated and soared above the cliffs, their size and the 'fingers' on their wing tips making them easily recognisable. The music of the morning was the gentle waves washing the coves below and the harsh cry of stonechats contrasting with the song of skylarks, background percussion was the incessant din of crickets. Ships far out at sea seemed hardly to move, whilst sailing boats nearer to the coast glided gracefully across the still water. A yacht was moored in Little Lantic Bay, the couple that owned it had the secluded cove to themselves.

Much of the coastline from Pencarrow Head eastwards is owned by the National Trust and their conservation work is undoubtedly important but once again we found ourselves wishing they would do more to maintain the path and control the vegetation. We crossed a stream at West Combe and began a quite level section of walking below Lansallos Cliff. Bracken closed in on the path, narrowing it considerably until we reached a wooden footbridge where we paused for a rest. I turned to look back the way we had come, just in time to see a vole scoot across the path.

Chris began reading the guidebook and informed me that Marie Stopes had once owned a holiday cottage in the area. I got confused and thought instead of Doris Stokes, asking, "Did she foresee how overgrown the path would become?"

"What are you talking about?" asked Chris.

"You know, she was psychic!" I replied.

"Marie Stopes. Not Doris Stokes!" said Chris, with exasperation. "Marie Stopes was involved with cancer research!"

"Oh," I said and began reading the path description, it didn't mention cancer research! "Birth control, not cancer research! The path description describes her as the pioneer of birth control!"

"Well, I knew it was something medical!" responded Chris.

From East Combe the path rose up the hillside, passing a daymark in the form of a huge white obelisk. Rough steps had been cut into the slope to aid walkers but these were totally obscured by the undergrowth. Bracken, nettles, bramble and yes, giant hogweed, grabbed at our legs as if trying to trip us, and slapped in our faces. We tried holding the vegetation aside for each other but it was a pointless task, there was just too much of it. Only a third of the way up the slope we rested against the daymark and waited for three German ladies to descend the slope. Their approach was heralded by much crashing of plants, thudding of boots as they slipped off the concealed steps and a considerable amount of cursing in German. We didn't understand the words but certainly agreed with the sentiments. They nodded curtly to us as they passed.

We turned and resumed our battle with the vegetation up the long flight of steps. The sun was shining strongly by that time, making a difficult ascent more tiring. I reached the top of the slope first, gasping for breath and dripping with perspiration. I needed to sit down! After a cursory inspection for creepy crawlies I collapsed for a well-earned rest on a grassy mound, the only clear patch at the side of the path for some distance. Chris appeared on the crest and staggered over to join me. Together we eased off our rucksacks, boots and socks and sat back to eat some cake, have a drink and recharge our energy levels. Chris turned and reached for her rucksack, but something had reached it first, the rucksack was moving away from her outstretched hands!

Ants!

Ants. Everywhere: climbing over the rucksacks and one even disappearing inside the leg of my shorts. Grabbing our socks, rucksacks, drinking bottles, cake and guidebook, we stuffed our bare feet into our boots and hastened along the path, bashing at any accompanying ants as we went. We scurried for nearly a quarter of a mile before the path widened out and we were able to sit down in ant-free comfort. It was a minor miracle that neither of us had tripped over a lace or stepped out of our boots during the hurried jaunt; thank goodness no other walkers were about at the time to witness our strange activities!

Thinking back to childhood holidays it was wasps that were always a major problem. Dad seemed to have a knack of parking beside shrubs that invariably sheltered a wasps' nest. Mum would then proceed to lay out a picnic and as soon as the first lid came off a Tupperware container, the wasps would descend. Sandwich in hand I would execute a rapid dance (usually in the style of St. Vitus) around the car in an attempt to outrun any wasp. This always failed. Mum would tell me not to be so silly. To which I paid no attention. And Dad would flap at any wasps that buzzed round him, with the immortal words "Leave them alone and they won't bother you." I so desperately wanted to leave them alone – but they didn't want to leave me alone! And Dad's flapping hands always seemed to send the wasps in my direction! Each lunchtime it was the same: Mum and Dad outside the car eating sandwiches and cake and fruit, ignoring the wasps and generally getting on with life; meanwhile, on a hot sunny day, I would be sat inside the car, doors shut, windows up and just in case (remember those killer bee disaster movies?) the air vents closed, with perspiration streaming down my face, eating my lunch, shuddering involuntarily each time a wasp landed on the windscreen.

So far we had not had any run-ins with wasps, and that was how I liked it! As we neared Polperro the path dropped down, levelling out before finally entering the village. Polperro is a tourist Mecca, tucked in a narrow valley with a sheltered inlet providing safe anchorage, walking from the coast path you literally turn a corner and step into it! Quaint and charming are just some of the adjectives the guidebook used to describe this typical Cornish fishing village but we arrived at a bad time. The narrow, traffic-free streets were crowded with holiday-makers, gulls soared between rooftops, shops competed to sell ice cream and postcards and worst of all the tide was out, resulting in a somewhat pungent aroma emanating from the festering seaweed.

We were hot, tired and in need of shade and a drink. We stopped briefly to buy a bargain batch of postcards (five for 50p – the cheapest so far!!) and then climbed the lane leading from the eastern side of the harbour. Several benches were set out overlooking the harbour and we settled thankfully on one sheltering in the shade of an old stone wall, for biscuits and a drink.

Twenty minutes later we felt ready for anything, almost, and we set off again following a very popular dog walking path up out of Polperro, passing many people all of whom seemed to be walking to Talland Bay. The stones along this well walked section of path had been polished smooth by countless numbers of feet.

"I bet these are slippery when they get wet!" I said, just before slipping on a dry stone.

At Talland, Chris continued along the path whilst I called in at the public toilets. By the time I emerged, Chris was a distant speck. I hurried to catch up with her, marching across a car park and towards a field. But in my haste I caught up with a family walking their two boisterous dogs. Before I knew it I was part of their group, walking along between the teenage daughter and her dopey boyfriend. As I negotiated a kissing gate, one of the dogs careered up to me, nearly knocking my legs from under me as I battled to get my rucksack through the narrow gateway. The dog was soaking wet, it must have been in the sea, and in the process of disentangling my two skinny legs from its four furry ones a lot of wet, smelly dog hair was exchanged!

East of Talland Bay a black cloud hung threateningly. By that stage we were accustomed to threats from black clouds, most of the clouds had failed to deliver and hopefully this one would be no different. Chris was only a few yards ahead when I passed an American couple. They were not taking any chances with the cloud and had stopped to put on their waterproof jackets. I could not help noticing their footwear. I have a thing about walking boots, believing that most people are conditioned into choosing an unnecessarily heavy, rugged (usually leather) pair of boots, when often a lighter weight pair would suffice. I will admit to a certain degree of prejudice, as I have not dared to wear heavy boots with a lot of ankle support after suffering a tendon injury. However, the lightweight pair that I now employ has proved to be very durable, incredibly comfortable, and easily capable of supporting me around the rugged South West Coast Path. So, I was especially pleased to note that both Americans were wearing the same design of boots as I was.

As I walked by the lady looked up from fastening her rucksack and said, "Hi."

"Hello," I responded and, as her husband looked up: "I like your boots!"

He returned my grin but had probably not understood a word I had said, the thick Lancashire accent always seems to be especially difficult for foreigners to comprehend! Chris would probably argue that it is just me that is especially thick and difficult! (What are friends for, if not to insult you at every opportunity?)

I finally caught up with Chris as the first fat drops of rain began to fall. The dripping tap scenario quickly turned to the gushing fire hydrant scenario and we got our cagoules on in record time!

"It's bound to pass," said Chris, "all the other heavy showers have."

She was right – all the other heavy showers had stopped almost as soon as they had begun. But she was wrong about this one! It didn't stop. And by the time it became apparent that it was not going to stop our legs and feet were saturated. We were wearing waterproof socks but because there was such a large volume of water running down our legs, it was soaking into the cuffs of the socks and getting inside them. I had taken Eeyore off my rucksack to prevent him becoming soaked again and had put him into the pocket of my shorts. But it soon felt as if he were peeing into my pocket, although it was actually rain wicking up my shorts!

For the next two hours we squelched along – cagoules on, hoods up, heads down and spirits low – into increasingly heavy rain. It was nearly all low level walking with what should have been good views across Portnadler Bay to Looe Island. The heavy rain cut down visibility and to lift our heads even for a second was unpleasant as the rain, falling with such force, stung our faces. At the western end of Samphire Beach, a swollen stream discharged its muddy water into the sea. All around the area the sea had been turned a dirty brown colour by the stream, and gulls circled and jostled one another for any invertebrate delicacies that had been washed down with the torrent.

At exclusive Hannafore the path merged with the road for a long mile into Looe. The American couple, with who we had been playing an alternating overtaking game ever since Talland, passed us for the last time near the coastguard lookout point (the first we had passed that had not been closed down).

"Are we having fun yet?" called the woman, splashing up water from a large puddle as she passed.

Did we look as if we were? If Chris had had the energy she may well have pushed the American into the sea at that point. Instead, all she could manage was a grunt and a weak flap of her arms.

Our B&B was in East Looe, across the river. As we walked through Hannafore and West Looe, passing numerous hotels and bed and breakfast establishments, I found myself wishing we were booked into one of them; tired and wet it seemed an awfully long way to East Looe.

We finally arrived on the doorstep of the B&B and rang the bell. Water dripped from our fingers and the bottom of our cagoules and ran down our legs. As soon as we stopped walking we began to feel very cold and by the time the door was opened our teeth had begun to chatter.

"Oh, you really are walking then!" said the landlord in astonishment.

No, we just thought we would park the car and then stand outside in heavy rain for three hours! Of course we were walking! We were walkers! What did he expect, a hovercraft? (Actually that would have been more appropriate considering the amount of water involved).

He led us inside and up to our first floor room; we followed, dripping all the way. Typically, as we were tired, soaked and at a low point, the B&B was not as good as the preceding ones had been; it was clean enough but the décor and furnishings were dated. Had we arrived in good spirits, dry and not tired, I do not think it would have seemed so bad. The owner took our boots and rucksacks away to dry, leaving us standing in the room on growing damp patches of carpet. We stripped off where we stood, wrapping towels around ourselves before Chris headed for the bathroom and I headed for the kettle.

Standing in front of the mirror, waiting for the tea to brew, I could not help but notice my reflection. The mirror was at thigh level. Was that cellulite? No, surely not. It was goose bumps - I was shivering after all. I put my glasses on and looked again. Oh, it did look a bit like orange peel! May be it was a touch of cellulite. (Could you have just a touch of cellulite? I didn't know. Was that like being a bit married or a bit pregnant?) Was the cellulite there before I came on holiday? And if it wasn't, then was it a result of too much clotted cream? I had to ask myself a vital question here: was cellulite a fair price to pay for the indulgence of clotted cream? For me, this was not a difficult question to answer. Yes. Well, life's too short to worry about a little bit of cellulite; all women have a layer of body fat, it's natural. Show me a woman who doesn't have cellulite and I'll show you an anorexic, unless of course she happens to be an international athlete or gymnast! (Or possibly someone in a pub at Thurlestone, but more of that later!)

It was my turn to do the laundry that night, so whilst Chris was in the shower I washed the usual array of clothing but the difficulty was trying to dry them. Fortunately our change of clothes in the rucksacks was dry, so at least we had something to wear! But we needed to get the washing dry in case the following day was wet or we would have no clean dry clothes for the next night. We could hardly ask to use the washing line and the landlord had said he did not have a tumble drier. Chris suggested we try to find a laundrette. It seemed like a good idea but in practice it proved impossible.

The landlord thought there was a laundrette in East Looe but he did not know where as it had recently moved. We searched East Looe before finally asking in the local supermarket. A boy filling shelves didn't know but he asked a cashier. The cashier wasn't sure, so she asked the lady behind the cigarette counter. The lady behind the cigarette counter waved a packet of Swan Vestas in the direction of West Looe and confidently declared there was a laundrette over the river. We took our bag of soggy clothes and crossed the bridge to West Looe. We passed one laundrette but that was closed, for good by the looks of things! We searched West Looe before finally asking in the local supermarket. There wasn't a boy filling shelves so, cutting out the middleman, I asked the lady behind the cigarette counter. She waved a butane lighter in the direction of East Looe and said there was a laundrette over the river. Okay, so it was going to be one of those days!

We crossed back over the river to East Looe and sought out a pizza takeaway. The garlic bread and spicy chicken pizza we shared that evening were the best thing about our stay in Looe.

After the food, I was feeling much better about our situation but Chris was still depressed and worried that our clothes would not be dry by morning. Necessity being the mother of invention, we rigged up a rather effective drying system from a hairdryer, several coat hangers and a chair. By hanging the clothes around the legs of the chair to form a tent and by positioning the hairdryer in front of the chair we were able to get the clothes at least nearly dry, although of course we could not leave the hairdryer switched on all the time. It was not just our clothes that were wet but our mobile phones, purses, stamps and even the guidebook. Rained had seeped into the rucksacks' pockets saturating everything inside them. Fortunately the phones had survived but some of the stamps were a definite write off and by the end of the week the guidebook had still not dried completely.

In the late evening the rain stopped and the nearby disco began. It competed with the resident seagulls to assault our eardrums late into the night.

"Do you think those Americans have dried out yet?" asked Chris sleepily.

"I don't know but I bet they are not having to listen to this racket!" I replied before shoving my head under the pillow.

"Do gulls go to sleep?"

"Pardon?" I asked raising a tousled head from the depths of the bedding.

"I said: do gulls go to sleep?"

Almost on cue, the gulls fell silent but just as Chris began to say I told you so, the screeching started up again with renewed vigour.

"Shift work! That will be the back shift starting."

Thursday 6th July

Breakfast was surprisingly good and included yoghurt and fruit and a choice of cooked items, we sat at a table by the window with excellent views over the rooftops and down into nests of the abundant herring gulls. The sky was a patchwork of white fluffy clouds and blue promising bits, dare we hope that there would be no rain to spoil the day?

"Oh, look!" I muttered sarcastically, "There's a gull feeding her chick on that nest. Yes, she's just regurgitated a nice, semi-digested dollop of fish guts."

"Do you mind!" said Chris, spearing a mushroom with her fork.

After breakfast we collected the rucksacks, they were dry but nothing else was. We packed the rucksacks, separating the damp clothes into a plastic bag, our shorts were almost dry so we just put them on, our body heat would soon eradicate any remaining dampness and if the day became warmer and we started sweating, the shorts would soon become damp again anyway. I suggested tying the tops and underwear to the rucksacks to dry in the sun but Chris had a better idea, a veritable brainwave in fact.

"We walk by a campsite this morning," she said, studying the guidebook. "They might have a laundrette."

We set off in wet socks and boots, but well fed and rested, the cold, clammy feeling surrounding our feet did not seem too bad. Chris confidently headed down the hill back into the main shopping area of East Looe, with me dutifully following her. When we reached the bottom of the hill, she checked the guidebook, turned round and walked back up the hill, with me dutifully following her. Two minutes later we passed our B&B and continued up the road. I forgave her the unnecessary walking and the steep ascent, she had just had a brainwave after all, and that must be very taxing!

The road climbed steeply, narrowing into a quiet lane as it reached the cliff tops above East Looe. Looking back at our route the previous day we were rewarded with fine views across the bay to Looe Island.

From there the path wound through Plaidy, passing a collection of nice houses with palm trees growing in the gardens, bullfinches flitted between the trees lining the lane. Following the signposts we dropped down some steps and into a campsite at Millendreath. The footpath went right by the door of the campsite laundrette and we thankfully made use of the facilities. We got strange glances from two women who were using the washing machines as we stood watching our clothes and hats tumbling about inside the drier. Every so often Buzz or Eeyore would appear in the window to glare out at us before being smothered by a shirt.

Beyond Millendreath Beach the path climbed an ancient rutted lane, once a medieval highway. The lane showed extensive evidence of the recent heavy rain, deep furrows were scored into the ground, made by a torrent of water as it washed earth, sticks and pebbles down the steep track, and miniature dams of twigs and leaves were strewn across the lane. Many other places along the coast path showed evident sign of their temporary status as rivers for the run-off.

We entered National Trust property above Bodigga Cliff and predictably vegetation closed in to clog the route. We battled and cursed our way through dew-soaked hogweed, nettle and bramble, our sore legs becoming wet causing them to sting even more. We saw still more bullfinches and thrushes and blackbirds and a large number of marbled white butterflies, presumably attracted by the thistles and brambles. After climbing several totally pointless and ridiculously height-ist stiles, the final one of which I slipped off, landing in a ditch at the side of the path, we dropped down into deciduous woodland. Unfortunately the humidity did not drop. Although the morning had grown quite sunny, the heat was causing the previous day's heavy rain to evaporate and walking in the humid, enclosed wood was uncomfortable, it was like hiking in a sauna. The scent of wet, warm earth and vegetation competed with the smell of wet, warm boots.

The guidebook foretold of 'excited shrieks' from the nearby monkey sanctuary but the only shrieking was made by us as our cut and blistered legs stung. For a short distance the wire boundary fence of the sanctuary ran along the landward side of the coast path. Presumably it was there to keep the public out rather than the monkeys in, they would be confined within cages, wouldn't they? Without being aware that we had passed through the fence we suddenly realised that it was now running along the opposite side of the path. Did that mean we were walking through the sanctuary? A crashing in the dense foliage below drew our attention, Chris stopped without warning and I walked right into her.

"What do you think was making that noise?" she whispered.

"I don't know."

It could have been a deer, it could have been a lost walker, or then again it could have been a monkey!

"Gorillas in the mist," murmured Chris.

"Thanks for those words of reassurance!"

Wild strawberries lined the path; I had munched my way through half a dozen of the tiny, sweet fruits before Chris said I would probably get the runs if I ate too many. On a coast walk with not many toilets, I decided that delicious though the strawberries were, they were not worth the risk. Besides, strawberries are really best eaten with lashings of clotted cream, don't you think?

The path cut up through a small coniferous plantation before joining the road and descending into Seaton, passing some exclusive housing along the way. Seaton is yet another little village lining a narrow wooded valley, with a stream flowing down to the sea. Some new development had recently taken place near the shore on the eastern side of the stream, replacing older holiday chalets. Local opinion was divided regarding the new housing, but we saw postcards of Seaton showing the old chalets and I must say the new housing looked far more sympathetic to the surroundings than the run down chalets had been.

We had a choice of two routes at Seaton, the first was along the road but the official one followed the sea wall and then continued along the beach. We were unable to decide which to take and so made a unanimous decision and headed for the toilets, quickly followed by the beach café. Now that we were away from the shade of the trees and other vegetation the morning felt hot rather than humid and we were both in need of some refreshment. We left our rucksacks at an outside table and went in to the café to buy a drink. Chris was diverted by a stand of postcards and I was diverted by the ice cream counter. I might not have had any clotted cream with the strawberries but I made up for it with the ice cream. We sat at the table, writing postcards and eating ice cream and soon began chatting to two elderly couples at an adjoining table. They were, like so many people we met, keen to know how far we were walking and where we had walked from. And they did, like so many people, express amazement at the distances but clearly had little concept of just how far we had walked from Falmouth. It was a common reaction.

We had been wondering what had become of our American couple, expecting them to be somewhere in front of us, but as we sat outside the café we noticed them walking along the promenade.

"Let's see which way they go," suggested Chris.

"And then go the other way, do you mean?" I asked, laughing.

"Well, the woman will probably ask us if we're having fun yet!"

The Americans stopped at the end of the promenade and seemed to be studying the guidebook. We were distracted by a question from one of the people at the other table and the next time we looked we could not see the Americans.

We made our way along the unofficial road route, not wishing to get our damp boots covered in sand along the official beach route. As we strolled up the road out of Seaton we turned back to take in the view and there, down below us, sitting on a bench were the Americans. The man spotted us and waved, we waved back.

"They're obviously having fun," said Chris.

Full of ice cream and fizzy drink I burped my way along the road through Downderry, each burp elicited a strange reaction from Chris that seemed to involve an involuntary rolling of the eyes and a tutting noise, she seemed to be doing rather a lot of that lately! It was a pleasant walk along the road and gave us two nosey parkers the opportunity to admire the houses and the church along the way.

Beyond Downderry the path left the road and turned up a track between tall hedges, to emerge in cliff top fields. It was somewhere in the middle of this large grassy field above Battern Cliffs that the path reached its highest point in south Cornwall at 462 feet, but as the climb had been gradual it did not feel particularly noteworthy.

The path joined a quiet road, the B3247, the main coast road along this undisturbed part of southeast Cornwall. With only a short break of off-road walking, we were to continue along this road for the rest of the day and much of the following day. The road was not unpleasant to walk along, for once we did not have to pay attention to where we placed our feet and the heat from the sun baking the tarmac helped to dry our boots.

The American couple caught up with us just after joining the road and for the next mile we walked together down into Portwrinkle, chatting about the walk, the state of the path, the unpredictable British weather and about California where they lived. I wanted to tell them how the South West Coast Path was the longest National Trail in the country and that it was equivalent to three times the height of Everest but they were having difficulty understanding my accent. Chris was doing a lot of translating, and it all seemed too much effort, coming from a country that has National Trails spanning thousands of miles they probably wouldn't have been very impressed. We left them in Portwrinkle, their destination for the day.

We made use of a bench overlooking the rocky beach to sit down, relax, have a snack and air our feet. An unpleasant smell drifted up to us, at first I thought it was coming from my socks but Chris reassured me it was from the uncovered seaweed drying in the sun. Fifteen minutes later the Americans were still in sight, asking directions to their accommodation from locals and their wives, roping in more and more people, until it seemed that the entire village must have been gathered around them! We did not meet those Americans again, although we were to encounter others in the second week.

Before setting off again Chris consulted the map.

"What does this red shaded area represent?" she asked, turning to the key for the answer.

"Oh nothing. It's blood. I was picking at my finger and things turned messy!"

From Portwrinkle the path climbed to the headlands once more, running along the edge of a golf course for the first half mile. We were part way across the course, and just contemplating hijacking a golf cart, when we were startled to hear a panicked shout, someone seemed to be counting.

"Fore!!"

We looked up to see a golf ball hurtling towards us. We stood frozen in shock, two startled rabbits in the glare of headlights, watching as the ball zoomed towards us, crossing into the air space of another fairway, and soaring worryingly close over our heads to land on the green behind us. Another golfer had ducked; we had just stood there! Too late came the messages from our brains commanding us to take evasive action, when the order did get through to our legs we turned and collided with one another.

"Sorry," called the abashed golfer with the loud voice and the poor aim, as he hummed past us in a golf cart.

"Well, at least he apologised," said Chris. "But why didn't he shout 'look out' or something instead of just shouting 'four'!"

"That's why he shouted. And it's fore. Not four."

"Well how are we supposed to know that fore doesn't mean four, it means watch out there's a potentially life threatening golf ball flying towards you?"

"I don't know why they shout fore," I said becoming exasperated. "Probably for the same reason they have bogies, birdies, eagles and albatrosses. It's a silly game, like cricket! When they're out they're in and when they're in they're out. And silly mid offs. And ghoolies – or is it googlies? And football's as bad, with off side, which doesn't mean the over-rated, over-paid

230

wally in long shorts is standing at the side of the pitch but actually is something to do with him being further up (or is it down?) the pitch than the other team when some other over-rated, over-paid wally kicks the ball to him! And then there's rugby! Why don't they use a proper ball, instead of a misshapen one?"

As I paused to draw breath Chris said, "I only asked! Have you quite finished now?"

"Well, since you ask..."

"Julia!"

"Yes?"

"Shut up."

"Can I just add...?"

"No."

"Oh. Okay. I'll shut up."

"Good." Then after a pause: "Silly mid what?"

After the golf course came the military fort and various notices directing us around the area and towards a road. I had been expecting an ancient monument type of fort, or at the least a relic from Napoleonic times, certainly not a leftover from World War II now used for training. At a stile onto the raised verge above the road we met a foreign walker.

"'Ow iz ze paff?" he asked.

"Oh, not too bad!" I responded cheerfully in an accent that he too, no doubt, failed to understand.

"Eet iz tres grassee furza on."

"What a nice German," I commented as we began wading through the deep 'grassee'.

"He was French!" sighed Chris.

Our views of the sea had gone, hidden by the extensive concrete of the fort but inland the fields rolled down towards the jagged fingers of land bordering the inlets of the river as it flowed into the estuary at Plymouth. Thick, dark green hedges marked out countless fields of lush grass, in one field adjoining the road a herd of Friesians grazed.

"Look at those cows!" I remarked. "There they are chewing the cud, turning it into Devon clotted cream. Er, then again, may be they aren't making clotted cream. I think they're all bullocks."

Soldiers moved across a neighbouring field, grouping and regrouping before making their way across the road to the fort. In the middle of the field a stand of shrubs grew together in an unusual shape, making us wonder if in fact it was a tank in disguise.

"All the soldiers are going for their tea," said Chris. "They must not be training tonight."

Indeed, it appeared that manoeuvres were over for the day, a few stragglers collected up the last of the equipment and watched by a man standing at the side of the road clutching binoculars, (who might have been an observer, or then again might equally have been a Soviet spy) they too crossed the road and entered the fort. An army Jeep drove by and then all was quiet.

Our B&B for the night was just outside Lower Tregantle and only a short distance from the main road and the fort. We found it up a drive, a large, modern detached house from the pebbledash school of architecture. It was not quite four o'clock when we rang the doorbell, as the ringing faded a car pulled onto the drive discharging several children in school uniform and a rather startled looking woman.

"Oh! Have you booked?" she asked.

No, please! Not again!

"Yes," replied Chris, sounding more confident than either she looked or I felt.

"That's okay then. It's just that this is my sister's house and I am only looking after things for the evening. Come inside and I'll show you where everything is."

She led us to a bedroom on the ground floor, pointed out the bathroom and, after telling us the evening meal would be at 6 p.m., disappeared into the kitchen to make us a pot of tea. There were no tea making facilities in the room, which meant we went without a drink before bedtime or before breakfast (a definite minus point in my book). The advertised drying facilities turned out to be the top of the boiler that, with the central heating turned down, was not firing up unless someone turned on a hot water tap. Chris and I spent a lot of time during the evening turning the hot water tap on! Our boots did dry on top of the boiler overnight but our washing, which we put on the washing line for at least an hour before the rain set in for the evening, did not dry. Breakfast the following morning turned out to be a 'cornflakes, grapefruit or orange juice?' kind of affair, as opposed to a 'there's the groaning sideboard, help yourself' kind of affair. Cleanliness was not an issue, we had no complaints on that score but the beds were rather old and saggy. We shared the tiny bathroom with four Belgian guests, an experience that resulted in much dashing to and from our room in the hopes of finding the loo vacant and also meant we got up extra early just to ensure we could get to use the shower! It was not until after breakfast that the owner of the house asked if her sister had shown us where the upstairs bathroom was; stable doors and bolting horses, and salt in wounds, sprang to mind.

When we arrived that afternoon, I was the first to head for the shower. I ventured out of our room into the large hallway but, faced with several closed doors, could not remember which one was the bathroom. I tried the first door I came to, opening it slowly and peering inside. A rather dishevelled bed faced me, with clothes strewn across its surface – oops – the other guest room! (Fortunately the other guests were not in it, although with the various garments

232

lying about I had wondered.) I had no better luck with the second door I tried – that was the broom cupboard, I reacted quickly enough to spare myself a bashing from an ironing board that began falling outwards as I opened the door. First flying golf balls and now household equipment trying to concuss me! Third time lucky and I found the bathroom, or rather the shower room; it was tiny and made my own five feet by seven feet shower room seem palatial.

As we lounged in our room writing postcards we heard the other guests arrive. Soon the peace of the evening was shattered, a whole tribe of children seemed to be playing in the garden, shouting to each other and running backwards and forwards past our window. Young English voices competed with young Belgian voices. The family dog was urged to join in the energetic activities and in his loyal way he tried to please but age and too many doggy chocs were against him. In the warm weather this old, overweight retriever with his long hair and arthritic joints, was pestered and chased around the garden.

"Max! Come here, Max."

"Max! Over here, boy."

It could only be a matter of time before his old heart gave up but, amazingly, in the morning he was still staggering around! For days afterwards one of us would wonder if Max was still alive.

This was the only night we were booked to have an evening meal, and that at least was good; shepherd's pie and runner beans, followed by cream meringues, and cheese and biscuits. The Belgian children were somewhat lacking in table manners, not, I suspect, representative of the nation as a whole but a poor reflection on this one family in particular. Each child left the table and visited the toilet at least twice during the course of the meal, and running round the room, kneeling on the chairs and shouting with their mouths full all seemed to be regarded as acceptable behaviour.

We went for a stroll along the lane in the evening, as much to escape the children tormenting the dog and generally being a nuisance as to find a post box. The escape was only brief as increasingly heavy rain drove us back indoors before we could find a post box. We slumped on the beds watching teams of interior designers ruin two couples' bathroom and kitchen, with Carole Smillie smiling throughout the half hour programme and trying to think of uplifting comments when the home owners viewed their 'new' rooms with horror. Then, rather appropriately, we watched a fly on the wall docu-soap about female army officer cadets being put through their paces in ridiculously out-dated and inappropriate skirts on the parade grounds of Sandhurst.

The news followed, it was depressing, a little girl was missing and police were not hopeful; her body was found days later. It seemed that every summer a child was abducted, always with the same tragic result. How did parents cope with the waiting, the uncertainty and the eventual grief? In the same programme a story about the Prime Minister's son was covered in great detail. It served to illustrate the biased way the media treats such stories when well-known people are involved and the emphasis placed on the perceived newsworthiness of these items. The story was of such irrelevance, particularly following the earlier news, as to be insulting. Basically the boy had been found drunk out of his head in Leicester Square, arrested on a charge of being drunk and incapable, and when questioned had given a false name. What did a charge of being drunk and incapable actually mean? Incapable of remembering his name, presumably! And why did the general population need to know? What relevance had it for anyone outside his own family? None. The television company were just using it to spice up their programme and score political points.

The local news followed with reports of flooding in Falmouth. One supermarket had been forced to close as water swept in through the automatic doors, ignoring the turnstiles and spurning the trolleys and baskets to sweep produce from the lower shelves and submerge the aisles. I pictured the vegetable aisle with mushrooms floating across it and apples bobbing in the currents, and the toiletries aisle with hundreds of rolls of loo paper and kitchen towel trying valiantly to soak up the flood.

The national weather forecast followed and Helen Young stood coyly in front of the map, smiled sweetly and told us we were going to get wet in the morning but would dry out in the afternoon. Do the Met. Office allocate work to the meteorologists depending on the type of weather expected? Miss Young always seems to get the rainy weather, Penny Tranter presents the sunny spells and for years they reserved poor old Michael Fish for the 'we aren't really sure but it's likely to be quite inclement if not downright horrible' sort of forecast. And for the really bad forecasts, the type that are always followed by the closure of Snake Pass, Ian Macaskill is brought out! Perhaps the pattern of forecasters and forecasts should be studied in greater detail; who knows, it might be possible to form your own weather prediction simply by identifying the person in front of the weather map.

At ten o'clock we settled down for the night, the children had eventually gone to bed, Max had collapsed somewhere and all was quiet and peaceful. A lone owl hooted somewhere in the fields, hunting for his supper. I was just drifting off to sleep when the firing began. At first I was at a loss to identify the sound.

"You awake?" I whispered.

"Hard not to be," replied Chris. "Did I foolishly surmise the army were not training tonight?"

"I think you did say something along those lines, yes."

I fell asleep before the firing ceased, so I do not know for how long it continued. But at 2 a.m. they brought in the heavy artillery!

BOOM!!

Chris and I were instantly awake and sitting up in bed.

"What the hell was that?"

A flash of light briefly illuminated the room before darkness returned, immediately followed by: BOOM!!

"Oh God, no! They're firing rockets or bombs or something now!"

"Great! Last night it was discos and seagulls, tonight it's World War Three!"

The shelling continued sporadically for some time. How did soldiers on active duty cope with lack of sleep and interrupted sleep? How could they possibly be able to fulfil their duties effectively after a night of constant shelling? More importantly for us, how would we manage to walk the ten miles to Plymouth if we did not get any sleep?

Friday 7th July

As we prepared to leave that morning and Chris paid the bill the landlady reminded us not to forget our boots. On a walking holiday we were hardly likely to set off in just our socks! Oh dear, these stones do feel sharp this morning! I wonder why? Oh, yes, now I remember, I've forgotten to put my boots on! Not really plausible, was it?

The children were still chasing Max around the garden, so he hadn't died of fright in the night when the shelling started! I supposed people living in the area became accustomed to it, as I was accustomed to the traffic noise and Chris was accustomed to the croaking frogs in her garden pond.

The drive was full of parked cars that morning. A large blue Ford headed the line, followed by a variety of cars of all shapes, sizes and ages until at the end of the drive a battered car brought up the rearguard. This last car could have been a Nova, but it was so covered in dents and expansive patches of rust and plastic body filler that it had morphed into a vehicle of indeterminate identity, it could just as easily have been a skip or a customised perambulator. The house had seemed full of people that morning, many more than the previous night: who were they all? Did they all live here? Were there even more guests than we had been aware of? Were any of them R.S.P.C.A. inspectors? We didn't know and we never found out, yet another of life's little mysteries.

It was very overcast as we set off along the road that morning. Mist hung over the fields and light drizzle threatened. We followed the road around the fort, passing a long line of soldiers walking along either side of the road, all wore battle dress and camouflage makeup (but none of it was very fetching, I think they needed to consider accessories – matching handbags, some costume jewellery and high heels possibly!) Some pointed their rifles at us making me jump until Chris assured me (in the confident manner of someone who has seen a lot of documentaries about army training) that the yellow things on the end of the rifles meant that they were not loaded. Other soldiers smiled and said hello as they passed. All carried packs and two were further weighted down with radios. Many of them seemed near the point of exhaustion, presumably it was these soldiers who had been running around shooting and bombing all night.

At Tregantle Cliff the road ran parallel to the coast once more, the path at that point actually following the road. It was easy walking along the road, good for the legs but hard on the feet which were aching by the end of the day. But it was not a particularly interesting walk along the road that morning, for much of the way we were able to see quite a distance ahead along the relatively straight highway, with only the odd point of interest to draw our attention. The first interesting distraction was marked on the map as The Grotto, which, the guidebook informed us was a cave hacked out of the cliffs just above sea level by an officer in the Navy as a cure for gout. Whether it cured his gout we were not told but the book did suggest that the detour down a long, steep flight of treacherous steps to view the cave was worthwhile. The cave had apparently survived for over two hundred years, until presumably some time between the guidebook being written and Chris and I venturing down the steps to look at it, because it had caved in! Having been unable to find anything but a rock fall we trudged back up the steps and rejoined the road to Freathy.

Freathy was another rather incongruous distraction for us that morning. It was a strange place, appearing to be just a scattering of wooden chalets that from a distance (especially when viewed later in the morning from Rame Head) resembled a load of rubbish that had been tipped down the hillside from the back of a lorry. Many of the chalets were rotting where they stood, some looked unfit for stabling a horse let alone housing people. But others were quite well kept and some even had UPVC double-glazing and satellite dishes.

At Wiggle Cliff the road turned inland, the path running out towards Rame Head following the curving line of the coast. We paused looking out towards the headland behind which lay Plymouth Sound. As we stood admiring the scenery a Royal Naval ship sailed slowly into view.

"It's very difficult to see that ship against the sea and sky," commented Chris. "If it was painted a brighter colour instead of that dull grey we would be able to see it much more easily."

"Perhaps the Navy just had a cheap job lot of grey paint."

We could joke about that first ship but by the end of the day we had become a little less tolerant of the heavy naval presence in the waters around Plymouth.

Rame Head is distinctive, its conical appearance and the six hundred year old chapel on its summit making it easily identifiable for miles along the coast. The chapel is apparently dedicated to Saint Michael – just imagine, six hundred years ago and someone had already thought about having a patron saint of shopping! Our arrival on Rame Head seemed to herald an improvement in the weather, the overcast morning vanished and the sun appeared. Looking back we were able to see the long white stretch of sand at Long Sands that had been covered by the tide the afternoon before. In the hazy distance, we wondered, was that Dodman Point? On a clear day, visibility from Rame Head was superb, little wonder it had been chosen as the site of a fort in Iron Age times, then a chapel in Mediaeval times and later still, in the mid twentieth century, as a World War II lookout. Needless to say the later building had not endured as well as the earlier constructions!

It seemed a long walk through the overgrown path towards Penlee Point and it wasn't even National Trust land! We were running on empty, a meagre breakfast and only a biscuit at Rame Head had done little to fuel our morning's walk. The promise of food at Cawsand beckoned. Penlee Point protrudes eastwards into Plymouth Sound and, only a short walk from a nearby country park, is a popular place. It boasts extensive views of the Devon coastline and numerous benches as well as a grotto built to commemorate the visit of Queen Adelaide. Leaving Chris reading the memorial inscriptions on all the benches, I made my way down the path to visit the grotto. Thankfully, this one had survived the years; it was a rough construction of stones cemented together with inbuilt stone seats, almost an extension of the cliff face. Inside it was welcomingly cool after the sudden warmth of the late morning. Spiders' webs festooned the rocky ceiling and woodlice scurried in the damp corners. Several arches looked out towards the Sound and the sea. I half expected to find graffiti boasting of the old Queen's visit: Queenie was here, or Adelaide rules OK, something along those lines, but there was nothing. It was easier to imagine this grotto being frequented by young lovers on a summers evening than the visit of a regal personage.

Retracing my steps, I joined Chris on Earl's Drive, a rough muddy pebble track that wound down into sycamore woodland towards Cawsand. We had gone only a few steps into the trees when I became aware of a buzzing sound. The nearer I was to Chris the louder it became.

What was it? A wasp? I stopped and the buzzing travelled down the path with Chris. I hurried to catch up with her and grabbing her arm, dragged her to a halt.

"What's the matter?" she asked.

"Can't you hear that buzzing?"

"No."

At that point a particularly loud buzz was emitted, it sounded like a wasp trapped inside a drum.

"Yes."

"It's there," I said pointing to Chris's rucksack.

"Where?" she said, turning round.

"There! On your rucksack."

A large bumblebee had become lodged inside the ventilated back of her rucksack, entangled in the bra she had wedged there to dry. Flicking at the bee with the corner of the guidebook had no effect, except to make it buzz more. Very quickly the rucksack came off but the bee was still wrapped in the underwear that in turn was wrapped in straps of the rucksack. Chris began shaking first the rucksack and then the bra but the bee made its way deeper into the folds of material and the buzzing intensified, this was becoming one very angry insect!

All my common sense told me not to worry - it was only a bee. But increasing panic told me it sounded like a giant wasp. A giant, irate, mean, nasty, evil wasp. I moved away from Chris and her rucksack and her bra and the bee, until I was standing on the edge of the wide path and could go no further. She continued to shake at her bra and the bee continued to become ever more entangled and to buzz even louder. I began dancing up and down with nerves and waving the guidebook, directing operations from the perceived safety of six feet away.

Chris finally succeeded in freeing the bee, which then flew in a tight circle and landed once again on her rucksack. She cursed, slapped at the bee, missed, dropped her bra into a patch of mud and cursed again. I continued to hover nervously, offering helpful bits of information like, "It's still there!" and "It's getting angry!" All of which Chris could plainly see for herself. Finally the bee freed itself, flying in increasingly large circles around us, (with me frantically ducking and squirming) until, with a final angry buzz it gained altitude and disappeared into the trees.

I breathed a long sigh of relief, Chris attempted to dust the mud off her bra, cursed again and swung on her rucksack.

"Thanks for your invaluable assistance," she said sarcastically.

"Any time," I replied, regaining my composure now that the crisis was over.

We began walking down the drive through the dappled shade cast by the canopy of leaves. Every so often the trees would thin, presenting us with views of Plymouth Sound. We could now see three Royal Navy ships lying at anchor; they sat there, going nowhere, with smoke rising from their stacks. What did they do all day?

"Look at that!" exclaimed Chris. "Three of them now! Wasting taxpayers' money. My money! What do they do all day?"

"Have you not seen that advert on telly?" I asked. "They catch drug smugglers and watch little green blips on radar screens!"

"They won't catch any drug smugglers sat in Plymouth Sound! Waste my tax, that's what they do!"

As we followed the path through a bank of sweet chestnut trees we got a different perspective of one of the ships.

"There's a front-on view of that ship," I told Chris.

"Hmm."

"Can you see it, or are the bushes in your way?"

"No, I have a perfect view of it through this gap in the leaves; an ideally shaped gap for seeing my taxes being wasted!"

We descended into Cawsand; it barely rated a mention in the guidebook, but together with its twin village of Kingsand was very attractive. In front of the old market cross a small collection of shops sold amongst other things, hot Cornish pasties, cakes, chocolate and cold drinks. We sat on a bench in the hot sun, eating our lunch and people watching. The beach at Cawsand is only small but it caters for a full range of activities. Families picnicked, children paddled, Navy vessels wasted Chris's tax and one man in baggy shorts and canvas shoes and sporting dark shades, long blond hair and a deep bronze tan rented out boats and canoes. A party of local school children were learning to sail – prompting me to ask Chris if she thought some of them would be the tax wasters of the future. We ate our last Cornish pasties in Cornwall, gulped down the cold drinks and sat relaxing in the sunshine. We had taken off our boots and socks, giving our feet a chance to air and to stretch our toes; already that day our feet were aching from the hard pounding on the tarmac road and Earl's Drive and we still had several miles of the same type of walking to come. I was eager to be off, my bare feet were beginning to burn and I was becoming too hot sitting there in the strong sunlight.

We walked along the quiet, narrow road through Cawsand, passing the old county boundary stone and into Kingsand. Kingsand had been part of Devon, until in the mid nineteenth century a re-shuffle of boundaries brought it into Cornwall. Cottages along the lane advertised B&B and we wondered if this might be a possible rest stop for our American friends that night, it would be nice to stay in such a quiet, pleasant village.

After buying postcards and ice cream at a shop in Kingsand we attempted to follow the directions to Mount Edgcumbe Country Park, through which the coast path ran, but we got lost. There's a novelty! It was Chris who figured out where we had gone wrong and soon we were on the right track and following the coast path towards Cremyll and the ferry point across the water into Plymouth. Mount Edgcumbe Country Park is noted for its various follies and its deer. The follies we saw, the deer we didn't, unless that is, they were a different sort of the short-legged, fleecy variety! The path under our feet had become red, a precursor of the distinctive red Devon soils to come. As it followed the undulating shoreline, through trees and down to little bays, views of Plymouth Sound, Drake's Island and the city itself were constantly changing. Every so often another Naval vessel would come into sight and Chris would mutter something about taxes.

A short ferry ride carried us across the Tamar and into Devon. Until recently the path through Plymouth had gone unmarked but lately investment by the City Council and the hard work of the Coastal Officer for the city had resulted in good way marking and points of interest directing the foot-tired coast path walker through the city, and improving the path as it left the city at Mount Batten Point and at Jennycliff on the eastern side of the Sound. The South West Coast Path Association had presented the official with its first annual award in recognition of his work and that of his team, an award that we thought was well deserved.

We followed lampposts displaying the Countryside Commission's acorn symbol until we approached the Hoe and began looking for our accommodation. As we neared a bar a man emerged and began weaving slowly up the street in front of us, he was clearly much the worse for drink and we hastened to pass him. But that proved somewhat difficult. We moved to overtake him on the right but he veered across the pavement, cutting off our route. We moved left but so did he! We tried to dart through a gap between him and some railings but, as if he had sensed our intention, he staggered to fill the gap. We tried going right again, but as before he weaved to block us. Resigning ourselves to the inevitable we strolled behind his meandering form until he turned right, narrowly missing a tree and a parked car, weaved between lines of honking traffic and disappeared down a side street.

Plymouth is remarkable as far as the South West Coast Path is concerned because it is the only city on the route. The large Naval presence resulted in an extensive bombing campaign by the Luftwaffe during the Second World War and much of the city was destroyed. Extensive rebuilding has created open traffic-free shopping malls and a large new commercial centre, whilst in the narrow residential streets around the Hoe much of the older housing remains but now with some open spaces containing parks and children's play areas on former bombed sites. Much of the historical parts of Plymouth remain, fortunately missed in the bombing raids: the Hoe, the Royal Citadel, the Barbican, with all their attendant history of Sir Francis Drake, the Armada, the various arrivals and departures of numerous epic journeys including in 1620 the migration of the Pilgrim Fathers to the New World.

The city is not only an important Naval base but a busy commercial port with regular ferry crossings to the continent and has a vast choice of hotels, motels, hostels, guest houses and B&Bs. We had plenty of accommodation to choose from and had chosen, with care, a guest house run by fellow walkers with the expectation that they would be in tune with our needs and sympathetic to our sweaty bodies and smelly boots. We found the street and walked past a laundrette and a small row of houses to the end of the row where our guest house was located. Chris knocked on the door and we waited expectantly. The door was answered by a motherly looking large lady and two somewhat boisterous dogs. But to our chagrin a mistake had been made by the woman's daughter and a double room had been reserved instead of a twin.

"I'm terribly sorry but it's a double room," said the woman. She then waited for us to say something, it was almost as if she expected us to say that a double room would be okay. Needless to say it wasn't and we didn't!

Following an uncomfortable silence, during which one of the dogs began to lick my scratched legs and I nudged it away (none too gently) with my knee, the woman went on to say she had reserved us a room at a hotel across the road, was very sorry about the mistake and would refund our deposit. She disappeared down the hallway to get her purse, returning clutching our £10 note and began asking Chris how far we had walked. The dog returned to lick Chris's legs this time and I kneed it away once more as Chris tried to make polite conversation in a tone of voice that I knew from experience was hiding how she truly felt. To say we were both annoyed and disappointed at being let down for a second time was an understatement!

Our little procession then made its way across the road and into the hotel. Our room was on the third floor. Great! We would have preferred to have found our own accommodation, in a city the size of Plymouth it would have been simple; but we now felt committed to staying in this hotel; no doubt the woman had thought she was acting in our best interests and trying to make amends. The hotel was clean and our room had en suite facilities but it was not what we had been expecting and the mix up had left us feeling dejected.

"How many more times could this happen?" I asked Chris, Eeyore, Buzz and the world in general.

None of them could give me an answer, which was perhaps as well. Sometimes it is best not to know what is in store.

"At least it's clean," comforted Chris. "But it's too hot!"

She flung open the windows and propped open the door in an attempt to create a draught of cool air. She was right, the room was incredibly hot and stuffy, in fact the entire city seemed to be baking in the late afternoon sunshine, it was amazing to think how cool and overcast the morning had been.

We made ourselves a cuppa using the only two cartons of UHT milk and the only teabag provided. When, assuming that there had been an oversight on the part of the maid, we later went to ask for more like a pair of modern day Oliver Twists, we were given a further two teabags and two milks by the landlady masquerading as Scrooge. So much for our great expectations! (The hotel wasn't called Bleak House was it?)

We showered and changed and then, bundling up our dirty laundry, we went down the road to the laundrette. Almost every item of clothing we were not wearing went into the washing machine, including our sweat-stained grubby sun hats. We left the machine to work its miracles and went off to the Hoe to buy some postcards.

Half an hour later we returned to the laundrette, loaded up one of the driers and sat waiting for our clothes to dry. Laundrettes are a good place to observe a microcosm of life. Two French ladies came in with lots of underwear, a scruffy young man had a load of football kits to be washed and a young English woman, bedecked with jewellery and body piercing sat waiting for her army surplus gear to be washed.

Our laundry having dried we dropped it off at the hotel and set off in search of some food. Our feet ached on the hot, hard pavements as we strolled across the Hoe towards the Barbican area with its nightspots, bars, pubs and restaurants. We walked along the waterfront, passing families clutching bags of chips and groups of young men clutching bottles of beer. We found a popular pizzeria in a quiet side street, serving excellent pasta and garlic bread, and stuffed ourselves silly!

Nearly two hours later we left the restaurant and headed for a convenience store to stock up on supplies for the following day. It was Friday night in Plymouth and the Barbican area seemed to be the place to be. All the bright young things were there, as well as some not so bright, and crowds thronged the streets and spilled out of the numerous bars and clubs. As Chris waited to be served a group of young men entered the shop, burping loudly and emitting beer fumes. I stepped out into the street to escape the second hand lager, only to almost collide with a man staggering past. It was barely nine o'clock and Plymouth seemed to be full of semi drunks.

Chris came out of the shop with a bag of groceries in one hand and a liquorice pipe sticking out of her mouth.

"I've got a pipe!" she grinned.

"I can see that."

"I didn't know you could still buy these. I must have been about nine years old when I last had one."

"Very nice but do you have to walk through the streets with it sticking out of your mouth?"

"Why? What's wrong?"

"You're showing me up, that's what's wrong. Why can't you just eat it like any normal nine year old? Next thing you know some pickled old salt will be offering to light it for you!"

We walked back towards our hotel, taking a short cut that Chris was sure would lead out onto the road the hotel was on. Ten minutes later and we were lost.

"We're lost." I remarked.

"No we're not, the hotel is just over there," Chris pointed towards the towering structure of the Forte Motel. "Just below that motel."

"It's nowhere near the motel! It's a few blocks beyond it."

We walked in silence until we eventually came to the hotel.

"My feet are aching," I moaned.

"So are mine and we've got to climb to the top floor!"

Saturday 8th July

The hotel breakfast was not the best by any means and we were soon on our way. We walked down to the Hoe, heading for Smeaton's Tower. Smeaton's Tower dominates Plymouth Hoe, it was originally built on Eddystone Rock, replacing the first two lighthouses there that had succumbed to the waves and a fire. In 1759 John Smeaton built the third lighthouse on the rock but it was undermined by the sea and removed to the Hoe, to be replaced by yet another lighthouse that is still going strong! Smeaton's Tower is a popular tourist attraction and when we had arrived in Plymouth I was hoping to recreate a childhood holiday experience. I was just seven when my Dad had taken me up the tower, and I had turned green at the top.

Twenty-six years later and I have a better head for heights but I was not able to climb the tower, it did not open until 11 a.m. and nor would it for several weeks - it was being renovated. I was dreadfully disappointed. I had wanted to go up, not just for myself but for Dad. He had died at the beginning of the year, leaving an enormous gap in my life filled with regret for all the things left unsaid, the missed opportunities, the love that I had taken for granted. Now, in my thirties, I had encountered a new experience, I was still learning and growing and sometimes the graph was too steep for comfort. As a good friend had said, it was a chapter of my life closed forever. Smeaton's Tower had symbolized all the good times and in the week before as I was walking towards it I had been walking towards a memory, one that I had profoundly wished to re-enact.

With the tower out of bounds we retraced our route of the previous night around to the Barbican where a water taxi would take us across the river. The water taxi set us down at Mount Batten Breakwater and we followed the way markings to the public toilets – too much tea at breakfast time! The area was undergoing a lot of renovation, good paths, posh housing and excellent signposting for the coast path made that stretch of urban walking rather enjoyable. Unfortunately the resident dog walkers then went and spoiled things by not cleaning up after their pets.

At the large car park at Jennycliff a group of teenagers had been set down by mini bus and were preparing to walk part of the coast path. We followed them through yet another popular dog walking area, in fact they walked ahead of us for most of the morning, dropping litter as they went. I was just bemoaning yet another crisp packet that had been jettisoned by the group in front when I stepped into a fresh, clinging pile of dog dirt, giving me two things to complain about. Which is worse – dog dirt or litter? Well, I suppose dog dirt is biodegradable as opposed to most litter, but that is not the first thought that springs to mind when you've got it all over your boot!

We climbed slightly through deciduous woodland, watching the clouds gather over Plymouth Sound and over the four Royal Navy ships that were anchored there. Chris was heard to mutter about taxes. Soon it began to rain, we had learnt our lesson on previous days and we quickly changed into waterproofs but within a matter of minutes the rain stopped. Having gone to all the effort of putting on the waterproofs, we kept them on, almost wishing the rain would return so that we wouldn't look like such idiots. A mile further on, with no more threatening spots of rain, we decided to remove the waterproofs, resting on a bench and having a biscuit whilst we were there. As we stood up to continue on our way the rain returned and we found ourselves unpacking the waterproofs and putting them back on. We were not particularly surprised when the rain stopped and so once more the waterproofs came off, for good that time for that day at least!

The low-level cliff top walk towards Heybrook Bay was pleasant; we had now walked beyond Plymouth Breakwater leaving the sheltered waters of the Sound behind. Directly west across the sea lay Penlee Point and Cornwall. A short flight of steps led down to a few houses where a lady clutching a furled but damp umbrella asked us if we were camping like the teenagers she had just met. But she answered her own question as she examined the back of Chris's rucksack for signs of a tent.

"Oh no, you're not," she said. "But I see you've got your little bunny or something."

Buzz bristled with indignation at the insult and both Eeyore and I had difficulty controlling our amusement.

More M.O.D. land was reached at Wembury Point, the location for the terrestrial base of H.M.S. Cambridge. As firing was not taking place that day we were able to walk along the real coast path in front of the site instead of following the alternative to the rear.

"No ships there to waste your taxes," I teased Chris.

But she wasn't listening, her attention had been caught by an unusual bird.

"What's that bird?" she asked pointing to a little feathered thing sitting on a nearby bush.

"That," I said confidently, "is a Cirl Bunting."

She looked at me and blurted: "You just read that on that information board, didn't you?!"

"Might have," I mumbled.

We stopped for lunch in the fields overlooking Wembury Point. The ripening barley waved in the fields and dancing blue heads of cornflower and greater knapweed grew in the field margins. Across the water, not very far from the shore, was the rising bulk of Great Mew Stone and looking east we could make out the mouth of the River Yealm not too far away, our goal that afternoon. The next part of the path ran over the low cliffs above the beach towards Wembury, the whole stretch of that coastline being the Wembury Marine Conservation Area. I have never seen so much litter in a conservation area before! Looking with distaste at the rubbish stranded on the high water mark, I failed to see that Chris had suddenly stopped, and collided with her. She hardly seemed to notice and hastily retraced her steps, making excited noises of the 'just seen something really interesting' variety. A £10 note speared to a bramble perhaps? No. A marine woodlouse, which is obviously very interesting to someone who has made a study of woodlice as part of her degree! That cute little woodlouse, which Chris very nearly squashed in attempting to pick it up, was the most remarkable wildlife we saw that day.

The National Trust owns the coastal land between Wembury and Warren Point and we were interested to see if this stretch of the Coast Path would be better managed and the vegetation controlled compared to the Cornish Trust-owned property. A Trust warden was posted in the car park at Wembury, drumming up membership and Chris approached him, keen to ask about the Trust's policy on footpath maintenance. She described our unpleasant experiences with vegetation and I modelled the various scratches, cuts and blisters. At one point he tried to tell us that the National Trust didn't own the footpaths – clearly untrue – and finally admitted to being unaware of the problem.

"Ah, that's Cornwall you see! But in Devon the footpaths are managed, I can assure you."

Hm, interesting. As far as we were aware the National Trust did not have political boundaries as the County Councils do! Was I being cynical or did the Trust invest more money on their houses and gardens than the footpaths because that was where the majority of the public went to spend their money? Invest in conserving the popular properties at the expense of the non-earning footpaths? I was not disputing the need for conservation and the important work undertaken by the National Trust in restoring and maintaining historic houses, gardens and so forth; but if the National Trust recognised the importance of preserving the beautiful coastline – and they clearly did or why else did Enterprise Neptune exist – why were the footpaths not being repaired and the vegetation trimmed? Money invested in path maintenance would prevent further erosion caused by walkers battling to cross muddy stretches or to avoid densely overgrown areas; not to maintain the paths was surely false economy.

The warden, under our barrage of polite but persistent complaints, assured us he would report our comments, whether he ever did or not we will never know. He told us he had recently walked the section of path from Plymouth to Salcombe and had not encountered any problems. Indeed, as our walk into Devon continued his words at first rang true but the further east we walked the worse the path became.

Having given the poor warden an ear bashing we visited the Marine Conservation Centre and looked at the exhibits of things to be found on a beach: razor shells, dead crabs, kelp, starfish, driftwood, trawler netting, plastic bottles, condoms and oil-smeared sea birds. Did you know that it takes a year for cardboard to degrade in the sea? A cleverly constructed life-size 'litter' man stood in one corner of the exhibition centre, he had been made entirely from litter collected from the beach. The thought occurred to me that an entire army could be made if all the litter was collected from Britain's coastline – you've heard of the Terracotta Army, this would be the Flotsam Army; what a sad reflection on our treatment of planet Earth.

The church at Wembury stands on a hill above the beach. It was supposed to be well worth looking at, still retaining parts of its Devon wagon roof dating from Medieval times, and we fully intended to visit it. However, what we intended to do was not what we actually did. Firstly, the path that set off in the direction of the churchyard fooled us completely by veering around and away from the church and leading us up an unnecessary hillside. Having followed the path for a few minutes we got a fine view of the church roof but from the outside! Retracing our steps we were still unable to find the entrance to the church, and this, combined with the fact that the church bells had begun to peal, made us decide to abandon looking around the church – we could hardly hike down the aisle in walking boots and sweaty clothes and sign the visitors book when someone else had just glided down the aisle in a white wedding dress to get married!

We made use of the public toilets at Wembury and before setting off took a few measures of the skin cancer prevention type by applying sun tan lotion and getting out our sun hats. After yet another overcast and damp start the day had become warm and sunny. The sun tan lotion went on no problem, the hats were a different matter. I crammed mine onto my head, where it perched precariously, for some reason it seemed a little small. Chris took one look at me and fell about laughing.

"Either your head's grown or your hat's shrunk!" she chortled.

I responded by yanking the hat firmly down over my ears and tried to look dignified. Chris laughed all the more.

"Now your head looks as if it has been vacuum packed!"

"Well let's see how yours fits."

Chris put her hat on, trying not to look silly. But she did look silly. Actually she looked ridiculous, which probably meant I looked preposterous.

"This is your fault!" I accused. "They must have shrunk in the tumble drier."

"They went in the tumble dryer at the campsite and didn't shrink," she responded. "It must have happened when they were washed!"

"Oh, fantastic! We've got shrunken sun hats, we just need two shrunken heads to fit in them."

"We can't tell your Mum!" said Chris with horror. "She bought us these, what will she say when she finds out they've shrunk?"

"I don't know. I'll blame you."

"Thanks!"

"What I do know is that I can't keep it on any longer, it's giving me headache. It must be cutting off the circulation to my brain."

"What brain?" muttered Chris, too quietly for me to be sure I had heard correctly.

"Pardon?"

"I said it is a pain."

"Oh," I said unconvinced but deciding to ignore the possible insult. "I could end up with gangrene of the scalp if I keep this hat on for any length of time. We'll just have to try and stretch them."

And that is what we did, walking along tugging and pulling at the hat brims, and fortunately it did seem to make them stretch although it took some time before they were quite as comfortable to wear as they had been before their encounter with the Plymouth laundrette.

A short walk along the coast and through gorse dotted fields of sheep pasture brought us out at the jetty where the ferry stops at Warren Point, overlooking Yealm Pool where Newton Creek and the River Yealm meet just upstream of the river mouth. On the northern side of the creek lies the village and popular sailing centre of Newton Ferrers, whilst the much smaller Noss Mayo was hidden from view on the south bank. The path did not go through either of these two villages but stopped and started again across the river at the ferry point downstream of the villages.

Newton Ferrers grew with the proposed coming of the railway, which never quite materialised and the village straggles out along the wooded river valley – a collection of pleasant houses, several quays, a hotel or two and some shops and a post office. Noss Mayo remains small with a couple of pubs, a chapel and some quaint cottages but has had some development thanks to investment by the Barings Bank bloke (not Nick Leeson) the first Lord of Revelstoke, otherwise known as Edward Baring. For some reason, the Lordly title always makes me think of Tarzan – it must be the 'Stoke' part of it! Both villages are very popular with the boating fraternity but on a much smaller scale than places like Salcome and Fowey. The river gave testament to their popularity: boats, dinghies and yachts cluttered the water, and somewhere in amongst them all was our ferry!

We stood on the tiny jetty searching for a boat that had 'ferry' painted on it but failed to see anything answering that description. Even through binoculars we were not able to make out a ferry, in fact the binoculars did not help at all, I seemed incapable of focusing on anything other than masts! So, as per the posted instructions by the landing stage, we waved our arms in the air – this was apparently supposed to summon the ferryman. No boats moved.

"It does run on Saturdays, doesn't it?" I asked Chris.

"Yep! According to the guidebook it runs Monday to Saturday in summer."

"Do we trust that book after what nearly happened at Fowey?"

"Of course we do! Just keep waving."

We stood there and waved, the trouble was we did not know what we were waving at, or even where we should be waving! Suddenly a boat emerged, weaving an erratic course between the many boats anchored in the river. Yippee! The ferry!

Getting on the ferry from the slipway proved difficult. The tide was in, making the steps completely submerged and we had to climb between the railings and drop down into the tiny boat. We were both nearly overbalanced by our rucksacks. I climbed into the bows of the boat, bending down to hold onto the gunwale but my momentum carried me forward and the weight of the rucksack added further impetus until it seemed that I would be catapulted over the far side of the boat. Having watched and learned from my experience, Chris tried a different tactic and somehow managed to launch herself from the jetty onto the bows of the boat.

The ferryman watched our landlubbers' attempts with amusement before commenting, "That was more like a controlled fall!"

Once safely aboard the boat we didn't pay the ferryman until he got us to the other side, (oh, oh!). Which was perhaps just as well or he might not have taken us! He had no change and we had insufficient money except a £10 note. Chris and I counted every penny from our purses but were still sixty pence short of the fare. Oh dear. After a bit of bartering he accepted what loose change we had and the remaining two of our fruit pastilles!

The ferryman had deposited us at the start of the coast path on the other side of the river, but we were not walking any further along the path that day and so turned left instead of right and began walking through Ferry Wood to reach Noss Mayo. As we arrived in Noss Mayo the same ferryman was also arriving with a boatload of tourists. The ferry was in fact a water taxi, had we but known we could have sailed up river to Noss Mayo and saved our legs!

We followed a narrow, leafy lane inland to the B&B with its own swimming pool and tennis courts. Tennis rackets would have taken up too much room in our rucksacks but swimming costumes had fitted in easily and we could not wait to go for a relaxing swim. Our host led us through the large farmhouse, passing a huge kitchen that would have made Delia Smith turn green, and down a maze of passageways. On one wall a framed collection of Victorian pornographic postcards caused me to raise an eyebrow in surprise. At this establishment the visitor did not just get an en suite room, no, no! We had a suite of rooms, spotlessly clean, beautifully decorated in a fresh country style and stocked with tea, coffee, bottled water and expensive toiletries. Each suite of guest rooms had been named, ours was called Misery but our stay there was anything but! The owner was not your run of the mill landlord but a successful businessman. Judging by his accent he had probably had a public school education but was not at all snobbish and he was the perfect host.

Having dumped our rucksacks, shed our boots and refreshed ourselves with a cup of tea, we hastened to take advantage of the one thing this B&B had that was the deciding factor when we booked it – a swimming pool. And we had it all to ourselves! None of the frantic dash to swim a mile or more before work on the early bird sessions three times each week at our local pool. Nor the rapid mile and a half at the weekend before children crowded the pool prior to their regular swimming lessons. No fighting for lane space. No dodging the graceless butterflies. No risk of broken limbs from the crazed chopping of the ignorant back-strokers. No little old dears somehow managing to propel themselves through the water whilst remaining upright and travelling at a rate of one length every forty minutes. No old men, wearing even older swimming trunks, whom you desperately try to avoid looking at because of the over-riding fear that the elastic is nearer the end of its life than they are. No floating plasters or sunken chewing gum. Just peace, the disinfectant smell of chlorine and some idiot choking and gasping because she's just inhaled half the contents of the pool: (me, not Chris). As we relaxed in the pool we both agreed that this B&B was the best yet, granted it was the most expensive but we felt we deserved a little luxury, we'd walked for it!

The walk back down the leafy lane to Noss Mayo did not seem as long as it had when we had been trying to find the farmhouse and we soon arrived at the pub. Way back in February when we had booked all the accommodation our host at Noss Mayo had asked if we would like him to book us an evening meal in his pub. Assuming he meant his local we had thought no more of it until, that is, we arrived at the door of the Ship Inn and noticed his name over the lintel. This really was his pub! Did he own the entire village? A modern day feudal landlord perhaps?

For the first time that day Chris had a signal on her mobile phone. Just as we were finishing our main course, the phone began to ring. It was Merv calling to see how she was. Ringing off she left the phone on the table. She had hardly put it down before a ringing began again.

Grabbing the phone and pressing a button, she held it to her ear and said, "Hello?"

The ringing continued. Chris stared at the phone as if it had just done a Mike Tyson on her ear lobe. It was my phone that was ringing! How she could have mistaken the two phones is difficult to comprehend as our phones have very distinctive and very different rings, mine is a catchy little ditty, whilst Chris's phone plays the theme from Laurel and Hardy, rather appropriate really!

Having made a fool of herself with the telephone, Chris must have decided to go all out for the biggest pratt of the evening award. Leaving me talking to Roger she went down to the bar to order desserts, squeezing through the crowd of smartly dressed, elegant diners. Smartly dressed the majority of diners may have been but none of them quite matched Chris when it came to accessories: it wasn't until she returned to the table that she noticed the napkin still tucked firmly into the waistband of her trousers!

Our dessert dishes were cleared by the landlord, our landlord, who had come down to the pub to check that everything was running smoothly on that first Saturday night.

"How was your meal, ladies?" he asked.

"Excellent!" we both replied, and meant it.

As the landlord crossed to another table and began chatting with other diners, Chris leaned across the table to whisper: "He must be a millionaire! To own the farmhouse and the cottages and to buy this pub and have it all renovated would have cost a fortune. Oooh, I've never stayed with a millionaire before!"

"He's married," I told her, "so don't get any ideas. And come to think of it, so are you!"

"A millionaire!" she squeaked gleefully, her eyes lighting up with little pound signs.

"I wonder if he saw you walking around with that napkin tucked in your trousers?" I pondered.

"Oh don't remind me!" groaned Chris with embarrassment.

As we left the pub it was, if anything, even busier. The car park consisted of the tidal creek – a big car park at low water but somewhat diminished when the tide was in. Never have I seen so many four-wheel drive off road vehicles actually off road, a rare sight indeed!

Sunday 9th July

There's nothing like an early morning swim to get the gastric juices flowing and breakfast that morning gave them plenty to flow over. We had a platter of fresh fruit, warm croissants, a beautifully cooked English breakfast, freshly squeezed orange juice, mountains of hot toast with delicious preserves and a teapot of tea that held gallons! It seemed like it would never end and that was fine by me! When my stomach and two hollow legs could hold no more I had to finally admit defeat, the teapot had beaten me.

There was a coast path waiting for us and we ventured out that morning into a fine drizzle and low cloud. It was 10 o'clock by the time we left, our latest start by far. Wrapped in waterproofs with the hoods up against the drizzle, we retraced our steps down the lane and into Noss Mayo and joined the lane back towards the ferry point. This lane was the start of Revelstoke Drive that, like the Hobby Drive near Clovelly, had been commissioned by the local landowner. But unlike Hobby Drive, this nine miles long drive had been built not by Napoleonic prisoners of war but by out of work local fishermen. The first part of the drive was now surfaced, providing easy access to a scattering of houses. We walked along accompanied by a robin that flew ahead of us, alighting on the fence occasionally until we caught up with him, when he would fly a little further before stopping again. He finally flew up into a tree and dropped his guano onto the road almost as a rather rude farewell gesture before flying further into the woods and out of sight. After watching the robin we began noticing other wildlife, or perhaps wild-lack-of-life would be a better description. Toads. Or were they frogs? It was a bit difficult to tell. We saw seven in all, scattered (or should that be splattered?) at varying intervals along the road. They had all been run over, making identification somewhat tricky. The unfortunate amphibians seemed a bit big for toads, but I suppose they would look bigger in two dimensions rather than three!

Beyond the landing stage and Ferry Cottage the surface of the drive reverted to a pebbly track. It provided pleasant easy walking, first through woodland and then out around Mouthstone Point and then Gara Point and along the bracken and gorse covered slopes near to the coast. On a clear day we would have been able to see Rame Head to the east, but the clouds were down and the constant drizzle reduced visibility across Wembury Bay, we could only hope the weather would improve later in the day, the prospect of spending an entire day in waterproofs was not appealing. The wide, now grass-covered, track continued at a high level, hugging the coastline through an area known as The Warren. The entire area was owned by one family and in past centuries had been partly walled off making the cliffs and the land for one field depth inland into a large warren, providing rabbits for his lordship's table. The wall still exists in parts, as does the Warren Cottage. What puzzled me was why the rabbits never burrowed under the wall.

A large chunk of the coastline from just before the mouth of the river Yealm, around the headland and southeast to Blackstone Point is now owned by the National Trust. Now if you are waiting for me to begin a lengthy tirade about the state of the path, I am sorry, but I am going to have to disappoint you. Thanks to Revelstoke Drive, which the footpath follows for a number of miles along this part of the coast, the walking was easy and pleasant, no need for us to watch our feet, no risk of twisting an ankle on uneven surfaces, no overgrown vegetation to do battle with. The fishermen had done a good job in creating the path and its wide level surface, covered with a thin layer of short-cropped grass, was a joy to walk on. We could walk along admiring the views without the risk of injuring ourselves or stepping off the path. What a shame the visibility had reduced the views to several hundred yards.

At Snellings Down we stopped for a break and to take a photo of the sea churning against the rocks around Netton Island. We had been walking in a big loop all morning and now our B&B was only two fields away inland from that point; the temptation to return to it was strong!

We left the official path at Stoke Point to detour to the ruins of St. Peter the Poor Fisherman. Like the church at St. Anthony this too was maintained by the Redundant Churches Fund, but it was little more than a ruin, albeit a deliciously enticing and sadly romantic one. The outer walls and even the doors remained intact but part of the roof had gone, leaving half of the church open to the skies. Ferns grew in the damp walls and moss almost obliterated many of the gravestones paving the nave, grass and dandelions grew in the gaps between the large stone slabs covering the floor and pigeons and swifts nested in the roof beams. For all that, the church still retained a spiritual air; the font remained and some of the windows, and through the heavy, iron-studded oak door the small churchyard was crowded with ancient overgrown gravestones. What a shame this thirteenth century church had been built slap-bang in the middle of a caravan site! Having said that, the site was only small and was well positioned, sheltering in amongst an old deciduous woodland.

We had our lunch in the shadow of the church's ancient walls before climbing the lane to rejoin the coast path on Revelstoke Drive. The sun came out for the first time that day and the persistent but light rain stopped, although the wind continued to gust, whipping up white horses far out into the Channel. We stopped and removed our waterproofs, stowing them in the tops of our rucksacks. The low clouds were lifting quickly revealing good views along the coast; Burgh Island was visible in the distance for the first time, prompting Chris to begin reminiscing of childhood holidays.

"We used to stay at Challaborough and take the tractor across the causeway to Burgh Island."

"We could go, we should have time tomorrow."

At Beacon Point the Drive turned inland and we continued along the footpath following the coastline. The path began a very steep descent down a still wet, grassy field. The sheep in the field must have gained considerable enjoyment from watching any walkers work their way, crab-wise, down the severe gradient. They stared at us, seeming to hope we would slip and tumble. We were half way down the near vertical slope and at the steepest point, when the rain began – a sudden heavy burst. Unless you have done it yourself you cannot imagine the difficulty of balancing on a steep slope, removing a rucksack and putting on waterproof leggings and cagoule, avoiding sheep muck and thistles and all the time maintaining your balance. We did it though after a considerable struggle and continued on our way. Two minutes later the rain stopped!

The rain continued on and off, but mostly on, for the remainder of the day and the wind continued to blow. However the visibility was superb, we could now distinguish the buildings on Burgh Island and in the distance Bolt Tail was visible across the deep blue and green waters of Bigbury Bay.

The path weaved up and down through numerous fields and the wet vegetation caused me to slip several times. There was nothing for it – I would have to use my walking pole. Chris unfastened it from the back of my rucksack and I began a lengthy battle to extend it. Tugging and heaving at the pole seemed to be having little effect. Oh for some WD40! Chris grabbed one end, I grabbed the other and our combined efforts resulted in the pole extending by about seven eighths of an inch. Some time later we had succeeded in extending it further but not much! I settled for a walking pole with a length of approximately three and a half feet, far from ideal – I had to bend over in order to lean my weight on it, thus throwing myself off balance, which rather defeated the object.

The occurrence of 'Private' signs was increasing, one particular farmer was very anti-walker if the barbed wire, broken signposts and poorly maintained stiles were any indication. He was also a bit of a litterbug. Black plastic sheeting littered the fields and collected, ensnared on the gorse. An empty drum of formalin lay discarded by the path.

The sea foamed around the rocks at Bugle Hole and soon the mouth of the River Erme came in sight. For much of the afternoon we had been walking up and down through fields, the nature of the path remaining constant. It is precisely that type of walking that seems to disorientate me, both in time and space. I had lost track of time and distance and had difficulty locating our position on the map. This was not an uncommon feeling for me; very often it was a case of when were we, as much as where were we! So it was a surprise to suddenly be overlooking Erme Mouth and to realise that the time was after 4 p.m.

A muddy path descended rapidly through woodland and we descended rapidly with it, sliding along its slippery surface, to emerge at the old coastguard cottages. Most of the land in the surrounding area and on both banks of the Rive Erme for some distance inland is owned (and jealously guarded) by the Flete Estate. You could not even sneeze on the beach, which incidentally is only open to the public three days each week, without prior consent of Flete Estate!

The River Erme had been the linchpin for our entire walk. No ferry operates on The Erme and the nearest bridge is several miles inland but it is possible to wade across the river at low tide. Would we reach it at a convenient time to wade across? And if we did, would we really want to wade across? The timing of our arrival at the river added complexities to the walk, and no matter how we broke down the daily mileage the river still had to be negotiated and suitable accommodation found. Low tide occurred at 5 p.m., if we waded across we would then have to find accommodation on the other side of the river. East of the Erme the nearest village was Bigbury-on-Sea four miles away, a distance that would take several hours on the strenuous coast path. We wanted to avoid late arrivals as much as possible and in any case we were both reluctant to wade the river encumbered with rucksacks. We were further deterred from wading the river after reading a different guidebook that stressed the dangers of doing so even in calm weather. There were no nearby bus routes, no nearby villages and even the paths following the river shown on the maps were private. We could walk inland on the country lanes, crossing the river by road and then follow the lanes back to the coast but that would add seven miles to our journey and we would still need accommodation on the eastern side of the river. The problem seemed insurmountable, escalating what should have been a medium-sized molehill to a dilemma of Everest-like magnitude. We began considering even the craziest of ideas. Someone at work was going on a sailing holiday in Cornwall, perhaps they could meet us and ferry us across? Could we flag down a passing frigate? (God knows there were enough of them doing nothing in Plymouth Sound!) Could we swim across? Could we rig up a breaches buoy from one side of the estuary to the other? The most practical of all our weird notions was to take our own inflatable dinghy!

The answer when it came was so obvious that we were stunned by its simplicity, how could we have failed to think of it before? We could abandon the walk and go to Tenerife instead! Just joking. If we planned the walk sensibly we could allocate time to walk inland on one day, stay overnight at a B&B nearby, and build in to the mileage for the following day the return walk to the coast. Looking at our breakdown of distances this made sense, and without too much difficulty we were able to choose a superb B&B near Ermington that featured in a book of exclusive accommodation. All the intricate planning had finally come good.

We sat on the beach that afternoon, enjoying the feeble warmth of a watery sun peeking through the clouds and looking forward to the luxuries to come. The inlet between the cliffs forming the river mouth was quite wide and with the tide out a large expanse of seaweed littered sand was exposed, the river itself was reduced to a deceptive looking trickle a few hundred yards away across the beach. Several people could be seen in the distance attempting to wade the river but we had no intention of joining them.

After a chocolate fix we left the beach and began the walk inland along the sunken lanes. A light drizzle began to fall, yet again, and we steamed inside our waterproofs as we followed the lanes climbing away from the coast. The lanes seemed very steep and hard underfoot after the soft springy turf of the fields. Our hosts for that evening had written to us acknowledging our deposit and offering to collect us if we so wished. We did not want to inconvenience them despite their kind offer but after trudging interminably uphill in the rain for some time we conceded that the prospect of a lift was very tempting and as we were not actually on the coast path at that point we would not be cheating. We decided to telephone our hosts to ask for a lift when we reached the village of Holbeton, it was not far – a sign we had just past said half a mile. Ten minutes later we passed another sign: 'Holbeton half a mile'. After a further ten minutes we had still not reached any signs of civilisation. The lane began to descend and the rain stopped, we walked on towards another sign: 'Holbeton quarter of a mile'. Were we ever going to arrive? Suddenly the lane levelled out and widen into a two-lane road and we were in the village of Holbeton. We sat on the wall below the church and telephoned for a lift. The gentleman who owned the B&B sounded very nice and assured us that his wife would be along to collect us in about ten minutes. Whilst we waited for her to arrive we took off our waterproofs, shaking off the rain and packing them into the top of our rucksacks so that they would not soak the interior of the car. We had no sooner put them away than a sudden and very heavy shower had us running for the shelter of the village toilets across the square, from where we kept a careful watch for our lift.

The house we were staying in that night was located down a rutted lane in secluded woodland, and had once been part of the Flete Estate. Our friendly and welcoming hosts made us feel very much at home, plying us with cups of tea and homemade cake. It was easy to see how they had featured in the exclusive accommodation guide. From the window of their dining room we watched with them as resident greater spotted woodpeckers came into the garden to feed. The couple could identify each woodpecker and had named them all. Chris chatted with the couple but I fear that for the most part I sat in a daze, gazing out of the window with a silly grin on my face, enchanted by the woodpeckers as they paraded their family before us on the bird table.

The standard of the accommodation was first class, everything from the furnishings to the food was superb. This was yet another wonderful place to stay, the second in a row and it is difficult to describe the sense of well-being and satisfaction, and the joy of being welcomed into such a home and into the care of genuine warm-hearted people. When you have been walking all day for a number of days it is places like this and people like these that make the walk all the more enjoyable and add to the pleasure of the holiday. With time, it is easy to forget average accommodation; the ones that stick in the mind are the extremes – the awful ones and the outstanding ones. The awful ones to be remembered with disgust and recounted with horror but the outstanding ones are the ones you recommend, the ones you hope to one day revisit to recapture the good memories, to relive good times. The trouble is that somehow you know the chances of ever getting back there are small and you have to be content with maybe, one day.

Our room under the eaves overlooked the garden, a vase of sweet peas added a delicate scent to the room, tea making facilities consisted of, amongst the usual tea and sugar, cafetiere coffee and a pint of fresh milk – no instant coffee and plastic-packed milk here! My turn again to do the laundry that night and after wringing out the clothes as best I could Chris suggested asking if there was a washing line available. Leaving her splashing about in the en suite bathroom (and making more noise than a basking shark) I ventured downstairs with an armful of damp laundry.

No sooner had I voiced my question than the laundry was whisked out of my hands.

"Don't worry about the washing, I'll put it in our spinner and then hang it in the boiler room. It will be dry by morning!"

Such a kind, simple gesture meant we would not have to worry about the washing still being damp the following day. Another kindness was their offer of a lift to a pub and their booking a table for our evening meal. As the journey to the pub was a distance of about three miles along twisting country lanes it was time consuming for them but once again of immense help to ourselves. They even told us to phone them when we were ready to be collected! So at a little before seven o'clock we appeared looking spruce and refreshed and were driven to a wonderful little pub in the village of Ermington.

As we climbed out of the car and thanked the lady, she leaned across the passenger seat to instruct, "I booked your table in the name of Foster. It saves confusion if we ever have foreign walkers with unpronounceable names. The pub landlord is used to us doing that and I'm sure you will be well looked after!"

She was right, we were. The pub was only small and tables cramped even the doorway, the tiny bar occupied one corner of the room and the jovial landlord seemed to have grown into the bar itself. His immense paunch flowed around a corner of the bar, giving me cause to wonder how he ever extricated himself from behind it. Groups of people crowded around the dining tables and two young waitresses hurried between the kitchen and the tables with steaming plates of food.

"We have a table booked for seven p.m.," said Chris squeezing a way to the bar.

The landlord gave her a knowing look, grinned and said, "Foster, is it?"

We grinned. He grinned. Three men leaning against the bar grinned. We order drinks and grinned again. He grinned back and then directed us to a table. A waitress appeared, presented us with a menu and grinned, we grinned, she grinned again and then disappeared into the kitchen. This was obviously a standing joke, we could just imagine the conversation each time the couple at our B&B telephoned to reserve a table.

Barman: "Save a table for two in the name of Foster."

Waitress: "More walkers staying at Goutsford then?"

(Prolonged laughter from various drinkers.)

Funny though the system was it worked! There was no mix up over names, no mispronunciation and, with the couple regularly sending their guests to the pub, it ensured we were well looked after. The menu was not your run of the mill pub food nor was it the posh nosh type of food that some pubs seem to favour; the choice was varied, the vegetables consisted of more than peas or carrots and the chef had mastered far more than just chips! The food was home cooked and delicious, and it came in hungry-walker sized portions. Chris admitted defeat after a huge beef and stilton pie with accompanying vegetables, but having finished lamb and leek pie, I was determined to sample the treacle tart with, yes you've guessed it, clotted cream. It was some time before I felt able to move after such a huge meal. We edged our way between tables to the bar, grinned at the barman and paid for the meal. He grinned. Oh, look, I'm not going through all that grinning again! You get the picture don't you? Everyone grinned. A lot.

Then we went outside and telephoned the B&B. We had time whilst we were waiting for them to arrive to walk through the village to the post box, passing on our way the church with its noteworthy leaning spire – Pisa has nothing on that church. At first I thought it was my eyesight, had I drunk too much scrumpy? Was it me that was leaning rather than the church spire?

"That church spire's got a lean on it!" commented Chris.

Thank goodness for that! It wasn't me then.

Arriving back at the B&B I walked into the bedroom and tripped over the rug. Must be careful, if I had landed on my walking pole it would have been painful! I went to the loo, came out of the bathroom and tripped over the rug again. Maybe I had drunk too much scrumpy after all!

Monday 10th July

We watched through the dining room window at breakfast time as the family of woodpeckers took it in turn to feed at the bird table. I couldn't speak for the woodpeckers but our own breakfast was superb – cereal, fresh fruit and yoghurt, croissants, fry up and toast. As we sat munching on toast and marmalade a sudden rattling and revving heralded the arrival of the milkman. Whatever happened to the gentle hum of the electrically powered milk floats? An open backed truck screeched to a halt in front of the window and the milkman leaped out, grabbing handfuls of milk bottles as he passed the back of the vehicle. The milk round obviously consisted of a lot of deliveries along very narrow overgrown lanes; with a chuckle Chris drew my attention to the proliferation of ferns and bracken trailing from the truck.

"That's the first time I've seen a camouflaged milk van before!" she laughed.

"Perhaps he is required to blend in with the scenery when he makes deliveries to the Flete Estate!"

Our kind hosts gave us a lift to Wonwell Beach where the footpath recommenced, saving us a couple of hours of tedious walking along twisting, steep, high-banked Devon lanes. We hoped this saving would give us time to spare to visit Burgh Island later in the day.

When we arrived at Wonwell Beach the tide was in, and the estuary looked totally different. The sand was underwater, the narrow trickle of the river now drowned in the rolling waves of the bay. Waving goodbye to our host we set off along the path that climbed above the submerged beach and out towards the cliffs. Climbing the cliff fields towards a prominent headland called The Beacon, we became aware of a strange noise gradually drawing nearer. It sounded like a motorbike but it couldn't be, then we saw the answer. Appearing over the brow of a hill inland and driving a running herd of cattle before him was a farmer on a quad bike. It was like a scene from a modern day version of The Big Country or Bonanza. The farmer was helped in his cattle drive by a black and white collie that charged around and in front of the herd but neither farmer nor dog seemed to have much control over the animals. We watched as the farmer herded his bullocks and one rather mature looking bull into the field behind us. The cattle stampeded through a gateway and made rapidly towards us as we stood on the edge of the cliff. The incident was becoming all too similar to an encounter we had with a herd of bullocks the previous summer, but now with the added dimension of a cliff and a long drop!

A little sign approximately eighteen inches high warned of cliff erosion and, with the cattle bearing down on us, Chris and I tried to shelter behind it. Only a stride away from the sheer drop to the sea churning on the rocks one hundred feet below, it was not an ideal place to stand! But in that narrow field and with those stampeding animals, the protection offered by a few inches of wood was marginally better than nothing. Just. This was probably it then! The end! To die so young, with all those cream teas left uneaten! I shut my eyes, waiting for the impact of a charging bullock and then the sensation of falling before final oblivion on the rocks below. I hate waiting! Why were they taking so long? I cautiously opened one eye, just in time to see the cattle swerve around both us and the sign before veering back towards the cliff and continuing their charge into the distance, some of the animals running within inches of the edge of the cliff. No wonder the cliff was eroding! The farmer ignored us completely, zooming by on his quad bike, continuing to herd the cattle until they were out of sight. We saw neither the farmer nor the beef again – did he leave them in an inland field, or did he drive them and himself over the edge of the cliffs?

From The Beacon views opened up back towards Rame Head and a grey blur in the far distance suggested Dodman Point, now a week behind us. This stretch of the path to Bigbury was very strenuous with some steep gradients to negotiate. I carried my semi-extended and consequently semi-useless walking pole; its shortened form offered some help in reducing the pounding on my knees but not much. A few spots of rain and some threatening looking clouds blowing in from the sea, caused us to don our waterproofs, and although the rain blew over quickly we walked in waterproofs until the early afternoon because they afforded a good degree of protection against the chilling wind.

Going down to Westcombe Beach was one hell of a descent; the drop so steep and the white Dartmouth slate cliffs so prominent that the view made it onto the front cover of the guidebook. We could now see Burgh Island clearly across the water, the white and green trim of the art deco hotel and the whitewashed walls of the ancient pub – The Pilchard – built in the fourteenth century, standing out clearly against the backdrop of the blue sea. The island is only small and owes much of its popularity to Agatha Christie who set one of her mysteries there. This rocky island stands a few hundred yards off shore, separated from the mainland by a spit of sand that is covered at all but low tide. At most states of the tide it is not possible to walk across to the island and in season a sea tractor plies a route across to the landing stage. The tractor is, too say the least, a strange looking beast; probably the best way to describe it would be to say it consists of a high level platform for the passengers and driver, an engine and associated running gear, four enormous tractor tyres and a gangplank-come-ladder all connected by a framework of metal that seems to be a cross between scaffolding and Dexion shelving, and with an open roof stuck on the top. This mechanical monster is extremely noisy, extremely dirty and extremely smelly but hey, it serves its purpose!

In several places along the path to Bigbury there was evidence of erosion, in fact, the route down the western side of Westcombe showed very recent signs of re-routing. As we descended into Challaborough and my idea of caravan hell, the path suddenly became overrun with people and clogged with dog dirt. No wonder this particular stretch had eroded so badly!

Chris gazed inland at the ranks of chalets and caravans, "It's dreadful! We had a few family holidays here when I was a child and I always remember it as being clean and pleasant. The chalets we stayed in are gone but it just looks so rundown!"

The only positive thing that could be said for Challaborough chalet land and caravan site was that it occupied a narrow valley and, tucked as it was into this little dale, it was quickly hidden from the view of anyone walking along the coast.

At Bigbury-on-Sea Chris relived her childhood memory and we took the sea tractor across to Burgh Island.

"This is the way to travel!" enthused an anorak standing next to me.

"Yes, isn't it just?" I politely but staunchly agreed, choking on a lungful of diesel fumes that a sudden gust of wind had blown in my face.

Once on the island the wind speed seemed to have increased by ten knots and everyone disembarking the tractor scuttled up the road and into the haven of The Pilchard. Everyone, that is, except us. Thirty years on, Chris sat on a grassy mound beyond the inn to pose for a photograph in exactly the same position and location as she had as a child, and then complained that the ship's figurehead was no longer there!

"No, you're standing in the wrong place!" she directed, determined that the present day photo should be taken from the identical spot.

"Here?" I asked, shuffling to the left.

"No, no, the other way."

"Here?" I moved a pace forward.

"Back a bit."

"Here?" I asked taking a stride backwards. This was becoming quite enjoyable, I wondered how long I could continue to tease her.

"No!" shrieked Chris, flapping her arms in a whirl of green Gore-tex. "To the left."

I moved left.

"No, my left."

"Well why the hell didn't you say so? At this rate I'll have walked another mile before I take the damn photo!"

"Move a bit to your right. Stop! Yes, I think that's where Dad was when he took the photo."

"How tall was he?" I asked, (if we were going to have accuracy we might as well have it through the horizontal as well as the vertical plane!)

"What? What's that got to do with anything? No, I don't want to know! Where's the figurehead gone? It isn't the same without it!"

"Shut up waffling and smile," I ordered.

She did and I took the photo.

"Actually you know, I think Dad was further over to the right. You'd better take another!"

"Eeurgh!"

"Pardon? Did you say something?"

"Never said a word! Just tell me where to stand and I'll take another picture."

Shivering inside our waterproofs and with the wind whipping sand into our faces and our sandwiches, we ate a packed lunch sitting on the beach. The sea tractor arrived, depositing another batch of holidaymakers and we boarded it to return to the mainland and commence the next section of the walk to the River Avon. Have you ever noticed how geography repeats itself? Place names keep recurring all over the country, all over the world even! This Avon wasn't *the* Avon as in Stratford-upon- or the Hampshire Avon but the lesser known Devon variety which rises on Dartmoor, flowing south, lingering for a while in the Avon Dam Reservoir before continuing on its way to empty into the English Channel just to the east of Bigbury.

Ferries across the Avon are sparse, operating only two hours a day, six days a week. When we arrived on the west bank of the river we had an hour to wait before the commencement of the afternoon service at 3 p.m. With an hour to kill and no food to eat I went for a paddle along the flinty estuary, Chris filled the time by curling up into a ball and falling asleep. When I could endure the cold water and the sharp flints no longer I limped back to Chris. She was still asleep. She looked so peaceful, so innocent even! It was strange how the sight of her sleeping form inspired me to think of how the walk had cemented our friendship, and led me to consider how much I valued that friendship in my life. I appreciated the easy-going nature of our relationship, the camaraderie, the trust, the reliability, the mutual respect. And then she farted.

"Oh please! You're disgusting!"

"What?" she muttered sleepily.

Once across the Avon we walked through the winding lanes of the small village of Bantham, hoping to find a shop selling postcards. But Bantham was closed. Chris hadn't got any postcards! What was she going to do? She bought postcards every day! Panic! Panic! I suggested she would be able to buy some at Thurlestone that evening but when we arrived there it too, was shut! A day without postcards – a catastrophe as far as Chris was concerned. She berated herself for the remainder of the day, she could have bought some at Bigbury but had forgotten to at the time.

Leaving Bantham, postcard-less, we walked through sand dunes around to the foreshore where surfers were enjoying the waves. The path climbed before levelling out to follow the low cliffs alongside Thurlestone golf course. Short tufts of grass bordered the path, and near to the edge of the cliff sea-carrot, vetch and the occasional orchid grew. Rabbit droppings littering the path made a pleasant alternative to the usual type of faecal matter we were accustomed to. We negotiated the golf course in safety, no one screamed 'fore' and no golf balls threatened to cut us down in our prime.

Our B&B was somewhere just beyond Thurlestone, but precisely where we did not have a clue. We stopped on the cliff top over looking Thurlestone Rock, a very distinctive boulder that protrudes above the waves and is notable for the large hole running right through it. The village of Thurlestone is named after the rock, 'thurle' being a distortion of 'thyrel', which (of course) is Anglo-Saxon for hole. How interesting the English language is! The way words have developed and changed over the centuries; phrases in common use today could be given a whole new slant by the use of old English. Shut your cake-thyrel, for instance; or, a thyrel in one (appropriate considering where we had just walked); or even, what an ass-thyrel! Well, perhaps not. But it did mean that for the last few days I had been walking around with a thyrel in my sock.

But, I digress; where were we? Oh, yes! Standing on the cliff top wondering where our B&B was. Chris took out her mobile phone and rang for directions. The lady who answered the phone instructed us to 'go across the beach and follow the road that went up by the beach café'. We set off to do just that, replacing the mobile in Chris's rucksack, but we had barely gone fifty yards before Chris suddenly threw off her rucksack with a haste that I have never seen before. Wasp in her bra? Bee back again? But no, she was frantically rummaging inside her rucksack, and I realised that her mobile phone had begun to ring.

The caller was the owner of the B&B. "You are walking aren't you? It just occurred to me, because you will never get a car over the beach!"

It was some time before Chris recovered from her laughing fit and was able to relay the conversation to me. The landlady must have panicked at the possibility of two guests determined to follow her directions to the letter and battling valiantly to drive their car across the beach, negotiating groynes and sand dunes, over the soft sand and up the lane to her house!

It was not quite five o'clock when we arrived at the B&B. The lady was still chuckling over a mental picture of someone attempting to drive a car over the rutted beach. Accompanied by two boisterous, yapping dogs, of the short and easy to trip over variety, she showed us to our room and then bustled off to make us a pot of tea. The dogs stayed, unfortunately, with it seemed, the unspoken intent of irritating us. Chris doesn't like dogs. I like dogs like I like children, that is, quiet and well behaved; these two sorry excuses for toilet brushes were neither. Also I am allergic to dogs; so as you can imagine, when the two mutts proceeded to jump onto every item of furniture in our room, we were quick to escort them to the door, not quick enough unfortunately to avoid one of the dogs jumping up at us and scratching our already sore legs. At that point, although of course little Roly didn't realise it, he came very close to becoming the second dog in orbit!

In a dog-free lounge we drank tea, ate biscuits, and chatted to the landlady. Then came the best bit – another swimming pool! Unlike the one at Noss Mayo, this one was outdoors and although it was heated, the blustery wind rapidly chilled any bits of our body that were not submerged. We splashed up and down the pool a few times before scurrying indoors, teeth chattering and bodies shivering, to a hot shower.

We were sharing a bathroom with some other guests. Not a problem, until that is, the lady told us they were a Belgian family. Belgians! Not *the* Belgians? But no, this family were quiet and we hardly knew they were there. A family that restored my faith in the people of this picked on little nation.

Chris did the laundry whilst I spent time administering second aid to my still sore legs. She returned from the bathroom with the washing but immediately disappeared down the hall, reappearing in the garden of the bungalow clutching an armful of washing and a peg bag – that night we did not have to worry about failing to dry the clothes. Returning to the room, Chris checked our two pairs of over-socks that she had draped across the windowsill to air, in the process she somehow managed to drop a sock out of the window.

Hearing her dismayed cry I looked up to see her bent double over the sill, attempting to reach the ground outside, it looked like a particularly masochistic way of trying to touch your toes. Without insulting her, Chris is a short-arm, there was no way she would ever reach the sock. Why not walk around and pick it up, you might ask? Well, that would have been far too sensible. Before I knew it, I was leaning out of the window, delicately balanced with my thighs on the sill, legs in the air and Chris acting as a counter-balance grimly holding my feet, as I tried to reach the sock. Somehow I managed to grasp a molecule-thin piece of sock between the very tips of two fingers and, like an old man tickling trout, hurled it over my shoulder where it sailed through the window and into the bedroom. I regained my feet just in time to notice one of the Belgians watching our antics with some curiosity as he crossed the drive to his car! He would probably go home with the firm idea that England was full of not only dog-dirt but eccentrics!

The landlady gave us a lift into Thurlestone, telling us we would have to walk back – no great trouble as with the coming of late afternoon the wind had dropped and the clouds vanished to result in a warm, clear summer's evening. We dined in the pub, a popular place with a limited but appetising menu. Waiting for the food to arrive Chris reminded me that I had not phoned Mum for several days. I dialled her number and waited.

"Hello?" came her voice through the ether, (I will never understand how that happens – how can sound travel like that from one aerial to another?)

"Hiya, it's me!"

"Oh, you've remembered my phone number then!"

Isn't it amazing that one word, one glance or one cutting remark from a Mum can make even the most responsible mature adult (not that I claim to fall into that category) feel like a six year old again?

"Oh, sorry," I mumbled apologetically, "There's poor reception on the coast." (What a pathetic excuse!)

Mum wanted to know where we were, I told her we were in a pub, and she asked if I was drunk! Did I sound drunk? Then with the knack that all Mums seem to possess, she changed the subject in mid sentence and said, "I'll have to go the cat's got a fur ball!"

We said hasty goodbyes and rang off. Next I called Roger. After quickly checking on his welfare and well-being I asked if he had remembered to feed the cats.

"Listen!" he commanded, sounds of slurping and chomping filtered weakly through the speaker. "Can you hear that noise? That is the sound of your cats eating. I have now had to open two cans of cat food!"

"Roger! I hope you're joking. I've been away over a week, two cans is nowhere near enough. If those cats look like rejects from a concentration camp when I get home I'll kill you!"

"There's hardly any cat food in the house," he said, and then I remembered! That was my fault, well actually no, that was Chris's fault. Allow me to explain. In the autumn of the previous year I had bought myself a new rucksack, determined that this summer I would not have a sweaty back. It was identical to Chris's in everything but price. Whilst I had saved Chris a fortune in the sales the previous year, I had saved myself £4 in the sales in October. Okay, so my rucksack cost £28 more than Chris's but I told myself I wouldn't regret it. It was worth every penny to be cool and comfortable. If I told myself this often enough eventually I would believe it. Wouldn't I?

I got a chance to try out my new rucksack on the Nidderdale Way at Christmas. Chris and I, together with her husband, finally finished a footpath that we had started the year before. Four days of walking around Nidderdale were just the thing to break in my rucksack and find the optimum adjustment of the various straps and fastenings, or so I thought.

By the first afternoon, my shoulders were aching and I was striding out leaving Chris and Merv panting to catch me.

"What's the hurry?"

"I just want to get back to the car. This high-tech, state of the art, ultimate in comfort rucksack is killing me!"

"Well what have you got in it?" asked Chris.

"A mobile phone, the remains of my lunch, my waterproof trousers and a sit mat," I replied, slumping onto the nearest rotting log.

"No wonder it's making your shoulders ache; all the weight, what little there is, is too low down," said Chris. And continued with a logic that clearly baffled Merv and left me wondering what she was on about, "you need more stuff in it."

"If it's heavier it will make her shoulders ache even more," said Merv.

"No it won't!" snapped Chris.

To avoid a domestic I hastily agreed to fill my rucksack for the following days.

Which is how on the remaining three days walking the Nidderdale Way, I came to be carrying four cans of cat food: rabbit and turkey, salmon and shrimp, lamb and kidney and beef and horse. Strangely, the cat food seemed to do the trick. One day I substituted the cans for baked beans. But beans were not as effective against aching shoulders and I quickly went back to cat food. Eight out of ten walkers, who expressed a preference, recommended cat food.

The cat food remained in the rucksack throughout the spring. I no longer endured aching shoulders, although I did occasionally suffer from concussion. The cans had a nasty habit of shifting in the top pocket of my rucksack, usually if I was climbing a stile; and I had to be very careful if I bent down to tie a lace or pick something up. It was easy to forget the cat food was there until a can suddenly impacted with the back of my skull, resulting in concussion and a dented can.

So easy was it to forget about the existence of four cans of moggie meat, that when we reached Cornwall and I began looking for a pen I discovered I had packed my rucksack with the cans still in it. No wonder it seemed heavier than last year! I left the cat food in Chris's car, I didn't think we would need it somehow. No, we didn't need it but my cats did!

Unwilling to admit to Roger what had happened to all the cat food, I told him all about supermarkets, what wonderful places they are and how, if you look carefully, you can find acres of shelving selling all types of food stuffs, including cat food!

As we came to the end of our meal the pub was rapidly filling up, mostly with locals. But one man, wearing an expensive suit, who looked as if he was a visitor to the golf club, or possibly here on business, was chatting up a tall, thin, woman dressed in skin-tight leather trousers and a skimpy top. From the tone of the conversation and the carrying voice of the woman, it was obvious to everyone in the pub that she was visiting the area. And from the gruff voice, arms that were a little too well-muscled and a little too lacking in any body fat, and the Adam's apple, it was obvious to everyone in the pub that she was a he. Obvious to everyone that is except the businessman. His body language suggested that, unaware of the true gender of the stunning creature before him, he thought that this was his lucky night – a little holiday romance was in the offing. And the stunning creature was giving him no reason to doubt this. Boy, was he in for a surprise!

We left the pub (and love's young nightmare) to make our way back to the coast, the shortest route back to our accommodation. Thurlestone has suffered a rash of development since the end of the Second World War and our path towards the coast led us between a particularly unsightly infection of ugly sixties-style houses. The decade that spawned concrete multi-storey car parks and tower blocks had left its blight even in this quiet corner of England.

Beyond the square, flat-roofed houses the golf course began. A notice instructed walkers to keep strictly to the footpath and follow the white marker posts. Well, that was just fine if we had wanted to walk back to Bantham, but we didn't! The white marker posts disappeared into the distance, keeping inland and heading in completely the wrong direction. Straight in front of us, a hundred yards away across a couple of fairways was the sea and the coast path. We had two choices: be good little walkers and follow the markers and end up goodness knows where, or ignore the markers, cut across the golf course and join the coast path which would take us back to the beach and the lane to the B&B. What harm could we do walking across a fairway or two? There did not seem to be any golfers about and so we scurried across the first open stretch of neatly trimmed grass until we reached a patch of rough consisting of buckthorn and gorse. Now only one fairway separated us from the path! So far, so good. We were just about to set off across the next fairway when we heard voices. We dived for cover behind the gorse; the voices seemed to be approaching. Peering cautiously over the bushes we saw four golfers, wearing ridiculous bright red trousers and green jumpers, walking across the fairway in front of us. We bobbed back out of sight to consider our options.

"We'll have to go back!" whispered Chris.

"It's miles. And we'll be seen if we go back now!"

"Well what are we going to do? We can't stay here all night."

"We'll wait until they go and then nip across."

"They could be ages."

Chris was right; the golfers messed about on the fairway only yards from our hiding place, taking ages to choose their clubs before finally whacking the balls a few yards further down the course. We took it in turns to bob up to check their progress. Every time it looked as if we were safe to proceed one of them would turn around and we would have to dart down again. When they finally moved away we cautiously emerged from our hiding place and scurried, bent double, across the fairway, anticipating an angry shout at any second, only slowing our pace and straightening when we reached the safety of the coast path.

Laid in bed with the light off that night, an eerie red glow came from the television in its standby mode. I got out of bed, trying not to wake Chris and in the dark groped my way to the TV. But without my specs, and unable to make out any details, I pushed the wrong button, turning it on instead of off and filling the room with sudden noise. Not only did it wake Chris but probably the rest of the house as well! I fumbled with the set before finally hitting the correct button and silencing the TV.

Having got back into bed and knowing that Chris was now wide-awake I commented on the moon, visible through the gap in the curtains.

"What moon?" asked Chris.

"That moon!" I replied, reaching for my specs to get a clearer view. And then: "Oh! It's not the moon."

"If it's not the moon, what is it?"

"Er, well, actually it's a lamp on the drive!"

Tuesday 11th July

The landlady wished us all the best as we set off that morning on the nine miles to Salcombe. It was bright and sunny and although it did try to rain a couple of times later in the day, for the most part we walked in just shorts and T-shirts, but the wind gusting from the north helped to make the day feel cool.

My walking pole, forever jammed at three and a half feet – too short to be useful and too long to be easy to carry – was by now really annoying me. I was fed up of carrying it and had been tempted on more than one occasion to hurl it, javelin-like, into the sea. In desperation that morning we experimented with it tied to the back of the rucksack, with the pointed tip sticking out above my head two feet into the air. It wasn't ideal but it was the best we could do and at least I now had both hands free. But each time I bent over and then straightened it threatened to impale Chris like a kebab, and her eyes became doubly precious!

A short walk behind a hotel and then along the edge of low cliffs led us into the twin villages of Outer and Inner Hope. A shop displaying postcards amongst its many bounteous wares beckoned Chris inside and I struggled to follow, manoeuvring in the narrow aisles and past racks of postcards. Chris crouched down to examine a low rack of cards, her knees gave way under the combined weight of breakfast and rucksack and it seemed likely that heavy lifting gear might be needed to raise her! After much heaving and pulling in a joint effort, with me gripping her rucksack and she clutching my elbow, we finally got her to her feet, by which time the shop had filled with locals who all seemed to be watching our antics with some amusement. Trying to appear nonchalant and eager not to attract any more attention, we selected cakes and chocolate for lunch, made our purchases, squeezed past the customers and headed for the door of the tiny shop. Having worn the rucksack for over a week I was used to making allowances for its size but I had completely forgotten about the walking pole. It was only thanks to Chris's quick reflexes as she followed me to the door, that a large inflatable toy hanging from the ceiling was saved from the sharp point of my pole. Otherwise I really would have gone out with a bang!

"I hope there's no lightning today!" she commented.

As we walked through Inner Hope, passing thatched cottages with exotic palms growing in the gardens, the walking pole seemed to be picking up Radio 2, or was it a shipping forecast? I don't know, but the feedback from the nearby radio masts was terrible!

From Inner Hope we climbed through a small wood where hawthorn dominated and ferns and ivy covered the ground. We soon emerged on the grassy slopes of Bolt Tail. Standing on the site of the only Iron Age hill fort on the South Devon coast, we looked back to the west. The visibility was superb that morning, and in a panoramic sweep of the coastline we saw Burgh Island, Stoke Point, Rame Head, Gribbin Head and Dodman Point and vast stretches of the coast in between, markers for our walk and reminders of the distance covered – now over one hundred miles.

Gorse and bracken dominated on Bolberry Down. This popular section of the path was busy with walkers as the route dropped to Soar Mill Cove, picturesque with its outcroppings of rock and small sandy beach. Honeysuckle scented the air and butterflies and bees fluttered and buzzed along between the wild geranium, sea buckthorn and bramble. As we reached the bottom of the descent into Soar Mill Cove Chris had a nosebleed.

"It's the altitude," she mumbled through a handful of tissues.

"Most people have nose bleeds climbing the Himalayas not making a two hundred feet descent on the South West Coast Path!"

All this was National Trust land but here, unlike in Cornwall, the path-side vegetation had been trimmed and the walking was relatively easy. With the spectacular views, the sunshine and the pleasant walking, the morning passed quickly and we soon found ourselves on Bolt Head. I explored the old World War II lookout point perched on the rocky pinnacle of the headland, before rejoining Chris who was still looking for the guidebook-promised ravens that were not there! As we rounded Bolt Head, Prawle Point came into view and a chill wind sprang up. We descended to the shelter of Starehole Cove for a lunch stop, passing numerous walkers who had presumably begun that day from Salcombe; one unfortunate chap was the dopple ganger of Adolf Hitler, although his appearance to some extent must have been a deliberate choice, why else would he cultivate such a silly little moustache? Resisting the temptation to salute and shriek 'Heil Hitler!' I goose stepped past him and hurried down the path.

Settling on a grassy knoll overlooking the blue waters of the cove we unpacked our lunch. As I began sharing out the food, Chris started to read from the path description, it waxed lyrical about the rocky outcroppings of Sharp Tor and we laughed so much at the colourful description of what was nothing more than exposed stone, that the cake I was cutting for lunch became flavoured with AB+ as my penknife slipped. The sharp blade cut easily through the cake and its foil tray and into my palm. Grunting in pain and surprise, yet still laughing, I thrust the cake at the by now hysterical Chris and fumbled with a tissue – I didn't want to get blood all over my nice new knife! As I sat mopping blood from my hand, my knife and the cake, Chris mopped tears from her face. It's so reassuring to go on a walk such as this with a person trained in first aid, so comforting to think that should the worst happen and an accident occur my travelling companion can be relied upon to fall about laughing and be totally useless!

"Please don't read any more!" I begged. "It's too dangerous."

It was 1 p.m. and with only two miles to Salcombe we had time to relax. Chris snoozed, I caught up with my diary, National Trust workmen repaired the storm damaged steps down to the tiny beach (and went some way to rebuilding my faith in the National Trust) and out in the bay someone on a jet ski created a furore of noise pollution rather spoiling the peace (although I have to admit it did look like fun!)

Leading into Salcombe, the path passed through a woodland of sweet chestnuts, which were proving rather populous on this year's walk, before joining the road at South Sands. The road rose and fell steeply from there into Salcombe. When we arrived the town was bustling with posh sailors, it was Rocket Week, an excuse – if one were needed – for the yachting fraternity to gather for fun and frolics and participate in the organised events taking place throughout the week. Salcombe, tucked snugly inside the river mouth, reminded me very much of Fowey, which had reminded me very much of Cowes; the shops were of the exclusive deck shoe, sou' wester, sailor's smock and ships chandler variety, with a few expensive delicatessens and wine merchants thrown in for good measure. And the yachts and dinghies at anchor in the river were equally elite. Maritime it might have been, Fleetwood and Mevagissey it was not! The narrow streets were thronged with families in matching nautical outfits; Chris and I were definitely not de rigueur with our walker's shorts, scabby legs and heavy rucksacks.

We wandered the streets, looking in shop windows, gasping at the prices of deck shoes and reading menus in the windows of the relatively few restaurants and bars. There was one shop we were determined to find – the chocolate factory shop – and believe me it took some finding. Eventually, after much fruitless (or should that be chocolate-less?) wandering, we decided to ask for directions in the Tourist Information Centre. Set in an old chapel, at the top of a flight of steep steps and totally without consideration for tired walkers, the TIC proved to be very helpful; as I staggered through the door a lady came around the counter to greet me (probably out of pity, or possibly concern that I did not tread mud into the carpet) and asked how she could be of help.

Well, I thought, you could get your car keys out and act as a free taxi service. But instead, I asked for directions to the chocolate factory, adding: "I've walked all the way from Falmouth to visit it!"

She laughed, not really believing me, understandable I suppose – she didn't know of my severe addiction to chocolate! Her directions were accurate but the route to the chocolate factory seemed circuitous, leading us down a residential street, back towards the waterfront and then on a long loop, passing a diving school and factory units before finally (thank you!) we arrived at the chocolate factory shop, only to find it was about to close. As with so many things that are eagerly anticipated, the outcome was somewhat of a disappointment. I had envisaged tours of the factory, with ample free tastings, ladles of melted heaven being offered for my delectation, money-off vouchers, lifetime membership to Chocaholics Anonymous and the glorious smell of chocolate wafting through the atmosphere for streets around. What I got was a small shop fronting an out-of-bounds-to-the-public little factory with a few display shelves artfully arranged with chocolate buttons, chocolate seashells, chocolate footballs, chocolate pyramids and chocolate sou' westers; and some rather heavy price tags! After much deliberation we bought a packet of chocolate buttons each and left in search of our B&B.

"Can I have some chocolate buttons, please?" I asked as Chris began putting the chocolate into my rucksack.

"You'll spoil your tea."

"It's ages before tea."

"Okay," she sighed and passed me one chocolate button.

I stared at it. "One!"

"Yes, that's one."

"One! What about two, or three, or four?"

"Oh, your maths is improving! Have you been practising?"

"Okay, okay – I know maths isn't my strong point – you can stop joking now and pass me some more buttons."

"I'm rationing them because you'll only whinge when we've eaten them all," she said firmly.

"Uh! This is like being on holiday with a reception class teacher! I can tell you are a mother!" I sucked slowly on the chocolate button, trying to make it last as long as possible. The trouble is Chris was right, and I knew it: I would whinge when all the buttons were gone!

Our B&B was inland up a hill, a hill that did not look like a hill on the two dimensional street plan we studied outside the Tourist Information Centre. Salcombe sprawls extensively up the hillside from the river; a strange town, in that at its hub is the small area fronting the river, whilst the majority of the land use is residential despite the town having only a small permanent population. The explanation for the number of houses in contrast to population is holiday homes, with over sixty percent of the residential properties falling into this category – an amazing figure for a town of its size.

Approximately one and a half miles from the river, the B&B was located at the far end of a small estate of modern detached houses and had been purpose built by the owners. To describe it as stylish, beautiful and, dare I say (particularly after my slating comments about some of the modern buildings at Thurlestone) in keeping, would not do it justice. The house was unbelievably wonderful with spacious rooms, elegant but comfortably furnished and attractively decorated, and as for the kitchen! And the bathroom!! And the garden!!! But overshadowing all this was the reception from the owners. Even the doormat had 'Welcome' written on it! (I have always hankered after one that said 'Oh no, not you again!') They ushered us into the lounge and wheeled in a huge teapot and a plate of biscuits, then proceeded to pour tea for us and showed a genuine interest in our walk. An hour later we were still sat there, with the teapot recharged for a second time (and my bladder rapidly approaching critical point) and chatting away as if we were old friends not casual paying guests. It was when the lady offered to replenish the teapot for a third time that Chris stepped in, saving me acute embarrassment, and said that we should really have a shower and change into fresh clothes.

Bladder emptied, laundry washed and showers taken, we returned to the lounge to ask if we might dry our clothes on the washing line. But the couple could not possibly let us use their line when they had a tumble drier in the basement! Before we knew it our damp laundry was whisked away, to be returned to us later that evening, dry and neatly folded. We asked if they could recommend somewhere to eat, only to find ourselves sitting in their Saab being driven back into town.

"Just give me a ring when you are ready to be collected and I will meet you back here!" said the gentleman as we clambered out of the car in the centre of Salcombe.

Thanking him and waving we watched as he turned the car and drove away.

"We have been so lucky with the B&Bs this year!" commented Chris.

"And such nice people, it really makes all the difference doesn't it?"

It was true. What is also true is that old adage about not counting your chickens before the end of the holiday!

The restaurant our kindly hosts had recommended was bulging at the seams so we ventured down the street to a garishly coloured, deliciously smelling pizza and pasta restaurant. This too was bulging at the seams but we managed to find a table in a corner and soon a waitress appeared to take our order. Feeling daring I ordered pasta in a cream and chilli sauce, Chris plumped for pizza. The walls were covered in a colourful mural, the music was loud (but then I did seem to be sat under the only speaker), the waitresses harassed but friendly, and the toilet door was just behind my chair. But none of that detracted from the atmosphere: the restaurant was vibrant and the food was delicious, but ooh! that chilli sauce was rather warm.

Have you ever noticed how all waitresses have been to the same training school? I'm not talking about their ability to carry five fully laden plates in one hand whilst erecting a folding table with the other hand and one foot, or their precise aim with the giant peppermill – it takes years of patient practice to be able to send specks of pepper cascading into your glass of wine. Nor am I referring to their knack of surreptitiously slipping a ramekin of baked beans into your handbag whilst serving fish and chips to a table of six – an unfortunate episode experienced by a friend of mine. What I am talking about is their uncanny ability to know just when you've got a particularly large chip or awkwardly shaped chunk of battered fish wedged across the roof of your mouth. It is at that precise moment that they home in on your table and utter those immortal words:

"Is everything alright with your meal?"

You nod frantically and grunt a reply, desperately trying not to spray masticated potato across the table, your cheeks bulging and your face turning red with the effort of keeping up the polite pretence, looking not dissimilar to a hamster that has just found its nether regions clamped in the jaws of a cat. You find yourself rapidly swallowing a bolus of food that really could have done with a bit more chewing and nearly choking on it in the process, just so you can politely reply, "Yes, thank you," when in fact the words which spring immediately to mind are anything but polite, particularly as you have a sneaking suspicion that you have just swallowed a fish bone.

What is even more annoying is that the waitress is not interested in hearing your reply. As soon as she has asked the question she is already turning away, seeking out other feeding victims, and as you finally manage to gasp out a response she is usually well out of earshot.

Well, the waitresses of Salcombe had certainly been to that training school. Our waitress hovered nearby, choosing her moment with infinite care, she waited until Chris was battling with strings of melted cheese and I was gasping over a particularly potent slice of chilli, before making her well-timed enquiry. However, this waitress had graduated with honours! Not only did she ask if everything was alright with our meal, she followed up with:

"Can I get you anything else?"

Chris mumbled something unintelligible through a mouthful of Monterey Jack, whilst I frantically shook my head spraying tears in all directions. Satisfied that she had completely humiliated us, the waitress departed to seek other victims.

After all the pieces of chilli lurking in the pasta I needed something to take the fire away, seeing no fire extinguishers readily to hand I followed Chris's lead and order an ice cream dessert. By the time we left the restaurant sated and happy a queue had formed outside that stretched away down the pavement, proving that modern day sailors prefer pasta to ship's biscuits.

We strolled along the road, looking in shop windows and feeling a little less sartorially challenged in our clean clothes and trainers than we had when we first arrived – all we needed was a pair of deck shoes and a Guernsey and no one would ever know we had not just stepped off a ketch!

As we retired for the night, the lady told us she would bring an early morning cup of tea for us. At that point I did not want to see another cup of tea ever again but Chris was more concerned with the possible shock she might get if she knocked and walked into our room.

"I had to endure your bare bum again this morning! Suppose she walks in carrying a tray of tea things and sees your naked backside poking out from the duvet? The shock might cause her to drop the tray!"

"Well, if we're woken to the sound of breaking crockery we'll know what's happened!"

The twin room we were staying in was usually reserved for children staying with their parents and was decorated accordingly. Stacked on the bookshelves over my bed was a range of Ladybird books that I had almost forgotten existed. As my eyes scanned the titles I was amazed at the number of identical books that I had owned as a child.

"Oh, look at this!" I exclaimed with rapture, "I had this 'The Green Umbrella' — *and* this 'Chicken Licken' this is wonderful! All these books, it's just incredible, what a coincidence."

"Yes, very nice. Goodnight," mumbled Chris.

"Have you read this one?" I asked thrusting 'Lost at the Fair' under her sleepy nose. "This was a favourite of mine!" I proceeded to share the thrilling story all about mice and elephant rides and a country fair with her, but by the time I had finished she was fast asleep. Oh! So that's how these bedtime stories work! It went a long way to explaining why I could remember the beginning and middle of lots of nursery rhymes and fairy tales but never the end!

Wednesday 12th July

I was awakened at 6 a.m. by a sound that for a moment I could not identify – was it breaking crockery? But no, my bum was modestly covered and no shrieking, traumatised landlady stood in the doorway. The sound came again, a metallic clanging noise from beyond the open bedroom window. It was the bird feeders knocking against the metal railings of the balcony and until the landlady brought us an early morning cup of tea, I watched the local birds having breakfast. No woodpeckers but plenty of thrushes and blue tits, a greenfinch and even a young robin still in the process of cultivating his red breast, feasted on the nuts and the bread that had been provided for them.

We ate breakfast at the huge pine table in the kitchen, with the landlady bustling around us and refilling the teapot each time we poured a cup of tea. There was no way, NO WAY, I intended draining the teapot that morning, any attempt to do so would have been an infinite loop of me pouring and drinking and the landlady refilling, and Chris would have had to continue the walk alone. But the couple were so very nice that Chris urged me to ask if they had any WD40. The question was barely formed before I found myself in the garage with the gentleman, engaged in a tug of war with my walking pole, a pair of mole grips, a vice and an aerosol can of silicon. Ten minutes later we emerged exhausted but triumphant – the walking pole was telescoping freely! I don't know who was more pleased, Chris or me, the previous day she had threatened to make me buy a new pole if we saw one in a shop at Salcombe, however sailors had no call for walking poles so nowhere in the town stocked them.

It was all down hill to the ferry point but the landlord still insisted on giving us a lift. As he dropped us off on the narrow main road within yards of the jetty we waved reluctant goodbyes. It was sad to consider that we had met so many genuinely helpful, friendly people who we would never see again but who, for a few hours, had made our holiday all the more special by their kindness.

Waiting for the ferry we were joined by three middle aged Americans, they too were walking the coast path and we struck up an acquaintance of the nodding and 'hi there, isn't it beautiful scenery?' type, as over the next two days we kept passing and being passed by them. We could not quite decide if they were all walking together or not, they seemed to set off from the ferry together and then gradually become separated and strung out, occasionally waiting for each other before dividing once more. The two men were carrying enormous packs and wearing woolly socks and heavy leather boots. The woman seemed to be the organiser of the trio, carrying a plastic map holder containing copious notes about accommodation as well as the map and guidebook.

The ferry carried us to East Portlemouth where we followed a narrow road passing secluded houses before the path entered woodland. Our approach disturbed a squirrel that darted across the leaf litter and climbed nimbly up into the branches of a tree. Pattering noises carried to us, was it more squirrels spilling their breakfasts or had it begun to rain? No, the sun was blazing down when we emerged from the trees onto the open land, so the noise must have been sloppy squirrels! In fact, the morning was becoming very hot, although not hot enough to tempt us to strip off our tops and walk along in just bra and shorts as the American woman was doing when she passed us a little while later.

Portlemouth Down was beautiful in the sunlight, bracken dominated with the occasional deep pink head of foxgloves and later wild geraniums and scabious; and on the beach below the

Gara Rock Hotel the blue sea gently washed the sand, tempting holidaymakers down onto the tiny beach. That was the first of several secluded, difficult to reach, tiny coves that the rocky path passed that morning. The underlying schist created a craggy backdrop to the route and made walking difficult on the uneven, rock-strewn path. We walked inland of Gammon Head, with Prawle Point coming into view and before it, the rusting hull of a wrecked ship stranded on the rocks of Black Cove. We paused at Prawle Point long enough to engage in a bit of view gazing and take a rest from stumbling along the rutted path. As we stood there a couple came in sight scrambling over the rocks, the woman wearing totally unsuitable (but very stylish) footwear and carrying a matching handbag which she frequently wind-milled in the air as her balance was threatened. Trying not to laugh at her unique style of walking we took encouragement, if she had made it to that point then surely the path would improve a little further along.

"Mrs Handbag can't possibly have walked a long way," commented Chris. "If she can get over those rocks then I'm sure we can."

"Yes but we've got heavy rucksacks," I replied. "Although, looking at the size of her handbag you could be right!"

Prawle Point is the most southerly point in Devon and can boast what must be one of the few remaining manned coastguard stations in the country. We descended from the coastguard lookout through a recently harvested field, along what had once been a raised seabed, very much like the path near Coverack. I had begun to think we would see no reptiles this year, having seen numerous adders, lizards and slow worms in previous years, and so I was suddenly surprised to see a slow worm in the middle of the path. I attributed it's lifelessness to the fact that it seemed to be lacking a head, which I'm sure you will appreciate can be crucial in matters of life and death. However, as I called Chris back to look at it, the slow worm began to move! It is truly amazing how much one end of a slow worm can look very like the other end!

We passed one car park, unfortunately for me without the added benefit of toilets, and continued along a popular section of coast path amidst a group of students on a field trip. The opportunities for an al fresco toilet stop none existent, each time I thought I had found a convenient spot another car park with its accompanying crowd of holidaymakers would appear. We walked in silence for some time, looking not only for privacy but for somewhere to stop for lunch.

"If I don't sit down soon, I'll fall down," said Chris. "But it's not very picturesque just here."

"Would you rather sit down here where it is unpicturesque, or fall down somewhere picturesque?" I asked. "There are a lot of people about who would witness you falling down somewhere picturesque but then again they might be busily occupied looking at all the picturesqueness and not notice you collapsing! Although it could have its compensations if you were to collapse: everyone would rush to your assistance and I would be able to sneak off and have a wee without being seen. Yes, that could work well! Off you go – collapse, create a diversion."

Unsurprisingly, Chris was reluctant to oblige and so we stopped for a snack at the edge of the path near Langerstone Point, with fields of barley on one side and the rocky shore on the other. Biscuits, fruit and one chocolate button each restored our flagging energy levels but nothing could be done for my bladder and we hastened toward Lannacombe Beach and the car park, praying for public toilets. Descending to Woodcombe Sand I slipped and nearly lost control, and seeing a white bullock in an adjoining field began singing 'Little White Bull' in an attempt to take my mind off things. Whilst my singing succeeded in taking my mind off my bladder (if you'll pardon the strange mental image that statement might conjure up) it seemed to be causing distress to Chris and to all the bulls, little or otherwise, in the field we were now passing through. Therefore it was with relief that we reached the car park, only to find there would be no relief – there were no toilets!

It was not until we had walked nearly a mile that we found relief at the interestingly named King's Head Rock, which looks nothing like a head, regal or otherwise, at a section of path marked on the map as The Narrows but which was actually rather wide. Had the original cartographer been drunk, or did he just have a warped sense of humour? As we emerged from the sheltered gap in the gorse, a wind blew in from the sea and fine rain began to fall. In the time it took us to unpack our waterproofs and put them on, the views had disappeared and the mist had closed in, deadening the sound of the waves and lending an eerie quality to the calls of the ewes and their lambs. With heads down we trudged on through grassy vegetation, following sheep tracks out towards Start Point. The views would have been fantastic had it not been for the weather. The lighthouse on Start Point was situated on a finger of land pointing out east into the English Channel, with sharp knuckles of rocks protruding into the air.

On reaching Start Point we turned north, descending below the level of the craggy hilltop; immediately the wind ceased behind the shelter of the peaks and the sea on that side was calmer, almost serene. A signpost pointed to Poole 164 miles away, and back to Minehead 449 miles behind us. Eeyore and I posed for a photograph under the signpost with the misty view of Start Bay arcing away at our backs. According to the path description, during the Plasticene Ice Age (sorry, I think that might be Pleistocene) South Devon was right on the doorstep of one enormous glacier, consequently its climate was rather chilly, and it was the result of these climes that created the Devon scenery we were walking through. It seemed as if a return to the Ice Age was imminent that afternoon, we were chilled, tired and in need of a nice cup of tea, or two.

Hallsands and the Trout Restaurant beckoned a little further along the path and we tramped off in anticipation of the tea and cake to come, listening to the foghorn baying dolefully from the lighthouse. Sitting in the conservatory at the front of the restaurant, with our waterproofs dripping gently all over the floor, we pigged out on chocolate cake and read with interest the numerous newspaper clippings adorning the walls. Both Hallsands and Trout's, as the building is known, have a remarkable history. The village of Hallsands shot to worldwide attention one stormy winter's night in 1903 when the outer row of houses was swept away by the sea; this had come about as a result of shingle extraction further out in the bay a few years previously. The authorities had believed the natural action of the currents would replace the dredged shingle, they were wrong. The beach dropped, buildings were undermined and the inevitable happened. Someone had the bright idea of building a sea wall but in 1917 history repeated itself when a violent storm washed away nearly all the remaining houses. Today little remains of the three-dozen houses that once stood above the shingle beach.

Trout's reminded me of the Minack Theatre for no other reason than 'girl power' had created it. The building was originally a hotel, taking its name from the sisters who owned it. A photograph showed the sisters standing in front of the hotel in its heyday. I had to read the caption twice before I could be sure I was looking at the right picture, two of the sisters were rather well built and manly looking (had they been alive today and competing in the Olympics they would probably have been tested persistently for drugs and testosterone) and it was these two beefy sisters who had quite literally built the hotel. Their muscle and determination had created a grand building overlooking Start Bay, and after the work was complete they had left the running to their more fragile sisters and gone out rowing around the bay and fishing and winning medals for rescuing sailors whose steamer had been hit by a torpedo! So, your average Edwardian ladies then!

From Trout's the path dropped to sea level, crossing the shingle beach in front of some rickety portacabin toilets. Oh yes! Aren't there always loads of toilets when you no longer need them? Why is that? We crossed the shingle, the loose pebbles tugging at our boots and I paused to collect a striped beige pebble that caught my eye. Mm, very pretty, that would look like nice in my bathroom amongst my pretty-little-pebbles-and-souvenirs-I-have-picked-up-on-a-walk collection. (Actually I had picked up so many similar souvenirs that my rucksack was beginning to bulge at the seams and the bathroom was becoming overcrowded, soon I would have to move the toilet out to make more room!) I slipped the pebble into my pocket and continued on my way – oh dear, that would probably mean another house somewhere being washed away!

After Hallsands the path began to climb through a ploughed field before joining a more obvious path running through dense bracken. A small herd of sheep took fright at our approach and tried unsuccessfully to penetrate the vegetation, they crashed around, leaping across the path trying to find an escape route before turning and running straight at us, at which point we leapt into the bracken and the sheep hurtled out of sight down the path! The route descended to run behind the sea wall at Beesands, which seemed as deserted as its ruined neighbour down the coast, although I think this was due to the weather as opposed to crass stupidity over shingle extraction.

It didn't look far on the map to our destination that night at Torcross. How many times had we thought that before? For a distance the path left the coast to divert around a National Trust owned disused quarry, now a haven for wild flora and fauna. The guidebook described the diversion as 'steep but not long, and interesting'. The climb was steep, it got that right, but to us it certainly seemed long and was definitely not interesting. Either the author had not really walked it, or had walked it at the beginning of the day and not, like us, at the end of a long one!

A series of steep steps between banks of valerian and montbretia brought us out in Torcross, a curious mixture of B&Bs, hotels and car park cramped together in a corner of land between the sea and a large body of fresh water called Slapton Ley. It is only thanks to its sea defences that this village too has not been washed away. Torcross seems peculiar as the road runs behind the houses and not in front, making the narrow promenade traffic-free and peaceful. We had booked a room in a B&B overlooking the promenade, paying extra for a sea view, unless the weather improved it looked as if our money would have been wasted!

Having checked in we did the usual chores of tea making, postcard writing and laundry. Our boots and outer socks were very wet, and after some thought we carefully improvised a drying rack using our extended walking poles to elevate our boots within range of the en suite bathroom fan heater. Leaving the heater blowing out hot air and turning the bathroom into a smelly sauna, we went out for a meal. The rain had stopped, the sun had come out and oh boy, so had millions of midges. I suppose the huge surface area of Slapton Ley is a prime breeding ground for midges. We walked along, our mouths shut for fear of being full before we found a restaurant, flapping our hands in front of our faces. Walking through the clouds of midges was like trying to battle your way through a pea souper, I began to empathise with people in smog-ridden 1950's London, but at least the midges were not life threatening.

My mobile began to ring, which is always vastly exciting because no one ever phones me, it was Roger and before I could ask (or nag as he would have you believe) he told me he was taking my Mum shopping the next day. He then went on to tell me the alternator was broken and he was having to bump-start the car. I kept visualising him sitting in the driving seat steering whilst my sixty-something Mum pushed the car around ASDA car park! It was not what I had envisaged when I had originally asked him to take my mum out for a drive.

"Don't forget her blood pressure!" I warned.

"Is it on the shopping list?"

Having eaten our fill in a nearby restaurant we made our way back through the midges to the B&B, where we learnt a hard lesson about counting chickens! Whilst we had been out Merv had telephoned the landlady after failing to get through to my mobile because it had been engaged and only reaching the answering service on Chris's mobile because its battery was being recharged. The landlady relayed a brief message that the owner of our B&B for the following night at Dartmouth had rung Merv to tell him they would be unable to accommodate us because water was pouring through the bedroom wall.

"Where were you staying at Dartmouth?" asked the landlady.

When we told her she nodded sagely and added, "It's very suspicious because this has happened to another of my walking guests who were booked in at that B&B, only then water was pouring through the bedroom ceiling!"

Feeling sick with disbelief we went to our room and telephoned Merv who told us not to worry because the landlord in Dartmouth had assured him he had found us alternative accommodation, was willing to pay any difference, and would drive us to our new B&B. Only slightly reassured we disconnected.

"It's happened again hasn't it?" I said. "I bet this chap has had the opportunity to rent the room for a week instead of one night, and so has decided to grab the chance to make more money and stuff us!"

"It sounds like it," agreed Chris. "And what is really annoying is that this B&B is the only one where we paid the full amount when we booked!"

"Well, we need to make sure he does pay for our alternative B&B and not try to keep the money. God! Why does this keep happening to us?"

"What I want to know is how did he get my home phone number?"

"Directory enquiries presumably. He probably didn't have the guts to let us arrive on his doorstep unaware. By ringing us with the bad news it means he doesn't have break it to us face to face. He can just apologise and get rid of us."

"Well at least we know the name of the B&B he has booked us into. We can suss it out before we go to see him and if it looks awful we can get our money back and find somewhere else."

"Good idea! There should be plenty of vacancies in a town the size of Dartmouth."

Feeling much better about the situation we made a cup of tea and prepared for bed, checking on the progress of the drying clothes and boots. To combat the growing dusk I switched on the ceiling light and suddenly the room seemed to be filled with midges! They streamed in through the partially open window from all directions, flying formations of midges converging on our lighted window from both ends of the promenade, forming a bottleneck as they fought to get into our room and then buzzing furiously around the glowing light bulb. The ones lucky enough to come within reach of the bulb were dazzled by sixty watts of brilliance and fell to earth, landing on my duvet where they crawled about. Marvellous! Midges all over my bed! Sitting in her own bed across the room, reading the path description, Chris seemed oblivious to the insectile invasion, until that is, I began swatting at the midges and thumping my bed with a magazine.

"What the hell are you doing? Do you have to be so noisy?" she asked.

"I'm trying to get rid of all these horrible midges!"

"They aren't doing any harm, leave them alone."

"Not doing any harm! You won't say that when you wake up in the middle of the night to find you've been eaten to death!" I responded, continuing to bat frantically at the duvet.

"If I've been eaten to death I'm not likely to say anything! Will you please stop it, you're making a real racket, you're more annoying than the midges!"

"But I'm the one who'll be eaten first. Have you seen them? They are all over my bed!"

"Once the light is switched off they will all go," explained Chris with exaggerated patience. "Now, if you stop swatting that magazine about I'll give you a chocolate button."

"Oh, well, in that case... make it two chocolate buttons and it's a deal."

I can be so easily bought that sometimes I am ashamed of myself! And though I hate to admit it, Chris was right – as soon as we turned the light off the midge invasion stopped.

Thursday 13th July

Please note the date! I know it's not Friday, but the date alone is bad enough, not that I'm superstitious or anything but sometimes events conspire to make you wonder if there might not be something in unlucky thirteen after all. The day did actually start off quite well, but by teatime it was turning into a nightmare neither of us could wake up from.

Our room was full of dead midges when I woke up that morning, the window sill was littered with little two-winged, six-legged corpses and I crushed hundreds underfoot as I made my way to the window to peer out at the calm, grey sea. This was probably the last chance I would have to go for a swim and whether it was raining or not (which it was) I intended to have a dip. Leaving Chris rubbing sleep from her eyes, I slipped on my costume, grabbed a towel and made my way downstairs, out of the still sleeping house and across the promenade to the shingle beach.

It was 6.30 a.m., no one else seemed to be awake in Torcross and I had the sea to myself as I eased off my trainers and dropped them in a heap with the towel before gingerly entering the water. The sea seemed icy cold as I let the waves wash over my ankles and the chill wind whipped at my exposed body. Goose pimples sprang up along my arms and legs and my teeth began chattering. I knew if I didn't plunge into the sea immediately I would change my mind and so with a deep breath, I steeled myself and ran out into the waves before plunging under the surface. That initial dive took my breath away and I surfaced gasping and coughing with shock. I probably only remained in the water for a few minutes, swimming rapidly up and down to generate heat. Having swam fifty yards in one direction I stopped, treading water and looking towards the promenade seeking the window of our bedroom; I found it easily – Chris was standing in the window, the camera in her hand! Leaving the sea I grabbed the towel, briskly rubbing myself to stimulate the circulation, my limbs had a somewhat bluish tinge, was I really that cold? But as I let myself back into the house and climbed the stairs I felt warm and very much awake.

"Is it as cold as it looks?" Chris greeted me.

"Yep! But I feel so invigorated now. You should have come with me!"

"No thanks. I could see you turning blue from up here!"

We shared the breakfast table with Mrs Handbag and her husband. At first I did not recognise them from the previous day and it wasn't until Chris mimed carrying a handbag that I realised who they were. A predictable conversation ensued with them advising us on walking the coast path and both of us wondering what the heck they knew about it! Why is it that some people walk a mile from a car park and think themselves experts on hiking? We nodded politely, listened to their comments and when asked where we had walked from told them Falmouth, which seemed to surprise them to say the least.

"Oh!" said Mrs Handbag and changed the subject.

We left the B&B that morning to find one of the Americans leaning against the sea wall. Was he waiting for us? No, apparently not, he was waiting for his two companions. We followed the road out of Torcross, passing the Sherman tank, a solitary reminder of the tragic events of 1944 when a passing German U-boat spotted US soldiers practising for the Normandy invasion and attacked the troops. The subsequent loss of life is commemorated with the recovered tank and a plaque. Further along the road near Slapton Bridge another plaque pays tribute to the sacrifice of villagers from the surrounding area who gave up their homes and farmland to enable US forces to practise. All along the walk this year we had come across evidence of World War II in the shape of lookouts and gun emplacements, but it was here at Torcross and Slapton that the human cost of the war was so clearly emphasised.

From Torcross, Slapton Sands stretched out in front of us for three miles, a long straight bank of shingle topped with the busy road and backed by Slapton Ley. The footpath followed the edge of the road and for most of the three miles we walked along the compacted shingle track where sea holly, couch grass, scarlet pimpernel and vipers bugloss grew. The Americans had overtaken us just outside Torcross and soon they were mere specks in the distance, striding out along the road. By comparison, we ambled along stopping to look at plants, at the Ley (me in the hope of seeing an otter, without success), at the sea and at the low clouds.

"I think it's going to start raining," said Chris.

"No, no, it won't. I told you it would have stopped by the time we had had breakfast and I was right. I predict a lovely sunny day to come!"

"It's not like you to be optimistic. Are you feeling alright?"

Half an hour later, as we were passing a group of college students on a field course, the sun began to peek out from behind a cloud and by the time we were following the road up a hill away from the coast and towards the village of Strete all the clouds had gone and the day was becoming very warm.

A big chunk of the walk from Torcross to Dartmouth is not actually along the coast. One particularly stubborn landowner has persistently refused access, as a result of which the path follows a circuitous route inland through villages, along lanes and finally across the fields before returning to the coast within a couple of miles of Dartmouth. Our progress along the road that morning was rapid, highlighting once again how the difficult coast path had slowed our pace on previous days: by 11.30 a.m. we had covered over five miles.

At Strete we walked through a small residential area of attractive detached houses before the path left the road to follow a badly overgrown bridleway that looped around the village. Eventually we rejoined the road and after checking the map decided to ignore any further signposting and stick with the road route to the neighbouring village of Stoke Fleming. Well, actually that's not strictly true! The truth is we were so busy gazing at the scenery that we missed the signpost directing us up a minor road to the left and by the time we realised our mistake we couldn't be bothered to go back. But by following the main road we were rewarded with excellent views of the coast as we dropped down to Blackpool Sands with its nice little beach café.

It seemed a good place to stop, have a break and enjoy an ice cream with clotted cream on top! Blackpool Sands takes this year's award for the Best Toilets, which was not that difficult because most of the public lavatories we had used since Falmouth were disgusting; however, the ones at Blackpool Sands were very nice: clean, colour co-ordinated with peach walls and beige doors, nicely tiled and with plenty of paper, soap, hot air and even a tampon dispenser. It was a wrench to leave them!

Relieved, rejuvenated and refreshed we set off up the A379 towards Stoke Fleming. We passed the Post Office, which seemed to be closed for lunch and turned a corner before passing a small general store. I was feeling rather thirsty, so, leaving Chris outside, I went in for a pint of milk. The only milk they had came in four pint plastic bottles. I wasn't feeling that thirsty! Perhaps I would just have a drink of tepid water from my rucksack instead. I turned and made my way back to the door but when I reached it found I was unable to open it: the door didn't have a handle on the inside! The shop was so full of shelves and racking that a one-way system was in operation and I discovered I had to make my way through a labyrinth of shelves displaying everything from drawing pins to cabbages before I reach the checkout and the exit door. Knocking over display racks and little old ladies with my rucksack and pole I squeezed my way through the congested, narrow aisles towards the exit. A barrage of shoppers blocked my escape through the checkout and I had to force a way through uttering a polite chant of 'excuse me please' and 'sorry about that' as my walking pole impaled one lady's hat brim and my boots bruised several toes protruding from someone else's open-toed sandals. In one final act of mischief the walking pole snagged a plastic bag of new potatoes and to an avalanche of cascading Jersey Royals I threw myself at the door and escaped into the street. Chris was standing on the main road in front of the shop, watching the door I had entered, and was rather surprised to see me scurrying to meet her from around the side of the shop.

"Quick! Let's get going!" I panted as I reached her.

"Why, what's the matter? How come you went in the front and came out the back? And where's your milk?"

"It's a long story. Let's just say that's the first time I've felt threatened by a bunch of bus pass wielding little old ladies!"

"Do you know you've got a new potato sticking to the sole of your boot?"

"Never mind that now, let's just get going. I have a feeling Stoke Fleming's lynching party are about to chase after us!"

Leaving the village we turned off the main road and onto a narrow lane that the guidebook described as uninteresting. It didn't seem too bad, at least it was an improvement on the bridleway.

"It is uninteresting," said Chris sarcastically. "On the A379 we could see red Fords, Green Volvos, Blue…"

"Yes, okay I get the picture. But at least dog dirt wasn't a problem on the main road!"

"Oh you haven't?"

"Yes I have! And you thought the new potato was messy!"

At the National Trust car park near Little Dartmouth we left the roads and turned south on a field-side track and back to the coast path proper. It was just after midday and the sun was beating down strongly. We had not applied sunscreen that morning and decided to stop and put some on. The lotion we had taken was different from the one we had used the year before,

279

this one was a leftover from a holiday Chris had taken in California and it was in the form of a gel which evaporated quickly without leaving any stick residue.

Chris applied the gel first and then passed the bottle to me. I squirted a blob into the palm of my hand, rubbed my hands together and then began to rub my arms.

"That's no good!" exclaimed Chris. "It will just evaporate on your hands. You need to put a blob on your arm and quickly rub it in with your finger tips, not go rubbing your hands together like you're auditioning for the role of Fagin!"

"You've waited until the next to the last day of the holiday to tell me that! For nearly a fortnight I've been putting it on wrong!"

"Well, you're supposed to be intelligent! I thought you would have realised how quickly it evaporates."

"It never occurred to me. No wonder everything's brown except my palms!"

A convenient seat at Combe Point was ideally placed for eating chocolate, which we did, taking the opportunity to change out of our waterproof socks into normal ones. Chris draped her socks on the bench to air and sat down swinging her bare feet and began to eat her chocolate. But a sudden gust of wind picked up one of the socks and blew it into the gorse and towards the cliff.

"Eek!" squeaked Chris and leapt up to chase after the sock, disappearing into a patch of gorse from where squeals and shrieks of pain could be heard as she was pricked by the needle sharp gorse.

The shrieking stopped, followed by a bit of swearing and Chris emerged from amidst the vegetation, clutching her sock. By this time tears were streaming down my face from laughing too much and I was in danger of choking on a chocolate button. But as often happens in these situations Chris had the last laugh. Before leaving we decided to make use of the seclusion for an al fresco toilet stop. Unfortunately I got a bit too near the needle-sharp gorse! My pained scream was 99% inoculation and 1% micturation, and was probably audible in Dartmouth.

From Combe Point the path hugged the cliffs all the way to Blackstone Point near the mouth of the River Dart. More conservation grazing was being carried out, this time by a herd of Shetland ponies, who unfortunately seemed unable to graze anywhere other than the edge of the path due to the density of the surrounding gorse. Their grazing had succeeded in widening the path, which was fortunate because we found ourselves trying to squeeze past them, having followed them for several hundred yards without finding any appropriate passing places! I had got past one rather fat little pony that would have been right at home on a Thelwell cartoon, only to hear a panicked squeak from Chris.

"Help!" she cried. "It's eating my boobs!"

I turned to find her backed up against the gorse with a pony thrusting its face at her, very much up close and personal!

"Just move round to your left," I advised. "He won't harm you."

"Easy for you to say!" she muttered, flapping the guidebook under his nose.

"That's right! Next thing we know he'll be eating the guidebook! How will we get to Torbay when the guidebook's digesting inside a pony in a field near Dartmouth?"

I gave the pony a shove, grabbed Chris's rucksack and dragged her along the path. And she calls me for being afraid of wasps!

Winding through bracken and gorse we passed the unseen Ladies Cove and Deadman's Cove and conscientiously followed the acorn signs as the path dropped towards the sea and suddenly disappeared into the undergrowth. The arrow pointed directly into a massive bank of bracken growing taller than six feet, and the footpath stopped at this green wall. Surely the path was not through the bracken? It seemed impenetrable! We looked around for another route but there wasn't one, we were on a tiny spit of land with the sea on our right and nowhere to go but either forwards into the bracken or back the way we had come. This had to be the worst case of overgrown path we had come across. There was no option: we had to wade into the jungle. Chris went first, plunging into the deep green gloom and immediately disappearing from sight as the bracken closed around her. Anxious not to lose her (she was carrying all the chocolate buttons) I dived in after her, becoming entangled in several giant fronds before I caught up with her and grabbed hold of a strap of her rucksack like a drowning sailor clutching at a lifeline. We floundered about in the bracken for several minutes before finding a way through to the other side and emerging once more into daylight, all the time I fully expected David Bellamy to appear and start expounding a theory about the ecology of bracken whilst eating bits of leaf!

At the mouth of the River Dart we passed the castle, perched on a rock high above the river; crowds of tourists sat in the sun and flocked around the information boards, the nearby road into the town was crammed with parked cars, a sharp reminder that we had reached civilisation once again. It was always a shock after walking in rural isolation to suddenly near a road or some other sign of civilisation. On this occasion the shock was not just rude but positively obscene. We could hear the incessant pounding of a car stereo and feel the vibration from the excessive bass, gradually becoming louder and louder and nearer and nearer, long before we actually saw the car as it zoomed towards us. The cacophony of the stereo and the speed of the car left windows rattling, lampposts vibrating and small trees uprooted as it charged past.

Dartmouth reminded me very much of Salcombe, which had reminded me very much of Fowey, which in turn had reminded me of Cowes; yet another yachting and sailing centre with all the accompanying boats, shops and people. Dartmouth has a history of naval daring do, from the Crusades up to the Normandy landings; and to the north of the town on a hill overlooking the busy river stands the Britannia Royal Naval College, not that you would have known it – we didn't see one sailor all the time we where there. Penzance had Humphrey Davy, Plymouth had Sir Francis Drake, Dartmouth had Thomas Newcomen. New who? Newcomen, maker of the first steam engine to be used in industry. A plaque on the wall of the Tourist Information Centre marks the achievement of Dartmouth's most famous son.

It was a long walk along the road into the centre of town, made all the longer by us loosing our way and finding ourselves on a jetty at the end of a street from where we had to retrace our steps to the main road. It was not quite three o'clock; we had walked ten miles and were looking forward to a dumping our stuff at our new B&B and having a leisurely afternoon looking around the shops and the busy waterfront. We felt we had made good time that day and were feeling rather pleased with ourselves if somewhat anxious about the problem with our B&B. But we kept telling each other it was a simple matter of checking out the alternative B&B and if it wasn't suitable we would just ask for our money back from Mr Leaky-Ceiling and find ourselves a better one. Simple!

However, just a quick reminder here: you haven't forgotten the date? Several things spring all too readily to mind; counting chickens; pride and falling; faecal matter and fans; and all those other apposite clichés that for the moment escape me. We picked up a town map and accommodation guide from the Tourist Information Centre and set off to investigate the alternative B&B. We found it easily and from the outside it looked rather nice, however, no one was at home but not to worry, first impressions were good. Somewhat reassured we made our way through the narrow streets of old buildings to our original B&B. And that's when things started going wrong.

A woman answered our knock, opening the door a fraction of an inch to explain she could not let us in because of the dogs; her husband was on the telephone but would be out in a minute to deal with us! The door shut in our faces and we were left standing on the pavement.

"It's as well we aren't staying here, or perhaps we would have to sleep on the pavement and have breakfast brought out to us!" I commented with amazement.

After a minute the door opened again and the woman, who had obviously had second thoughts, let us in, struggling as she did so to control two large, baying hounds. We stepped inside and waited with growing reluctance before her husband finally appeared from an upstairs room. He apologised expansively and led us out to his car, an ancient jalopy of indeterminate age and colour, parked under a tree and covered in sap and seagull droppings. The inside of the car was as dirty as the outside and we perched on the edge of the seats reluctant to contaminate our sweaty, mud-covered walking gear with muck, oil and dog hairs.

"After I spoke to your son last night I was not able to get you a room in the B&B I had told him about," he explained.

Neither of us corrected his mistake; Merv hardly sounded like a teenager!

"But don't worry," he continued, "I have found you a very nice one just up the road. It's £3 more than we charge but I have paid the difference, it's the least I could do."

Yes it was!

Just up the road turned out to be about a mile up a rather long hill. When we arrived we were literally dumped on the doorstep, briefly introduced as Mrs Ashton and Mrs Merryweather (you would think someone who has just badly let you down would at least have the courtesy to get your names right) and escorted to a room where we were given no chance to decide whether we wished to stay or not before the man departed, leaving us standing in a bedroom that had changed little, if at all, since 1970.

"Breakfast is at nine," barked the elderly landlady. "If you intend being out after eleven o'clock tonight you will need to get a key on your way out. I lock up at eleven."

With orders issued she left. We stood looking around the room. It was awful. The décor was dated, the beds old and saggy, goodness knew how many times the bed linen had been used, and the furniture was battered. I fully expected the en suite bathroom to contain a tin bath, it didn't but the towels were small, thin and well worn. The only concession to twenty first century tourism was a tray containing tea making facilities but closer examination revealed a miserly two teabags, one coffee sachet and two plastic cartons of milk.

Chris sank down onto the bed in despair, a bad move as she was nearly catapulted off the uneven mattress and onto the floor.

"What are we going to do?" she moaned, turning into a despairing, incapable wreck.

"This is just like Falmouth," I commented unhelpfully.

The despairing, incapable wreck sat on the bed looking at me, waiting for me to make a decision and deal with the situation.

"Do you want to stay here?" I asked (a silly question).

"No, but will we be able to find anywhere else?"

I grabbed my mobile phone, intending to ring the Tourist Information Centre to see if there were vacancies elsewhere, but my mobile was out of signal range; Chris's mobile, on a different network, had no signal either. I scratched my head and looked around the room again, my gaze settling on the hospitality tray. Two teabags! I reminded myself. And silly as it sounds I think that was the deciding factor – this dump was charging £23 per person per night and was only providing two teabags. For £27.50 we had wallowed in luxury at Noss Mayo, there was just no comparison.

"What are we going to do?" moaned Chris again.

"Leave!" I almost shouted. "You stay here while I go down and get our money back."

At the foot of the stairs I met the landlord and I launched into an assertive statement about how we were not happy, we had been given no opportunity to discuss in private whether we wished to stay or not, and the B&B was too far from the town centre. The last point was an excuse as I could hardly tell him we wanted to leave because it was an overpriced dump. If he could please refund our money we would leave.

"What money?" he responded.

Gulp!

"The other gentleman told us he had paid you in full," I replied trying to stay calm.

"He hasn't paid us!"

"Yes, he has," I said with more conviction than I felt.

"No he hasn't."

Double gulp!

"Yes he did. He paid me," said a disembodied voice.

The man moved into the doorway of the lounge, where his wife was sitting watching a quiz show on television.

"They want their money back!" the landlord told her, nodding in my direction.

His wife stood up, reached into a pocket of her apron and brought out a wad of bank notes.

Seeing my chance I addressed her: "We're not bothered about the extra, you can keep that, but can we please have the £40 we paid the other gentleman?"

She handed it over, almost as if she were glad not to have the bother of paying guests. Her husband turned white and I thought he was going to try to snatch the money from me, I hastily tucked it deep into the pocket of my shorts.

"Thank you," I said and turned to go back upstairs.

"That's not your money," yelled the man.

"Yes it is, we paid in full when we booked our accommodation. And he has paid your wife. So it is ours."

"No, it's not. Give it back. I will return it to him."

"It's our money!" I was beginning to loose my temper. What would it take to get through to this idiot?

"It's our money!" he bellowed. "You've broken your contract with us and used the room!"

"We never had a contract with you! And we haven't used the room, all we've done is sit on the bed and put our rucksacks on the floor."

"Let me have the money and I'll return it to him."

"It is not his money. We paid him, in full, for one night's accommodation, which he was not able to provide. Therefore the money is ours."

Do you know the feeling when no matter what you say you know that it won't make any difference? It's that old familiar banging your head against a brick wall feeling. Know the one I mean?

I had had enough of this pointless heated discussion and I was not prepared to argue further. Either the guy was deliberately mis-understanding to try and make an easy £40 (as I am sure he had no intention of returning the money to the other man had I given it to him) or he was genuinely stupid! With the money safely in my pocket I rushed upstairs, effectively ending the row, and burst into the bedroom.

"What's happening? What's all the shouting?" asked Chris.

"I'll explain later. Come on, we're leaving!"

With that I almost threw Chris's rucksack at her, dragged her off the bed, grabbed my own rucksack and headed downstairs, pulling a bemused Chris behind me. The man was waiting at the bottom of the stairs!

"You're not leaving with that money!" he barked.

"Yes we are," I replied.

"It's our money," added Chris. "We have the receipt to prove it."

I expected him to try and stop us leaving but he didn't, and we thankfully escaped into the street and began walking back to the town centre. We had gone no more than fifty yards before we heard running footsteps and shouting. He was chasing after us! My instinct was to carry on going but Chris stopped and I had no option but to stop as well. Passers by were beginning to stare and the whole situation was becoming not only frustrating and embarrassing but also rather frightening.

"I can't let you take that money!" he screamed. "You people want it all ways!"

"For the last time, it's our money!" I replied.

"I don't believe you, hand it over and I will return it to the other chap. You've broken your contract, used the room and are now refusing to pay us!"

"Make your mind up! Either you think we should have paid you or you think the money belongs to the other man!" I had done well to keep my temper for as long as I had but now I had lost it. Uncaring of the audience our little scene was generating, I shouted: "The money's ours, so do what you want, I don't care; report us to the police or the Tourist Information Centre. Come on Chris, we're leaving."

I turned and began marching down the street, trying to drag Chris with me but she wouldn't budge. At first I didn't understand why she was staying put, until I saw her rummaging in her pocket, from which she produced the receipt from Mr Leaky-Ceiling.

"Look!" she said, thrusting the paper towards the landlord, "This is a receipt and it clearly says we paid in full for the accommodation. Therefore, the £40 is ours!"

Faced with proof the chap shut up. Now why had I not thought to show him the receipt earlier? Good old Chris. We left him standing on the pavement and carried on down the hill and back to the Tourist Information Centre. Both of us were shaking, it had been a horrible experience. At the TIC, the lady behind the counter recommended another B&B, telephoned them to check their vacancies and booked us a room.

"Now, this is a nice place?" I asked as I filled in the booking form.

"Yes, we have had several people come back to tell us how much they enjoyed their stay," she told me.

"You promise? You're absolutely sure that it is nice and clean and comfortable and well decorated?"

"Well, I can only tell you what other visitors have reported, but I'm sure you won't be disappointed."

Whilst I signed the booking form and paid a deposit I became aware that Chris was chatting with someone. Bent over a low table with pen poised above the booking form I glanced down and to my left to see a pair of very white feet, clad in sandals, attached to a pair of very brown legs. I followed the legs up – shorts, T-shirt, smiling deeply tanned face – it was our American friend! Chris was busy telling her all about our recent experience. I completed the booking formalities and we moved outside, continuing to chat about our day's walk, comparing notes on footpath and vegetation.

"Where are you walking to tomorrow?" Chris asked.

"Somewhere called Paginten," replied our new friend.

Chris and I looked at one another. We thought we were familiar with every town and village name on the South Devon coast but we had never heard of that one before.

"Where?" I asked, perplexed.

"Paginten?" repeated the American. "P. A. I. G…"

"Oh, you mean Paignton!"

"What did you say? Paint-what?"

"Paignton! It is a rather silly spelling."

"Is that how it's pronounced?" asked the lady. "Geez, we wondered! You Brits have such strange place names, you know?"

We knew: we had fallen foul of odd place names ourselves on the walk, particularly in Cornwall!

"Listen, I gotta go. But if this new B&B doesn't work out for you guys, then I know the place we're staying has vacancies. So try there! It's really nice!" She told us the name of her B&B and where it was, and then with cheery goodbyes we parted. We never saw the Americans again, rather sad really; they must have set off earlier than we did the next morning. We often wondered how they had got on, they were walking to Poole Harbour, the finish of the South West Coast Path, it would have been nice to know if they made it but I'm sure they would have. Too late, it occurred to us we should have asked for their email address.

Our new B&B was an improvement on the previous one – difficult to be otherwise really! But it was not what we had been hoping for, it was clean but rather run down and very expensive compared to some of the other places we had stayed. But the beds were very comfortable and the hospitality tray was generously supplied with tea, coffee and fresh milk – much nicer than those little plastic cartons of UHT stuff! By the time we had showered and changed and ventured out in search of a restaurant all the shops had closed. The afternoon had gone in a whirl of accommodation hunting and arguing: wasted! We salvaged the evening as best we could by finding a busy restaurant overlooking the river that offered a carvery menu and eating until we were stuffed.

Before going to bed I decided to strip down my walking pole, clean it all up and reassemble it. Chris warned me not to – said I was better just leaving it alone – but I didn't listen. Five minutes later I was surrounded by bits of metal and plastic and two broken clips from the telescoping mechanism. Now how the hell had I managed to break them? And were they vital to the operation of the pole? I reassembled the pole and the telescoping mechanism worked well, there was just one slight problem – it would not stop telescoping! So, yes, I guess the two clips were vital to the operating mechanism! I must buy a new walking pole before next year.

"It's not been a very auspicious end to the day has it?" asked Chris, watching me fumble with the walking pole. "Why do you think the accommodation is more expensive in Dartmouth? I would expect that in a larger resort competition would keep the prices down but it doesn't seem to be the case here."

"It amazes me the quality of accommodation that some people are prepared to offer!" I replied.

"Yes, and there must be people prepared to accept it! I would be ashamed to let rooms like that 1970's one."

"Well, obviously not everyone has our high standards, unfortunately for us. It isn't easy being perfect in an imperfect world."

"No, it's not," agreed Chris.

Friday 14th July

Breakfast was very good, particularly the jam. We had a choice from countless jars of preserves ranged along the sideboard: whiskey marmalade, plum jam with brandy, chunky Seville orange marmalade, blackberry and apple, as well as all the usual favourites. Proper jam! The trend seems to be for most hotels and guest houses to offer their visitors little packets of jam, and I really don't like them. The teaspoon of preserve inside looks anaemic, especially the marmalades, and it always seems to taste of the plastic carton it comes in. I suppose that hygienically the cartons have the advantage over a jar that everyone has dipped into, but they seem so cheap and so environmentally unfriendly, a waste of packaging.

The shops were just beginning to open as we walked through the town to the ferry point that morning. We crossed the river to Kingswear, our last ferry crossing of the holiday, and Chris hadn't thrown up once! A short section of road walking took us out of the village and into woodland. It was a beautiful sunny morning, wrens darted amongst the trees and the sea played a distance background symphony.

Back in the spring of 1982 I was sitting in an 'O' Level English class studying media, looking at how the various newspapers were covering the major news story of the time. Also in 1982, the author Mark Wallington was walking the South West Coast Path, his story of which would eventually inspire me to walk the path. And thousands of miles away in the South Atlantic, the afore-mentioned major news story was unfolding. Britain and Argentina were at war over the Falkland Islands. Until Argentina invaded this tiny group of islands, few Britons had even heard of the Falklands, let alone knew where they were. But all that changed in just a few weeks. Argentina's struggling Junta, led by General Galtieri, ordered the invasion in an attempt to divert attention from their falling popularity. Some might say the invasion had a similar effect on Margaret Thatcher's governing Conservative Party. Whatever the political effect, the affect on human lives was more far reaching. Almost one thousand lives were lost in total from both sides, hundreds more were injured and heroes emerged; men like the incredibly brave Simon Weston, and Lieutenant Colonel H Jones. When the second battalion of the Parachute Regiment took Goose Green seventeen British soldiers lost their lives, among them 'H' Jones as he led an attack on an Argentine machine gun post. His bravery earned him the Victoria Cross.

Why the sudden history lesson? Well, H Jones had strong connections in the area and two years later this section of the coast path was opened by his wife as a lasting memorial. We passed the commemorative plaque and descended a length of wooden steps that can only be described as spectacular, dropping to Mill Bay Cove before climbing The Warren. This was a particularly beautiful part of the walk, with views through the branches of Monterey pine trees and across the mouth of the River Dart; I could think of no more fitting a memorial for anyone.

I was intoxicated by the views and kept looking back across the water towards Blackstone Point. The sun was shining, the sea a palate of blues and greens, sunlight sparkled on the water and the branches threw waving shadows across the path. All that was missing was some chocolate.

"How about a chocolate button?" I asked Chris, hurrying to catch her up.

"Now? You've only just had breakfast!"

288

So that was that! Great views. Shame about the chocolate.

We got lost at Inner Froward Point, and when we get lost we do it with style! A network of paths shot off in various directions amongst the derelict buildings that were once a World War II defence battery. The guidebook directions were confusing to say the least, but after some consultation between ourselves (and much cursing over the lack of signposts), we confidently took a path down between two buildings and then a second path along the cliff-side before reaching a fork. Did we go left and upwards or right down a narrow track that more closely resembled a sheep run than a footpath? We chose left, to emerge ten minutes later, with trembling leg muscles, racing hearts and heaving lungs back where we had started, amongst the buildings! The prospect of retracing our steps down the steep hillside was far from appealing, so we cheated, taking a different route, which although more overgrown and farther from the coast, linked up with the coast path a little further along. We could have been spared all our needless efforts had the footpaths been properly maintained and adequately signposted. Now, I'm not going to mention the landowner, that wouldn't be fair but suffice it to say that we came across a National Trust owned Land Rover parked by a stile. There was no sign of any ranger and I suspect he was probably hiding in the undergrowth (and there was no shortage of that!) awaiting our departure, eager to avoid a confrontation with two irate walkers who were vociferously telling each other just how fed up they were of walking in circles on jungle-like paths. Seeing the Land Rover but no one to moan at, we crossed a ridiculous squeeze stile and set off for Coleton Fishacre.

And that's another gripe: stiles! There we were on the longest National Trail in the country, not the only people walking the route – hundreds do it every year – a few all in one go but the majority, like us, walking for several days or a couple of weeks at a time. And what is the one thing all these walkers and backpackers have in common? Rucksacks! By no means were all those walkers in the long-legged, beanpole body shape category. So what does that leave us with? Short people, shapely people, people who are not just broad shouldered but broad from front to backpack. People unable to leap tall-stepped stiles in a single bound. People wearing bulky rucksacks to throw them off balance if bending, twisting or leaning. And the stiles? What variation on a theme have we got with these? Some are nice, like the simple gates, I like gates – these are my favourite! (All except the ones that seem to be built of mahogany or lead and whose hinges have dropped). Then we have the wall stiles – you know the sort – stone walls with stone slabs running through and sticking out, running in steps up the wall at a right angle. With no handrail to hold on to, and the stones often slippery with rain, these type of stiles are a problem for the shorter walker and can throw you off balance if carrying a rucksack. Next are the ladder stiles, the main problem here is the distance between the steps, but fortunately there had been few of these on the walk this year. The popular one for this year had been the traditional stile with two steps passing through wooden fence posts (often decorated with barbed wire or electric fencing). For me, with my disproportionately long legs, these had been okay but for Chris, who is short (but not record-breakingly so) the steps were often too high to reach comfortably. Squeeze stiles are a bit rarer and are designed to allow a person to squeeze their legs through but prevent a fat woolly sheep from pushing through to get to the greener grass. All the ones we had come across had been tall, made from upright slabs and boulders they were too tall. We had to squeeze not only our legs through but our upper bodies and the rucksacks as well. Imagine being suspended by your rucksack in a V-shaped stile! But the all time worst stile is the kissing gate. I am not sure why they are so popular, they may hinder bicycles – but they also hinder prams – and in any case, a determined cyclist could lift the bike over. The major trouble with kissing gates is the angle, it is never wide enough to let you stand there in your rucksack and close the gate past you. It is so easy to get in and then get stuck. The number of walker's corpses we had seen hanging, stuck in kissing gates, suspended by their rucksacks! Just like gallows, some kissing gates! And without fail all stiles have nettles growing around their base and almost obscuring the last step! It's true.

The path improved as it twisted round to the north and out towards Scabbacombe Head. We stopped for lunch on a conveniently sited bench. We needed those calories for what was about to come. At Scabbacombe Sands the path dropped to sea level and then rose steeply to a height of four hundred feet, we rose slowly with it. The whole process was repeated minutes afterwards at Man Sands, only that time the four hundred feet ascent to the top of Southdown Cliff was even steeper. As we went up, three pensioners were slithering down, dressed completely inappropriately courtesy of Debenhams: high heels, tights, skirts and navy blazers. How they had not sustained laddered tights and broken ankles I could not imagine.

At Sharkham Point we met Mr and Mrs Idiot. Seeing our walking poles the man asked where we had got them, adding that he had never seen any in the shops. I wanted to ask what sort of shops he had looked in, fishmongers perhaps, because you can't go into any outdoor shop without falling over massive displays of walking poles, they seem to be the latest trend. Then he asked where we had walked from and our response elicited the usual comments. His next question was the ignorant one we had encountered a couple of times before – were we mother and daughter? Chris turned an irate shade of burgundy and I half expected her to give the twit a closer inspection of her walking pole via his bottom. How anyone not in possession of a guide dog could mistake us for relations is beyond comprehension. Physically, we are total opposites and, with the exception of colour, as far removed from one another as possible whilst still being of the same species! We don't even have the same accent. His wife cringed with embarrassment and attempted to throw herself off the cliff; sensing his acute case of foot in mouth disease he changed tact asking where we were from.

"Chris is originally from the Midlands and I'm from Burnley," I replied.

"Burnley!" he exclaimed. "I was in Burnley in 1956, I remember it snowing and I thought I've got to get away from here. Has it changed much?"

"Well, it's stopped snowing," I said dryly.

Despite what Mr and Mrs Idiot had said, we did not find the next bit easier. The steepness had gone, to be replaced with twists, dips and long straight bits, which at the end of the day seemed to drag interminably. A familiar story: on the map Brixham, our destination for the day, seemed very near but in reality we had to skirt the deep concave sweep of St Mary's Bay and round past Durl Head to Berry Head before turning west on the home straight.

Around St Mary's Bay the path followed the perimeter fencing of a huge holiday camp. As we trudged along, climbing steps and squeezing through narrow stiles, hordes of screaming children disgorged from the camp and raced along the path; all, it seemed, were intent on tripping us up or knocking us flying. I allowed myself the luxurious daydream of a particularly obnoxious child becoming impaled on my walking pole. But alas! The walking pole was behaving itself at that point – unlike most of the children. Perhaps Good Manners and Conduct should be included in the National Curriculum.

Berry Head sticks out eastwards into the English Channel, marking the southern tip of Torbay. The headland is a nature reserve and a S.S.S.I., and an important breeding ground for lots of noisy fulmars, kittiwakes, guillemots and er, pigeons, most of which seemed to be flying rather worryingly over our heads. On Berry Head there is a Country Park, a nature trail, a now disused quarry, a tearoom, a little visitor centre, a large car park, a Coast Guard lookout point, a lighthouse, a rather interesting orientation table, some toilets and a Napoleonic Fort. We played a little game of which came first: the lighthouse, the Country Park or the Fort? Then we went in to use the toilets and realised that they must have been there when the Devonian limestone was still forming and had not been cleaned since! To describe them as filthy and disgusting falls far short of accuracy; I've been in some pretty crappy toilets – no pun intended – but these were the worst ever. What must foreign visitors to this country think of our facilities?

The view to the north from Berry Head was an open panoramic sweep of Torbay. As the view of what was to come the following year for our final section of the Coast Path, it was not exactly inspiring. The sea looked nice. Torquay looked er, not very nice. Urban. Big. Sprawling. And heavily populated. After two weeks of rural isolation with very few large towns, our first glimpse of Torquay was not very appealing. I was getting depressed, our holiday for this year was nearly over and for the last few miles of our walk we would have an almost uninterrupted view of suburbia! We entered Brixham and Torquay briefly hid behind the next small headland.

Brixham had changed somewhat since I had been with my parents many years before. A new red brick multi-storey car park had sprung up but the replica of the Golden Hind was still anchored in the harbour, and the Wimpy (which my Dad had once absent-mindedly walked out of without paying, only to have the manager chase him down the street) had gone, to be replaced with an amusement arcade. But the most noticeable difference was the litter and the general run-down feel of the place. It was doing its best – a brass band played in the evening and hanging baskets and trendy street furniture in the shape of cast iron benches and litter bins adorned the pedestrianised thoroughfares – but perhaps the number of tourists thronging the small resort, clutching silly hats and ice creams and dropping litter were too great for the cleaning services to cope with. Perhaps, like so many other English seaside resorts, Brixham was suffering a slump in the British holiday market; with less money coming into the town, less could be invested in maintaining services. The Borough Council had obviously initiated the belt tightening strategy with the toilet cleaning on Berry Head!

If Brixham was a bit of a let down, the Guest House we had booked into was not. We arrived at the same time as two other walkers and after being shown to our room (on the top floor – oh joy!) we relaxed in the lounge with a pot of tea and plate of biscuits. There was no laundry to wash that night, with only one day of walking left before we returned to the car at Falmouth, we had clean clothes for the following day in our rucksacks and a fresh change of clothes for the last day awaiting us with the car. But habits are hard to break and Chris had to stop me from rolling up my sleeves and getting down to a bout of the Widow Twankeys! We used the extra time to unwind, criticise Mr and Mrs Idiot and write some postcards. Then we set out in search of an evening meal.

Brixham was somewhat quieter than it had been a couple of hours earlier when we arrived, the happy campers presumably having gone back to chalet heaven to be fed and entertained on site. We wandered up and down the quiet streets, looking in shop windows, reading menus and listening to the brass band and the raucous herring gulls. We were struggling to decide where to have a meal, there seemed to be a vast choice of not a great deal, but we finally ended up in a fish restaurant overlooking the harbour. I could not be bothered with the 'is the fish skinned?' rigmarole and expectantly ordered a large battered haddock, chips and mushy peas. When the fish came it had skin on it!

Saturday 15th July

A gorgeous blue sky heralded the earliest breakfast of the walk, at 7.30 a.m. We shared it chatting to a retired couple who were walking from Poole to Plymouth. At last: someone who really knew what it was like to walk the coast path!

By the time we set off, we had lost some of the advantage of our early breakfast, having chatted for nearly an hour over cooling pots of tea and extra rounds of toast. On this day of all days, timing was everything. We had to reach Paignton by two o'clock at the latest in order to catch a bus that would link with a coach at Plymouth. The coach was the last one running that day from Plymouth to Falmouth and we had pre-booked our tickets to be sure of a seat. The path from Brixham to Paignton is five miles long, we expected to arrive in Paignton with plenty of time to spare but we were determined not to take any chances, hence the early start.

Brixham was just beginning to wake up as we left, passing the harbour and crossing a car park before joining a woodland trail just beyond the breakwater. But signposts were not at a premium, and without realising we soon left the coast path becoming lost in the woods. Despite what you might think of all our bickering, it was actually at this point that we came closest to having a disagreement. Chris thought we had wasted too much time wandering around the wood, tripping over tree roots and complaining about the lack of signposts, she proposed we leave the wood and join the road. I thought we should retrace our steps and find out where we had gone wrong, in the desperate hope that in doing so we might stumble on the correct footpath. The drawback to Chris's plan was that any roads were just off our maps. The drawback to my plan was the sheer number of interlinking footpaths that were running through the wood. Whilst we were standing in limbo, unsure whose plan was the least flawed, I became aware that I really shouldn't have drunk quite so much tea at breakfast. So what's new? As things turned out, that was one occasion that an al fresco toilet stop proved useful. I ducked behind a nearby wall to discover that from my crouched position I could see an information board with a map of the woods on it!

We scrutinised the map, trying to memorise the network of paths and then set off down a track running down a slope, back into the heart of the woodland. A mile later we stumbled back onto the Coast Path, only fifty yards from where we had left it, at Churston Cove. What should have been quite a nice secluded little inlet had been totally spoiled by a group of campers. Being one herself, Chris thinks the word campers is inappropriate for the people defiling the cove that morning. Dossers, litterbugs, scum, drunks, druggies: take your pick, any and all are apt. Sometime the previous day presumably, they had erected three tents, smashed a large collection of beer bottles, had several campfires using a wide-ranging choice of fuels from saplings to lager cans and scattered litter over an extensive area of ground, before finally collapsing into an alcohol (and very probably drug) induced stupor, from which, when we arrived, they had yet to come round. Their 'camp' was an utter desecration of the cove. We hastily clambered out of the cove, trying to forget the scene behind us. So far the morning was not going well.

For the next mile, the view of the sea on our right was hidden by trees. Well, you can't have everything. For the same mile, the view of the golf course on our left was also hidden by trees. Which just goes to show there are always compensations in life if you look for them!

Broad Sands and its multi-coloured beach huts appeared. We used the public toilets there; they reminded me of the ones in Weston-Super-Mare. Many happy childhood holidays had

293

been spent on the beach, building sand castles, riding donkeys and flying a kite with Dad. Mum always maintained I spent enough money on donkey rides to buy one of the animals. These toilets were just the same as the ones from 1970's Weston. A fine patina of sand covered the floor, trodden in from the beach and crunching under foot as I made my way into the narrow cubicle with the low porcelain pan. Memories of Weston came rushing back: the sand swept clean every morning by huge JCBs, the tide seemingly miles away across the smooth beach and the way, twice a year, the moon's influence on the tides would cause the sea to coming surging in to crash against the sea wall and hurl sand across the promenade. The days on those holidays were always hot and sunny, I'm sure it must have rained at some time but if it did I don't remember; all too soon the week would end and we would pack up the car and return home. Those holidays seemed as far away now as the distant sea had appeared then.

Leaving the toilets and the 1970s behind, we took the road under the Torbay and Dartmouth Steam Railway line, climbed some steps and turned to follow the path as it ran parallel to the tracks. A nearby bench provided a convenient stopping place for a rest and a drink. As we sat there, a toot heralded the approaching locomotive.

"Ooh! Quick! Take a photo," urged Chris.

But from where we were sitting not a lot of the line was visible.

"Stand on the bench!" she insisted as the train drew nearer.

"I can't do that. People have to sit on here after we've gone. Suppose my boots are mucky?"

"Your boots are fine. Just stand on the bench before it's too late!"

I stood on the bench. From up there, all of six inches higher, not much more of the line was visible, the curve of the embankment hiding most of the track. Copious amounts of smoke and increasingly louder chuff-chuffing noises indicated the imminent approach of the engine. Not having enough time to run down to the bridge for a clear shot, I just stood on the bench on my tip toes and hoped for the best.

"If I could balance one foot on the back of the bench and the other on your head," I suggested to Chris, "I might be high enough to see the whole track."

Her terse reply indicated a certain reluctance to try and so I had to be content with a photo of the loco's chimney, a lot of smoke and quite a lot of carriage roofs, which, when the film was developed, could only be made out under strong magnification!

On reaching Goodrington Sands, past the extensive sprawl of a caravan site, we were reminded of what the majority of people come to the South West for: sand, sea, ice cream and structured entertainment. We were entering the English Riviera and all that came with it: arcades, fun parks, cheap cafes, expensive ice creams, campsites, hotels, B&Bs, screaming kids, stressed out mothers and frustrated fathers. No wonder our guidebook suggested catching a bus through Torbay! We passed hastily through Goodrington, but not before sampling the ice cream.

Paignton drew near and with it the end of our walk for that year. All we had to do was walk down into the town and find the bus station. Yet after less than half an hour in this urban environment I was already wishing for rural peace. I had had all I could tolerate of suburbia with its organised fun, noisy amusement arcades, dog dirt and out of control children. Like, for instance, the child who had just thrown ice cream across the path! A small dollop landed on the strap of Chris's rucksack, a second, larger dollop splattered my arm, some hit my shorts and the rest of the white runny mess hit the pavement. Chris was beginning to swear. I was just looking round for the Mr Whippy hurler (hoping to give either child, parent or both a piece of my mind) when my brain began to register a frantic message that my nostrils had been sending. What was that horrible, festering, fishy smell? Since when did Mr Whippy come in fish flavour?

Seagull excreta! We'd been hit! Pooped on! Oh yuck! Oh no! Oh great! Oh sh… ame! And it stank!

Faced with a generous application of the white smelly stuff (which on closer inspection revealed bits of green and yellow things in it) there is a limit to what you can do with one paper tissue. At the first toilets we came to we hurried inside and began a mopping up and damage limitation operation. Some minutes later we emerged looking cleaner but not smelling particularly pleasant and completed our walk to Paignton promenade.

The beach at Paignton was busy, its fine white sand attracting hordes of families clutching buckets and spades, cool boxes full of sand sandwiches and bottles of wasp-attracting fizzy drinks, and struggling to erect colourful striped windbreaks in the soft sand. We bought a Styrofoam cup of tea and a strawberry cream scone from the one hundred year old refreshment hut on the promenade – if you are ever in the area I recommend you try their scones! We walked delicately onto the beach, trying but failing to keep sand out of our walking boots, and with our rucksacks lying in the sand and Buzz sitting embarrassingly on Chris's head, we celebrated the end of our walk for that year with our takeaway cream tea.

We had arrived in plenty of time for our bus and relaxed on the beach (keeping a wary eye out for flying gulls) passing time making phone calls to everyone we could think of.

"Hiya Mum! We've done it! We're sitting on the beach at Paignton, smelling of seagull muck."

"Well done! Never mind about the seagull, it's supposed to be lucky!"

That of course, made me feel a whole lot better and very grateful to the kindly seagull. After all, it could have chosen to dump on anyone!

We took our time, people watching and writing postcards. I offered to bury Chris in the sand, she refused and eventually we set off in search of the bus station, catching the bus to Plymouth where we had over two hours to wait before the coach left for Falmouth. Plymouth was hot and crowded, full of shoppers on that busy Saturday afternoon. We made our way down to the Hoe and visited the Dome, a relatively new visitor attraction overlooking the waterfront, refreshing ourselves with a cool drink and a sandwich. Looking out, down Plymouth Sound, it seemed strange that we had walked that coastline only one week earlier. Oh, to be able to wind back the clock! Our holiday was almost over and I was full of regrets that time had gone so quickly.

The late afternoon found us back at the bus station, we had arrived in good time and stood watching increasing numbers of coaches draw in but none of them were ours. One by one, the coaches filled with people and departed. Still our coach had not arrived. A harassed official eventually appeared to inform us all that the coach had been delayed by an hour. We had no choice but to wait. There were no seats nearby and we dared not leave the immediate area to find a seat in case the coach made up time and arrived without us knowing, and, worse still, left without us on board! The time dragged, the temperature in the claustrophobic concrete dungeon that Plymouth calls a bus station increased and everyone's patience decreased. One boy continually zoomed up and down the concourse on a scooter, the 'in' thing of that summer. I think he single-handedly succeeded in annoying everyone there. When he wasn't whizzing by on the infernal aluminium contraption, he was messing about with its telescopic handlebars, a habit I found particularly irksome in view of my own lack of success with my telescopic walking pole. The coach arrived at an opportune moment, saving the child (had he but know it) from an especially messy death involving his beloved handlebars and a certain part of his anatomy. By 8 p.m. when we finally arrived in Falmouth my tolerance of any form of transport other than walking was gone.

We hastened to the hotel, showered, changed into the fresh clean clothes that we had left in the car and rushed out for a meal. The hotel owner had recommended a popular restaurant on the main street but at nine o'clock on a Saturday evening it was very popular and very full. The pubs seemed to be full of groups of young men, possibly all sailors, and were rather noisy. By wandering up the main street and into the quieter part of the town, climbing a gentle hill away from the waterfront, we came across a quiet, gently lit little Italian restaurant. They had a table available and for the first time all holiday (can you believe it?) we indulged in a three course meal. Boy, do those Italians know how to make a chocolate mousse!

The travelling by bus and coach had tired me more than any walking and I was exhausted. Whilst Chris slept brokenly I woke only once, just before I drowned in front of the Eddystone Lighthouse in freezing seas whilst struggling to put on a lifeline. I had no sooner woken from the watery dream, to find Chris awake and pouring a glass of water, than I was asleep again (shouting apparently) and that time dreaming of babies and zombies. Perhaps all my shouting was the reason for Chris's bad night!

The following morning we travelled through sunshine, stopping for a few hours to visit The Lost Gardens of Heligan before continuing our long journey home. We planned to walk the next section of the South West Coast Path, from Torbay to Poole Harbour, the following year, for me, although not for Chris, the conclusion of my journey on Britain's longest National Trail. In between times we had work, family holidays, work, Christmas and more work. But for this year at least it was all over and we were going home.

"It seems ages away until next summer."

"Yeah."

It wasn't.

Torbay to Poole Harbour

In summer 2001 Chris and I were due to walk our last section of the South West Coast Path, a distance of approximately 130 miles from Torquay to Poole Harbour. It was to see the completion of the coast path for me, although not for Chris – who, as you will remember, had missed the first part of the path due to a leg injury. Full of our usual excitement and anticipation we began planning the walk in January. By the end of the month we had booked all the accommodation and sent off deposit cheques totalling over £300.

In February Foot and Mouth Disease was found in animals at an Essex abattoir. In a knee-jerk reaction the Government imposed restrictions on the movement of farm animals and appealed to the general public to stay away from the countryside. Seemingly overnight the countryside became a no-go area sprouting 'Keep Out' signs and disinfecting points across roads and farm tracks. By the end of the month hundreds of cases had been confirmed throughout the country with Cumbria and Devon the worst hit areas; rights of way were closed even in unaffected regions and Britain's farming industry was once again the pariah of Europe.

By March, the Government was declaring their stringent precautions had brought the disease under control. A claim that of course had nothing to do with the forthcoming general election. Hundreds of thousands of sheep, cattle and pigs were awaiting slaughter on infected farms and those in the immediate vicinity. Hundreds of thousands had already been slaughtered – of those many had been burned on controversial pyres - were the dioxins released in the burning process more harmful than the virus and did the burning aid the spread of this airborne virus? But most carcasses were piling up in bloated putrefying heaps, still awaiting disposal. Children lost pet lambs, petting zoos lost their pets, farmers lost entire breeding herds and slowly the Government lost its credibility. Clearly Foot and Mouth Disease was not yet under control.

Farmers' Unions talked of compensation, hauliers complained of not getting any compensation and a quiet voice in the background gradually began to gain more and more volume – the tourist industry. By the beginning of April it was apparent that Foot and Mouth was affecting tourism far more than it was farming. Since the start of the outbreak millions of tourist pounds had been lost, the tourist industry provided jobs for a greater number of people than farming, and tourism generated many times more income than agriculture. How did the expected financial loss of Britain's European meat trade and the cost of fighting a prolonged battle of culling and burning and compensating, balance against the very real financial loss to Britain's tourist industry?

With the approach of Easter the Government was confusing everyone with its U-turns as Spin Doctors laboured to turn a mess of sows' ears into silk purses (first problem was finding any sows that had not been slaughtered!) The Prime Minister declared the countryside was open; what he failed to grasp was most people wanted to go to the countryside to visit the country – perhaps do a bit of walking, that sort of thing – not to spend an entire week's holiday driving between craft shops and tea rooms whilst attempting to divert the kids' attention from piles of rotting corpses or smoke from the world's largest barbecue! Footpaths and other rights of way remained closed, Britons were staying away from the countryside and foreign tourists were staying away from Britain.

By the end of April confirmed Foot and Mouth cases numbered in the thousands but finally it really did seem that the outbreak was in decline. Confirmed cases each day dropped from over fifty to fewer than ten. Somewhere down in the tunnel of despair that Britain had slipped into a light had begun to glimmer.

Chris and I had followed the progress of the outbreak with sympathy, frustration and dread. Sympathy for the farmers, their animals and the tourist industry. Frustration over the handling of the crisis. Dread, selfish dread I will admit, that our walking holiday was at risk. Would the Coast Path be re-opened by July? If it wasn't, how much of the route could we follow along roads and promenades? Should we cancel? Should we wait and see? Could we afford to cancel? With every new confirmed case we too sank further into the tunnel of despair. I considered investing in disinfectant manufacturers and indeed, had I had any spare money to invest I might have been tempted, but all my money was tied up in holiday accommodation deposits. Colleagues constantly asked us if the walk was still on and depending on the number of cases that day we replied with dogged stoicism or bitter depression.

Our frustration was perhaps a more difficult emotion to deal with. Our scientific backgrounds gave us a clearer understanding of the outbreak, the way the virus spread and the manner in which the crisis was handled. Lessons that should have been learned from the FMD outbreak in 1967 were ignored, vaccination was seen as an unworkable solution purely on the grounds of future economics, when in fact the vaccine was readily available, inexpensive and produced at labs in this country. Meanwhile Holland, who also had an outbreak, was quick to use the vaccine. Vaccination could have controlled the spread of the disease but the Government and the Farmers' Unions were against it on the grounds that there would no longer be a European market for British meat, if livestock were vaccinated the animals would carry Foot and Mouth antibodies and therefore would not be regarded as FMD-free. How quickly they forgot about Europe's reaction to British beef in the wake of the BSE crisis! Europe wouldn't want British meat now even if it could be proved to come from a strain of FMD-resistant dinosaur!

A television journalist summed up the whole crazy fiasco when he said 'The Government have taken a non-life threatening disease that is harmless to humans and turned it into a major catastrophe'.

By May a turning point was seemingly reached. As cases continued to decline and funeral pyres continued to burn, the authorities were struggling to cope with the backlog of carcasses. Two and half million animals had been slaughtered. The Army was rumoured to be considering the use of napalm. And then another outbreak occurred in an area bordering Lancashire and Yorkshire, was there to be no end?

At the end of May MAFF admitted that walkers posed no risk of spreading the disease, although some farmers still seemed reluctant to believe this; the truth was the virus was more likely to be spread by wild animals and birds and borne on the wind. Slowly rights of way were re-opened, and Chris and I tentatively began to hope that maybe our walk would take place after all. Many farmers were still reluctant to have walkers on their land and local authorities were busy carrying out risk assessments on re-opening the many hundreds of miles of footpaths in their areas. We monitored the web sites of Devon and Dorset County Councils; every opened path was a cause for further celebration.

What was not in doubt was that this year's walk would be undertaken in a countryside very sensitive to the perceived risks walkers might pose and very different from the rich dairy farms and sheep-filled pastures of previous summers. To what degree had this disease affected the countryside we would be walking through? How would blighted Devon compare to disease-free Dorset? As our walk progressed we were to experience first hand the aftermath of the disease in terms of environmental and human costs, and to hear some chilling tales of selfishness and greed. The legacy of the 2001 Foot and Mouth outbreak was to remain with Britain for years to come.

By the end of June we knew of only one small part of the coast path that remained closed as a precaution against Foot and Mouth. Our next concern was to what extent the heavy winter rains and the resultant landslides in much of Dorset had affected the route of the path. There was only one way to find out and so at the end of June we set off on what was for me, although not Chris, the final part, the completion of the South West Coast Path.

Friday 29th June

In preparation for the long drive to Dorset I had filled up the car, checked tyre pressures, oil and water levels and even emptied the ashtray of sweet wrappers. The car had been serviced and, for its nine years and 114,000 miles, was running well. It was just unfortunate that the exhaust started blowing as we joined the M6. For the entire journey it sounded like I was driving a hot rod, and my embarrassment when we eventually pulled into the car park of our hotel in peaceful Lulworth was extreme.

Remembering our nightmare journey on the final day of the walk the previous year we had given much thought to where we should leave the car this time. Lulworth Cove was a convenient stopping point; near to the end of the walk it would be an easy bus ride to return from Poole at the end of the coast path, and a bus and train journey at the beginning of our holiday would take us to Torquay, our starting point this year. Initially we had intended to leave the car at the start in Torquay but we quickly hit a major problem. After telephoning countless hotels and guest houses in the town we began to realise that nowhere in such a busy seaside resort were willing to take a single night booking and allow us to leave a car occupying valuable space in their car park for two weeks. It had been Chris's idea to look further afield and she had found a very nice hotel at Lulworth. In the aftermath of Foot and Mouth I expect we would have had no problem finding somewhere in Torquay, hindsight is a wonderful thing.

We arrived in the late afternoon to find the Dorset coast draped in a heavy sea mist. A taste of things to come perhaps? Starting as we intended to continue, our first task was to make a cup of tea. Suitably refreshed we wandered down to the cove to admire the sea mist.

So much of the South West Coast Path consists of textbook geology and nowhere more so than at Lulworth Cove. The coastline here is rich with curious geological phenomenon created by the sea's erosion of softer rocks, leaving two enfolding arms of limestone that reach out to hug the cove, almost meeting. The layering of softer rocks, mainly clays, with harder limestones along this part of the Dorset coast and the eroding action of the sea has resulted in some spectacular scenery. The area around Lulworth is a geologist's heaven with impressive sculptured cliffs, folded rock formations and fossils. I had never seen cliff formations like these before and looked forward to walking this part of the coast path. Why had I ever thought the scenery in Dorset would be dull in comparison to what I had experienced earlier on the coast path? Dorset was totally different in character from Devon and Cornwall, even inland the scenery seemed disparate as the land contoured in folded hills and hidden valleys stretching away from the coast in a rippling patchwork of fields and wooded hillsides. A large section of the East Devon and Dorset coastline has recently been designated a UNESCO World Heritage Site; a status it shares with the Pyramids, the Great Barrier Reef, Yosemite National Park and the Great Wall of China to name but a few.

Leaving the tiny fishing boats bobbing gently in the cove, we headed off in search of an evening meal. Not surprisingly fish was a popular choice on the menus of nearly all the pubs and restaurants, of which there were not very many in the little village. But we found a pub at the far end of the village with a diverse menu and a rapidly filling bar, and enjoyed a generously proportioned main course that left us too full for any desserts. We promised ourselves that we would return on the last night to sample the desserts.

Saturday 30th June

An infrequent bus service carried us to Dorchester with an hour to spare before our train to Torquay. As I got on the bus at Lulworth I somehow succeeded in spearing my leg with my new walking pole. Having broken my previous one I had received this one as a Christmas present and because of all the Foot and Mouth restrictions had been unable to try it out until now. I had yet to become acquainted with all its idiosyncrasies and by the time I got off the bus at Dorchester I had two scratches on my legs from its unsheathed metal tip. I could see that this walking pole was going to be no less problematic than my previous one had been. What I needed was a rubber tip to go over the end but we didn't really have time to find one, first priority was locating the train station.

We found the station only to be told by a lady waiting for her friend's train that there was a delay at Castle Carey. That was where we were due to change trains, and it was vital both our trains ran, without either we would be stranded. We spent an anxious thirty minutes until our train arrived. Our connecting train was running ten minutes late but at least it was running.

It was almost 3 p.m. by the time we arrived in Torquay for the start of our walk that year. We had been walking for barely five minutes when Chris spotted a shop selling postcards. Having selected a handful of cards, she began groping about in the pocket of her shorts for her purse. She dragged it out amidst a shower of tampons that scattered across the pavement without her noticing.

"Excuse me," whispered a lady, hurrying towards us. She had spotted the sanity shower at the same moment I had, Chris meanwhile was still oblivious as we hurried to collect her 'litter'.

Passing an outdoor shop by the harbour I was able to buy a rubber tip for my walking pole. Then we battled our way through the crowded pavements and along the road to join the quieter path that climbed up to Daddy Hole Plan.

Memories of wonderful childhood holidays came rushing back. And if wishing alone could have turned back the clock I would surely have been eight years old again, wearing the red trouser suit Mum had made for me and racing Dad down the steps to Meadfoot Beach.

We had a nine-mile walk that afternoon to our hotel at Maidencombe and we were prepared for a late arrival. Torquay sprawls across a wide area, and its suburbs branch out to fill the numerous headlands and picturesque coves. On the path that evening we were never far away from built up areas but only at Babbacombe was this apparent. The path closely followed the wriggling line of the coast; Hope's Nose followed Meadfoot and then came scenic Ansty's Cove with jet skis and fishing boats. Craggy red sandstone cliffs dipped into the sea and lush woodland grew on the gentler slopes. When we arrived on the grassy cliff tops near Babbacombe we called the hotel to inform them we would be late arriving.

"We are just above Redgate Beach," I advised the landlady.

"Oh, it won't take you long from there!" she answered superciliously.

"I bet she's never even walked this part of the path," muttered Chris.

We estimated we were approximately three miles away but the nature of the path and the fact that Chris was having a bit of a problem with a painful knee would, we knew, slow us down.

Our knees protested through the steep climbs and uneven steps of Babbacombe and Oddicombe and the evening was drawing on. The beach at Oddicombe is at the bottom of a very steep hill, a road snakes down to the beach but parking is restricted and a cliff railway, similar to the one at Lynmouth, runs down to the beach. At Oddicombe, for the first of many times that year, we lost our way; insufficient signposting at the end of a long day being to blame, we felt, for our unnecessary hike to the top of the hill and the subsequent hike halfway back down, hopefully in the direction of the coast path.

Maybe it was time to summon the help of Chris's latest gizmo. Earlier that year Chris had purchased a GPS - a Global Positioning System. Using signals from satellites it enabled her to plot our location precisely. Technology had progressed and prices had come down until what had once been expensive, bulky, hi-tech equipment for the likes of the armed forces and yacht owners, was now affordable to the masses and as compact as a mobile phone. The GPS was Chris's new toy and she loved it, in fact she had been playing with it ever since April when it had dropped through her letterbox following her successful bid for it on an Internet auction.

"It can tell us exactly where we are to the inch!" she enthused.

"I can see where we are just by the simple act of looking around," I replied, as I psyched myself up for a sarcastic Chris baiting session.

"So why are we lost?"

"That is due to your dodgy map reading."

She chose to ignore that comment. "It can tell us our altitude as well!"

"So can I. At this precise moment we are standing on the beach, so I would guess we must be pretty near sea level."

"When I was at home practising how to use it," she said, ignoring my sarcasm, "I plotted where we keep our toilet rolls."

"Do you not find it more helpful to tell guests to look in the bathroom cabinet if they need more loo paper rather than giving them a six figure grid reference?"

She wasn't to be deterred. "It can plot our course even if we are travelling at anything up to 950 miles an hour!"

"So unless you are running to a cream tea shop it should be able to cope then?"

"I don't think you're taking this seriously! Talking of cream tea shops, I can set an alarm to go off when we are close to pre-set co-ordinates, such as cream tea shops!"

"Oh, yes!" I exclaimed, immediately forgetting I was pretending disinterest. "You never said it would be that useful. Why stop at tearooms? What about pizzerias, fish and chip shops, ice cream parlours, free toilets..." A tinny electronic alarm began to sound cutting into my tirade. "Come back! Where are you going?"

"To the tea room," she called over her rapidly disappearing shoulder.

We never did find the tearoom, instead an unwelcome and badly signed diversion near Petit Tour Point took us out onto the road and added yet more distance and time to the long day. Watcombe came and went in the gathering twilight to the accompanying squeaks and rustles of small mammals in the woodland undergrowth, (or it might have been teenage lovers). A slowworm wriggled lethargically out of our way and into the ivy and dogs mercury at the side of the path.

At 8.45 p.m. we reached the lane into Maidencombe and staggered into the exceedingly crowded pub. We expected to be too late to order food although this was not the case but on hearing there was a one and a half hour wait for meals I thanked Chris for her brainwave. It's not often she has one but this was a beauty! Takeaway sandwiches.

I approached the bar with some trepidation, if the wait for meals was so long was it not likely that they were too busy to rustle up a couple of takeaway sarnies? But hunger is a serious motivator and, determined to give it my best shot, I turned on the all the charm I could muster.

"I wonder if there is any possible chance that you could do some takeaway sandwiches for two weary walkers, please?" We both did our best to look exhausted and on the point of collapse, which wasn't difficult.

The bar tender was happy to oblige and cheerily took our order, asking us where we had walked from and where we were walking to. A mere three weeks later we found ourselves eating a meal in this very same pub, having returned to Devon with Chris's family whilst her daughter, Clare, attended an induction day for her gap year before starting university. On that weekend the pub was equally busy, the staff equally pleasant and they seemed genuinely interested to know how we had fared with our walk.

Whilst we waited for the sandwiches that evening we took a couple of drinks out into the beer garden. Alcohol and I rarely meet and after we had collected our sandwiches, the effect of half a pint of cider on an empty stomach resulted in me staggering up the road to the hotel, giggling hysterically at something Chris had said.

The foyer of the hotel displayed a Welcome Host Award. But our welcome was rather cool, maybe it was something do to with the smell of alcohol that must have emanated from us. Maybe the landlady assumed we had spent the last few hours in the pub, although this was certainly not the case. Or maybe she was like that with all her guests?

Once in our room we made a pot of tea and sat down in the easy chairs by the window to eat our supper. The sandwiches were delicious, made all the more so by our lethargy and hunger, I only wished I had ordered more than I did.

Sunday 1st July

That morning the landlady's husband served us breakfast in the large dining room and he was certainly more cheerful and welcoming than his wife, so perhaps it was he that had won the award. The reception desk was empty when we went to settle the bill, so I gave the bell a smart ring as per the posted instructions. The landlady appeared, and huffed and puffed her way through taking my cheque and writing out a receipt. We left with the impression that we had been a great inconvenience to her. We would view any future Welcome Host signs with much scepticism.

It was a warm and humid morning on the difficult path from Maidencombe to Shaldon. The path dipped steeply running near the cliff edge and beside birch, hawthorn and blackthorn hedges. Honeysuckle and wild roses attracted marbled white butterflies, the first of hundreds we were to see this year. Industrious bumble bees fed on drooping foxglove flowers. The path veered inland at Labrador Bay, climbing steeply through a field to briefly join the road before returning once more to the coast.

Some very peculiar noises announced our nearness to the small zoo at The Ness, where we descended to Shaldon and crossed the river by ferry to Teignmouth. We bought yet more sandwiches and went down to the beach to have lunch. Our rustling sandwich wrappers soon attracted the attention of half the herring gulls in Devon. They loitered nearby hoping for some food and seemed to be rather well behaved for a bunch of scavengers until, that is, one gull spotted an apple bobbing on the waves. Obviously a healthy living animal, aware of the need for five pieces of fruit and veg a day, this gull wasted no time in rescuing the Golden Delicious and proceeded to eat it just in front of us. However, all the other gulls were equal health freaks and did their best to steal the apple. But the first healthy eater was jealously guarding it and not prepared to share it with anyone. Eventually, after much pestering he lost his temper and turned on one of the other gulls. We watched amazed, and it has to be said a little sickened by the level of violence involved, as the gull set about one of the would-be thieves. Meanwhile all the other gulls rushed in to help themselves to his abandoned apple. The fight began to turn nasty when the first gull managed to pin the other one on his back on the sand and proceeded to try and rip a wing off. I was just looking round to find a pebble to throw to break up the fight when the first gull suddenly realised what was happening to his apple. With an outraged squawk he forgot about the fight and flapped back to reclaim his lunch. One look at his approaching figure and all the other gulls scarpered and both he and we were left to finish our meals in peace.

With a short exception at Holcombe, the rest of the walking that day was along the flat, hard promenade from Teignmouth through Dawlish and round to Dawlish Warren. The afternoon had grown hot. Crickets chattered in the shrubs and high speed trains thundered by on Isambard Kingdom Brunel's railway line that ran parallel to the promenade.

We stopped to buy a drink at Dawlish. I left Chris watching the famous black swans as I went off to try and find a shop that was still open. Most of them were just closing for the day. Already I had lost track of the days and remembered with a jolt that this was Sunday. I attempted to rush into the supermarket but the manager barred the doorway, it was four o'clock, closing time. Having been successful with my weary walker routine at the pub the night before, I tried it again but to no avail. I could see I would get nowhere appealing to his better nature, he clearly didn't have one, and so I sprinted down the street until I came to Woolworth's, which was fortunately still open. Returning to Chris I was concerned to see her popping painkillers. Her knee was obviously troubling her, although she had said nothing to indicate the severity of the pain she was in. I spent the rest of the day surreptitiously watching her.

Dawlish Warren seems to exist solely as a holiday resort; it consists of a scattering of small shops, a few houses and vast acres of caravans and campsites. Along the spit of sand reaching out into the Exe estuary there is a golf course and a large amusement park, as well as a nature reserve. Happy campers abounded amongst the arcades, novelty shops and ice cream stalls. The sight of a stand selling hot banana fritters had Chris reminiscing happily about family holidays spent here when Clare was a small child.

We now had four miles of walking along a busy, narrow road to reach our B&B beyond Kenton. Watching Chris hobbling along and feeling my own feet aching from the pounding along the pavements, I was suddenly struck by a brainwave of my own. We could catch a bus! The resulting twenty-minute journey saved us an awful walk. We alighted from the bus at Kenton, slightly unsure of the precise location of the B&B.

A lady was watering her hanging baskets, and I decided to ask for directions.

"Come with me," she said, ushering us into the garden at the rear of her cottage. "I'll ask my husband."

She called his name a few times and waited for a response.

"Sorry dear? Did you call?" said a man springing into view.

Not only did he sound like Basil Fawlty he looked like him too! Fortunately the resemblance ended there and he was able to confidently direct us up the road. But his estimate of half a mile turned out to be only half correct. It was a mile before we eventually reached our destination.

We were greeted with a pot of tea on the lawn and then, much to our relief, an offer of a lift to the pub and collection afterwards, which we wasted no time in accepting. Whilst I did our usually laundry chore and made use of the washing line, Chris began chatting with the owner. This was a working farm and the conversation naturally turned to the Foot and Mouth crisis. The lady was very pragmatic about the situation, knowing first hand how the closure of footpaths and warnings to stay away from the countryside affected the tourist trade. By that time many rumours were flying around regarding unscrupulous farmers deliberately selling infected sheep for over £100 to other farmers who cared more about the amount of compensation they would received than their animals. And whilst it was easy to pass these off as just rumours, there undoubtedly were farmers who would go to any lengths with no regard for anyone just to make money out of the situation. The landlady told us of one such farmer in Devon who had put his sheep's feet into bleach and poured boiling water into their mouths and then telephoned MAFF. Hardly surprisingly when the vets inspected the animals they found blisters. His flock was slaughtered and he no doubt received the compensation he had conspired for. Unfortunately for all his neighbours their herds were culled as a precautionary measure. In total ten farms had their herds wiped out as a result of one farmer's greed. Several of these farms had breeding herds going back several hundred years. This manipulation of the system served to highlight the flaws in the Government's handling of the Foot and Mouth outbreak. How many more so-called cases were really the result of dishonesty and abuse?

We returned to the B&B later in the evening, replete with a superb meal. So far, so good: three out of three for good accommodation and three out of three for excellent evening meals. This just couldn't last.

By the time we were ready for bed that evening Chris's knee had swollen somewhat.

"Look at my knee!"

I looked up from writing a postcard. Chris was sitting on her bed. Where her knee should have been there was a football. If I was worried earlier in the day I almost panicked on seeing her knee. Would the swelling have gone down by morning? And if it hadn't how could she possibly walk? But I could not dissuade her from continuing. To rest up and catch the bus for a few days would be to fail. I would have felt exactly the same. The best I could do was to carry some of her gear and thus lighten her load, hopefully that would be enough to ensure she could continue and complete the walk. For the rest of the holiday both of us were secretly worrying that she might do permanent damage to her joint.

Monday 2nd July

Frantic cheeping woke me the next morning. At first I thought it was Chris squealing with pain but fortunately her knee was back to normal size. The cheeping sounds were coming from the open window. House martins had built their nests just under the eaves and were busy flying in and out feeding their young. Leaning backwards out of the window and peering towards the roof I counted four neat little mud nests. A fifth nest directly above my head housed not martins but sparrows. This nest looked in danger of falling down and was in dire need of repair but the sparrows didn't seem to mind. I wondered how the house martins felt with squatters living next door?

After breakfast we waited at the side of the busy road for the bus to take us back to Starcross. From there we took the ferry across the mouth of the river Exe to Exmouth. The coast path does not seem to make sense at Exmouth, for some reason it does not actually start until one and half miles along the promenade from the ferry point. We wandered along the prom in the sunshine, watching the holidaymakers and looking out for any coast path signposts. The guidebook and the path description seemed to contradict one another's directions and we were left to try and figure it out for ourselves. Eventually we noticed a sign pointing away from the road and climbed a path to reach Orcombe Point, from where we could look back across the Exe estuary towards the red cliffs of Teignmouth and Dawlish.

That morning we had the first of several army ranges to negotiate. The path cut between the rifle range and a sprawling holiday park where row after row of static caravans marched away up the hill inland. On the farther side of the rifle range we stopped for a break and were passed by two middle-aged men carrying heavily laden rucksacks. It was the start of a relay we were to continue with them for the next two days. Further on we passed them sitting on the side of the path, camping stove burning merrily as they made a pot of tea.

To the west of Budleigh Salterton the path levelled out, although the walking was no less easy because of the narrow rut of a path. The rut was only just wide enough for one foot and was filled with loose stones and grit, soon my boots were full and I found myself constantly stopping to empty them. Gorse lined the path, the seedpods popping quietly in the heat. Walking that path was like walking a tightrope; one false move and you fell sideways to be impaled on the gorse. Ahead a stand of pine trees heralded a descent and an improvement in the path. But we were in no hurry to continue as at that moment two Peregrine falcons began calling to each other. One was perched conspicuously on an exposed branch, whilst the other circled constantly overhead.

As we sat on a bench in God's waiting room, otherwise known as Budleigh Salterton, a sea mist rolled in and that was that for the scenery for the rest of the day. Budleigh Salterton is a quiet, genteel resort, obviously appealing to the older generation both for holidays and retirement. The centre of the town seemed to be concentrated just inland of the promenade, and as we set off along the prom it was almost like stepping back to a time when a holiday by the seaside was an altogether more dignified experience. We passed couples sleeping in deckchairs, other couples snoozing in their cars and then a row of prettily painted beach huts with yet more slumbering occupants. No amusement arcades, no bouncy castles - thank goodness but, unfortunately, no ice cream vans either!

The path veered inland to cross the River Otter. The area was a nature reserve and information boards along both banks detailed plants, bird life and the history of this much silted up river mouth. I kept a sharp eye out for any of this bounteous wildlife but had to be content with a single heron. Apparently the mud flats and reed beds were home not just to mink but also to aquatic snails that were thought to number twelve times the population of Great Britain. A similar parallel could, I thought, be drawn with the snails in my garden.

As we crossed the bridge over the river we were expecting to see diversionary signs, as when we had started the holiday this part of the path was closed because of the perceived risk walkers posed of spreading Foot and Mouth to a nearby pig farm. The pigs were free range and their field extended to the edge of the cliffs, taking in the footpath. Having been prepared for a diversion we were somewhat worried at the absence of signs – would we reach the farm only then to find the path closed and be forced to retrace our steps? From our experience of the organised manner in which Devon County Council had re-opened paths we were surprised to find no forewarning of any possible diversion, and so hoping for the best we continued along the footpath down the eastern side of the river. We were half way along this path when our way was barred, not by a sign, a barrier or an irate farmer but by a fledgling. The tiny bird with pathetically few feathers stood square in the middle of the path, cheeping furiously. It didn't move at our approach and we cautiously edged past it and carried on our way. As we passed an elderly couple walking towards us I felt I had to warn them about the little bird. They too had to inch cautiously past it.

There was much new fencing along the path, put up hastily in the last few weeks to separate farmland from the footpath, without it much of the coast path would have remained closed. We could only admire the hard work of the team of County Council employees who had been responsible, for without their efforts we would not have been able to complete the walk. Dorset County Council had undertaken similar measures. We were pleasantly surprised to arrive at the pig farm to find the path was now open. The fencing here must have been put up within the last couple of days.

"Halloo!" I greeted the pigs.

"Julia!" Chris responded. "Have you forgotten you are not supposed to come into contact with the livestock? It said so on that website."

"That didn't include talking to them did it?"

"Yes it did. You could be breathing on each other and passing the virus."

"What if I just whispered?"

"No. I knew your Doctor Doolittle role would cause problems."

"Can I wave?"

"If you must," she sighed.

It didn't feel right walking past a herd of cows or a flock of sheep without talking to them. I did an awful lot of waving that year, but I did talk when I thought Chris was out of earshot!

We walked along a wide and grassy path all afternoon, passing the two guys brewing yet another pot of tea. Their pace seemed as slow as ours, which was generally unusual for men, we had found that most men walking together set a blistering pace. If ever male walkers overtook us you could guarantee we would not see them again. But these two ambled along and seemed to stop frequently for cups of tea.

Ladram Bay came into view, well actually it didn't – it was too misty. But we knew we had arrived when we collided with another caravan park. Leaving Chris sitting on a bench I went off in search of some refreshments and found myself down by the cove. Red sandstone stacks dominated the bay and numerous gulls nested on them. With the sea mist swirling round the stacks and the muted cry of the gulls the atmosphere was rather eerie.

We had two steeps hills to negotiate before we would arrive at our B&B in Sidmouth. The first hill was topped with mixed woodland. Squirrels played amongst the branches as we tramped up the steep path. Leaving the wood we crossed a field and then began the next ascent to the top of Peak Hill. Inland the mist had lifted to expose rolling fields full of sheep. But looking out to sea the mist lay thickly over the English Channel. Standing on the cliff top over five hundred feet above sea level, we were actually above the mist and could look down onto the top of the clouds as you would in an aeroplane, it was a novel experience.

Cliff slides at Sidmouth had actually affected the road which had been rerouted a short way inland. For some reason the footpath still followed the line of the old road, now worryingly near to the edge of the cliff. By this time we were beginning to suffer Last Mile Legs, a condition other walkers may recognise, the symptoms manifest themselves in a weakening of the knees and jellying of the leg muscles at a point in the day's walking when the end is just around the corner.

Fortunately our B&B was right by the path and we found it without even looking. The building was now owned by the National Trust and presumably rented by the family who ran it as a Bed and Breakfast business. A little too large to be described as a cottage, it sat just above the pebble beach, with its own access direct from the garden. Arched windows, cream paint and blue lintels were set off by the magnificent thatched roof and numerous gables. We were shown inside and led along a parquet corridor and up a sweeping wooden staircase to our room that looked out over the sea mist. We had a private bathroom with the largest bath I have ever seen standing proud in the centre of the room on cast iron clawed feet.

"Will you be joining me for an early morning dip in the sea tomorrow?" I asked Chris.

"No need to," came her reply from the bathroom, "I can have a swim in this bath!"

It was quite late in the evening before we ventured out in search of a meal. No one was around as we left the B&B although we could hear voices coming from an inner room. Just in time I remembered we had been asked to lock the door if we went out.

"It's unlocked at the moment," I told Chris as I opened the door.

"Well maybe you should leave it unlocked."

"Mm, but they did say to lock it."

"Was it this door?" she asked. We were standing in a large porch and there were in fact two doors, one leading into the house from the porch and the other leading directly onto the street.

"Well the other door was unlocked as well."

"Perhaps you had better leave them both as we found them," Chris advised.

"Yes but suppose someone breaks in? It would be our fault for leaving the door unlocked."

"There's someone in the house, I think the doors will be okay unlocked."

"No, better to be safe than sorry." And with that I flipped the Yale latch and followed Chris onto the street, shutting the door behind me. I gave a cursory glance at the keys we had been given and with mounting horror realised that there wasn't a Yale key.

"Oh no!" I groaned.

"What?" sighed Chris. "What have you done now?"

"We don't have a key for this door!"

"Oh Julia! I told you not to lock it, didn't I? Now what do we? Ring the bell!"

"I'm not ringing the bell. They'll think we're total idiots!"

"Speak for yourself, this was nothing to do with me."

"No, no. I've had an idea."

"Oh, great. That's reassuring!" Chris moaned sarcastically.

"There are no vacancies, correct?"

"Yeeess…"

"That means that when the other guests come back…"

"How do you know they are out?" she interrupted.

"Well, they're more than likely having a meal somewhere. There are two other rooms. At least one of the other guests is bound to be out! So by the time we get back from having something to eat, chances are the other guests will have come back, found the door locked and rung the bell! Then when we come back the door will already have been unlocked!" I said triumphantly.

"You really think so?"

"Trust me."

"You had better be right because I don't fancy spending the night on a park bench or the beach."

We left the locked door behind and set off for the town centre. We found a nice little restaurant on one of the main streets and enjoyed a good meal. It was ten o'clock before we returned to the B&B. The door was still locked.

"Yes, well, your plan has worked a treat!" Chris muttered.

"Okay, we will just have to ring the bell. Perhaps we could blame one of the other guests – you know 'Oh someone must have locked the door, wonder who would be daft enough to do a thing like that?'"

"I wonder! This is going to be so embarrassing."

I rang the doorbell. We waited. A minute went by and no one came to answer the door. I rang again. It had to be working, it worked earlier when we had arrived! We waited another minute and it became apparent that no one was going to let us in. All the windows seemed to be in darkness.

"They've probably gone to bed. I don't suppose they get many people ringing the bell after ten o'clock," sighed Chris.

A few yards further along the high garden wall was another door. But that too had a Yale lock. Could we climb over the wall? Out of desperation I tried the second door and discovered to my surprise that it was unlocked. Breathing sighs of relief we scuttled into the garden closing the door behind us. But this had still not got us into the house. We now had to get into the porch but fortunately the door from the garden into the porch was unlocked. Once in the porch we were facing the large, oak front door. Suppose it was locked?

"Presumably one of the keys on that ring is for this door," said Chris reading my thoughts.

She was correct and we quietly let ourselves into the house. Not a sound came from any of the rooms, only the ominous ticking of a grandfather clock in the dining room broke the silence. We sneaked quietly upstairs, hoping to get to our room before anyone saw us and realised who had been responsible for ringing the bell. We made it and slumped wearily on the beds. That was quite enough stress and adventure for one day.

Tuesday 3rd July

My invigorating, not to mention chilling, early morning swim was followed by a gargantuan breakfast. I was too full to contemplate lunch but I knew that by midday I would be hungry and so we set off in search of a bakery before leaving the town that morning.

If Budleigh Salterton was God's waiting room then Sidmouth seemed to be the antechamber. As we made our way through the busy shopping streets we were amazed by the number of elderly people disgorging from hotels and embarking onto numerous coaches. Sidmouth attracted Victoria before she became Queen and has plenty of appealing Georgian and Victorian architecture to recommend it. The town has won numerous Britain in Bloom competitions and it was easy to see why, every lamp post was festooned with colourful hanging baskets and the Connaught Gardens to the west of the promenade seemed to have millions of plants crammed into a relatively tiny space. Larger than Budleigh, Sidmouth still manages to retain an air of gentility whilst at the same time catering for a large number of visitors. The town even boasts it own annual International Folk Festival.

I had visited Sidmouth a few years ago and remembered an energetic climb to the cliff tops on the east of the town. However, the cliffs had become unstable since then and the first part of the path was routed a little way inland, passing a select collection of houses before crossing a field and rejoining the coast. We were in for a difficult walk that day. Looking at the map we estimated that in the ten miles it would take us to reach Seaton that evening we would climb the equivalent of Snowdon. To make the walking all the more difficult Chris was still having problems with her knee and my foot was causing me some pain. As if all this was not bad enough the day was hot and humid.

We paused at the orientation point on the top of Salcombe Hill Cliff, feeling exhausted although we had only reached our first summit. It was to be the first of seven arduous climbs before we reached Beer Head. We counted five climbs from sea level to over or nearly five hundred feet. The gradients were steep, in some places the path was badly signed and what should have been fantastic views were for the most part restricted by haze.

At one point we entered National Trust property where a sign told of the conservation work being undertaken using Shetland ponies. Very admirable, those ponies had done a superb job of the fencing.

At Salcombe Mouth my inability to differentiate between the words 'coast path' and 'foot path' resulted in us going on a long and unnecessary detour. Only when it became apparent that the path we were following was curving away inland and heading west did I realise something was amiss. We retraced our steps to the coast with me apologising profusely to Chris. I couldn't even read a signpost properly, heaven help us if we ever had to rely solely on my map reading skills.

Our steepest climb came from Weston Mouth to the summit of Weston Cliff at 526 feet above sea level. It seemed to have been a morning of labouring up hill and staggering down. Our calves ached from the effort and our toes hurt from the pounding they had received inside our boots on the steep descents.

At Coxe's Cliff the official route veered inland to cut out a hanging valley but temporary fencing blocked our way. We had little option but to negotiate the almost sheer drop into the valley and then climb out the other side. This seemed like a good time to have a break and by unspoken agreement we stopped for lunch. As we sat there munching pasties the two men we had seen the previous day caught up with us.

"That's right! Have a cup of tea, ladies," one of them said as they passed.

"How on earth did we get in front of them?" asked Chris.

"I've no idea," I replied. The last time we had seen them was when they had overtaken us near Ladram Bay the previous afternoon. We had certainly not expected to see them again.

From there to Branscombe Mouth, the path moved inland a little way passing ancient earthworks and some old chalk pits. The fertile soil supported a wide variety of flowering plants and orchids, and woodland had colonised the abandoned workings. The picturesque village of Branscombe could be seen through the trees, once it had been busy with spinners and weavers in the wool trade but now like so many such villages it survived mainly thanks to the tourist industry. The path dropped through the woods on West Cliff, passed a hidden sewage works and arrived at the crowded car park at Branscombe Mouth. Leaving Chris still coming painfully down the hill, I went ahead to buy chocolate and drinks at the little store.

Sitting on staddle stones edging the grassy foreshore we noticed the two tea-drinking walkers. They were in conversation with another walker but he soon left them and continued in the direction of Beer. So far those three were the only other walkers we had met on the coast path, a telling reflection on the impact of the Foot and Mouth outbreak. Before we had finished our milk the tea drinkers had packed up and disappeared into Under Hooken. This is the name given to an area of the cliff below Hooken Cliff, which collapsed sometime in the late eighteenth century. The official route goes through this plant rich undercliff, dipping and twisting between chalk pinnacles before climbing to the top of Beer Head. Beer Head stood out white and brilliant in the late afternoon sunshine, the first chalk cliff you come to heading east along the south coast.

Chris opted to climb directly to the top of Hooken Cliff, fearing for her knee on the more strenuous undercliff. I meanwhile went on the lower level. At one point I turned and looked back. I had a clear view of the cliff top and could not help but notice someone standing on the edge, waving. I waved back before stopping to wonder if it was Chris, or was it someone else waving not at me but at the woman I had just passed? But it was Chris and we met up again at the top.

"I've found a fossil," said a delighted Chris, holding out her hand to show me a tiny piece of rock with something non descript patterned on it.

"Oh," I replied, trying to sound impressed. "I've found a map!" And brandished an Ordnance Survey Pathfinder.

"Those two tea drinkers had one like that sticking out of their rucksack."

"Yes, I think they are intending to camp just further along here, they've marked it on the map," I said. "If they do, then we should be able to catch them and return the map."

As the path neared the campsite at Beer Head we saw the two walkers in one of the fields with some other campers. Diverting into the campground to return the map, I was not surprised to see that the first thing they were doing was brewing a pot of tea. Their camping gear lay scattered about the grass, whilst the kettle whistled merrily on the stove.

"Hello! Have a cup of tea," came the greeting when they saw me.

"I might take you up on that tomorrow," I laughed, handing them the map.

As I waved goodbye and hastened back to catch up with Chris I could hear them discussing which one had lost the map. I had noticed they had marked a campsite at West Bexington for the next night. That was quite a distance along the path and I felt it unlikely we would see them again, to walk so far in one day they would surely be having a very early start the next day.

At Beer, yet another unstable cliff meant the path had been rerouted. Today we were suffering Last Two Mile Legs and the walk along a tarmac path beside cliff top fields was incredibly tiring. I dawdled along watching rabbits playing at the edge of the fields in the evening sunlight. We reached Seaton at 7.30 in the evening and found the B&B without too much difficulty. From the outside it looked very nice but as we approached the front door we noticed a Welcome Host sign. Oh no! Not another huffing and puffing landlady, please! But we were in luck. This landlady was deserving of the award and showed us upstairs to a pleasant room overlooking the garden and the bay with the cliffs at Beer visible above the trees. For our evening meal she recommended a friendly pub owned by a butcher, which proved to serve excellent food.

After a very tiring day what we needed was a good night's sleep and all the ingredients for just that were available: comfy beds, hot chocolate and a packet of biscuits. We watched the news and weather sitting up in bed drinking and munching before settling down for the night.

I was awoken at 1.30 a.m. by a loud explosion that seemed to shake the house. As I had been asleep I couldn't possibly have broken anything so my first thought was we were near an army firing range. A flash of brilliant light lit the room, followed immediately by another tremendous bang, and with drowsy realisation came the knowledge that we were in the middle of a colossal electrical storm. The miracle was that I had not awoken any sooner; the storm had apparently started at midnight. Chris and I sat up watching the pyrotechnics for the next hour. The lightning and thunder continued non-stop for four hours. Bang followed flash with rapid succession. With each flash of lightning not only the room but the garden, the cliffs and the sea beyond were illuminated. The storm remaining directly overhead throughout that time, it was without doubt the worst thunderstorm I have ever witnessed. Across the South West this phenomenal electrical storm, the biggest the country had experienced for many years, brought chaos to thousands of homes and businesses. Houses on Bodmin Moor in Cornwall were without electricity for several days and many other properties had their fuses blown and several buildings were reduced to smoking pyres after receiving direct lightning strikes. For the first hour it was thrilling to witness the power of the storm and the heavy deluges of rain that would stop and start at intervals, but after a while we began to worry that we would get no sleep that night. Then our thoughts turned to the tea drinkers in their little tent, to them it must feel like they were in the middle of the storm. I drifted in and out of sleep, not wishing to miss the spectacular light show and its accompanying percussion. Eventually the storm ceased and I went back to sleep. At half past five Act II began, every bit as impressive as Act I but this time lasting only an hour.

Wednesday 4th July

Everything looked jet washed that morning. The storm had ceased and the rain had stopped, but we worried that the storm might have caused more landslides and possibly brought down trees. We were due to walk another undercliff that day but this one stretched for over six miles to Lyme Regis and once in there was no way out until you got to the other end. If the path were blocked we would have to retrace our steps and face a lengthy and very inconvenient diversion.

The storm had left behind a heavy mist that draped the town, the coast and the fields inland. It was to be a damp day but fortunately the storm did not return. The damp mist was cooling and not wet enough to necessitate waterproofs, the only time we wore them that day was when a wind sprang up in the afternoon, making the trees shed the moisture collected on their leaves.

Our walk that morning led us across the River Axe, up a long steep hill and across the golf course. Climbing a lane leading up to the golf course I kept my eyes on the ground, my heavy rucksack seemed to be trying to push me into the rutted tarmac. Chris and her knee followed gamely along behind.

"Julia, look up!" Chris suddenly called.

On hearing my name I turned to see what she wanted, then realised what she had said and looked skywards. All I could see was some overhanging branches and the grey misty sky. By the time I figured out she was indicating up the hill I was only just in time to turn and see a deer's bottom disappearing into the bushes. Typical. Apparently it had strolled slowly across the lane from one side to the other – and all I got to see was its bum!

As we reached the clubhouse one of the grounds men was just setting off up the hill in an open backed buggy that was stacked full of tools. He was a very nice looking young grounds man and the hill was very steep so it seemed like a good idea to try and thumb a lift. But as he drew level with us he misjudged the width of the lane, forgot about a rake that was sticking sideways out of the back of the buggy and proceeded to snap the wooden handle of the rake in half as it snagged on a wall. With a loud splintering crack the end of the handle ricocheted past our heads. The grounds man looked hastily around hoping his boss had not witnessed the incident, and then did actually offer us a lift. But having witnessed his skill with the vehicle we gracefully declined and followed him and the buggy up the track, keeping well clear.

From the top of the track we turned right between hedgerows, crossed a field and entered the Axmouth to Lyme Regis Undercliffs National Nature Reserve. This spectacular area of coastline is the result of landslips. Permeable layers of greensand and chalk lie on top of impermeable clay. The layer of clay on this part of the coast slopes slightly seawards. After heavy rain, such as the downpour we had experienced the night before, and such as the country had experienced most of the previous winter, the top layers of rock become saturated and heavy, the clay becomes slippery and landslides are often the result. Little landslides happen fairly often. However, in the winter of 1839 a major landslip occurred that was responsible for the shaping of the Dowlands Undercliff at the western end of the Nature Reserve. Almost fifteen acres of land slid seawards, opening up a chasm 195 feet deep and almost one and a half miles long. Terrified locals thought it was an earthquake. An area known as Goat Island was left standing following the slip, surrounded by chasms. A crop of wheat remained growing on the top and was later harvested. The farmer was not slow to miss an opportunity and was soon selling certificates with the ears of wheat encased within a frame. One such frame can be seen in the museum at Lyme Regis. The locals at the time made the most of the landslip as it attracted a lot of interest and became a bit of a tourist attraction; even Queen Victoria came and had a look. Admission tickets were sold by one farmer who owned the land, other locals set up refreshment stalls and into the twentieth century a tea room still existed selling beverages to walkers but unfortunately it had gone by the time we got there.

Plants and wildlife have been left to themselves in the undercliff. With hardly any intervention from man, no agriculture, no building and no land management of any kind other than the maintenance of the footpath, in less than two hundred years a rich ecosystem has become established. It was startling to consider that all the trees, shrubs and flowering plants had invaded the area - none had been planted. The undercliff today exhibits a wide variety of vegetation, many rare species of plant, and is rich in birds, mammals, insects and other wildlife. That said, the only animal life we saw were bees, flies, midges and one squirrel. But the plants were spectacular. Creepers hung down from the high branches, ideal for any budding Tarzans. The deciduous woodland was rich with elm, ash, oak, hazel, honeysuckle and hawthorn. Ivy, ferns, mosses and liverworts thrived on the damp woodland floor. Dogs mercury, wild garlic, red campion, stinking iris and wild strawberry were just a few of the flowering plants that grew in wild tangles.

For several hours we wandered along, twisting and turning with the path. We searched for old stones covered in moss and nearly overgrown, the only remaining evidence of the few people that had lived in the undercliff many decades ago. We found very few of these old dwellings and could only conclude that they had been entirely swallowed up by the undergrowth. The scenery was beautiful in a totally different way from the normal coast path: the panoramic views replaced with woodland. It was very disorientating because of the twisting path and all the many plants, and very soon we had no idea just how far we had travelled through the undercliff.

A flight of steps reinforced with logs added variety to the route and a little excitement, not to mention a touch of entertainment for Chris. I was leading and half way down the steps when my foot skidded on a wet log. Before I knew what was happening I found myself lying on the path, gazing up into the trees.

"Mind these logs, they are little on the slippery side," I warned.

"Have a cup of tea while you're down there!" came the amused response.

The tea-drinking walkers had caught up with us. We had been expecting them to be miles in front and were surprised by how suddenly they had materialised behind us. Until that moment we had no idea anyone had been following us, hidden as they were by the thick woodland. As I picked myself up and tried to brush the mud from my shorts, succeeding only in rubbing it further in, we chatted about the thunderstorm; they did not seem any worse for wear for their night under canvass in an electrical storm, although they confessed to suffering sleep deprivation. They passed us and that was the last we saw of them.

An ominous rumbling sound shortly after brought us hastening to the nearest fallen log. My stomach gave its second bellowing rumble and we stopped for lunch. One sausage roll later and I still felt ravenous. Half of Chris's pasty later and I still felt ravenous. Even a bar of chocolate had little effect. Never mind, tonight we intended to dine in an Italian restaurant in Lyme Regis. We carried on our way with visions of garlic bread and pasta as initiatives.

A slow and mild ascent brought us out into the open at the end of the Undercliffs near Underhill Farm. We had passed numerous small and more recent landslips as we climbed out of the woodland, and spared a thought for the risks that residents of the farm faced every day

We were leaving Devon and entering Dorset, the last county on the South West Coast Path. If I had been hoping for a boundary stone, I was to be disappointed, none existed and we crossed the county line unaware.

The path wandered about near Devonshire Head just to the west of Lyme Regis. Numerous footpaths joined it and we successfully found the correct one that would lead us inland to a car park just off the main Sidmouth Road. There seemed little point continuing down into the centre of Lyme Regis only to climb back up the hill to our B&B.

Ahead of us was a two-night stay at the B&B at Lyme. We had planned this into the walk that year, knowing that with less total mileage we could afford to have a day off to just relax, recuperate and have a break from carrying heavy rucksacks. And hopefully the day of rest would be beneficial to Chris's knee.

The B&B was quite a way inland up a steep hill. The mist had not lifted and any views that we might have had over Lyme Bay were blanked out. Having found the B&B and been shown to our room we relaxed with a pot of tea (our walking friends would have approved) and a tin of very nice handmade biscuits that were provided. The usual argument over whose turn it was to do the laundry ensued. I lost, did the laundry and then we set off into town for the Italian restaurant. For quite a small town, Lyme Regis can boast (quite deservedly) two good Italian restaurants. That night we tried the first we came to. Set down a narrow cobbled alley near the bottom of the main street, the restaurant was tiny and rather crowded. The delicious aroma of garlic wafted down the alley, attracting not just us but a lean black cat that sat determinedly on the doorstep meowing piteously. The cat obviously had good taste even if he didn't get shown to a table, the food was delicious, filling and reasonably priced. I had been looking forward to an Italian meal at Lyme and I was not disappointed.

As we walked slowly back up the long hill to our accommodation nearly all the shops were shut. We called in at a little convenience store for a few provisions and as we emerged onto the street Chris caught sight of a sign pinned up in the shop window. Chris is terrible for reading any type of notice that she comes across, be it planning applications, adverts for car boot sales, lost and founds and especially the plaques on memorial benches. She began to avidly read the notice advertising guided fossil walks.

"Oh, I bet that's good!" she said. She was very keen to go fossil hunting the next day, Lyme being rich in fossils. But then her face fell when she read the date. It was yesterday.

"'Every Tuesday evening'" I read. "We could have gone if it had been tonight."

"Oh."

To say she was disappointed was an understatement.

"Well never mind," I chivvied, "we can still have a look on our own tomorrow."

"It won't be as good though," she sulked. "Look it even says that you will be guaranteed to find a fossil."

"Well it's bound to say that or nobody would go!"

"Cynic!"

She remained miserable for the rest of the evening. Really! The fuss some people make over a bit of old rock!

Thursday 5th July

Another misty morning, but this time it didn't matter too much because we were not walking. We enjoyed a late breakfast before setting off down the hill to explore the town. We followed the directions provided by the owner of the B&B to reach the town centre by a quiet back road. As we followed a narrow winding lane we passed the first of Lyme's many fossil shops. A notice was pinned to the wall and true to form Chris stopped to read it.

"Guided fossil tours," she breathed, her eyes lighting up. "The next one is at 11 o'clock today!"

"Well we can go on a tour if you would like to but just be aware that this one does not guarantee you to find a fossil," I pointed out.

"Oh, we're bound to find one, I bet the beach is covered in them," Chris gushed.

"Yes and the streets of London are paved with gold!" I replied. "Okay, let's go in and book a ticket, but don't be disappointed if we spend half the day up to our armpits in sand and pebbles and come away with nothing."

"You don't have to come with me if you don't want to, I wouldn't mind."

"No, I'll tag along if only to watch dozens of people frantically scratting about in the sand, all hoping they are going to discover a complete Tyrannosaurus Rex skeleton."

I think I heard Chris call me a cynic again as she hurried into the shop to purchase two tour tickets before I could change my mind.

At the appointed hour we set off with various assorted holidaymakers, following the tour leader through the winding streets of the town as if he were the Pied Piper. I ambled along at the back of the group, hoping Chris wasn't going to be disappointed but suspecting that she would be. I was working on my principle of 'expect the worst and then you are never disappointed', whereas Chris seemed to me to be exhibiting blind faith in the plaentological hype of Lyme Regis.

Our tour guide led us through the local churchyard and stopped to show us the grave of Mary Anning. In the nineteenth century this local girl eked out a living selling shells and small fossils that she found on the beach. It wasn't until she found the complete fossil of an Ichthyosaur that she became famous. Her knowledge of the fossils and her recognition of their importance, together with her continuing fossil finds both large and small at a time when some chap called Darwin was wandering round the Galapagos Islands theorising about a new science he termed 'Evolution', resulted in her being recognised nationally. On a slightly more frivolous note it is to her that the tongue twister 'she sells sea shells' refers.

I had sarcastically joked about becoming the next Mary Anning but as the guide led us down onto the beach and began to explain the geology of the area, I remained unconvinced that I would be fortunate enough to find even a fossil fragment. The guide's knowledge was extensive and his style light-hearted and informative but standing at the rear of the group I have to confess that my mind began to wander and I started to admire the scenery, look at the way the mist was clearing over the coast and to people watch. Chris turned to see me staring down the beach and has forever after tried to convince anyone who will listen that until events transpired to awaken my interest, I was totally bored by the whole idea of fossils.

"She's not at all interested in fossils," were to be her oft-repeated words.

After a couple of minutes the guide set off to lead us a mile down the beach to an area of recent landslip below Black Ven cliff where, he assured us, a large number of fossils had been exposed. The landslip had taken place much earlier in the year, surely all the fossils would have been collected by now? All we would find, I thought, would be mud, pebbles and litter left by previous fossil hunters!

"Here's a good spot," enthused the tour guide, "remember to carefully pick through the pebbles in front of you. You're looking for mainly grey bits of rock. Once you have carefully scoured a small area move on a bit. If you find anything interesting or something you are unsure of call me over."

With his words everyone fanned out a little bit and assumed a bent double posture as they began picking up pebbles and examining each one diligently. Chris was full of excitement, scrabbling about with everyone else in a mad, expectant frenzy hoping to find ammonites, belemnites and any other nites. I began to move a few pebbles about, not too sure what I was looking for. What was that grey thing? I picked it up and it smeared between my fingers – clay! Wonderful – now I had dirty fingers. I moved on a bit and tried again. Another grey thing. Rock or clay? Rock this time, it had one rough side.

"What do you think this is?" I asked Chris holding it under her nose.

"Just a rough pebble," she replied.

"Not a fossil then?"

"No."

"Uh! I knew we wouldn't find anything."

"Julia, you've only just started looking. You've no patience." She bent to pick up a nondescript little pebble and then squealed with excitement. "I've found an ammonite!"

In her hand she held a flattened grey rock with the imprint of a curled shell, very much like a snail's.

"He probably came here first thing this morning and just scattered a couple about to fool people," I suggested.

But no! Soon everyone was finding fossils except me. Maybe there were fossils here after all! I picked up and rejected various grey pebbles and several more chunks of muddy clay. I tried a new patch and suddenly seemed to strike it lucky. The next rock I picked up contained an ammonite. Hey! This was great!

"I've found one!!" I shrieked.

"Thank goodness for that," sighed Chris.

Then I found a belemnite and several more ammonites. This fossil hunt was beginning to get exciting after all! After a few more minutes I came across a strange shaped pebble that looked a little like a nut, nut as in nut and bolt that is, not nut as in Brazil. It was about one inch across with a slight dimple in the middle and had several sides.

"What do you think this is?" I asked Chris, who was by this time clutching a handful of small fossils.

"Mmm, not sure."

"Oh, it's probably a bit of corroded metal off a ship. I'll just chuck it away."

"No, don't do that. Go and ask the guide."

I wandered off to find the guide surrounded by people all hopefully showing him various oddments of rock.

Feeling a bit of a twit and sure of having my find laughed at, I approached the guide who was gently breaking the bad news to a small boy that his proffered fossil was in fact a sea shell.

"Excuse me, please can you tell me what this is?" I asked, giving him the rock.

His face split into a huge grin. Wait for it, I thought, he's about to fall about laughing and tell everyone I've found a nut. I was wrong.

"Star find! Star find!" he shouted, jumping up and down with excitement and waving my 'nut' in the air.

Everyone rushed over to see this star find. I had found an Ichthyosaur! 195 million years old, and one and a half metres long, according to the tour guide. Okay the bit I had found wasn't that long. But I had found an Ichthyosaur vertebra. Everyone crowded round to have a look at my find; they all seemed very impressed. Feeling very pleased with myself I proudly showed it to Chris.

"Isn't that amazing? Aren't you impressed?"

"Life is so unfair!" she responded. "Here am I, mad keen to go fossil hunting, really interested in fossils and geology. There are you – ten minutes ago you were bored out of your head! And now you've gone and found an Ichthyosaur vertebra. It's just… it's just… Not Fair!"

"Sorry. I thought you'd be pleased. At least we've both found some fossils. You've got loads of really nice ammonites, they're far nicer than mine."

"Yes, but I haven't the star find, have I?"

"You're jealous!" I said in amazement.

322

"Too right I'm jealous!"

"You can look at it whenever you like, hold it if you want to!"

"No, I don't want to see it ever again. I don't want reminding. I'm not speaking to you now! Life is so unfair."

"So you don't want to have another look at it?"

No answer.

I think she was sulking, very unreasonable, especially to suggest I had no interest in fossils. I had always shown a keen interest in this fossil hunting caper. Hadn't I? Wasn't it me who encouraged her to partake of the guided fossil hunt?

The fossil hunt ended at one o'clock and we retraced our steps down the beach. After lunch we sought out the Tourist Information Centre. A large landslip had occurred just to the east of the town and our route the following day was diverted onto the main trunk road for several miles. Having studied the map and spoken to a member of staff we decided the most sensible option would be to catch the bus to pick up the diverted route where it left the busy main road.

We spent the remainder of the afternoon in the local museum, located in a revamped building on the seafront. And a very interesting and informative museum it proved to be. For such a small town Lyme Regis has had a colourful past. Scene of fires, Civil War battles, landslips and filming, it was the setting for Jane Austen's Persuasion and for the French Lieutenant's Woman. The Cobb, an old harbour wall, juts out into the English Channel providing safe anchorage for the numerous small fishing boats that still survive, making a living from the sea. Today tourism is the main industry with fishing playing a small part in the town's economy, an economy that for several centuries was rich thanks to the wool trade, the Napoleonic Wars and trade with the West Indies. Fossils are another claim to fame for Lyme Regis, (did I mention my Ichthyosaur?) In 1685 the Duke of Monmouth landed in the town on his way to try to reclaim the English crown, as things turned out he would have been better off staying in France because after a few fisticuffs and defeat in Somerset his head eventually parted company with his body at Tower Hill.

We concluded what had been a very educational day off in the second of the town's two Italian restaurants. We judged it to be very good, but not quite as good as the first one. It was the first time I had been in an Italian restaurant that did not serve pizza; a culinary contradiction comparable to that of a vegetarian carvery, I felt.

Settled in our room that night, we sat up in bed watching the late evening news and drinking hot chocolate. We heard two other guests climbing the stairs, chatting noisily; they seemed to have stopped outside our room. Next second we heard a key being inserted in the lock.

"Someone's trying to get in!" exclaimed Chris, drawing the duvet up under her chin.

"Did you lock the door?"

"No. Do something!"

I drew my own duvet up under my chin and then called, "Excuse me, I think you have the wrong room!"

The key continued to rattle in the lock, we heard it turn – effectively locking the door – and someone tried the handle.

"I can't unlock the door," came a man's disembodied voice from the landing.

"Hello! Excuse me! You have the wrong room!" I called again.

More rattling of the door handle followed my apparently unheeded cry.

Chris and I exchanged worried glances.

"Go and tell them!" I whispered.

"I've only a little nightie on, you go and tell them!"

"I'm not getting out of bed, my nightie's littler than yours!"

"You've got the wrong room!!" we bellowed together.

The rattling stopped.

"I don't think this is our room," we heard a woman say.

"Oh my God, it's not!" said the man.

We heard them move off down the landing to their own room and breathed a sigh of relief. What was it with us and locked doors this year?

Friday 6th July

Mist lay over Lyme Bay; trees in the garden were barely visible from our bedroom window that morning. The mist soon lifted to reveal cloudy skies but the day was warm and very humid. At breakfast that morning we sat around the large dining table, waiting for one of the other guests to mention their blundering error of the night before, only the loud ticking of the grandfather clock in the hall broke the silence between the three unknown couples. When the landlady had settled us all with pots of tea, an Australian gentleman cleared his throat and in rather embarrassed tones asked to whom he owed an apology. It broke the ice and resulted in a rather jolly and prolonged breakfast time. Eventually realising we had a bus to catch we crunched our last piece of toast, drained the teapot and took our leave.

We needed to get off the bus at the far side of Charmouth but when we named the lane where we wanted to alight the bus driver did not seem to know it. As the bus climbed the steep hill out of Lyme Regis we decided we would get up and stand at the front when the bus reached Charmouth, hoping to spot the lane before we were carried too far from our route.

"I don't know where this lane is," grumbled the bus driver unhelpfully as he accelerated away from Charmouth, "why don't you ask some of the passengers?"

"By the time we've spoken to the passengers we will probably be in Weymouth at the speed you're driving," I muttered.

"There it is!" Chris had spotted the lane just ahead of us on a bend.

The driver grudgingly pulled over to the side of the road and we got off. Our feet were barely on the ground before the driver had closed the door and was setting off down the road with an angry revving of his engine.

"Miserable old sod!" Chris said, "he was even worse than the grump driving the bus at Lulworth."

The colossal landslides that had taken place around Lyme Regis and Charmouth earlier in the year had made headline news. We estimated some three miles of coastline had been affected. It was unfortunate for us that our diversion took us away from a beautiful stretch of coast. The landslides had been even more unfortunate for the poor people who were actually walking the coast path when the earth began to move. Newspaper and television accounts of the incident related how many walkers had turned and fled inland as enormous areas of land began sliding down the cliffs and into the sea, it must have been a terrifying experience. The police were relying on people being reported as missing as the only way to know if anyone had been buried beneath the cliffs.

We trudged up the very long and very steep lane until we finally reached some National Trust land and a car park above Cain's Folly. Diversion signs were not at a premium, dog dirt was. We had a choice of paths, all winding off to disappear into heather and bracken, and it was sheer luck that we found ourselves on the correct one that led us back to the coast path near a farm. Lapwings flew gracefully overhead, making a pleasant change from the squawking herring gulls and black-headed gulls we had become familiar with in Lyme Regis.

We followed a winding path through open fields of short-cropped grass, bounded by low banks of stunted hawthorn and gorse. Golden Cap, the highest point on the south coast of England at 626 feet, loomed ahead of us. But before we began its ascent we diverted from the coast path to visit what was marked on the map as 'Saint Gabriel's Church (remains of)'. Apparently the main road had once passed this way, through the village of St Gabriel and close by the church, but landslides had done away with the road many years ago; the few houses that remained were in an enviously quiet and very secluded location. But where was the church (remains of)? We found it tucked away around a corner of the track. One very ruined ruin.

We left the thirteenth century ruin of the tiny church and climbed a well-maintained path to the summit of Golden Cap. Up here gorse had given way to heather and large patches of white-flowered sea campion. Despite the low cloud the views both ways along the coast were tremendous – west beyond Lyme Regis and east to Chesil Beach, inland the deep valleys and wooded hills rolled away towards Chideock and beyond. On a clear day, according to the guidebook, the Isle of Portland was visible. More visible and much nearer at hand was a paper bag containing two flapjacks emerging from Chris's rucksack; needing no further prompting I stopped taking photos of the coastline and joined her for elevenses.

From the summit the coast dropped away to the east, tiny Seatown huddled at the foot of Golden Cap. We descended to Seatown along a gently sloping path. Oh, that all the ascents and descents were like those of Golden Cap! Half way down the hillside we came to an unusual double stile that consisted of two stiles side by side in the one fence. It suggested this was a popular route to the summit of Golden Cap, we could only surmise that the second stile was there to alleviate congestion.

Seatown is not, as the name implies, a town. The hamlet consists of a small collection of thatched cottages, an inn and a small campsite that had won a conservation award. It was one of the few campsites on the South West Coast Path that I could honestly say I liked. Small, secluded, well maintained and clean, the site occupied a few acres of land dipping down to a stream, with woodland and a tiny lake stocked with fish. The site buildings were sympathetic to their surroundings and the shop sold excellent ice cream. I wasted no time buying milk and ice cream, whilst Chris wasted no time in asking the staff to send a campsite brochure to some friends at work who spend their summer holidays with their three children camping somewhere in the south west and often ask us which areas we can recommend and which they should avoid.

"This is a really nice site," enthused Chris when she joined me at a picnic bench. "They could take the children on a fossil hunt one day and it would be nice to walk up to the top of Golden Cap - it's not too far for the kids to manage, the beach looks clean and apparently it's safe for bathing."

"The ice cream's not bad either," I added, carelessly dropping some into my lap. "Actually I wouldn't mind staying here myself."

"I saw a sign for a farmhouse tea room just along the coast, so they could walk to there one day for a snack."

"Well, that's the Rowan family holiday organised for next year. All we have to do now is persuade them they want to come!"

After Seatown came three progressively longer climbs up the cliffs, culminating at Thorncombe Beacon, so called because it is the historic site of a beacon, last used for the Millennium celebrations. Landslips were once again in evidence. Rabbits and sheep grazed near to the edge, reminding me of an old letter we had seen in the museum at Lyme, written at the time of the great landslip in 1839 by a gentleman who blamed the burrowing rabbits for destabilising the land and causing the landslide. Fortunately for the rabbits, more is now understood about the cause of such landslides. Where no grazers, roamed the wildflowers and grasses were spectacular, great clumps of thrift were still in flower and coloured the cliff edges pale pink, it was unusual to see so many late blooms when their main flowering season was in May.

Rabbits were everywhere at Eypes Mouth, running through the caravans on yet another campsite, this one with its own golf course. As we crossed the stream we observed two rather unusual occupations on the coast path, the first was a group of people litter picking, the second was a cyclist. For me the litter pickers were a welcome sight, there had not been a lot of litter on the path this year which could only be due to the prolonged closure of the path. However, for several days we had been following someone who had a liking for one particular kind of sweet but who was totally ignorant of the 'leave only footprints' philosophy. We never caught up with the littering sweet eater but by the end of each day we had collected a pocketful of his discarded sweet wrappers. I felt like I should congratulate the litter pickers, saying there was nothing I hated more on footpaths than litter, with the possible exception of cyclists. I dearly wish I had told them because it was at that moment that a yob on a mountain bike whizzed down the footpath from the cliff top, passing a sign that read 'cycling forbidden', maybe he would have overheard and felt guilty? No, probably not, some people just don't care. The use of cycles on footpaths must have been a problem in Dorset, we saw many signs forbidding cycling on footpaths but we also saw many tyre tracks suggesting these signs were frequently ignored. Perhaps I should pen a letter to the local paper implying cyclists were responsible for landslides?

At West Cliff we passed an old limekiln and yet more rabbits before crossing fields down to West Bay. As we reached the first houses we were somewhat startled to observe that one house had its roof held down by ropes with heavy concrete weights suspended from the ends. Was the purpose of the weighted ropes really to hold down the roof? Surely not! But the fence was bedecked in the same manner. I knew the winds could be strong on the coast but this was taking things a bit far, all the remaining houses seemed to survive the strong winds without need for these guy ropes!

It has to be said that I did not like West Bay. Actually I think it rates as my least favourite place on the entire coast path, even below Newquay - which after all did have some redeeming features (give me time, I'm sure I'll think of some… beaches! it had lovely beaches.) West Bay reminded me of a small run down northern seaside resort. It had none of the ugly yet vibrant attractions of a larger resort such as amusement arcades and takeaways, but all of the ugly, dreary elements: concrete - acres of the stuff, a sprawling, sardine-can squash of a caravan site, dirty toilets, concrete pre-fab holiday chalets, landscaped concrete open areas and old, past their best, tall, angular hotels and boarding houses. The short, scruffy beach was bordered by a concrete promenade at one end and a large, empty gravel car park at the other. Through the middle of what was once a busy commercial harbour, famous for its shipbuilding, the River Brit flowed through concrete channels. West Bay's later claim to fame was as the location for the television series 'Harbour Lights'. I expect it looked quite a nice place on telly. Thank goodness we had been unable to find accommodation in West Bay, I wasn't inspired to stay ten minutes let alone overnight.

Turning north we hurried through the caravan site, following a path that paralleled the river into the centre of Bridport. Once a major producer of rope for the shipping industry, the town has now, like so many others, diversified. But the old brewery still brews traditional ales and the old open-air market still does a roaring trade, as we were to discover the next morning. We located our B&B at the end of a terrace of large rambling Victorian houses in the Allington district of Bridport. Run by a friendly middle-aged couple, it was clean and bright and, as we were to discover, served probably the best breakfast in Dorset.

After the obligatory cup of tea and laundry session, I headed for the adjacent bathroom with its power shower positioned over the bath. Unfortunately the shower was very powerful and the screen was very short, a combination of facts the significance of which did not occur to me until I had finished my shower. Stepping out of the bath I stepped into a flood. The bathroom, the toilet, the towel rail and my clean, dry clothes were under several feet of water! Even the window was awash. I spent the next several minutes splashing about attempting to mop up the Noah-like flood with every towel I could lay my hands on. If the water went through the ceiling the owners would be sure to notice as the bathroom was directly above the front door. I think I got away with it, although they probably puzzled how two walkers could manage to use so many towels.

Saturday 7th July

As we sat in the bus shelter at Bridport that morning a fine drizzle began to fall. We put on cagoules in expectation of a damp and dismal morning but on arrival in West Bay the rain had stopped. The cagoules were put back in the rucksacks and gradually the clouds lifted on another hot and sunny day.

A group of army cadets were just leaving the town and ascending to the top of the cliffs heading off in the direction we intended to take. We expected to be closely behind them all morning, dogging their steps and dodging their litter but we need not have worried. It was a sharp climb out of West Bay and by the time we had reached the top of the cliff the cadets were disappearing into the distance, making us feel less than fit. We tried to blame the weight of our rucksacks but the cadets' packs were bigger. Ah yes, but our legs were older than theirs!

Once past East Cliff (yet another original name!) the route became more level. A charm of goldfinches swooped ahead of us from one clump of thistles to another, calling noisily to each other as they flew along. Each time they came to rest on a thistle, clouds of wispy seeds were released to float away on the breeze. We passed a golf course, then a campsite where we got lost by nosying at the tents and caravans when we should have been keeping a look out for a signpost. Retracing our steps we were soon climbing a slight rise, then suddenly the land sloped down to sea level and we reached Chesil Beach.

Chesil Beach, or Bank, is eighteen miles long and stretches from west of West Bexington east along the coast to the Isle of Portland. It is a natural ridge of pebbles that at its highest is sixty feet above sea level and no more than two hundred yards across. The pebbles have been graded by the action of the currents, so that at the western end of the beach the pebbles are quite tiny whilst at the eastern end they are the size of potatoes. Behind the bank for much of the way lies the Fleet, a trapped body of water, and an excellent breeding ground for waterfowl and midges. Hardy maritime plants colonise the bank and their flowers were an artist's palate of differing colours, we identified yellow horned poppy, silverweed, sea vetch, sea holly and mallow in just a small area alone. It would be almost impossible to walk the eighteen miles of its length, and a terrible, painful and arduous walk that would be. The coast path ran along the inland edge of the beach for a couple of miles until it reached West Bexington, by which time we had had quite enough of tramping over the shifting pebbles, it was a tiring process. A lunch stop was needed to fuel our aching legs.

A small car park right on the edge of the shingle bank had attracted an assorted collection of cars and campervans; and an assorted collection of families and elderly couples wandered about on the shifting pebbles, eating sandwiches and looking miserable. One little boy busied himself with the removal of the wooden coast path marker, wiggling it backwards and forwards in the ground until he could successfully pull it free. A modern day, vandalising King Arthur: whosoever shall pull this stump from the shingle shall be crowned a right little nuisance. His grandmother eventually called him away before either Chris or I could reprimand him. More's the pity.

A large, gas-guzzling four-wheel drive vehicle pulled into the car park and ground to a halt in a spray of shingle. Doubtless that was the first time it had ever been taken off road, I thought cynically. Four elderly people stumbled out, struggling with the high sills and their arthritic hips, and then began to walk a short way along the pebble-covered path. Having covered fifty yards they turned and walked back to their car, discussing where they might find a pub. Obviously the coast path was not to their liking.

This particular part of it was not much to our liking either but we had no choice and so, packing up the remains of our picnic, we continued along the shingle. After a little way the loose shingle transformed into an unmade, hard packed dirt track. We were unable to see the sea because of the elevated bank of pebbles. Fields on the left rose gently up to the Ridgeway further inland, the Ridgeway – get this – being the alternative inland coast path between West Bexington and Osmington Mills! This alternative was apparently for all those coast path walkers who had an aversion to walking through a bustling holiday resort, namely Weymouth. If you were to follow that logic to its reasonable conclusion you would expect to find alternative inland routes dotted here and there all the way around the South West peninsular; in fact, the coast path would not even be able to start at Minehead!

We followed the track until a car park and refreshment hut were reached just where the first marshes indicated the beginnings of the Fleet. It had been a hot afternoon so far and we were very much in need of a pot of tea.

"I quite fancy an ice cream," I said, wandering over to the freezer cabinet. But having seen the prices I soon changed my mind. "A pound! I'm not paying that for a tiny tub of ice cream."

"You skinflint!" said Chris. "It's made in Dorset, using the finest clotted cream."

"I don't care if it's made in ancient Egypt by Cleopatra herself using sterilized milk from sterilized asses, or mules or whatever they were. I'm not paying a pound for such a little tub; it will have melted before I get the lid off!"

Later in the week, in a most un-Scrooge-like reckless moment, I did pay a pound for just such a little tub, and I am forced to admit it was money well spent.

The path looped inland to reach Abbotsbury, presumably because the nearby Swannery owned the land bordering the Fleet and did not want walkers going through their visitor attraction without paying. This small loop did not matter to us as our accommodation that evening was on a farm in the village.

We found the very pink farmhouse quite easily and a lady who seemed to be setting some new kind of makeup trend finally answered our prolonged knocking. Foundation and mascara had been generally applied in roughly the right areas but the lipstick was remarkable; the bright red war paint seemed to have been daubed onto the middle of her lips, leaving the outer corners nude. Holding a conversation with her was very disconcerting as our eyes were continually drawn to the splotch of scarlet. She led us into the house and pointed out a dining room that at first glance was swamped with clutter: dolls, toy prams, a rocking horse, China ornaments and frilly things of indeterminate use, there was barely room for the dining tables and chairs.

Leading the way upstairs she suddenly said, "Please mind your rucksacks, I don't want anything knocking over."

Easier said than done. The stairs were sloping; the risers of differing sizes and the third step up had a neat trick of catapulting you into the wall. To add to this assault course the walls were hung with various dead animal heads, corn dollies, framed photographs of horses and ugly children and more frilly things. Our room was very pink and very frilly. I have a natural aversion to frills. The frilly litter bin, frilly toilet roll holder, frilly curtains, frilly pelmet, frilly pillow case, frilly duvets, frilly teapot, frilly lampshade and yet more frilly things of indeterminate use were nearly too much for me. However, it was clean, which I felt, considering all the dust-catching frills, was quite an achievement. A frilly notice on the frilly dressing table asked guests not to smoke as the family had lived in the farmhouse for several generations and would like to live in it for many generations to come, and a misplaced cigarette could cause tremendous damage to a wattle and daub, timber and thatched property, (especially with so many frills hanging about).

That evening we eagerly escaped the frills and headed out to explore the historic village. Abbotsbury was around before Domesday and was once home to a large Benedictine monastery. Henry VIII's policies, in view of his predilections for several wives and the Catholic Church's proscription of divorce, led to the dissolution of the monasteries and the demolition of this one; but evidence of many of the other elements from this period in history remain, such as the ancient track ways and field systems, the Swannery – once an important food source for the monastery, Saint Catherine's chapel, the Tithe barn and some old cottages and manor houses.

We were keen to see the barn, one of the largest in the country, although only half of it now remains. We wanted to get a feel for the history of the place and eagerly made our way down the winding track and past the last remaining standing wall of the ruined monastery. But we were in for a shock. Big green signs were everywhere, promoting the newly dubbed 'Smuggler's Barn'. Beyond the gate stood the Tithe Barn, no mention of its history, now nothing more than a children's miniature theme park. What had happened to the exhibits of a country life now past: the farrier's trade, the thatcher, the cooper, and all the other elements of traditional skills once vital to rural life? According to the path description the Tithe Barn had housed displays of rural crafts and an informative history of Abbotsbury. All that had obviously gone. The building might have remained structurally intact but for us it was spoilt by the blatant commercialism. I felt it would have been better to let it fall into ruin than succumb to this: a children's petting zoo and adventure playground! That could have been set up in any old field, not in this magnificent old building. We turned away in disgust from the advertised delights of milking Molly the mechanical cow, driving toy tractors and cuddling Dolly the lamb, no concern about Foot and Mouth had closed this attraction – well at least Molly need not worry.

Grumbling, we took the lane leading to the old church with its Civil War musket ball scars. The door was locked. What next? No food at the inn?

Sunday 8th July

"The bacon could be crispier," read the entry in the visitors' book. We had sat down to breakfast in the deserted dining room some ten minutes earlier and were gradually working our way through all the comments in the book. We were nearly up to date before the landlady appeared. By the time breakfast had arrived and been consumed we empathised with the comment. It was one of the worst breakfasts ever. The bacon was barely cooked never mind crisp and the mushroom (singular – a blessing actually) had a very peculiar flavour, quite possibly it had been fried in cod liver oil. Throughout the meal a variety of odd noises drifted in through the frilly net curtain covering the window. What on earth was going on?

"Billy's hungry," explained the landlady vaguely, bringing in a rack of cold toast. "He always does this when he thinks I've forgotten his breakfast."

Billy was an African Grey parrot and apart from various wild bird impressions he also mimicked cats, dogs, horses, squeaking doors, zippers and flushing toilets.

With the Tithe Barn no longer on our list of 'must visits' and not wishing to drive tractors, milk a robotic cow or play at being smugglers whilst parting with an entrance fee of £5.20, we turned right instead of left and climbed the hill to visit the free, ancient, historic, unchanged, untainted, unsullied, uncommercialised and (unlike the church) unlocked Saint Catherine's chapel.

From there we descended to the coast path, used the toilets at the entrance to the over-priced, over-hyped but historic Swannery (run by the same company as the Tithe Barn – sorry, Smuggler's Barn) and then headed along two miles of unusual but panoramic inland coast path. At first we followed a high ridge, climbing dilapidated stiles and ducking under low hanging blackthorn branches, walking through fields of sheep that were separated from the path by the most rudimentary of 'dead' electric fencing. In this part of Dorset at least, the farmers were far more reasonable about the perceived risk of walkers spreading Foot and Mouth Disease, however, unfortunately for us, this state of affairs was to change.

From the elevated vantage point of the ridge we could see the whole of Chesil Beach and most of the Fleet. The Swannery appeared very tiny, the hundreds of swans mere specks of white on the water's edge. From the ridge the path struck off sharply down hill and followed the edge of a small coppice before returning to the banks of the Fleet near Langton Herring.

At a field boundary we stopped to chat to two other walkers, members of the local Ramblers Association. This was one of their favourite parts of the coast path, although I have to say it was not one of mine. Whilst scenic in its own right, the path along the Fleet was totally different from any other parts of the coast path, and after the staggering cliffs and tiny coves, the pounding waves and crashing breakers, I found it tame, nice but tame, and a little bit smelly with all the festering seaweed and algae that lay in stagnant inlets along the edge of the Fleet. But the ramblers loved it!

"We think this is just the best section of the whole of the coast path," the chap enthused. His wife nodded vigorously and began untying her shoelace.

"Are you walking round the Isle of Portland?" he demanded. His wife raised a questioning eyebrow, loosening the lace.

"Er, no," replied Chris.

"You're missing the best part of all!" he shook his head in disbelief, his wife nodded violently in agreement with her husband and pulled off her boot.

"It's not yet part of the official coast path," I chipped in. His wife dropped her boot with shock at such heresy.

"That doesn't matter!" he cried aghast. "It's beautiful! Isn't it Kath?"

Kath was too busy to answer, hoping about on one leg whilst trying to pick up her boot.

"It didn't sound particularly scenic when we read the guidebook," ventured Chris.

"Of course it's scenic! It's rocky and stony and... and... positively Grecian!!"

"Well it's a quarry, isn't it?" I mumbled.

"Oh, yes but a wonderful Grecian looking quarry. I used to work there," he added. His wife nodded vigorously and with one wild hop grabbed her boot and began to shake a stone out of it.

"Oh, dear," said Chris, "it sounds like we've made a mistake to miss it out."

"You must make a point of coming back and completing it!" urged the chap, unaware of the appeasing nature of Chris's comment. His wife jammed her foot back into the boot and nodded her agreement.

We left them to their boots and headed off in the direction of Greece. From this distance Portland didn't look anything other than an off-white lump of land in the hazy distance. Perhaps it would improve as we drew nearer.

We followed the wandering banks of the Fleet, keeping to the edge of arable fields. In some the wheat had already been harvested, leaving only the sharp stubble in regimental rows. In others the wheat was still ripening under the hot sun. In the furrowed ridges the soil was hard, dry and cracked. We walked for an hour or more, looking for somewhere suitable to stop for lunch; a shady, grassy spot would be nice, but this was proving hard to find.

Whilst Chris watched for a likely lunch spot, I scanned the waters of the Fleet for wildlife. There must be some, I reasoned, for the Fleet and Chesil Beach are a nature reserve. All I can report from this ecological site are a black-headed gull (wow, last time I saw one of those was at the local landfill site!), a crow and three small egrets. According to an information sign we passed there should have been Arctic terns, small terns and a plethora of other birds. Uh! Mind you, would I have known what they looked like? I could just about recognise a funny turn when I saw one. While I was musing on the absence of feathered friends, four mute swans flew past in formation, low across the water, the sound of their powerful wing beats carrying noisily to us.

"I bet they've decided to leave the Swannery for a bit of peace from all those tourists."

With the exception of those few birds we saw no wildlife that day, disappointing considering the ecological importance of Chesil Bank and the Fleet lagoon. It wasn't until that evening when we were walking along a road to the pub that we saw the most exciting piece of wildlife of the day – a brown rat crossing the road.

Resigned to the total lack of shade, Chris decided we would stop for lunch in a corner of a field where a footpath from inland came down to meet the coast path. Glad to take off our heavy rucksacks, we slumped down on the grass, eased our hot, tired feet out of our boots, removed our damp, smelly socks and set out our lunch. I have to say it was not one of the most nutritionally balanced lunches we had, consisting of a chocolate bar each, followed by another chocolate bar each, and, in case we were still hungry, another chocolate bar each. Sod nutrition! And anyway wasn't chocolate one of the major food groups? Just a pity it had such a low melting point.

After a very delicious, high calorie and very messy lunch we just sprawled in the grass and digested for a little while. We were in no hurry that afternoon. The B&B was only a short distance away and there was no urgency to arrive early. The sun beat down and I think it must have gone to our heads a little. I might have snoozed, I'm not sure, but I do remember that at one stage we were both flat on our backs with our legs in the air, waving our feet about and discussing blood flow, veins, valves and lymphatic systems. Goodness knows what the people walking down the footpath to the Fleet made of four naked feet waving in the air!

Our socks had aired by the time we packed up and were ready to set off once more. The sun was strong that afternoon, prompting Chris to nag at me about wearing my sun hat. She already had her hat on, reasonable I suppose, if I had paid as much as she had I would want to make sure I got my moneys worth! The hats we had worn the previous year, hats that my Mum had kindly bought for us, had not survived a hot wash in a Plymouth laundrette.

"Well, you fools!" my Mum had said on hearing about the mishap, "don't you know cotton shrinks! And I thought you were supposed to be educated!"

With some birthday money Chris had purchased a Tilly hat. It looked like a rather grand safari hat, with a practical broad brim, chinstrap and ventilation holes. I had offered to let Chris have one of Roger's fishing flies to stick in the brim but she didn't seem impressed. Instead Chris had adorned it with some plaited, colourful shoelaces.

"Are they spare?" I asked, on seeing them for the first time.

"Spare? What do you mean spare?"

"You know, in case your laces break, you can just unthread one and lace your boot up!"

"They're not for that!"

"Well, why have you got them wrapped round your hat? Seems a bit pointless if you're not going to use them."

"I am using them!"

"Well make your mind up!" I objected. "You just said you weren't."

"They are for decoration!" she said in an exasperated tone.

"It's extra weight to carry. You would have been better off with a fishing fly."

"I don't want a fishing fly!"

"They're very colourful you know. Some of them are really quite attractive. Roger has some called baby dolls. And then there are hare's ears, suspender buzzers, rusty rats, grey ghosts, muddlers, boobies, deceivers… although you'd think all fishing flies would be called deceivers, wouldn't you? I mean that's what they are designed to do – deceive the poor little fish."

"I don't want a fishing fly!"

"What about some nice feathers? I'm sure we could find plenty of feathers. Or how about a flower, or some ears of wheat, or some grass?"

"You just don't seem to realise this hat has class. Everything about it says style, comfort, practicality."

"Which brings me no nearer to understanding why you've wrapped some shoe laces around it."

"This hat," continued Chris, ignoring my interruption, "has been eaten by an elephant three times, and come out the other end each time looking as good as it went in!"

"I thought it looked a bit grubby but I didn't like to say anything," I muttered. "Let's be realistic here, it couldn't look just as good as when it went in. There must have been some degree of sh…"

"Not this precise hat!!" snapped Chris.

"But you said 'this hat…'and as I was about to point out there must have been some degree of shabbiness about it after passing through an elephant three times!"

"Yes, there must have been but it didn't happen to this precise hat. When have I been near an elephant?"

"Chester Zoo?" I ventured timidly.

"This make of hat was worn by a keeper in an elephant house. And one of his elephants used to eat it on a regular basis. And the keeper just waited for it to re-emerge, so to speak, before putting it back on."

"Didn't he wash it first?"

"The company use this as a selling point," she added, ignoring my interruption once again.

"Oh," I said, putting my own sun hat on. "Mine cost £4.99 in Millets and I don't care if it gets eaten by an elephant, I still wouldn't put it on my head afterwards!"

For all its cheapness, my own hat had taken much more finding than Chris's up-market one. I had deliberated long and hard over what type of hat to buy. A baseball cap was Roger's recommendation because it would conceal my big nose (I didn't quite know how to take that comment), but a baseball cap wouldn't keep the sun off my ears. All the floppy hats I tried seemed to be either too big or too small. On a hot Sunday in June Chris, Merv and I walked along the promenade from Fleetwood to Blackpool. With two weeks to go before the walk in Devon I had still not chosen a sun hat.

"Why don't you buy one in Blackpool," suggested Chris.

"Blackpool! Nowhere in Blackpool will sell walking gear."

"There are lots of shops in Blackpool selling hats."

"Oh, no!" I retorted, suddenly realising what she was getting at. "There is no way I am going to go on a walking holiday wearing a hat that says 'Kiss me quick' emblazoned across the front!"

"They won't all have that on," offered Merv. "I'm sure there will be some that say 'Snog me slow' or something!"

Eventually I did get a hat. But not in Blackpool.

At Butterstreet Cove we turned inland, passing the stunted remains of the old Fleet church. In 1824 a severe storm caused the sea to breach Chesil Bank, the enormous, powerful waves sweeping away half of the nave. What remains is a repaired squared-off version of the original church. The row of cottages behind the church was also badly damage, and this too was rebuilt.

We took a moment to visit the little church before following the track inland to join a lane. Our B&B in a modern but beautiful farmhouse was only a short walk along this lane. Our knock on the front door provoked a furious chorus of barking from inside the house, and we glanced nervously at one another. A young woman's voice could be heard shouting at the dogs, then silence. The door opened onto a huge entrance hall with a winding staircase and not a dog in sight, and a very friendly girl in her late teens led us upstairs to our room. Her mother, she explained, was out at the moment but would be back later.

By the time we had congratulated ourselves on another excellent choice of accommodation, made a pot of tea, showered, changed and done the laundry, the missing mother had returned. We bumped into her as we were heading out for an evening meal. Even friendlier than her daughter she recommended a pub that all the locals frequented and gave us directions – a short walk along the lane towards Chickerell – adding that she hoped we were hungry.

When we found the pub it was very busy, always a good sign, and the food was certainly of the hungry walker sized portion, and certainly more than made up for the un-crispy bacon and cold toast of that morning's breakfast.

Arriving back at the B&B we encountered once again a problem with doors and locks. We had been given a key ring holding two keys: one for the bedroom door and one for the door to the farmhouse. The first key I tried in the front door didn't fit the lock, so I tried the other key. That one looked like it would fit but it didn't want to go in.

"What's up?" asked Chris, as I rattled the key against the lock.

"The key won't go in!" I replied bending down to examine the keyhole. "Oh! No wonder I can't get it in! There's a key on the inside!"

"Here we go again!" sighed Chris.

"What do we do now? Is there another way in?"

"What was round the back? The drive goes round to the back of the building."

At that moment we heard laughter from inside and a voice called out: "Hang on a minute girls!" A key rattled on the inside and the door swung open.

We stood shamefacedly on the doorstep, feeling very foolish as the lady explained the key was actually for the back door.

"Did my daughter not tell you?" she asked apologetically.

"No," we mumbled.

"That is the last time I take responsibility for locks and doors," I asserted as we made our way to our room. "From now on you can look after any keys. It's just far too stressful!"

Monday 9th July

It was inevitable that breakfast conversation at this farmhouse would cover the topic of Foot and Mouth. The landlady was realistic about the situation; part of her income was reliant on the tourist industry. As we ate the delicious crispy bacon she told us of one dog walker who had ignored the 'footpath closed' signs and when stopped by the farmer had told him that her dog could not possibly carry Foot and Mouth disease because it was a pedigree!

A light drizzle accompanied us on the walk back to rejoin the coast. With not many miles of the Fleet left to pass until we reached Weymouth, that morning seemed to be full of MoD ranges and soldiers. The first firing range we came to near Tidmore Point was cordoned off, with sentries posted around the perimeter to direct walkers along a safe route. The first sentry directed us inland to the next sentry box, where a rather nice soldier in combat fatigues waved a vague hand across an open area of grassland in the general direction of a gate in a wooden fence. Busy nattering and watching the soldiers on the firing range we were not really paying much attention to his directions and we set off across the grass. We were in the middle of an open area, with the live ranges to our right when we heard a yell.

"Oi!"

Really! Did soldiers do nothing but scream at one another?

"Oi!"

Apparently they also screamed at walkers who were straying from the path.

"That way!" shrieked the soldier waving his arm about.

We looked round. Oops! We seemed to have wandered off the path a little. There was a second gate in the fence further inland and it was that gate we should have been heading for, not the one nearer to the ranges. Feeling rather foolish we adjusted our course, passed through the gate, along a little track and to the next sentry box where we were directed back to the coast.

But Chris had not finished trying to attract the soldiers' attention. We were half way along the narrow rutted path and still within sight of the sentry box when Chris suddenly threw herself into the blackberry bushes at the side of the path.

"Are you okay?" I asked solicitously before dissolving into laughter at the sight of her lying on her side, legs kicking, unable to get up because of the weight of her rucksack.

"I'm fine. You just stand there laughing!"

"You went down so fast I thought you'd been shot," I chortled.

"Oh yes, very funny – Chris's been shot!"

We resumed our walk with Chris stopping every so often to pull bits of bramble out of her clothing. The sun came out as we passed a holiday camp. Then we rounded a small hill to find ourselves overlooking the Royal Engineers Bridging Hard, where the Royal Engineers were busy building bridges. Portland glimmered in the distance, looking very Grecian. A cormorant flew past, which was quite exciting – definitely wildlife on the Fleet then!

At Ferry Bridge the Fleet came to an end. To our left was Weymouth and to the right the Isle of Portland. In front of us was a busy main road, a rude welcome back to suburbia.

"Doesn't Portland look Grecian?" muttered Chris.

"Not."

As we came to the Weymouth Borough boundary stone all foot path signs ceased, we saw no more until we had passed through the busy town and left the borough at another marker stone at Bowleaze. The path into Weymouth followed a cycle route; my abiding memories of that route are buddleia, bindweed and dog dirt. It seemed ages before we finally reached the crowded town centre streets and found a bakery where we bought some lunch.

We sat on a bench on the promenade, watching all the holidaymakers strolling past. The children dragged buckets and spades with them, the parents dragged children with them and the pensioners dragged fat little dogs on extendable leads. All of them could be heard to comment on how Grecian Portland looked. Bench space was in demand, and we were lucky to find somewhere to sit, so were the people who sat down next to us, although they probably thought differently when Chris proceeded to remove her boots and socks to air her feet. Still, I could only detect a faint odour of festering socks as I ate my sausage roll and chocolate fudge brownie.

We walked nearly six miles of hard concrete to get from one side of Weymouth to the other. At times the walk seemed tedious, at others annoying, as the promenade was crowded with holidaymakers. Leaving the town along the top of the sea wall to Bowleaze had felt very hard underfoot and the Grecian views to our right did nothing to ease the monotony.

We weaved our way through an amusement area to the path at the back of Bowleaze, passing a grand hotel that would have been more at home in Florida than Dorset. The weather at the time was anything but tropical, clouds had begun to gather and a cool wind had sprung up, raising goose pimples along my arms and legs. For the first time that year I stopped and put on my shirt.

As I was struggling to find my shirt at the bottom of the rucksack, Chris was gazing out to sea.

"Doesn't Portland look Grecian?" she muttered.

"Under grey skies? Definitely not!"

More landslips nearby meant that once again we followed a diverted route inland, rejoining the coast path near to a children's holiday centre. The kids were obviously enjoying themselves playing football, although whether they found the aerial slide quite so much fun is debatable. The top of the slide towered above the camp buildings, looking more like a form of punishment to me than an activity to be anticipated with eager excitement.

"Have you seen the height of that slide?" I asked Chris. "You wouldn't get me up there."

339

"Yes, it is rather high. But I bet you would get a fantastic view of Grecian Portland from the top!"

Yet another landslide at Black Head had meant the path was closed and a diversion posted along a lane. That was okay by us, we were staying a little way inland at Osmington that night and the lane emerged in the centre of the village. We walked along the road looking for the B&B but a sign posted to a telegraph pole soon distracted Chris and, being Chris, she just had to stop and read what it said.

"Ooh! Look!"

"What? Is it a memorial to someone who 'loved this place'? 'Ebenezer Grim: he loved this telegraph pole and so did his little terrier Piddles. Died together in the Great Landslip of 2001. R.I.P.' Or is someone having a car boot sale?" I asked.

"There's no need to be like that – be sensible for once! Come and read it."

I did. The sign was advertising a talk by a gentleman from the County Engineers Department on landslides, and it was taking place in the village hall that evening. In view of all the landslides we had been diverted around we felt the talk would be interesting and decided to go along. It did not start until seven o'clock, which gave us plenty of time to find the B&B, have a cuppa and get showered and changed. This B&B was our first vegetarian one which meant we didn't have to worry about the state of the bacon, soggy or otherwise. The modern bungalow was located down a quiet lane and the landlady showed us to a pleasant room with a luxurious private bathroom and a supply of fresh fruit and chocolate biscuits to augment the usual tea and coffee.

At 6.45 we made our way to the tiny village hall. A handful of villagers were already there setting up rows of chairs and brewing vast quantities of tea. They seemed to be expecting a disproportionate number of people for the size of the village. However, by 7 p.m. the hall was full and the engineer was talking to a packed and avid audience. The locals had to live day to day with the risk of landslides, whereas we were only walking through the area, and the talk highlighted the fragility of the cliffs and the constant threat of coastal erosion. As the talk continued a frightening fact emerged: the landslip that occurred at Black Ven could just as easily have occurred at Lyme Regis itself, the whole town was built on old landslip sites. So, much as I liked Lyme Regis I don't think I will ever buy a house there! Basically the message of the talk was while the engineers do all they can to monitor high risk areas, there is not a lot that can be done to stop landslides and with the increasingly wet climate the risk of more landslides occurring is likely to increase. If the villagers were hoping for cast iron guarantees they must have been very disappointed.

We left the village hall nearly two hours later and hurried to the nearby pub for an evening meal. We had barely seated ourselves when the whole room seemed to darken as a sudden heavy downpour began. Having just heard about the contributory effects of rain on coastal erosion we were left wondering if there would be anything left of the coast path by morning.

Tuesday 10th July

It must have rained all night. It was still raining steadily as we left the B&B that morning and made our way back to the coast. With our newly acquired knowledge about landslips it was easier to identify susceptible areas and to spot old landslips. Perhaps we were lucky to be able to walk the path while it was still there!

A donkey stood sad and lonely in a field at the side of the lane, reminding me of Eeyore. So I leaned across the fence and patted him. He didn't want patting and I should have taken the hint, but no, I persisted, only to discover he had been rolling in the mud. Well, I hoped it was mud, as I tried to clean my filthy hand on some wet grass. We stocked up with supplies at Osmington Mills, emerging from the village store to find the rain had stopped, and then turned east to rejoin the coast path by the side of the thirteenth century Smugglers Inn.

Another landslide, this time a minor one, and another diversion at Ringstead took us through a small woodland of coppiced hazel. Sheltered from the wind it was quiet amongst the trees and quite by chance we came across a young deer. How long had she watched our steady progress before we saw her?

Just to the east of Ringstead the path climbed along the back of Burning Cliff, named for the time when the bituminous oil shale of which it consists spontaneously ignited. We came across a small church perched near the edge of the cliff. Built of wood and barely larger than a garage, it seemed too fragile to survive any strong winds. The tiny graveyard contained the remains of several drowned sailors whose bodies had washed up in the coves below. One severe landslide and these seamen would find themselves back in the sea!

We were only walking six miles that day, but it was six miles of breath-taking scenery, a chalk roller coaster of sheer cliffs and tiny coves. Wild flowers and hay meadows were constantly battered by the high gusting winds. Harebells, orchids and ladies bedstraw provided dancing flashes of colour. With each ascent of grass-topped white cliff came another awesome view, the white cliffs stretched on for miles, stacked and folded one behind the other. Middle Bottom followed West Bottom until we arrived at Bat's Hole, where a distant dark patch on the side of the cliff face revealed itself as we drew nearer, to be a colony of nesting cormorants. After watching the cormorants we set off for Scratchy Bottom. Honestly.

If I had been allergic to the honey pot of Bedruthan Steps near Newquay, then the spectacle that greeted us at Durdle Door was sufficient to induce anaphylactic shock. A motorway of a path surged over the chalk hillside, swarming with tourists by the coach load.

"There'll be four Wallace Arnolds in the car park at Lulworth!" As it turned out I was right about the number but not the company.

The quantity of tourists with their clicking cameras was out done only by the quantity of litter. There were no litterbins in sight, which I suppose would be because of their intrusive appearance but the litter was even more intrusive. Drinks cartons, cans and bottles rolled about blown by the wind. Crisp packets, sweet wrappers and sandwich bags flapped crazily overhead, tossed about by the wind like demented ghostly gulls. Carrier bags crammed full of litter had been impaled onto the fence posts as make shift bin bags and then left there uncollected. With some determined litter picking on the part of the landowners, Lulworth

Estates, the majority of the rubbish could be collected; however there was a large amount of litter that had been blown part way down the cliffs, and that was surely where it would stay until the next storm blew it either inland or carried it out to sea. We were both disappointed by the sudden presence of so many people and disgusted by the sheer volume of litter.

"Litterbugs deserve to be kneecapped!" I grumbled.

"Julia! That's taking punishment a bit far. What would your Mum say?"

"Birch them, probably."

I had been looking forward to arriving at Durdle Door and hoping to be able to swim from the beach towards this natural limestone arch. Whether the currents would have permitted this is another matter, but I didn't get my longed for swim, there were too many people about and the wind chill factor was just a little too much, changing into a swimming costume at that point no longer appealed.

If you could learn to ignore the tourists and the litter and just concentrate on the scenery, Durdle Door was indeed a spectacular sight. J. Meade Faulkner, author of Moonfleet, described the sea as 'gleaming like a mackerel's back', and what an apt and accurate description that was, for even with the grey sky overhead and the wind whipping up the sea into creaming waves, still the colour remained a bright, shimmering mixture of blues, greens and greys.

A cobbled highway of a path carried us down from Durdle Door, dropping behind the cliffs at Dungy Head to emerge in the huge car park at Lulworth Cove. How busy Lulworth now seemed compared to the Friday evening at the end of June when we had arrived; people thronged the single main street and crammed into the visitor centre. We battled our way through the crowds, feeling distinctly windswept and dishevelled and headed for our hotel.

We had chosen to stay in a different hotel to the one where we had left the car. There were two reasons for this. This first was in case the original hotel had turned out to not be very good, therefore we would not find ourselves staying longer than necessary in a dump. The second reason was because we felt that by returning to the same hotel part way through the walk, it would reinforce the feeling that the walk was drawing to a close.

Our room at this second hotel was on the ground floor, a twin room with en suite shower room, equipped with a disabled bath/shower, which seemed practical. It ceased to seem practical for disabled people when I attempted to use it. I know my knees were aching but even so I could not be described as disabled. But did I have trouble getting into that shower cubicle! How on earth, I mused, were people with disabilities expected to negotiate the two large steps down? Slipping as I climbed out, I nearly crippled myself. If it had not been for my forehead coming into contact with the edge of the sink I would have found myself sprawled in a jumble of limbs across the cold lino.

The hotel had a swimming pool and having missed out on a swim at Durdle Door I was keen to use it. However, the pool was outdoors, the wind was bracing and the water only just heated. Much against her better judgement Chris accompanied me to the pool. Each time we brought any part of our anatomy out of the water the wind immediately turned it to a block of ice. Our swim was brief and our return to the warmth of the hotel room almost supersonic.

We ate in the hotel that evening and then spent some time exploring the eroded rock formations of Stair Hole and the cove itself. The weather had improved; the wind finally blowing the clouds inland and the sun was setting in a red sky behind Portland.

"Doesn't the Isle of Portland look Grecian this evening?" Chris was heard to mutter.

We returned to the hotel in time to watch the evening news. However, the television in our room had other ideas. Whether we were just unfortunate with that particular television set or whether Lulworth suffered from especially poor reception I do not know. When we first switched on the TV the picture was clear and the sound good but as soon as we sat down to watch it the clear images of the opening titles of the ten o'clock news were replaced by snow. Chris stood up and began to wiggle the aerial. This had zero effect on the picture quality.

"Can you put the kettle on while you're on your feet, please?" I asked.

Chris obligingly switched on the kettle and immediately the TV picture cleared. We watched two minutes worth of news until the kettle boiled and the picture disappeared to be replaced once again by snow. In between making and drinking a cup of tea, Chris spent the next thirty minutes parading around the bedroom, waving her arms and even her walking pole in the air in a crazy attempt to improve the picture. Whenever the reception did improve she would freeze until the sound turned crackly and the picture snowy, and then the whole farce would begin again. At one point she resembled a demented drum majorette twirling her walking pole baton in the air and almost tearing the overhead light from the ceiling in the process! The news ended to be replaced by the weather forecast, which seemed to be predicting snow.

Wednesday 11th July

Seven o'clock saw me determinedly getting my moneys worth at the hotel, by swimming up and down the tiny pool. When I had suggested an early morning swim Chris had mumbled something about being mad, before turning over in bed and going back to sleep, a response I took to mean she didn't feel like a swim that morning. Having immersed myself in the leaf littered, chlorine-smelling water I was beginning to have second thoughts myself. The British sun had just gone behind a big cloud, the wind gusted and I was an idiot. Nothing new there then.

A beautiful section of coastline runs from Lulworth Cove to Kimmeridge, seven and a half miles of spectacular limestone cliffs and bays layered with colourful clays. Grass, gorse and heather-covered ridges roll away inland, dotted about with the sites of ancient hill forts and Roman remains and long barrows. The area is rich in geological interest and marine wildlife, and a rare fossil forest, designated a Site of Special Scientific Interest, lies near the path. Another prominent and unusual aspect of this part of the coast path is the proliferation of yellow marker posts. And it's important to take note of these when walking this part of the path, because the posts indicate the safe route through one of Britain's largest Army ranges.

The Ministry of Defence owns 7500 acres of land stretching from the coast some way in land between Lulworth Cove and Kimmeridge. At certain times of the year public access to the footpaths and the roads crossing this land is permitted. At all other times the range walks are closed to prevent walkers being run over by tanks or blown up. The Army doesn't work weekends and have a long summer holiday in August. We were walking on a weekday in July. This was one occasion when we definitely could not ignore any signs of the 'Footpath Closed' variety.

Instead of a lovely section of coast path walking we were facing a ten-mile inland detour, mostly on roads, and the forecast was for rain and wind. It was windy all right, so much so that perhaps we were fortunate not to be on the exposed cliff tops; but as for the promised rain – what rain? We walked under clement skies.

The Ministry of Defence first commandeered the Lulworth Ranges in 1917; over the years further land was added to this until in 1943 the MoD acquired the largest parcel of land including the village of Tyneham. Fishermen and farmers and the residents of the village were evacuated, it was to be their sacrifice for the war effort, they fully expected to be able to return one day. This has never happened, despite much publicity and their best endeavours the village remains empty. It is possible, on days when the ranges are open – as we did the following Sunday before beginning our journey home – to visit the abandoned church and the bomb blasted cottages, and to wander into the old school, now housing an historical exhibition of the village children's work. We were astounded to read examples of their work from the 1920's. Their local knowledge of the surrounding countryside and its wildlife led us to wonder if perhaps we are now educating our children too globally, instead of teaching them to appreciate the world around them.

But visiting Tyneham is a sobering experience. This tiny village, with its nearby manor house, once a listed building, lies in ruins. Used as a target by the Army and having taken numerous direct hits, the manor house was deemed unsafe some years ago and was demolished. Tyneham was a village with a history predating the Domesday Book. Today few of the villagers remain to fight the battle to be allowed to return.

It is hardly surprising, therefore, that the Ministry of Defence is frequently criticised for its ownership and subsequent closure of vast tracts of land. However, while the human costs of such land management are often various and controversial, there can be some startling benefits to wildlife and the environment. Without intensive farming and with restricted human contact the wildlife on the MoD land benefits. We saw three deer grazing in a clearing on the heath within earshot of the Army's guns and later we watched a herd of sika deer running across a meadow. In fact, the Lulworth Ranges are home to the largest herd of sika deer in Britain. Whilst you might expect the frequent shelling and gunfire to scare off any wildlife, the animals are thought to regard all the noise as just another thunderstorm and they learn to avoid the more heavily used areas of the ranges. The flora, too, benefits from the Army's tenure. Some grazing is allowed at certain times of the year and in some areas. But without intensive grazing, application of herbicides and pesticides, and with no harvesting taking place the land is actually being managed in a much more traditional way than most of the agricultural land in Britain. The wild flowers bloom, literally. And with the rich variety of wild flowers comes a wide diversity of insects, small mammals and birds.

Our inland route that day led us past Lulworth Army camp, then Lulworth Castle and up a very long, very straight road. At first it seemed that the Army were having a day off, and we wondered if this was due to the tragedy on Salisbury Plain the day before when a tank had overturned killing two of the soldiers inside. We had walked for several miles along busy minor roads before hearing the first explosion of the morning. Chris had just commented on the apparent lack of activity when a huge boom seemed to shake every tree, every bush and even us.

"They sound to be firing in this direction!" I squealed. "Now I wish I hadn't drunk so much tea at breakfast."

"Go behind that bush," suggested Chris.

"No way, I might get blown up!"

With each subsequent explosion or rattle of machine gun fire my bladder seemed to shrink a little more. And I could hardly climb over the fence – suppose I trod on an unexploded shell?

We arrived at the old farmhouse B&B in the late afternoon. We had been somewhat anxious about the quality of this particular night's accommodation, it had been the last of several we had tried to book into, all the others had been unwilling to take a single night's booking, and the price of this one seemed a little too cheap in comparison to the others. As is often the case it turned out to be one of the best. The farmer's wife greeted us with a big smile and an even bigger pot of tea and plate of biscuits. And then gave us the bad news. There was a section of coast path to the east that remained closed due to the risk of Foot and Mouth Disease.

"It's about a quarter of a mile long," she told us. "Apparently the other walkers that are staying with me found out about this closure only yesterday when they tried to walk it."

"Oh, great," I muttered.

"Is there a diversion signposted?" asked Chris more practically.

"There is, but it's nearly four miles long. You have to go right inland to the road, then along that for a mile or so before turning down a bridle path to get back to the coast path."

"But there aren't any cases of the disease in Dorset. Do you know why the diversion is in place?" I asked.

"The farmer's just being awkward, that's why!" declared this farmer's wife. "I telephoned him to ask what he's playing at and he said the cattle in the field which the coast path runs through have to cross the path to get to a trough."

"Well, couldn't he move the trough or something? We've walked through loads of fields with animals in, all those farmers are being more realistic about the risks of walkers on their land."

"He's just being stupid, and I've told him so. Have you a long walk tomorrow? If you want I could meet you on the road and drive you round to rejoin the coast path at the other side of the diversion."

It was a very kind offer and had we planned on walking to Swanage the next day we would have gratefully accepted. Fortunately the following day's walk was a short one to the next village of Worth Matravers and the additional four miles would not add too much to our day.

Our large bedroom with its tiny mullion windows overlooked the fields. Shedding boots and socks I unpacked whilst Chris went off to the huge and luxurious bathroom for a shower. With a long hot day on the hard roads our feet had taken a pounding, with four socks, four boots and my pair of naked feet let loose in the room the air suddenly seemed to be full of toxic fumes. I barely made it to the window to let in some fresh air!

The landlady gave us a lift to the nearest village pub for our evening meal and sat waiting in the car until we were safely inside. This proved to be rather embarrassing as we suddenly encountered yet more problems with doors. With Chris leading the way we headed for the pub entrance. But Chris couldn't open the door.

"May be there's another door, this one seems to be locked."

Grinning vacuously at the landlady still watching from the car, we went around the corner of the building. No door there.

"May be there's a door on the other side," suggested Chris.

Shrugging my shoulders and rolling my eyes at the watching landlady I followed Chris to the other end of the pub.

"No door here either," she said.

"It can't be shut," called our landlady.

"Try the door again," I suggested and we trudged back to the front door.

Chris heaved at the old iron latch but still the door would not open.

"You have a go!" she eventually said in frustration.

Whereupon I succeeded in opening the door first time.

"How did you do that?" demanded Chris.

Thursday 12th July

The flock of baaing sheep separated from their lambs only the previous day failed to disturb my sleep that night. We woke to blue skies and grey skies depending on which window you looked out of. The optimist preferred the view from the south-facing window.

The breakfast was one of the best: huge, various and prolonged. We chatted for nearly an hour with the landlady and the other walkers. Having eaten up, packed up and paid up, the landlady offered us a lift to the coast, saving us a mile on the winding narrow lane. She deposited us near to the Kimmeridge Marine Centre and with a cheery wave, turned her car around and sped off.

We had heard a lot of good reports about the marine centre, this area of the south coast is a rich wildlife reserve and even has an underwater nature trail, but unfortunately we had forgot to pack our scuba gear. Never mind! We could still visit the Marine Centre. The door was open and we headed eagerly towards it, only to be met by a marine conservation worker carrying a notice board.

"Sorry ladies, we are closed this morning whilst we sort out our glass fibre." With that he set up the notice board: 'Open at 1 p.m.' it said. Typical!

Leaving the closed Marine Centre behind we climbed the cliffs to reach the old and now dangerously derelict folly of Clavel Tower. Looking back down into Kimmeridge Bay we watched the nodding donkey of the little oil well working quietly. Further to the west we could see Grecian Portland and to the east the jutting promontory of St Aldhelm's Head. The guidebook urged us to be on the lookout for snakes and puffins but we saw none, although we did see two deer hiding in a wheat field a little way inland. And once again we heard the guns of Lulworth Ranges.

The cliff was crumbling in places, the path running very close to this precarious edge. Once again I had drunk too much at breakfast time and was beginning to be in urgent need of relief. With no trees or bushes to hide behind Chris suggested I chose a spot in the middle of a long straight stretch of path where I could see if the path was clear in both directions. Tactfully admiring the view in the other direction Chris dawdled behind whilst I hurried on in front for the first alfresco toilet stop of the day. For reasons of safety I finally chose a flattened area of grass at the side of the path, rather than anywhere too near the edge of the eroding cliff.

I had barely finished and signalled to Chris to catch up than an elderly couple appeared heading towards us. By the time Chris had joined me so had this couple. We exchanged the usual 'hellos' and the gentleman began chatting.

"We've done this walk once and now we've come back to take photographs because we didn't have time before, we were walking too fast," he explained.

I wondered why he hadn't just walked slower in the first place but I didn't like to ask him.

He began fumbling with a camera, throwing the map he was carrying down onto the grass at the side of the path. *The* grass. The *wet* grass! I stood frozen with horror – would his map be wet? Chris and the couple continued to chat and I continued to stare with disbelief and embarrassment at the map lying on the grass. I breathed a sigh of relief when we moved on, leaving them still standing there taking photographs, with the map still lying on the grass.

The path dropped to almost sea level at Freshwater Steps where a small waterfall tumbled into the sea. It was there that we met two more walkers and this couple seemed to dawdle even more than we did. Each had a pair of high-powered binoculars swinging from their necks and pockets stuffed with identification books. The lady expressed sadness that the cliff falls and landslides were causing rare orchids and wild flowers to be lost. We genuinely sympathised but began to feel rather ignorant as she proceeded to name countless flowers and butterflies they had seen that morning.

"We've noted fifteen species of butterflies since Swanage," she enthused.

I muttered something inadequate about seeing three marbled whites and felt an even bigger fool. Meanwhile her husband was using a hand lens to examine a tiny beetle perched on the top of a sea carrot flower. Until we met them we had felt relatively confident about our ability to identify flora and fauna. Oh well, at least we could identify the dozens of noisy birds flying from bush to bush as stonechats. And Chris could always be relied upon to find an ant's nest to sit on!

A very steep climb brought us to the top of Houns-tout cliff where the diversion began. What was particularly annoying was the fact that we could stand at the start of the closed off path and look across the intervening valley to the end of the closed section. It all seemed so frustrating. Having expended energy getting to the top of the cliff we took advantage of the stone seat to have a break for lunch. Portland was beginning to look a little less than Grecian: a large black cloud was covering it. Whilst we sat eating, the large black cloud began heading our way, picking up speed and appearing to get blacker by the minute. We packed up our things and set off on the diverted route. Two minutes later the cloud caught up with us and a sudden heavy deluge began. It took us about two minutes to get all our waterproofs on. A further two minutes later the downpour ceased as the cloud moved away down the coast. We were left clad in full waterproof regalia looking a little overdressed in the hot sun.

Through a wood and onto a road, we walked along the diverted route. We passed through the little village of Kingston, getting our first sight of Corfe Castle across the deceptively named Isle of Purbeck. The castle ruins sat on a small hill, looking like an island in a sea of pasture. In the far distance was the grey conurbation of Poole and Bournemouth, our first reminder that we were nearing the end of the South West Coast Path. The diversion from the road was badly signed; we followed a bridle path back to the coast before arriving at a track where all signs petered out. A discussion ensued, a difference of opinion followed and we set off in different directions along the track. There is a reason that I usually leave all the map reading to Chris: she's better at it than I am. Remembering this I turned around and hurried after her.

Two hours after leaving the coast path we rejoined it on the eastern side of a bay called Chapman's Pool. A brief cliff top walk soon plunged to sea level before ascending a long flight of steps to the 350 feet summit of St Aldhelm's Head, where another stone bench was conveniently located. This one was inscribed with a name and the line 'Time passes, listen, time passes'.

"I expect this bench marks the spot where the poor chap collapsed and died having tackled all those steps," I said wearily.

349

"What's that inscription mean?" mused Chris.

"May be it's to remind all the walkers that they aren't getting any younger."

"I don't like the way you looked at me when you said that."

"You're only as young as you feel."

"I've a forty-something's body with a ninety-something's knees!"

"So young?" I laughed.

She's got a frighteningly good aim with her walking pole.

A Norman chapel dedicated to St Aldhelm stands at the top of the cliff that takes its name. Near to the chapel are the barely discernable remains of the army buildings erected during the Second World War. The chapel door stood unlocked and we entered the dark interior, giving our eyes time to adjust to the dimness. We expected the chapel to smell of damp but instead were surprised to find it full of the scent of fresh flowers, vases of which were arranged around the font. Chris began to read an information leaflet but I was intrigued by the graffiti of dates and initials carved into the central buttress. Some of the inscriptions dated back to the seventeenth century. I don't like vandalism and would never condone such graffiti, but I had to ask myself at what point does vandalism such as those carvings become history?

The coastline from St Aldhelm's Head changed substantially. Gone were the layers of limestone, clays and shales of the previous undulating cliffs, to be replaced with lower cliffs of Purbeck limestone. Small caves and abandoned stone quarries were dotted along the cliffs. At the hanging valley of Winspit we turned inland, passing along a green lane and up through fields where the strip lynchets of ancient field systems could still be clearly seen as uniform ridges in the sheep-grazed fields.

Our B&B at the inland village of Worth Matravers had sounded wonderful when we had telephoned earlier in the year to book our accommodation. But as with many things in life, it was a disappointment. We received a somewhat less than warm welcome, made all the worse when compared to the friendly farmer's wife of the night before. The house smelt strongly of dog, although our room, thank goodness, did not. Initially the couple that ran the B&B offered us a lift to the pub in the next village, a distance of about two miles.

"But you will have to make your own way back," added the husband.

"Oh, okay," we replied, somewhat bemused.

The owners of so many guesthouses we had stayed in over the course of the walk had offered their services as a taxi, and this was obviously a common courtesy extended to any walkers who stayed with them. We had always been very grateful, although not expectant of this charity. However, it was rare indeed to be grudgingly offered only a one-way lift. When we had first made the booking with them we had been led to believe that they would happily transport us to and from the pub. That evening we had no option but to accept the lift if we wanted to eat, there being nowhere else in the immediate area that served food. Chris's knee was once again troubling her and so the prospect of a further two miles walking that day was not particularly pleasant. However we were barely settled in our room when the lady called upstairs. They had decided to dine at the pub themselves that evening and, providing we were finished eating when they were ready to leave, would give us a lift back. They intended leaving for the pub in about an hour, that gave us time to have a cuppa, get showered and changed and do our laundry.

Feeling hot and sticky and very much in need of a cool shower we investigated the bathroom. There was a bath, with a shower over, a selection of moderately expensive shampoos, conditioners and shower gels, and some rather small towels.

But the tiny, windowless bathroom seemed to be rather hot; was the radiator on? No. A glance at the ceiling revealed the reason.

"Which idiot put a 250 Watt spot light in a small, low ceilinged bathroom?" I asked in amazement, blinking under the hot powerful light.

"The same one who hasn't heard of tumble driers and fabric conditioner!" exclaimed Chris as she inspected one of the rough towels.

The spotlight might have made the bathroom temperature, well Grecian, but it was rather useful for drying the washing, which we draped from the top of the door and the shower screen.

Our lift to the pub in the very cramped back of a very smelly car seemed a far longer journey than the two miles they had said. Fearful of missing the return journey we gobbled our scampi but I still had some way to go before clearing the plate when the man appeared.

"We're going now. Are you ready?" he asked eying my half finished meal.

"Very nearly," replied Chris.

"Okay," he said and disappeared through the doorway.

"Oh hell!" I mumbled scoffing chips and scampi.

"It's alright, I can see their car from here," Chris said, peering through the window. "If I suddenly leap to my feet and run out, you'll know they are starting the engine."

"I guess we're foregoing a dessert then?" I gasped, reaching for the remainder of my half of cider and beginning to gulp it down.

Having finished the meal in indigestion-risking record time we made our way out of the dining room and into the bar area, only to find the couple leaning against the bar with full pints in their hands! All that rushing for nothing!

"We thought we probably had time for another drink," they explained.

A southwesterly wind blew up that evening. The bedroom door, yes – yet another problematic door – would not stay shut. Merely pushing the door firmly closed did not make it shut. We tried propping walking boots and rucksacks against it, and even jammed a piece of folded up card under it but each time there was a strong gust of wind the door blew open. We even considered wedging a chair under the handle!

"There must be a window open somewhere in the house," mused Chris as the door blew open yet again, nearly knocking me flying in the process.

"Maybe it just needs a good shove," I said. Putting words into action I leaned against the door. I shoved until the carpet started wrinkling up under my feet and the panelled door began to creak in protest, but the latch steadfastly refused to click into place.

"You're going to break the door!" warned Chris.

Giving up, I slumped back against the door exhausted by my futile efforts. Click! It shut!

Friday 13th July

Within fifteen minutes of setting off that morning it began to rain. Initially we tried sheltering under a tree but the tree was not big enough for two. True to form, the rain stopped just minutes after we had put on our waterproofs.

That day we had a ridiculously short, easy walk of six miles from where we rejoined the coast path at the old Winspit quarries to Swanage. St Aldhelm's Head blocked our view of Grecian Portland, but another isle was now in sight, the Isle of Wight. The sun came out to make the walk a pleasant leisurely summer stroll along the low cliff tops. Caves and old quarries abounded along that part of the coast. A group of school children were climbing the old quarried cliffs at Dancing Ledge.

Much of the walk that morning was through National Trust land. In the middle of one field a National Trust van was parked and the ranger was working nearby.

"What's he doing?" asked Chris.

"I'm not sure."

He was kneeling in the middle of the field, surrounded by nothing but short grass, and seemed to be hammering at the ground. As neither of us was willing to ask him what he was doing we never found out, but it was certainly different from the usual tasks of footpath and stile maintenance.

A flotilla of small sailing ships appeared, presumably having sailed from Poole harbour. Soon we began to meet more and more walkers, suggesting we were nearing Durlston Country Park. This part of Dorset seemed to be the most relaxed about the risk of walkers spreading Foot and Mouth. Most of the morning we walked through herds of cattle, unfenced from the path. Having negotiated a particularly inquisitive herd of bullocks we dropped into a sheltered spot where gorse bushes provided a natural windbreak.

"Here looks like a good place for lunch," suggested Chris.

Agreeing, I sat down next to her and removed my rucksack. I had taken my first bite of flapjack when Chris leapt to her feet and began swearing.

"What? What?" I demanded. Had she sat in something one of the cattle had left?

"Every time! I do it every time!" She was hastily flapping at her shorts.

"Do what?"

"Sit on an ant nest! And one has just gone up the inside of my shorts!"

"Ugh! Poor thing. You!" I added hastily as Chris glared at me.

With her innate sense of inappropriate picnic spots she had chosen to sit on the ant equivalent of Mexico City. The grass seemed to be full of the scurrying insects. Ants were running over our boots and swarming across our rucksacks. Lunch was put on hold until we found an ant-free zone.

We passed the lighthouse at Anvil Point, failed to find what the guidebook described as 'the excellent information centre' and instead found ourselves in Durlston Country Park. We decided to stop for a pot of tea in the ant-free tearooms at the castle, built as a folly by a wealthy Swanage merchant in the nineteenth century.

Leaving Chris at an outdoor table I went inside to buy the tea. The interior was filled with interesting displays of the area's natural history, and was a rather grand building. It has been my experience that the posher the place the more likely I am to show myself up, and Durlston Castle was no exception. Having ordered and paid for a pot of tea for two, I was turning to carry the tray of tea things outside when I noticed a bundle of serviettes lying on a table next to some cutlery and sachets of sugar. I missed deep embarrassment by a mere whisker as I dropped and, fortunately, caught a teacup from the tray I was carrying. Serves me right for trying to grab a serviette to blow my nose on!

"How much do I owe you?" asked Chris, when I appeared with the tray of tea things.

"Well, there's some from yesterday as well as this. I have it written down somewhere." Getting a scrap of paper and a pen I began to add it up. "Okay, that's all from yesterday and then there's half of £2.30 from today. Er, that's forty one pounds."

"How much? Are you sure?" asked Chris, not without good reason, it did seem rather a lot.

Handing her the piece of paper I watched as she went down the list checking my maths.

"Julia! What's half of £2.30?"

"£1.15."

"So why have you written £15?"

"Oh! Have I?"

"Yes, look!"

She was right, I had.

"Well, I got the fifteen bit right, I just wrote it on the wrong side of the decimal point. Sorry. It's a good job you checked."

She has since taken great pleasure in telling everyone about my mathematical mix-ups. Whenever I now start to do any maths at work, some clever swine always pipes up: "What's half of £2.30?"

Cliff falls beyond Durlston soon had us diverted into Swanage. Unable to walk around Peveril Point we entered the town along residential streets before descending the green towards the sweeping sea front of Swanage Bay. In general we do not enjoy the urban areas after walking miles of wonderful solitude, but Swanage was rather nice. Genteel is probably the best word to describe the uncluttered sea front of this quiet Victorian resort. My only criticism of Swanage would be the toilets, which I had little choice but to use, having drained the teapot dry at Durlston. They were clean, no complaints there, but they were costly – well to a skinflint like myself 20p is expensive when you've been used to using free bushes!

That weekend a Jazz festival was taking place in the town. When we had tried to book accommodation we had found that everywhere was fully booked. We had been forced to look for accommodation further afield, gradually widening our area until we had finally found a B&B with vacancies in the inland village of Corfe Castle. Corfe Castle was quite a way from the coast at Swanage but there were frequent bus services between the two places and the old Swanage Railway line, now run by volunteers, also travelled to Corfe Castle.

The romantic appeal of the old railway and the fact that a train was just about to depart when we found the station, made the decision of train versus bus an easy one. So we took the old train to Corfe Castle and a leap into the unknown, for we had little information about the B&B other than a vague address.

The ruins from which it takes its name dominate the village of Corfe Castle. The castle was originally built in the ninth century using wood but was rebuilt using local limestone in the eleventh century. King John did a little bit of modernising a couple of hundred years later and when Henry III came along, he too rolled his sleeves up and added a few extensions. Eventually the castle passed to the Bankes family. In the English Civil War it took a bit of a battering, enduring a few sieges until finally it fell to the Roundheads. Presumably looking a little worse for wear, it remained in the Bankes family until they finally bequeathed it to the National Trust in the 1980's.

When we arrived in the village, it was nearly closing time at the Castle. We followed a footpath around the perimeter of the castle grounds, getting a good view of the castle from all sides except the inside. We browsed the shops and read menus posted outside various expensive inns and hostelries, and searched in vain for a road bearing the name of the address of our B&B. Finally we resorted to asking in a newsagent's shop. Neither the owner nor his son had heard of the B&B, but the son knew where the road was and directed us out of the village and along a busy road.

Following the directions we tramped up a road, squeezing into the hedge every time a car or tractor roared past. According to the leaflet we had received from the owner of the B&B, the cottage was located half a mile along this road from its junction with the main road. We inspected every gateway we passed (all two of them) but saw no familiar house name or B&B sign. We walked nearly a mile, still searching in vain, wondering if perhaps we could be on the wrong road. Where the road widened out at a junction we stopped to phone the B&B.

"You don't think it could have been that gateway we passed with no sign on it, do you?" Chris asked me.

"Possibly, but what sort of B&B wouldn't advertise their presence?"

"An awful one?" She began tapping the number into her mobile phone. It rang for ages before it was finally answered.

"Hello, we are trying to find your B&B," Chris said. She screwed her face up and rolled her eyes at the reply. "Yes, we are at the top of the hill."

Another brief pause and then: "Is there a sign outside?" More eye rolling. "So we've walked right past it! Okay, we'll be there in about ten minutes."

"Thanks for nothing!" she muttered as she put the phone in her pocket.

We retraced our steps down the busy road until we reached a gateway.

"This must be it," I sighed. "I've got a bad feeling about this."

"Me too."

"I've had a bad feeling about this ever since we booked it. Oh God! What's it going to be like? They can't even be bothered to put a sign up."

"If you're trying to reassure me, it's not working!"

We turned in at the gateway and began walking up a rough gravel drive towards a distant bungalow. A dilapidated old truck was parked nearby and a jumble of breezeblocks, cement mixers, tools and timber surrounded a half constructed building to our left.

"Maybe our room's not finished yet," Chris joked weakly.

Suddenly, from behind the bungalow, a baying hellhound appeared and began charging straight at us. Large, black and mean he looked like a cross between a Rottweiler and Anne Robinson. We both jumped with fright and instinctively moved closer together. The slavering dog kept coming and, for some strange reason, we kept walking.

"Just keep going, don't let him know you're scared. I'm sure the owner will appear and call him off at any second," I muttered.

We continued to advance slowly down the gravel drive, whilst every nerve and muscle in our bodies was telling us to run for our lives. The dog reached us and began circling, still barking and snarling and slavering, his hackles raised all the way from the tip of his tail to his head. His lips were drawn back to show his teeth, and they all looked incredibly sharp. Almost clinging to each other with terror, we inched slowly down the path, the dog's manic howls and barks deafening us.

Suddenly a man appeared in the doorway of the bungalow.

"Oh, thank God!" mumbled Chris, "he's going to call the dog off."

But he didn't. He began walking towards us, obviously enjoying our fright. When he reached us he grabbed the dog's collar and pulled the animal back a little. Unable to circle us, the dog then reared up on his hind legs, bringing his jaws on a level with our heads. We found ourselves looking into his open maw, with the saliva dripping off the huge fangs, and down his throat.

"Is this the B&B?" one of us squeaked.

"Yeah," came the monosyllabic response and with a jerk of his head the man motioned us to follow him to the bungalow.

He showed us inside, leaving the dog growling menacingly in the doorway, and pointed out our room and the neighbouring bathroom. Then he turned and left us. We closed the door of the bedroom, effectively shutting out the growling and the underlying doggy smell. The bedroom seemed quite clean which was one consolation. However, neither of us liked the atmosphere, after our less than welcome first impression of the landlord we were both feeling uneasy about the prospect of staying overnight under the same roof. I checked the bedroom door and was much relieved at finding a bolt on the inside. This was one place I would definitely not like to stay in alone.

"I think I preferred the welcome we got last night," said Chris.

"Yes, do you think this B&B will ever qualify for a Welcome Host award?"

"Depends if the inspector is the same one who visited the hotel at Maidencombe. Never mind, at least the room seems clean. And there are tea making facilities."

"Oh goodie. Let's make a cuppa, things always look better after a good cup of tea."

Our attempts to make the best of the situation were undermined when we took a drink of the tea. With no milk and only coffee whitener in the room, the resulting brew could only be described as undrinkable. Abandoning the idea of a nice cup of tea, we decided to shower and change and then walk back down into the village for a meal. Five minutes after going to the bathroom Chris was back, looking wet, red and flustered.

"I've just had a happening!" she exclaimed, shuddering.

"What? That odd bloke never walked in on you did he?"

"No. But the bathroom's full of hairs! I didn't know where to put my clean clothes, or my dirty ones for that matter. And when I was getting dried I found a hair on me!"

"Not one of yours, I take it?"

"No! I think it was a dog hair!"

"Urgh! That's put me right off having a shower. What state is the toilet in?"

"Well, you know the horrible one at work? It's worse than that."

"So what you're saying is that if I want to use the loo I would probably be better off finding a bush in the garden?"

"Yes, except the dog might get you!"

"Okay, I'm going in!" I said, psyching myself up. "It probably won't look too bad if I take my glasses off."

Chris was right, there was not one square inch of clean, hair-free surface in the bathroom. I finally resorted to piling my clothes on top of my boots. With my specs resting on the windowsill the bathroom still looked dirty but in an out of focus kind of way. The compensation was the powerful shower and the various shower gels, shampoos and conditioners available. But getting dried, I too, found a non-native hair on me. Then I found another. Then another. Then a whole lot of others. Where the hell were they all coming from? The towel! I shook the towel and the bathroom seemed to be full of floating hairs. Batting at my skin to knock off all the hairs I could find, I resorted to scrubbing myself with my own T-shirt before getting dressed.

"See what I mean?" asked Chris when I returned to the bedroom.

"That's decided me. I am not having a shower in the morning. No way. Nothing is going to induce me to put my body anywhere near those towels ever again!"

When we arrived back in Corfe Castle later that evening all the tearooms were closed. The few hotels and pubs bordering the market square looked expensive: gentlemen in suits and ladies in evening dress were going in and out. In casual clothes, with our hair still damp from the shower and with no makeup we felt distinctly underdressed for such exclusive-looking establishments. Nevertheless we stopped to read some of the menus posted outside.

"Mules…what does that say? Are they serving horse meat?" I asked, reading one of the menus, which seemed to be written entirely in French.

"It's mussels," explained Chris.

"Well, of course it's muscle. Most meat is muscle, unless it's offal!"

"No, not muscle. Mussel – as in shellfish!"

"Yuck, those black things covered in barnacles? I don't fancy that do you? It would be like eating snails. What's this one – escargot?"

"Those are snails, you idiot!"

"Let's find somewhere else. Somewhere that serves proper food, the sort that has legs."

We had to walk away from the centre of the village before finding a pub that served traditional English fayre of the steak, chicken and curry variety! The pub was small, busy and crowded with locals as they prepared for their regular Friday night karaoke session. We found a quieter table in the beer garden and enjoyed an excellent meal that was entirely invertebrate-free, with the possible exception of the greenfly, which I think got eaten along with some lettuce. Feeling decidedly full we set off back to the B&B, hoping to get some milk from the shop. But the shop had closed for the night.

"I'm sure there is a sachet of hot chocolate somewhere that we brought from the B&B last night," I said. But when we arrived back at the B&B and searched through our things we could not find it anywhere. We both agreed the tea was totally unpalatable if made with coffee whitener and so went to bed rather thirsty. A couple of weeks later I found the sachet of hot chocolate at the bottom of my rucksack! How typical is that?

Lying awake that night I found myself pondering on a local Dorset delicacy that I had seen in various cake shops and supermarkets. I had been wondering for some days what they actually tasted like because they certainly did not look particularly appetising.

Voicing my thoughts I said, "They're rather hard you know!"

"What are?" asked Chris sleepily.

"Dorset knobs!" Feeling that perhaps I should elucidate, I added, "I gave one a prod and they're rock hard."

Chris dissolved into fits of giggles, and I quickly followed.

"Let's buy some tomorrow and take them back for the people at work."

We did buy a packet of Dorset knobs the following day, taking them to work the next week. But I have to say they were not a success! Chorley and Eccles have rather nice little currant filled cakes, Bakewell has its tarts, Switzerland has its rolls, Yorkshire has its puddings, Grasmere has its gingerbread and Dorset has some tasteless, tooth-chippingly hard, dry little buns with a rude name. Our colleagues were not impressed, and having paid over £3 for a packet of the horrible things, neither were we.

Saturday 14th July

We woke up to find neither of us had been murdered in our sleep, which was a relief. We did not shower that morning – we could barely face the bathroom even to clean our teeth! Dreading what we would find at breakfast we took a deep breath and went into the dining room. A lady greeted us, presumably the wife of the miserable man, but where the husband had been morose and monosyllabic, she was cheerful, chatty and pleasant. The breakfast was rather good, much better than at Abbotsbury; and we found it difficult to associate this neat lady with the horrors of the bathroom.

An early bus left Corfe Castle at 8.45 a.m. We could just make it if we hurried. We reached the village centre at exactly 8.45, but could not find the bus stop. Logically it had to be somewhere along the main road, so we hurried down the street until we caught sight of a bus shelter in the distance. At that moment the bus appeared around a bend in the road behind us. We both began running, no easy task with full stomachs and even fuller rucksacks, but there was no way we would reach the bus stop before the bus overtook us. I turned to face the bus, stopped running and stuck my arm out, flapping it up and down. The bus kept on coming, with no discernible reduction in speed. It wasn't going to stop! The next bus was not for another hour, we would save so much time if we could only catch this one. In desperation I clasped my hands together in a gesture of prayer and looked beseechingly at the driver. And miraculously the bus began to slow down, passed us and drew to a halt in the bus stop. We raced down the road, half expecting the bus to set off before we reached it, but it didn't and we clambered hastily on board, thanking the driver profusely. What a nice man, so much better than the miserable driver at Lyme Regis; he even slowed down to let a rabbit, which was running in circles in the middle of the road, get out of the way.

The shopkeepers of Swanage were just swinging into action for another day's assault by holidaymakers as we arrived in the town. We toured the shops, buying provisions for lunch and a packet of Dorset knobs and choosing our final postcards. As we began our walk along the promenade we passed two young men walking in the opposite direction. The first guy had dark, curly hair, the second had a thatch of blond wavy hair, reaching almost to his shoulders, both were wearing day sacks and carried walking poles. We all 'hello-ed' fellow walkers and continued on our way.

"I wonder how far they are walking?" Chris said.

"Well Kimmeridge is about eighteen miles. Although if they are going as far as Kimmeridge I hope they are aware of the diversion."

We soon forgot about the two walkers as we reached the end of the promenade and lost all traces of the coast path. There were no way markers to be seen and we desperately read the guidebook for any clue as to the correct route. Following the very vague description in the book, we walked inland, turning along various side streets and following an alley between houses until we came to the conclusion we were lost in what felt like the largest housing estate on the south coast. Noticing a sign for a bridle way that pointed in roughly the right direction, we set off along a narrow lane that eventually led to open fields on a hillside above Swanage. We were rewarded with splendid views of the town and the bay, and in the distance we could just make out the coast path, approximately half a mile away across three dramatically sloping fields.

360

After twenty minutes of difficult walking across the steep slope, we finally rejoined the coast, climbing the last hill on the South West Coast Path to reach the trig point at Ballard Cliff, where short cropped grass and a few scrubby bushes almost concealed the old earth works. It was a strange feeling to know that from here there would be no more knee-straining ascents, no more gasped 'just admiring the views', from here it was downhill all the way. The panoramic views from the top of Ballard Point stretched into the distance: across the Isle of Purbeck, back along the coast to Durlston Head, out to sea towards the Isle of Wight and finally across the finger of land at Studland Bay to the finishing point of the walk at South Haven Point, with Poole Harbour and the town itself in the background. The end was now literally in sight. Finally after 630 miles of walking, along Britain's longest National Trail, I was gazing across the last few miles of the route. For the last three years I had been imagining how South Haven Point would look, now for the first time I could actually see it.

We descended to Old Harry Rocks and the limestone sea stacks of The Pinnacles, watching as a large black cloud began to empty its contents over Bournemouth and The Solent. Would the cloud move this way, or would we end the walk in sunshine? A lot of people were walking along the path that morning, exercising their dogs, themselves and their children. The path at that point was a bridleway and several people were out cycling. A lady passed us on a green shopper's bike, with a little basket attached to the handlebars. But at the time I was not taking much notice of anything other than the hundreds of sand wasps that were flying around our feet and disappearing into holes in the path. Did they sting like normal wasps? I was just about to ask Chris when a man on a green shopper's bike with a little basket attached to the handle bars, hurtled past us, pedalling furiously. Had he stolen it from the woman? We watched with apathy as the possible thief sped out of sight.

"That looks just like the bike that woman was riding," said Chris.

"Does it?" And that was as far as our crime fighting went.

The little village of Studland is dominated by the National Trust. A few thatched cottages and a hotel, a narrow, yellow-line decorated lane and several rather large car parks seemed to be all the village consisted of. The path ran along the beach and on that busy summer Saturday the sand was full of families. We walked along, dodging sandcastles, kites, footballs and small children. The black cloud had grown tired of soaking holidaymakers in Bournemouth and had begun to head towards Studland. Just as we found a quieter spot on the beach to have our lunch, the first fat drops of rain began to fall. We put on our waterproofs and sat eating lunch, watching as the sudden shower had people frenziedly packing up and running to the car park. Most of the tourists had loads of luggage – cool boxes, windbreaks, beach tents, towels, holdalls and picnic baskets; more luggage for a day on the beach than we had for a fortnight of walking. Families scurried along the beach dragging all their paraphernalia and their children with them in a desperate attempt to reach the dry comfort of their cars. Within a matter of minutes the beach was empty except for ourselves and one man who was strolling along near the waterline.

"He's a walker," said Chris.

"How do you know?" I asked.

"Because he's hardly any luggage." She was right, all he carried was one small rucksack.

The shower stopped as suddenly as it had started. We remained the only people on that part of the beach, although in the distance, there were still quite a number of people.

"I guess those people are the naturalists," Chris said.

"Naturalists? Ooh, do you think we might meet David Attenborough and Tony Soper?" I laughed.

"Okay, okay. I mean naturists."

"Obviously they're not concerned about the rain, it's not like they would have to worry about their clothes getting wet!"

We were not really looking forward to entering the naturist beach. We had read a report of some walkers being verbally abused by naturists and did not wish to have any unpleasant encounters. The coast path ran through the beach, so we had no choice but to walk that way, hopefully we would get through without experiencing anything too unpleasant, although the thought of naked bodies so soon after lunch was hardly conducive to digestion.

After lunch I decided to take advantage of the nearly empty beach to go for a swim. Chris could not be persuaded to join me but watched as I tested the water before taking the plunge. The sea at Studland felt much warmer than it had at Sidmouth and the swim was rather pleasant. At their own end of the beach, some of the naturists were also venturing into the water, sans swimming costumes, unlike myself. The down side of swimming in the sea is all the bother of getting dried and dressed. And it was not helped on this occasion by my miniature towel and the sudden appearance of four people walking along the edge of the beach. After a brief struggle with my clothing, and a little help from Chris, I managed to get dressed without too much loss of dignity and we prepared to continue our walk. A large prominent sign announced we were entering the naturist section of Studland beach and Chris stopped to fiddle with her hat.

"I'm adjusting my hat brim," she explained.

"Oh, so that you can't see any nudists?"

"No! So that it doesn't obscure my view!"

If we were hoping for dashing, virile, athletic, young men we were disappointed. The nudists were old; in fact, the average age must have been about eighty. The four people who had passed us earlier were already naked, having shed their clothes before even putting up their beach tent. I was reminded of some of the rams we had encountered. We tried desperately to look anywhere other than along the nudist beach but it was a bit like driving past a serious road accident, you can't help but look, even though you know it just isn't going to be pretty! We looked at the blue sea, we looked at our feet and we watched the enormous ferries as they came and went into the mouth of Poole harbour, like an optical illusion they seemed to be sailing straight into the sand dunes.

Hidden behind the dunes lies one of England's most important wildlife habitats, Studland Heath. A National Nature Reserve of ponds, marsh, woodlands and heath it is home to a wide variety of flora and fauna, including all six of Britain's native reptiles. We saw two herring

362

gulls and a few crows. Although the crows were actually quite entertaining as they balanced on top of litter bins on the beach and, using their beaks and feet, hauled the dustbin liners out of the bins to reach the remains of sandwiches at the bottom.

We paddled beyond the reaches of the naturist beach and around the corner into Shell Bay with only a few hundred yards to go. And then that was it. We stepped up onto the road where the ferry docked, breathing in the exhaust fumes of a long line of cars waiting to cross to Sandbanks. Six hundred and thirty miles walked over a period of eight weeks in four summers. No fanfares. No balloons. No reception committee. Not even a sign saying 'Minehead – that way – 630 miles'. Disappointment. Anticlimax. We later found out that the South West Coast Path Association, the voluntary body that does much to promote, improve and maintain the route, were at that time fundraising for a memorial sign to be erected at the end of the path. Apparently since I began the walk they have installed a sculpture at the start of the route in Minehead. Which means there is only one thing for it – I will have to walk the South West Coast Path all over again.

We crossed to Sandbanks on the rattling chain-driven ferry and then we did see a sign, a pathetic little green one, pointing in the direction of South Haven Point with the words 'South West Coastal Path' and the symbol of a walker on. Having completed the walk I felt I had to pose under something and took up my position leaning on a railing under the sign. Chris risked getting run over as, dodging between cars and lorries going onto the ferry, she planted herself firmly in the middle of the road to take a photograph. As it turned out, it was worth the risk. The snapshot shows me leaning against the signpost, the wording clearly visible; I'm grinning idiotically, my face is brown, my arms are brown, my legs are brown and my sandal-clad feet are glaringly white.

We caught a bus and then a train back to Wool and then a taxi to return to the hotel at Lulworth, where we received a warm welcome from the hoteliers. In clean clothes that we had collected from the car, we set off for a last excellent meal of the holiday. As we walked through the quiet lanes of West Lulworth we passed a signpost pointing up a track, part of the South West Coast Path. Two young men were just emerging from the track and we nearly collided with them. The first guy had dark, curly hair, the second had a thatch of blond wavy hair, reaching almost to his shoulders, both were wearing day sacks and carried walking poles. We all 'hello-ed' fellow walkers and continued on our way. But they looked vaguely familiar.

"Hang on a minute!" I exclaimed, stopping them in their tracks. "Didn't we see you in Swanage this morning?"

"Oh yeah. But you look a bit different," said the dark haired one, puzzled.

"Yes, we're clean now," explained Chris.

A conversation ensued. When we finally went our separate ways we realised with amazement that the two men had walked over twenty-five miles that day. And on the coast path, believe me, that's quite an achievement. Sitting in the beer garden that evening Chris was still marvelling at their feat.

"Yes but that's nothing to what you have managed to achieve considering how swollen your knee was and how much pain you've been in. I was seriously concerned you would do some permanent damage."

"To be honest, I didn't think it I'd be able to finish it at times," replied Chris. "I kept thinking if I get back to Lulworth it will be a miracle!"

"Well, here's to miracles!"

The End

Er, well, actually it's not. Chris had yet to complete it – and I couldn't let her do it on her own, now could I? So July 2002 saw us setting off on Chris's final leg, this time in reverse (so it would look different for me) from Padstow to Minehead. But even that wasn't The End. There are lots of adjectives to describe the South West Coast Path – beautiful, dramatic, ever-changing, windswept, glorious, wonderful, stunning… And how would I describe it? Addictive!

Copyright Julia R Merrifield 2003

Acknowledgements

I owe thanks to a number of people without whom this book would not have been possible.

Thanks to my Mum, Rose May, for introducing me to the West Country, for encouraging me not to give up and for her constant worrying! Thanks to Chris for her encouragement and friendship, not only does she work with me but she chooses to spend two weeks holiday with me as well – I could have done it without her but it wouldn't have been half as much fun! Thank you to the Mervyn Ashford Laundry Service. Thanks to Clare for her kind words of encouragement – keep up the bridge building!

Thanks also to Tracy Wild for the title. Thank you to all the accommodation providers, magazine editors etc for their help in promoting and marketing this CD Rom. And finally thanks to all those who have suffered, supported and encouraged me on the numerous occasions when I have felt like giving up.

Very many thanks to Max Keuper, without whom the CD ROM version of this book would not exist, and to Tom Graham for his help in bringing Max and I together.

Thanks to B&B owner Peter Tamblin, Hemingford House Bed and Breakfast, 21 Grenville Road, Padstow, Cornwall PL28 8EX http://www.padstow-bb.co.uk/ for his help in promoting this book and for his excellent B&B.

Did you Know?

The South West Coast Path is 3 times height of Everest.*
At 630 miles, the South West Coast Path is the longest National Trail in Britain.
The South West Coast Path is the equivalent distance of walking from Aberdeen to Plymouth, (although as that mileage is calculated along main roads and motorways, should you try it you are unlikely to get beyond a Scottish Intensive Care Unit).
On average each year 7 miles of the coast path are subject to landslides.*
The South West Coast Path celebrated its 25th birthday in 2003.
The South West Coast Path only goes through one city – Plymouth.
Part of the coastline is a world heritage site – ranking alongside the Pyramids.
Over the four years of walking the coast path, Chris and I have encountered numerous pleasant and not so pleasant experiences:

- Number of blisters – 2
- Number of adders – 3
- Number of basking sharks – 3
- Number of foxes – 1
- Number of French walkers met – 3
- Number of American walkers met - 7
- Number of times Chris said: "Come away from the edge!" – 9
- Number of full English breakfasts – 62
- Number of stiles – 916*
- Number of steps – 26,655*
- Number of gates – 489*
- Number of ferries – 15
- Number of times Chris said: "I don't like boats!" – 15
- Number of times I received electric shocks – 4
- Number of cream teas – a disappointingly low 7
- Number of ice creams – 22
- Record number of cups of tea drunk by me at breakfast – 8
- Number of times I said: "I wonder where the nearest toilets are?" – 57
- Number of times I want to walk the SWCP again – countless.

(*Courtesy of the South West Coast Path Association)

Equipment List

rucksack, Berghaus 35 litre Freeflow – containing:
waterproof over trousers, Sprayway
waterproof kagool, Sprayway
sandals, Merrell
nightie
trousers for evening (lightweight)
walking trousers or shorts (one of which would be worn depending on weather), Columbia
shirt, long sleeved, Crag Hoppers
shirt, short sleeved, Regatta
sun hat
knickers (one pair)
socks, Coolmax (one pair)
socks, thicker, Coolmax (one pair)
socks, waterproof, Sealskinz (one pair)
bra
walking boots, Salomon Low II Exit, size 7.5, rather smelly
(Worn when walking would be another set of socks, knickers, bra and short sleeved shirt which was washed each evening and worn clean the following evening, walked in the day after that and then washed again).
toothbrush
toothpaste
deodorant (partially full bottle)
moisturiser (small bottle)
shampoo (small bottle)
shower gel (small bottle)
comb
nail clippers
sun glasses
swimming costume
first aid kit
walking pole, Brasher (the second one – not the one that let me down)
water bottle, plastic, 1 litre, Platypus
pedometer
pen
notebook
mobile phone and charger
camera
binoculars
wild flower identification book, Collins Gem
Eeyore

By the Same Author:

Walking Pembrokeshire with a Fruitcake
© Julia R Merrifield 2004
https://tinyurl.com/ycnuhgev

Two friends deliberated where to choose for their next walking holiday. How about somewhere different? How about somewhere exotic? How about somewhere foreign? How about Wales? But with countless people advising them where to walk that summer and with neither of them speaking a word of Welsh, had they made the right decision? On a hot August day they set off to walk the 180 miles of the Pembrokeshire Coast Path, starting from somewhere unpronounceable and finishing at a little place called Amroth, passing on the way lots more places they would struggle to enunciate.

Wales, a proud land with a proud past; a land steeped in history, a land of myths and magic, castles and cromlechs, dragons and double consonants, male voice choirs and Aled Jones. Follow their adventures as they search for ice cream vans and a Welsh dictionary.

Pedals, Panniers and Punctures
© Julia R Merrifield 2005
https://tinyurl.com/ybyfn8to

One woman, one bike, no backup and 1477 miles on a unique End to End adventure.

Since when did cycle touring become an extreme sport? Since it involved travelling by train. When one woman, more accustomed to long distance footpaths than long distance cycle rides, set out to cycle from Land's End to John o'Groats the first obstacle she faced was getting to the start. Between the start of her journey and the finish, 1477 miles later, she encountered not only ups and downs of terrain but mental and physical highs and lows as well.

Cycling the End to End is so much more than just sitting on something no bigger than, and as hard as, the sole plate of an iron and pedalling, as Julia was to discover. Every experience seemed to be about extremes: Cornish hills, Cheshire plains, busy Devon lanes, empty highland roads, downpours, droughts, smooth cycle tracks, hazardous cattle grids, psychedelic B&Bs and homely hostels. And when the terrain and the weather weren't against her the wildlife was: terrorising Labradors, formation herding sheep dogs, kamikaze squirrels, plagues of midges and road-senseless sheep.

With no backup, and just a bike and a puncture repair kit for company, that strangest of traveller, the lone female, set off to tackle the ultimate British cycle ride. If only she had got a pound for every time someone told her it was all downhill the other way she could have bought a lot more chocolate. As it was, sustained by copious quantities of tea and as much chocolate as she could carry she finally reached her wet and windswept goal.

Walking with Offa
© Julia R Merrifield 2006
https://tinyurl.com/yd73j3q8

Ever heard of a bloke called Offa? King of Mercia, he instigated the building of a defensive dyke. Twelve centuries later a long distance path was laid out, roughly following the line of Offa's Dyke, and thirty years later still two friends set out to walk it.

How difficult could it be, walking from one end of Wales to the other? Loaded down with maps, guide books and global positioning systems they were soon to find out and only five minutes after leaving Chepstow were monumentally lost! Soon they were enjoying the scenery, watching the wildlife and overdosing on dried apricots. Staying in haunted English castles and heavenly Welsh guest houses they made their way north.

By the same author but writing under her new name:

Cycling Across England
© Julia R May 2012
https://tinyurl.com/yc62pful

Two women, two bikes, no backup on a Sea to Sea adventure.

At the beginning of the twenty-first century two friends set off to cycle from coast to coast across England. For one, it was to be the first of many long distance cycle rides.

Cycling Across England is an account of the fun, the food, the mountains, the moorlands and the mathematics the two friends encountered along the way. From the Irish Sea, through the mountains of Cumbria and the Pennine uplands they travelled through a landscape of contrasts to finish their journey in the industrial northeast on the North Sea coast. Broken glass, slugs and arduous ascents were relieved by blackberries, an excess of pizza and delightful descents. Join them as they cycle across England on this iconic ride.

I've Cycled Through There
© Julia R May 2012
https://tinyurl.com/ybxf3gfj

That strangest of traveller, the lone female, is at it again. This time cycling through the heart of England from Bath to London to her home in Lancashire. For such a small country England was proving to be a land of contrasts and surprises; from the leafy lanes of Berkshire to the bleak moorlands of the north, spectacular scenery and post-industrial mill towns, dead divas and murderous mad men.

Throughout the six hundred mile cycle ride there was much that was quintessentially English: Georgian architecture and thatched cottages, William Shakespeare and Samuel Johnson, Bath buns and Yorkshire pudding, canals and Roman roads, Magna Carta and the Houses of Parliament, oh, and Maharajah's Wells and teams of huskies!

Share the experience, the food, the fun and the frustrations. Funny and factual by turns, this is a true account of a cycle journey home through the heart of England.

Walking with Hadrian
© Julia R May 2012
https://tinyurl.com/y9929ggz

A walk through time and fog along Hadrian's Wall.

Built almost two thousand years ago on the orders of the Emperor Hadrian and marking the northern-most boundary of the Roman Empire, Hadrian's Wall is one of Britain's most enduring ancient monuments and a UNESCO World Heritage Site. In 2003 a footpath following the line of the Wall was designated as a National Trail running 84 miles across England from the Solway Firth to the North Sea. Since then walkers have been coming to enjoy this long distance path in the wild landscape of northern England, and a few years later inadvertently choosing the foggiest week she could, Julia finally got round to walking the Wall.

Factual and funny by turns, 'Walking with Hadrian' is an accurate account of the history, culture, scenery and wildlife of Hadrian's Wall Path. Battling fog, maps, social networking and the encroaching perils of middle age, the author has added another book to her collection of traveller's tales.

Cycles and Sandcastles
© Julia R May 2013
https://tinyurl.com/yba8rbqz

Running two hundred miles from Newcastle to Edinburgh, the Coast and Castles Cycle Route promised to be a journey through millennia of turbulent history and fabulous scenery. It proved to be more than just ruined castles and wild coastline. More industrial heritage, more rain, more cross dressing stag nights, more stunning beaches, more wildlife, more grave robbers, more railways, more tea rooms and the Moorfoot Hills.

Close encounters with seagulls, precocious children, warrior-like toddlers and bathroom cleaning products were all in a day's cycling for the author as she pedalled north, passing remote beaches, wooded river valleys and more castles than you could shake a bicycle pump at.

Written with self-deprecating humour and a wry eye for detail, Cycles and Sandcastles is a narrative of the history, the scenery and the flavours of a bike ride through Northumberland and the Scottish Borders.

A Week in Provence
© Julia R May 2014
https://tinyurl.com/y7pruz4x

A much needed autumn break walking in the Verdon Gorge region of Provence turns into a fraught lesson in how not to speak French as the author gets to grips with the language of love, romance and strange combinations of Cs, Qs, apostrophes and genders. Written with her by now trademark self-deprecating humour, this, the author's tenth travelogue, recounts the beauty, the peace and the quieter way of life to be found walking in idyllic rural France.

Never a successful student of languages, but believing you ought to try, Julia displays an enthusiastic if dreadful grasp (or should that be stranglehold?) of the French language as the week unfolds. Whilst coping with a lack of underpants, some rather smelly food and the intricacies of French, A Week in Provence tells of the walks walked, the food eaten, the language butchered and the stretched patience of her long suffering partner as they embark on a walking holiday in south east France.

Bicycles, Boats and Bagpipes
© Julia R May 2014
https://tinyurl.com/y7hrnokp

Having cycled the length and breadth of the British mainland, it was time for a change. After seeing a little blue cycle route sign on the west coast of Scotland, Julia was struck with inspiration. The islands of the Outer Hebrides beckoned. There was just one problem, her boyfriend wanted to go too! Looking on the bright side he could be responsible for navigating and could take most of the luggage. Well, that was the plan. Little did she realise that with her boyfriend there also came his smelly footwear and holey cycling leggings.

Bicycles, Boats and Bagpipes is a detailed and often amusing account of a 500 mile cycle journey through the beautiful and remote islands of the Outer Hebrides and along the mountainous northwest coast of the Scottish mainland.

But it wasn't all about the cycling; there were the rare flower-rich machairs of the Western Isles, idyllic white sandy beaches, blue seas, wild moorland and ancient historic sites to explore. Wildlife to watch. Ferries to sail. Cake to eat and tea to drink. And throughout the trip the experience of isolated communities going about their daily lives, such a contrast from the hustle and bustle of home.

Bicycles, Beer and Black Forest Gateau
© Julia R May 2016
https://tinyurl.com/yctr5bbg

Not many people would consider cycling hundreds miles through Europe to be a relaxing holiday. Mike certainly didn't. But Julia did, she was peculiar that way. There was a challenge to be had in following the River Rhine from its source high in the Swiss Alps, through Germany, France and the Netherlands to the North Sea. But if Mike could not be convinced by mention of the varied scenery, the cultural diversity and the cake, what would change his mind? Finally it was mention of the hundreds of breweries in Germany that convinced him. Who knew, it might turn out to be very relaxing after all?

But as the couple were to discover, cycling on the continent can be very different to cycling in Britain. It was not just the language that would prove difficult to get to grips with, the rules of the road, the navigation, the continental heat and the alpine thunderstorms would test their patience as would tractor drivers and mosquitoes. But most challenging of all would be two weeks without a proper cup of tea. Would beer, gateaux and chocolate be enough to compensate?

Dawdling Through The Dales
© Julia R May 2018
https://tinyurl.com/y8kew292

The Dales Way long distance footpath runs for over eighty miles from Ilkley to Bowness-on-Windermere, encompassing the beautiful scenery of North Yorkshire and Cumbria and two National Parks. It is a varied walk of ever-changing scenery of lush river valleys, limestone

371

pavements, moorland and mountains, and one undertaken by thousands of walkers every year.

When two friends decided to walk the Dales Way over a series of weekends they expected to complete it within a year, but life got in the way. For one of them, the Dales Way would remain an uncompleted long distance footpath.

With details of the scenery, the natural history and anecdotes about the walk, this book will give you a true flavour of walking this often overlooked yet delightful footpath. Light hearted but also darker at times, Dawdling through the Dales, like all of Julia's books, will make you laugh, but it might also make you cry. It is a true tale of walking, divorce, betrayal, depression and enduring friendship.

Cycling Through a Foreign Field
© Julia R May 2018
https://tinyurl.com/yc3rv2y7

In an overheated room in a sheltered housing complex in Burnley there is a small, carved wooden box. The box is a depository for memories, half remembered or forgotten entirely. Inside this box are two life times of old photographs, some sepia, some black and white, known and unknown ancestors; and laid carefully on top of them all sits a newspaper clipping, faded and torn at the edges, over one hundred years old now.

The clipping was taken from the Burnley Express which in 1916 was running a regular feature of Burnley families and the contributions they were making to the First World War. The clipping shows eight head and shoulder photographs of mother and father and six of their sons. One son is in a reserved occupation, one son is too young to fight. The other four sons are in uniform, serving soldiers in the Great War.

The occupant of this hot, stuffy little room and keeper of this box of memories is a lady in her late eighties, frail now and suffering from Alzheimer's Disease, her memory is fading like the contents of the box. She is my mother, Rose. The youngest son in the old newspaper clipping is her father.

In spring 2018 my partner and I set out to cycle the battlefields of Flanders and The Somme; to retrace our forefathers' footsteps and to find out a little of where they served, the conditions they endured and what had become of them during the First World War.

Find me on Facebook:

For excerpts from my books, photos and more information.

Julia R May Books on Kindle & Kobo

https://www.facebook.com/JuliaRMayBooksOnKindle?ref_type=bookmark

If you like what I do – let people know. If you don't – shh! ☺

Printed in Great Britain
by Amazon

50551277R00214